Complete
Spanish Grammar

Complete
Spanish Grammar

PREMIUM THIRD EDITION

Gilda Nissenberg, PhD

New York Chicago San Francisco Athens London Madrid
Mexico City Milan New Delhi Singapore Sydney Toronto

8 9 10 LHS 21 20 19

ISBN   978-1-259-58419-0
MHID   1-259-58419-4

e-ISBN 978-1-259-58420-6
e-MHID 1-259-58420-8

Interior design by Village Bookworks, Inc.

McGraw-Hill Education products are available at special quantity discounts to use as premiums and sales promotions or for use in corporate training programs. To contact a representative, please visit the Contact Us pages at mhprofessional.com.

McGraw-Hill Education Language Lab App
Audio recordings and flash cards are available to support your study of this book. Go to mhlanguagelab.com to access the online version of this application, or to locate links to the mobile app for iOS and Android devices. More details about the features of the app are available on the inside front and back covers.

Other titles by Gilda Nissenberg
Practice Makes Perfect: Complete Spanish All-in-One
Practice Makes Perfect: Intermediate Spanish Grammar
Practice Makes Perfect: Spanish Sentence Builder
Practice Makes Perfect: Spanish Vocabulary Games

Contents

Introduction

Practice Makes Perfect: Complete Spanish Grammar is designed as a tool for review and advancement in the language for the advanced beginner and intermediate learner of Spanish. In each unit, clear grammar explanations include comparisons with English grammar followed by practical examples and exercises that provide ample practice of the material and appropriate, useful vocabulary. Instructions for the exercises are typically in Spanish to prepare the learner to anticipate the task that follows while practicing vocabulary in context. The variety of exercises suits different learning styles and includes open-ended exercises to encourage the learner to produce creative answers and increase confidence in using Spanish for daily communication.

Each unit can be studied independently to suit individual needs in a specific area and to provide opportunities to learn and review Spanish grammar for those who need additional practice at the high school or college level or for those wishing to continue to learn Spanish.

Learning another language requires dedication, time, and, ultimately, frequent practice. Using what the students already know, making connections with their first language, and building on that base strengthen the foundation on which to advance their learning. For this reason, the vocabulary selected includes numerous cognates of English words, giving the advanced beginner and intermediate learners ample opportunities to reinforce what they already know while advancing their knowledge of Spanish.

New vocabulary is incorporated within the exercises or is highlighted in boxes. The glossaries include words appropriate to this level of learner and make it easy to quickly review or learn new vocabulary. Finally, the Verb tables serve as a quick grammar reference.

This Premium Third Edition is enhanced with digital resources via app and online: audio recordings of the Answer key, flash cards of all vocabulary lists in the book, and an auto-fill glossary for quick reference.

PRACTICE MAKES PERFECT®

Complete
Spanish Grammar

The present tense of regular verbs, irregular verbs, and verbs with spelling changes

·1·

Before studying the present tense of Spanish verbs, let's review some grammatical terms you will find in the units related to verbs. To conjugate a verb in the present tense or in any other tense, you will need the root of the verb and the particular ending that expresses information about the action you wish to communicate. You will find the root (or radical) of the verb in its infinitive form. It is easy to spot an infinitive in English because it is preceded by the word *to*: *to shop*, *to learn*, *to receive*, etc. Infinitives in Spanish are not preceded by a particular word but can be recognized by one of three endings: **-ar**, **-er**, or **-ir**. The infinitive endings are attached to the root of the verb: **habl + ar, beb + er, decid + ir**.

The three groups of infinitives are called the first, second, and third conjugation, respectively. To conjugate a verb in Spanish, drop the **-ar**, **-er**, or **-ir** and replace it with the corresponding ending that agrees with the subject doing the action.

Vender

> **Vendo** pólizas de seguro.　　　　　　　*I sell life insurance.*

Because conjugation endings tell who the subject is, subject pronouns in Spanish are usually omitted. The **-o** of the form **vendo** reveals the subject is **yo** (*I*). But conjugated verb endings tell more than just who does the action. Usually, these endings tell the tense (or time) actions take place: the present, past, or future.

Salir

> **Sales** muy temprano.　　　　　　　*You leave very early.*

Sales (*you leave*) is like **vendo** (*I sell*); each indicates an action in the present. The **-es** ending can only refer to the person **tú** in the present tense of the indicative mood. However, endings convey additional information. With **vendo** and **sales**, the speaker indicates that these actions are perceived as a fact or reality: *I sell*; *you leave*. This is called the indicative mood (**modo indicativo**) of the verb. The mood expresses the attitude of the speaker. The examples **vendo** and **sales** are in the indicative mood, because these verbs communicate actions perceived as factual or real. Later on, you will study other moods, such as subjunctive, conditional, and imperative.

Thus, the endings attached to the stem of a verb hold a lot of information: who does the action, when it takes place, and the attitude or perception of the speaker.

1

Regular verbs in the present tense

To form the present tense, drop the **-ar**, **-er**, or **-ir** from the root (or radical) of the infinitive and add the ending that corresponds to the subject. The following verbs can be used as models for all regular verbs in the present tense.

comprar (*to buy*)		**aprender** (*to learn*)	
SINGULAR	PLURAL	SINGULAR	PLURAL
compr**o** *I buy*	compr**amos** *we buy*	aprend**o** *I learn*	aprend**emos** *we learn*
compr**as** *you* (fam.) *buy*	compr**áis** *you buy*	aprend**es** *you* (fam.) *learn*	aprend**éis** *you learn*
compr**a** *he/she/it buys, you* (for.) *buy*	compr**an** *they buy, you buy*	aprend**e** *he/she/it learns, you* (for.) *learn*	aprend**en** *they learn, you learn*

recibir (*to receive*)	
SINGULAR	PLURAL
recib**o** *I receive*	recib**imos** *we receive*
recib**es** *you* (fam.) *receive*	recib**ís** *you receive*
recib**e** *he/she/it receives, you* (for.) *receive*	recib**en** *they receive, you receive*

In the following conjugations, note the *subject pronouns*, as well as the English equivalents.

yo compr**o**	*I buy, am buying, do buy*
tú compr**as**	*you* (fam. sing.) *buy, are buying, do buy*
él compr**a**	*he buys, is buying, does buy*
ella compr**a**	*she buys, is buying, does buy*
usted (**Ud.**) compr**a**	*you* (for. sing.) *buy, are buying, do buy*
nosotros compr**amos**	*we* (masc., masc. & fem.) *buy, are buying, do buy*
nosotras compr**amos**	*we* (fem.) *buy, are buying, do buy*
vosotros compr**áis**	*you* (masc., masc. & fem. pl.) *buy, are buying, do buy*
vosotras compr**áis**	*you* (fem. pl.) *buy, are buying, do buy*
ellos compr**an**	*they* (masc., masc. & fem.) *buy, are buying, do buy*
ellas compr**an**	*they* (fem.) *buy, are buying, do buy*
ustedes (**Uds.**) compr**an**	*you* (for. pl.) *buy, are buying, do buy*

Study the conjugations above and remember that

◆ the first-person singular **yo** has the same ending in all three conjugations.

◆ in the **-er** and **-ir** verb conjugations, all three third-person singular forms have the same endings.

◆ the subject pronouns are usually omitted in Spanish. Verb endings give information about the subject.

Some commonly used regular verbs appear in the following list.

-ar		-er		-ir	
bajar	to step down	**beber**	to drink	**abrir**	to open
cocinar	to cook	**comer**	to eat	**compartir**	to share
comprar	to buy	**comprender**	to understand	**cubrir**	to cover
conversar	to talk	**correr**	to run	**decidir**	to decide
cooperar	to cooperate	**creer**	to believe	**discutir**	to discuss
dibujar	to draw	**leer**	to read	**escribir**	to write
escuchar	to listen	**responder**	to answer	**repartir**	to distribute
limpiar	to clean	**romper**	to break	**subir**	to climb, go up
preparar	to prepare	**temer**	to fear	**sufrir**	to suffer
sacar	to take out	**vender**	to sell	**vivir**	to live
sumar	to add (up)				
trabajar	to work				

EJERCICIO 1·1

La familia Gómez. Escribe la forma del presente del verbo entre paréntesis.

1. Pedro Gómez ____vive____ (vivir) con su familia en mi edificio de apartamentos.

2. Lucía, la esposa de Pedro, no ____trabaja____ (trabajar) todos los días.

3. La hija, Mercedes, ____estudia____ (estudiar) en la universidad.

4. Lucía y su esposo ____planean____ (planear) una visita a Mercedes esta semana.

5. Pedrito, el hijo, ahora ____sube____ (subir) a su apartamento.

6. Pedrito ____sube____ (sacar) a su perro a caminar todos los días.

7. Y tú, ¿____conversas____ (conversar) con los Gómez?

8. Pedro ____necesita____ (necesitar) una persona para cuidar su apartamento esta semana.

EJERCICIO 1·2

Práctica. Escribe en español.

1. *I prepare dinner.* Preparo la cena

2. *The children climb the stairs.* Los niños suben la escalera

3. *My cats drink milk.* Mis gatos beben la leche

4. *The customer adds up the bill (la cuenta).* El cliente suma la cuenta

5. *Carli's mother talks to the reporter (el/la reportero[a]).*
   La madre de Carli conversa al reportero

6. *The actress fears the critics.* La actriz teme los críticos

7. *Your friends eat fajitas.* Tus amigos comen fajitas

When is the present tense used in Spanish?

The present tense is used in Spanish

- ◆ to describe an action happening now. Often, it is translated with the *-ing* form in English.

Ahora, **veo** a Anna.	*Now **I see** Anna.*
Louis **llega** a la puerta.	*Louis **is arriving** at the gate.*

- ◆ to express actions that take place regularly, in a habitual way, although the actions may not be occurring in the present. Expressions of time and other adverbs are often used to indicate that these actions take place routinely in the present.

Normalmente, compro las frutas en el supermercado.	***Usually, I buy*** *fruit at the supermarket.*

- ◆ to describe events that will take place in the near future. A reference to the future may appear in the context or sentence.

Mañana discuto el plan con ustedes en la reunión.	***Tomorrow, I will discuss*** *the plan at the meeting.*
Este verano, viajo a Alemania.	***I will travel*** *to Germany **this summer**.*

- ◆ to ask questions, especially questions requesting permission or someone's opinion or preference.

¿**Bebes** café o té?	*Do you **drink** coffee or tea?*
¿**Abro** la puerta?	***Shall I open*** *the door?*
¿**Compramos** la casa?	*Do we **buy** the house?*

Keep in mind that the auxiliary verb *do* in English is not translated. In Spanish, an auxiliary verb is not needed to ask a question.

Often, the context or words surrounding a verb help pin down information about the time the action takes place. The following are some expressions of time used frequently to refer to actions that take place customarily in the present.

Vocabulary

al mediodía	at noon	**nunca**	never
de vez en cuando	from time to time	**por la mañana**	in the morning
el lunes, el martes, etc.	on Monday, on Tuesday, etc.		*or* this morning
		por la noche	in the evening
esta semana	this week		*or* at night
este mes	this month	**por la tarde**	in the afternoon
hoy	today	**siempre**	always
los lunes, los martes, etc.	on Mondays, on Tuesdays, etc.	**todos los días**	every day

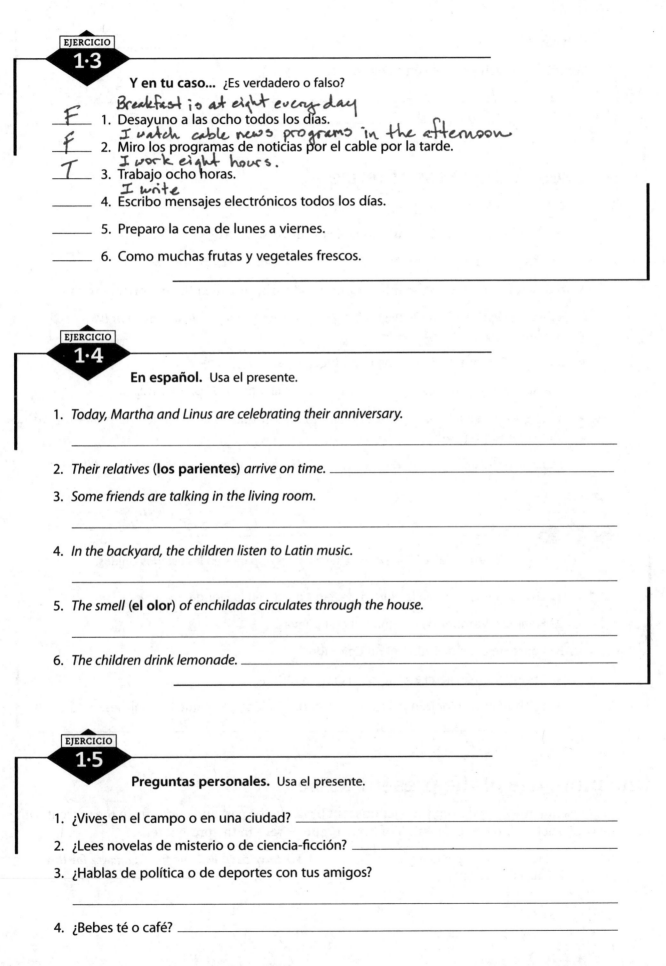

EJERCICIO
1·3

Y en tu caso... ¿Es verdadero o falso?

Breakfast is at eight every day
__F__ 1. Desayuno a las ocho todos los días.

I watch cable news programs in the afternoon
__F__ 2. Miro los programas de noticias por el cable por la tarde.

I work eight hours.
__T__ 3. Trabajo ocho horas.

I write
_____ 4. Escribo mensajes electrónicos todos los días.

_____ 5. Preparo la cena de lunes a viernes.

_____ 6. Como muchas frutas y vegetales frescos.

EJERCICIO
1·4

En español. Usa el presente.

1. _Today, Martha and Linus are celebrating their anniversary._

_____

2. _Their relatives (**los parientes**) arrive on time._ _____

3. _Some friends are talking in the living room._

_____

4. _In the backyard, the children listen to Latin music._

_____

5. _The smell (**el olor**) of enchiladas circulates through the house._

_____

6. _The children drink lemonade._ _____

EJERCICIO
1·5

Preguntas personales. Usa el presente.

1. ¿Vives en el campo o en una ciudad? _____

2. ¿Lees novelas de misterio o de ciencia-ficción? _____

3. ¿Hablas de política o de deportes con tus amigos?

_____

4. ¿Bebes té o café? _____

The present tense of regular verbs, irregular verbs, and verbs with spelling changes   **5**

5. ¿Trabajas de día o de noche? _____

6. ¿Compartes tu tiempo libre con tu perro o con tu gato?

_____

_____

Other uses of the present tense

The present is also used

- ◆ to tell facts considered unquestionable or universal truths.

    Cinco más quince **son** veinte.   *Five plus fifteen **is** twenty.*

- ◆ to describe a past event, making it more vivid. This is called the historical present.

    En 1969 el primer hombre **llega** a la   *The first man **gets** to the moon in 1969.*
    luna.

- ◆ to express hypothetical actions introduced by **si**.

    Si llega el tren, salimos.   *If the train **arrives**, we leave.*

- ◆ to refer to possible consequences from an action that took place in the past with **casi...**
  (*almost*) and **por poco...** (*nearly*).

    Sacó la pistola y casi me **mata**.   *He drew the gun and nearly **killed** (**kills**) me.*

EJERCICIO
1·6

¿Verdadero o falso? Un poco de historia: los hispanos en los Estados Unidos.

_____ 1. Los españoles fundan la ciudad de San Agustín en la Florida.

_____ 2. Francisco Vázquez de Coronado llega a Texas.

_____ 3. Ponce de León descubre el río Colorado.

_____ 4. Cristóbal Colón llega a México en el siglo XVI.

_____ 5. Los hispanos colonizan parte de los Estados Unidos antes que los ingleses.

One more use of the present tense

The present tense is used to express actions that began in the past and continue in the present with
the construction **hace** + expression of time + **que** + verb in the present tense.

    Hace tres años que esperamos   *We have been waiting for an answer for three*
    una respuesta.   *years.*

This construction has two other variations that carry the same meaning.

- Verb in the present tense + **hace** + expression of time

Esperamos una respuesta **hace tres años**.

We have been waiting for an answer for three years.

- Verb in the present tense + **desde hace** + expression of time

Esperamos una respuesta **desde hace tres años**.

We have been waiting for an answer for three years.

Note the following questions using each of these constructions. They all have the same meaning.

¿Cuánto tiempo hace que observas las estrellas?
¿Desde hace cuánto tiempo observas las estrellas?
¿Desde cuándo observas las estrellas?

How long have you been watching the stars?

EJERCICIO
1·7

En español. Responde a las preguntas.

1. ¿Cuánto tiempo hace que estudias español?

   _____

2. ¿Desde hace cuánto tiempo usas la computadora?

   _____

3. ¿Cuántos años hace que los Estados Unidos son una nación independiente?

   _____

4. ¿Cuánto tiempo hace que usamos la Internet?

   _____

5. ¿Desde cuándo escuchas música clásica?

   _____

EJERCICIO
1·8

Tu propia experiencia. En español, completa la oración con tu información personal.

1. Hace una semana que _____.

2. Desde hace un año _____.

3. Hace diez días _____.

4. Desde hace un año, no _____.

5. Hace tres meses _____.

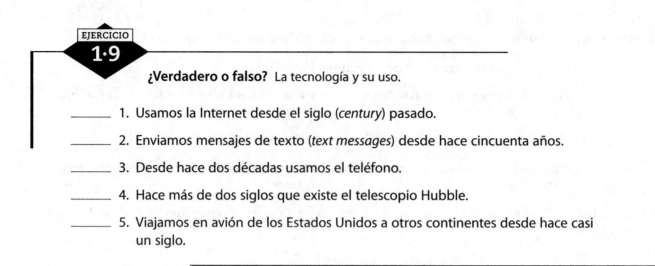

¿Verdadero o falso? La tecnología y su uso.

_____ 1. Usamos la Internet desde el siglo (*century*) pasado.

_____ 2. Enviamos mensajes de texto (*text messages*) desde hace cincuenta años.

_____ 3. Desde hace dos décadas usamos el teléfono.

_____ 4. Hace más de dos siglos que existe el telescopio Hubble.

_____ 5. Viajamos en avión de los Estados Unidos a otros continentes desde hace casi un siglo.

Irregular verbs in the present tense

Many Spanish verbs do not follow the patterns of the regular verbs you have just studied. Instead, they change the root (or radical) of the verb, the conjugation endings, or both. Because they follow different patterns, they are considered *irregular* verbs. Since irregular verbs are so commonly used, a good strategy to identify and learn them is to focus on similarities, grouping them into patterns. Study the following groups of irregular verbs in the present.

◆ Verbs with irregular first-person singular only; all other forms in the present are regular.

caber	to fit	**quepo**	**saber**	to know	**sé**
caer	to fall	**caigo**	**salir**	to leave	**salgo**
dar	to give	**doy**	**traer**	to bring	**traigo**
estar	to be	**estoy**	**valer**	to be worth	**valgo**
hacer	to do	**hago**	**ver**	to see	**veo**
poner	to put	**pongo**			

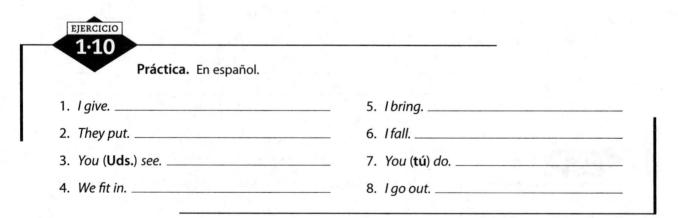

Práctica. En español.

1. *I give.* _____

2. *They put.* _____

3. *You (**Uds.**) see.* _____

4. *We fit in.* _____

5. *I bring.* _____

6. *I fall.* _____

7. *You (**tú**) do.* _____

8. *I go out.* _____

The compounds of these verbs are also irregular in the **yo** form only; they add the consonant **g** between the radical and the verb ending. Compounds are easy to spot, because they show a prefix (**des-**, **dis-**, **com-**, **con-**, etc.) preceding the radical. Here is a list of frequently used compounds of **hacer**, **poner**, and **traer**.

componer	to compose	**compongo**	**proponer**	to propose	**propongo**
deshacer	to undo	**deshago**	**rehacer**	to remake	**rehago**
disponer	to arrange	**dispongo**	**reponer**	to replace	**repongo**
distraer(se)	to distract	**distraigo**	**suponer**	to suppose	**supongo**

EJERCICIO
1·11

En español.

1. *I write (**componer**) songs for my friends.* _____

2. *I propose a toast (**el brindis**).* _____

3. *They replace the money in my account.* _____

4. *You (**Ud.**) distract the audience.* _____

5. *The girls undo the puzzle (**el rompecabezas**).* _____

EJERCICIO
1·12

Pareados. Escribe la letra de la respuesta más lógica.

_____ 1. Sé	a.	a mis compañeros de trabajo.
_____ 2. Distraigo	b.	que trabajas mucho.
_____ 3. No quepo	c.	música para mis canciones.
_____ 4. Compongo	d.	en esa trampa (*trap*) a menudo.
_____ 5. Propongo	e.	de la conferencia ahora.
_____ 6. Pongo	f.	una solución para tu problema.
_____ 7. Salgo	g.	el agua en un vaso.
_____ 8. Caigo	h.	en estos pantalones.

Other verbs with irregular forms in the first person

◆ Verbs that end in a vowel followed by -cer and -cir change c to zc in the first-person singular only. They are conjugated like conocer.

Conozco muy bien a Margo.   *I know Margo very well.*

-er VERBS LIKE conocer

agradecer	to thank, be grateful	agradezco
aparecer	to appear	aparezco
complacer	to please	complazco
crecer	to grow	crezco
establecer	to establish	establezco
merecer	to deserve	merezco
ofrecer	to offer	ofrezco
padecer	to suffer	padezco
permanecer	to remain	permanezco
pertenecer	to belong	pertenezco
reconocer	to recognize	reconozco

-ir VERBS LIKE traducir

traducir	to translate	traduzco
conducir	to drive, lead	conduzco
producir	to produce	produzco

EJERCICIO
1·13

Práctica. Escribe la forma correspondiente del verbo entre paréntesis.

1. Yo _____ (conducir) el coche.

2. Marta y tú _____ (salir) de casa juntos (*together*).

3. Yo no _____ (conocer) a esa familia.

4. ¿Quién _____ (ofrecer) más por este cuadro?

5. ¡Yo no _____ (merecer) este regalo!

6. Las asistentes del director _____ (obedecer) sus órdenes.

7. ¡Tú _____ (pertenecer) a una familia muy famosa!

8. Marcia _____ (conocer) a los padres de Luisa.

¿Y yo? Escribe en español. Usa el presente.

1. *I deserve a raise.* _____

2. *Do I go out now?* _____

3. *I am grateful for your friendship.* _____

4. *I do not belong to this group.* _____

5. *I translate the instructions.* _____

6. *I seldom impose my ideas!* _____

7. *I remain quiet (**callado**[a]).* _____

Other frequently used verbs with irregular forms in the present tense

Study the conjugations of the verbs that follow. They have irregular forms in the present tense.

decir (*to say*)		**ir** (*to go*)		**oír** (*to hear*)	
digo	decimos	voy	vamos	oigo	oímos
dices	decís	vas	vais	oyes	oís
dice	dicen	va	van	oye	oyen

ser (*to be*)		**tener** (*to have*)		**venir** (*to come*)	
soy	somos	tengo	tenemos	vengo	venimos
eres	sois	tienes	tenéis	vienes	venís
es	son	tiene	tienen	viene	vienen

Note that **haber** is also irregular. One meaning of **haber** is *to have*. However, in the present as well as in other tenses, **haber** is more frequently used as an impersonal verb in the third-person singular form. The present tense form is **hay**. It means *there is* and *there are*.

Hay tres sillas en la sala.   ***There are** three chairs in the living room.*
Hay una posibilidad solamente.   ***There is** only one possibility.*

Compounds of **tener** have the same irregular forms.

VERBS LIKE **tener**

contener	to contain	**contengo**
detener	to detain	**detengo**
mantener	to maintain	**mantengo**
obtener	to obtain	**obtengo**
retener	to retain	**retengo**
sostener	to sustain	**sostengo**

En español.

1. *There is one person.* _____

2. *There are ten programs.* _____

3. *I'm going now.* _____

4. *I do not hear music.* _____

5. *Do you (**Ud.**) see the bus?* _____

6. *I tell the truth.* _____

7. *You (**Uds.**) have time.* _____

8. *They stop the car.* _____

¡Mira quién baila! Escribe la forma correspondiente del presente.

1. Mi amiga Alicia _____ (estar) en el estudio para ver el programa *¡Mira quién baila!*

2. Aquí, en el estudio, _____ (haber) muchos aficionados (*fans*) al baile.

3. Todos los aficionados _____ (llegar) al estudio para ver esta competencia de baile.

4. Marcos _____ (ser) uno de los participantes y yo _____ (decir) que Marcos va a ganar hoy.

5. Muchas personas _____ (venir) para escuchar la música.

6. Marcos _____ (tener) a su hermana aquí y baila con ella.

7. Si vienes al programa, tú _____ (oír) los comentarios de los jueces.

8. ¡Todos ustedes _____ (ir) a querer bailar aquí, en el estudio!

Verbs with spelling changes in the present tense

In the present tense, certain verbs have spelling changes. These are determined by Spanish rules of pronunciation to preserve the sound appearing in the infinitive. The following groups of verbs have spelling changes before the verb ending -**o**, in the **yo** form only.

- Verbs ending in **-ger** or **-gir** change **g** to **j** before the **-o** ending.

coger (*to catch, grab*)		**exigir** (*to demand*)	
cojo	cogemos	exijo	exigimos
coges	cogéis	exiges	exigís
coge	cogen	exige	exigen

VERBS LIKE **coger**

encoger	to shrink	**encojo**
escoger	to choose	**escojo**
proteger	to protect	**protejo**
recoger	to pick up	**recojo**

VERBS LIKE **exigir**

dirigir	to direct	**dirijo**
fingir	to pretend	**finjo**

Other **-gir** verbs have stem changes as well. Check the sections on stem-changing verbs in Unit 2.

- Verbs ending in **-guir** change **gu** to **g** before the **-o** ending.

distinguir (*to distinguish*)	
distingo	distinguimos
distingues	distinguís
distingue	distinguen

VERBS LIKE **distinguir**

extinguir	to extinguish

Other **-guir** verbs have stem changes as well. Check the sections on stem-changing verbs in Unit 2.

- Verbs ending in **-cer** and **-cir** change **c** to **z** before the **-o** ending.

convencer (*to convince*)	
convenzo	convencemos
convences	convencéis
convence	convencen

VERBS LIKE **convencer**

ejercer	to practice (*a profession*)	**ejerzo**
vencer	to overcome	**venzo**

Some -cer and -cir verbs may have stem changes as well: **e** changes to **i** and **o** to **ue**.

elegir	to correct	**elijo**
torcer	to twist	**tuerzo**

"Yo también..." Marlo hace todo lo que Ramón hace. *Write the present tense of the* **yo** *form of the verb that is underlined.*

1. <u>Exige</u> una explicación. _____

2. <u>Escoge</u> los colores. _____

3. <u>Extingue</u> el fuego. _____

4. <u>Recoge</u> los periódicos. _____

5. <u>Vence</u> los obstáculos. _____

6. <u>Protege</u> sus derechos (*rights*). _____

7. <u>Convence</u> a sus amigos. _____

8. No <u>finge</u>. _____

Dar, haber, hacer, and tener in expressions with a special meaning

In this unit, you have studied **dar**, **haber**, **hacer**, and **tener**, verbs with irregular forms in the present. These verbs appear frequently in idiomatic expressions. Many are formed with a conjugated verb + an infinitive, called **formas perifrásticas** or **perífrasis verbales** in Spanish.

Other idiomatic verbal expressions will appear in other units. Learn them as lexical (vocabulary) items.

Note the use of the present tense in the examples with **dar, haber, hacer,** and **tener** that follow. Keep in mind that, in different contexts or surrounded by expressions of time referring to the past or the future, these idioms may also be used in other tenses.

◆ **Dar**

dar un abrazo *to hug, embrace*

Le da un abrazo a su amigo.   *He hugs his friend.*

dar gritos *to shout, scream*

La multitud da gritos.   *The crowd screams.*

dar la hora *to strike the hour*

El reloj da la una.   *The clock strikes one.*

◆ **Haber**

hay que + infinitive *to be necessary* (to express obligation)

Hay que estudiar para aprender.   *It is necessary to study in order to learn.*

haber sol *to be sunny*

Hay sol por la mañana.   *It is sunny in the morning.*

haber neblina *to be foggy*

Hay neblina esta mañana.   *It is foggy this morning.*

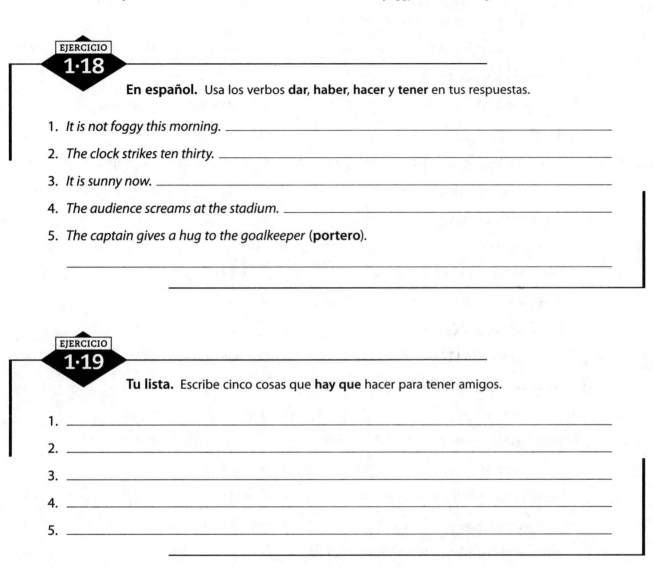

EJERCICIO
1·18

En español. Usa los verbos **dar**, **haber**, **hacer** y **tener** en tus respuestas.

1. *It is not foggy this morning.* _____

2. *The clock strikes ten thirty.* _____

3. *It is sunny now.* _____

4. *The audience screams at the stadium.* _____

5. *The captain gives a hug to the goalkeeper* (**portero**).

_____

_____

EJERCICIO
1·19

Tu lista. Escribe cinco cosas que **hay que** hacer para tener amigos.

1. _____

2. _____

3. _____

4. _____

5. _____

◆ **Hacer** in expressions that refer to weather conditions

hacer calor, hacer fresco *to be hot, to be cool*

Hace fresco, no hace calor.   *It is cool; it is not hot.*

hacer viento *to be windy*

Hace viento.   *It is windy.*

hacer un viaje *to take a trip*

Lina hace un viaje a las Bahamas.   *Lina takes a trip to the Bahamas.*

◆ **Hacer** in other expressions

hacer una visita *to pay a visit*

Marcus hace una visita a su tío.   *Marcus visits his uncle.*

The present tense of regular verbs, irregular verbs, and verbs with spelling changes   **15**

hacer daño *to harm, damage*

Beber mucha agua no te hace daño.   *Drinking a lot of water does not harm you.*

hacer caso a *to notice, pay attention (to)*

Los niños no hacen caso al maestro.   *The children do not pay attention to the teacher.*

hacer el papel de *to play the role of*

El actor hace el papel de Hamlet.   *The actor plays the role of Hamlet.*

◆ **Tener**

To express obligation with a conjugated verb, use the formula **tener** + **que** + infinitive.

Tenemos que salir.   *We must leave.*

tener frío *to be cold*

Tengo frío.   *I am cold.*

tener hambre *to be hungry*

¿Tienes hambre?   *Are you hungry?*

tener miedo *to be afraid*

No tienen miedo a las serpientes.   *They are not afraid of snakes.*

tener razón *to be right*

Yo tengo razón.   *I am right.*

tener sed *to be thirsty*

¿Tienes sed?   *Are you thirsty?*

tener prisa *to be in a hurry*

Mi esposo tiene prisa.   *My husband is in a hurry.*

tener la culpa (de) *to be to blame (for)*

El sospechoso tiene la culpa de este accidente.   *The suspect is to blame for this accident.*

tener lugar *to take place*

La reunión tiene lugar los domingos.   *The meeting takes place on Sundays.*

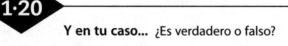

EJERCICIO
1·20

Y en tu caso... ¿Es verdadero o falso?

_____ 1. Tengo miedo a los fantasmas (*ghosts*).

_____ 2. Nunca tengo prisa.

_____ 3. Tengo que hacer la cama todos los días.

_____ 4. Hago caso a las buenas sugerencias de mis amigos.

_____ 5. No tengo mucho sueño ahora.

_____ 6. Siempre hago una visita a mi familia en diciembre.

EJERCICIO
1·21

En español.

1. *Are you (**tú**) hungry?* _____

2. *We are thirsty.* _____

3. *Lori pays a visit to her cousin.* _____

4. *Mario hugs his friend.* _____

5. *They are in a hurry.* _____

6. *You (**tú**) are right this time.* _____

7. *I am not afraid.* _____

8. *Are you (**Ud.**) cold?* _____

EJERCICIO
1·22

Conecta la letra. Escribe la letra de la expresión apropiada.

_____ 1. ¡Quiero dos hamburguesas!   a. Tengo razón.

_____ 2. Obedezco a mi médico.   b. Hago caso.

_____ 3. Bebo dos vasos de agua.   c. Hago una visita.

_____ 4. Estoy en lo cierto.   d. Tengo prisa.

_____ 5. Tengo diez minutos nada más.   e. Tengo hambre.

_____ 6. Quiero dormir.   f. Tengo sueño.

_____ 7. Voy a ver a mi amigo.   g. No tengo la culpa.

_____ 8. Soy inocente.   h. Tengo sed.

La vida diaria. Traduce. Usa el **Vocabulario útil.**

I hate Mondays. We start another week with the same routine. I talk to my neighbors about the weekend, our family, and our habits at home. My husband sometimes helps me with the household chores. He vacuums the floors and he sweeps the terrace. Juan, Lidia's husband, washes the clothes. They have a new washing machine and a dryer! And Juan likes to iron his shirts. Marta's husband, Mauricio, prepares dinner almost every night. He has a new grill on the patio, a gift from Marta for his birthday. Now, Marta does not cook! My other neighbor, Susana, lives with her mother-in-law and she helps, too. I need more help from my husband, my mother, or the electric appliances. I work too hard!

Vocabulario útil

birthday	**el cumpleaños**	mother-in-law	**la suegra**
cleaning	**la limpieza**	routine	**la rutina**
custom	**la costumbre; el hábito**	to hate	**detestar; odiar**
dryer	**la secadora**	to iron, press	**planchar**
electric appliances	**los aparatos electrodomésticos**	to sweep	**barrer**
		to vacuum	**pasar la aspiradora**
grill	**la parrilla**	to wash	**lavar, limpiar**
habit	**el hábito; la costumbre**	vacuum cleaner	**la aspiradora**
household chores	**los quehaceres de la casa / domésticos**	washing machine	**la lavadora**
		weekend	**el fin de semana**

The present tense of verbs with stem changes

You have learned that regular verbs, when conjugated, keep their stem (also called root or radical), drop the **-ar**, **-er**, and **-ir** infinitive endings, and add the corresponding endings for the respective subjects (**yo, tú**, etc.). However, stem-changing verbs do not follow the regular verb patterns of conjugation. As their name suggests, they change a vowel in the stem. Remember that stem changes affect all persons in the singular and in the third-person plural. The exceptions are the **nosotros** and **vosotros** forms, both plural forms.

Although they do not always use the same system, vocabulary and verb lists in textbooks and dictionaries usually indicate stem changes: **e > ie, o > ue**, etc., following the infinitive in the entry. For example, **empezar** (**e > ie**) tells you the present tense is **empiezo, empiezas**, etc.

Stem-changing verbs are grouped according to the infinitive endings and the patterns of change in the stem vowels. Several lists of stem-changing verbs appear in this unit for you to use as reference and vocabulary building. You will see (**se**) attached to some of the infinitives, indicating they are used as reflexive verbs with the reflexive pronouns (**me, te, se, nos, os, se**). You may wish to review the unit on reflexive verbs (Unit 8) as you study stem-changing verbs.

Verbs ending in -ar and -er

◆ **-Ar** and **-er** stem-changing verbs with the stem vowel **e** change to **ie**. Remember that the stem changes occur in all forms except the plural forms **nosotros** and **vosotros**.

cerrar (*to close*)		**querer** (*to love; to want*)	
cierro	cerramos	quiero	queremos
cierras	cerráis	quieres	queréis
cierra	cierran	quiere	quieren

The following is a list of commonly used verbs that follow the pattern of **cerrar** and **querer**.

-ar		-er	
acertar	to guess	**defender**	to defend
atravesar	to cross (over)	**descender**	to descend, go down
comenzar	to start, begin	**encender**	to light up
confesar	to confess	**entender**	to understand
despertar(se)	to wake up	**perder**	to lose; to miss
empezar	to start, begin		
encerrar	to lock in, contain		
fregar	to wash dishes; to scrub		
gobernar	to govern, rule		
helar	to freeze		
negar	to deny		
nevar	to snow		
pensar (en)	to think (of, about)		
recomendar	to recommend, advise		
remendar	to mend, patch		
sentar(se)	to sit down, seat (oneself)		
tropezar (con)	to stumble (into, across)		

Keep in mind that **helar** and **nevar** are impersonal verbs used in the third-person singular only.

Podemos esquiar si **nieva**.   *We can ski if **it snows**.*
La carretera es peligrosa cuando **hiela**.   *The road is dangerous when **it freezes**.*

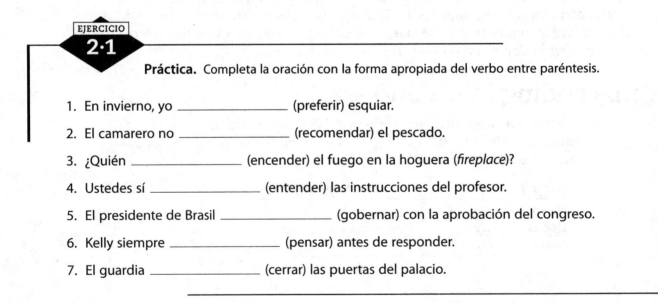

EJERCICIO
2·1

Práctica. Completa la oración con la forma apropiada del verbo entre paréntesis.

1. En invierno, yo _____ (preferir) esquiar.

2. El camarero no _____ (recomendar) el pescado.

3. ¿Quién _____ (encender) el fuego en la hoguera (*fireplace*)?

4. Ustedes sí _____ (entender) las instrucciones del profesor.

5. El presidente de Brasil _____ (gobernar) con la aprobación del congreso.

6. Kelly siempre _____ (pensar) antes de responder.

7. El guardia _____ (cerrar) las puertas del palacio.

¿Qué hacen estas personas? Escoge (*choose*) el verbo adecuado para comunicar el mensaje de cada oración. Después, escribe la forma apropiada del presente para cada respuesta.

comenzar   entender   helar
defender   gobernar   sentarse

1. El presidente _____ desde la Casa Blanca.

2. El abogado _____ al acusado ante el jurado (*jury*).

3. ¿A qué hora _____ el partido de béisbol?

4. Cuando _____ las temperaturas descienden.

5. ¿Quién no _____ la pregunta?

6. Nosotros _____ en el salón para ver la televisión.

◆ **-Ar** and **-er** stem-changing verbs with the stem vowel **o** change to **ue**.

contar (*to count; to tell, retell*)		**volver** (*to return*)	
cuento	contamos	vuelvo	volvemos
cuentas	contáis	vuelves	volvéis
cuenta	cuentan	vuelve	vuelven

The following is a list of commonly used **-ar** and **-er** verbs that follow the pattern of **contar** and **volver**.

-ar		**-er**	
acordar(se) de	to remember	**conmover**	to move (*emotionally*)
acostar(se)	to go to bed	**devolver**	to return (*something*)
almorzar	to eat lunch	**doler**	to hurt
aprobar	to approve	**llover**	to rain
colgar	to hang (up)	**morder**	to bite
costar	to cost	**mover**	to move (*an object*)
demostrar	to demonstrate; to prove	**oler**	to smell
encontrar	to find	**poder**	to be able to
jugar (a)	to play (*a game or sport*)	**resolver**	to solve
mostrar	to show	**revolver**	to shake
probar(se)	to try; to taste; to try on	**soler**	to be accustomed to
recordar	to remember		
rogar	to beg		
sonar	to ring, sound		
soñar (con)	to dream		
tronar	to thunder		
volar	to fly		

Keep in mind the following.

- ◆ **Jugar** (*to play [a game or sport]*) is a **u** stem verb conjugated like **contar**. (It is the only **u** > **ue** stem-changing verb in Spanish.)

- ◆ Spanish spelling rules require **h** to precede all present tense forms of **oler**, except **nosotros** and **vosotros**: **huelo, hueles**, etc.

- ◆ **Llover** and **tronar** are usually used in the third-person singular only, **llueve** (*it's raining*) and **truena** (*it's thundering*) except when used in figurative speech.

  Le **llueven proposiciones** de negocios.   *The business **propositions are pouring in**.*

- ◆ Some stem-changing verbs have spelling changes as well. **Torcer(se)** (*to twist*) and **cocer** (*to cook*) change the stem **o** to **ue** and the **yo** form follows the pattern of -**cer** verbs with spelling changes.

  Me tuerzo el pie si no tengo cuidado.   *I'll twist my foot if I am not careful.*
  Si **cuezo** los vegetales, podemos   *If I cook the vegetables, we can eat soon.*
     comer pronto.

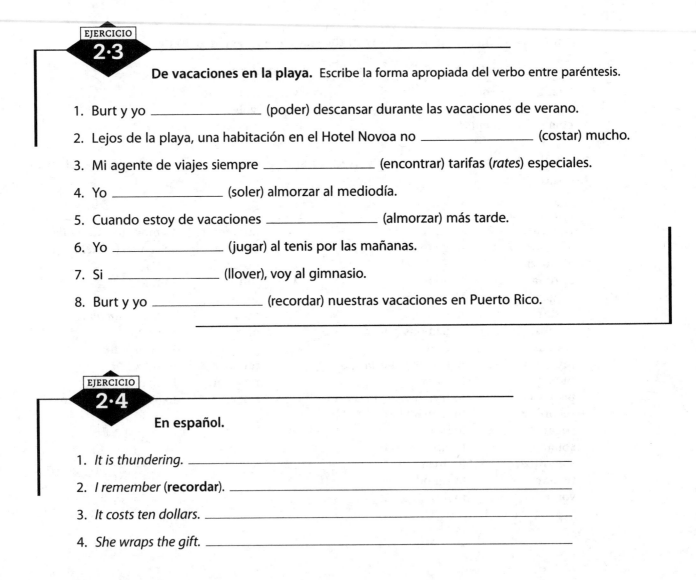

EJERCICIO
2·3

De vacaciones en la playa. Escribe la forma apropiada del verbo entre paréntesis.

1. Burt y yo _____ (poder) descansar durante las vacaciones de verano.

2. Lejos de la playa, una habitación en el Hotel Novoa no _____ (costar) mucho.

3. Mi agente de viajes siempre _____ (encontrar) tarifas (*rates*) especiales.

4. Yo _____ (soler) almorzar al mediodía.

5. Cuando estoy de vacaciones _____ (almorzar) más tarde.

6. Yo _____ (jugar) al tenis por las mañanas.

7. Si _____ (llover), voy al gimnasio.

8. Burt y yo _____ (recordar) nuestras vacaciones en Puerto Rico.

EJERCICIO
2·4

En español.

1. *It is thundering.* _____

2. *I remember* (**recordar**). _____

3. *It costs ten dollars.* _____

4. *She wraps the gift.* _____

5. *Silvia counts the bills.* _____

6. *We play now.* _____

7. *You (**tú**) show the photo.* _____

8. *They smell the flowers.* _____

Verbs ending in -ir

In the present tense, stem-changing verbs ending in **-ir** are grouped in one of three patterns according to the change in the stem vowel: **e** to **ie**, **o** to **ue**, and **e** to **i**. As with all stem-changing verbs, the changes occur in all forms except the plural forms **nosotros** and **vosotros**.

◆ **-Ir** verbs with the stem vowel **e** change to **ie**.

preferir (*to prefer*)

prefiero	preferimos
prefieres	preferís
prefiere	prefieren

VERBS LIKE **preferir**

advertir	to notify, warn	**presentir**	to forebode, predict
convertir	to convert	**referir**(se) a	to refer to
divertir(se)	to have a good time	**sentir**	to regret
hervir	to boil	**sentir**(se)	to feel
mentir	to lie		

EJERCICIO
2·5

Práctica. Usa la forma apropiada del verbo entre paréntesis.

1. Elsa _____ (preferir) café.

2. Ese hombre _____ (mentir).

3. Los jugadores _____ (presentir) ya la victoria.

4. Los funcionarios del gobierno _____ (advertir) el peligro a la población.

5. ¡Tú _____ (mentir)!

6. Yo _____ (sentir) mucho su ausencia.

7. ¿Por qué Uds. no _____ (convertir) los dólares a pesos?

8. La nota en el libro _____ (referir) a la página 225.

En español.

1. *The water boils (is boiling).* _____

2. *Martha doesn't lie.* _____

3. *He feels fine.* _____

4. *They have a good time.* _____

5. *You (**Ud.**) are lying.* _____

6. *We prefer to play chess (**ajedrez**).* _____

♦ **-Ir** verbs with the stem vowel **o** change to **ue**.

dormir (*to sleep*)

duermo	dormimos
duermes	dormís
duerme	duermen

Morir(se) (*to die*) is conjugated like **dormir**.

♦ **-Ir** verbs with the stem vowel **e** change to **i**.

pedir (*to ask for, request*)

pido	pedimos
pides	pedís
pide	piden

VERBS LIKE **pedir**

despedir	to fire (*from a job*)	**repetir**	to repeat
despedir(se)	to say good-bye	**seguir**	to follow; to continue
impedir	to avoid, prevent	**servir**	to serve
medir	to measure	**sonreír(se)**	to smile
perseguir	to pursue; to follow	**vestir(se)**	to dress; to get dressed
reírse (de)	to laugh; to make fun (of)		

Note the spelling changes of **seguir** and its compounds where the soft **g** sound is followed by **e**: **sigues, sigue, siguen**. All forms of **reír** and **sonreír** have an accent mark on the stem vowel **í**.

Práctica. Los modales en el trabajo. En español. Usa el presente y la persona **tú**.

1. *Do you smile when you see your colleagues?*

_____

2. *Do you follow the rules at work?* _____

3. *Do you measure your words when you speak with your supervisor?*

_____

4. *Do you make fun of your friends?* _____

5. *Do you dress appropriately?* _____

6. *Do you say good-bye when you leave at the end of the day?*

_____

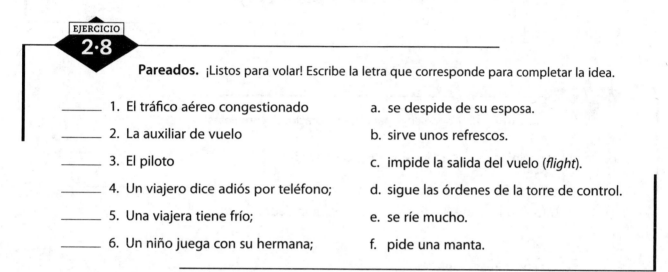

EJERCICIO
2·8

Pareados. ¡Listos para volar! Escribe la letra que corresponde para completar la idea.

_____ 1. El tráfico aéreo congestionado   a. se despide de su esposa.

_____ 2. La auxiliar de vuelo   b. sirve unos refrescos.

_____ 3. El piloto   c. impide la salida del vuelo (*flight*).

_____ 4. Un viajero dice adiós por teléfono;   d. sigue las órdenes de la torre de control.

_____ 5. Una viajera tiene frío;   e. se ríe mucho.

_____ 6. Un niño juega con su hermana;   f. pide una manta.

Verbs ending in -uir

Verbs ending in **-uir** add a **y** following the **u** in all forms except the **nosotros** and **vosotros** forms. The indication (**y**) reminds you of this change in verb lists and glossaries.

incluir (*to include*)

incluyo	incluimos
incluyes	incluís
incluye	incluyen

Note that verbs ending in **-guir** are not included in this group.

VERBS LIKE **incluir**

atribuir	to attribute	**distribuir**	to distribute
concluir	to conclude	**huir**	to flee
contribuir	to contribute	**influir**	to influence
destruir	to destroy	**sustituir**	to substitute

¿Verdadero o falso?

_____ 1. Generalmente, un policía distribuye el correo.

_____ 2. Los huracanes destruyen árboles.

_____ 3. La comida influye en la salud.

_____ 4. La ciencia contribuye al progreso.

_____ 5. La temporada de fútbol americano concluye en octubre.

_____ 6. Las vitaminas sustituyen la comida saludable (_healthy_).

Tu turno. Responde en español y con oraciones completas.

1. ¿Influye la opinión de tus amigos en tus decisiones?

   _____

2. ¿Contribuyes con tus ideas o tu tiempo a tu comunidad?

   _____

3. ¿Concluyes tus tareas a tiempo?

   _____

4. ¿Huyes de tus responsabilidades?

   _____

5. ¿Atribuyes tus problemas a la falta de tiempo?

   _____

¿Verdadero o falso?

_____ 1. Colgamos la ropa en el armario.

_____ 2. Los perros vuelan.

_____ 3. Después de terminar mi llamada de teléfono, cuelgo.

_____ 4. Casi todos los americanos sueñan con tener su casa.

_____ 5. Los cajeros (*cashiers*) cuentan el dinero.

_____ 6. Las personas bilingües entienden más de una lengua.

EJERCICIO
2·12

La palabra apropiada. Entre paréntesis, subraya (*underline*) el verbo que tiene sentido en cada frase.

1. ¿Quién no (entiende | espía) este párrafo?

2. Tú (quieres | pierdes) ganar la lotería.

3. Nosotros siempre (nos referimos | nos resfriamos) en invierno.

4. Si esta conferencia (actúa | continúa), ¡me voy a dormir!

5. (Enviamos | Confiamos) los regalos por correo aéreo.

6. La venta especial (cuenta | concluye) mañana.

EJERCICIO
2·13

Una visita al siquiatra. Traduce. Usa el **Vocabulario útil**.

I have an obsession: I read and write novels about detectives. When I dream, I can write more novels. On Wednesdays, I have a session with my new psychiatrist, Dr. Salazar. She suggests hypnosis therapy for my well-being. I prefer not to talk about the treatment. I confess it is difficult to write novels. I show her a chapter of my novel. She listens. I suggest reading the text aloud. Dr. Salazar does not respond. I feel nervous. I bite my nails while I describe my hero. I want to defend the ideas in my novel. Dr. Salazar does not respond. I continue to read my novel. The detective, my hero, is six feet tall. In this chapter, he follows his client's wife, a beautiful woman, but she disappears. All of a sudden, the phone rings and Dr. Salazar wakes up! I say good-bye. Outside the office, I laugh. The power of my words can hypnotize my audience. Dr. Salazar sleeps while I talk!

Vocabulario útil

all of a sudden	**de repente**	nail	**la uña**
aloud	**en voz alta**	obsession	**la manía; la obsesión**
chapter	**el capítulo**	power	**el poder**
client	**el cliente, la clienta**	psychiatrist	**el/la psiquiatra**
dream	**el sueño**	treatment	**el tratamiento**
hypnosis therapy	**la terapia de hipnosis**	well-being	**el bienestar**

Ser and estar

Similarities and differences between **ser** and **estar**

◆ Learning the different uses of **ser** and **estar** in Spanish may present some challenges for the English speaker. Both **ser** and **estar** are equivalent to the English *to be*, and they are frequently used in daily communication. A comparison of **ser** and **estar** will help highlight some similarities and differences.

◆ Both **ser** and **estar** are irregular verbs in some tenses. For the sake of comparison, let us look at the present tense forms.

ser (*to be*)		**estar** (*to be*)	
soy	somos	estoy	estamos
eres	sois	estás	estáis
es	son	está	están

See the Verb tables at the back of this book for the other tenses of **ser** and **estar**.

◆ Both **ser** and **estar** are used as the main verb in a sentence.

Soy de los Estados Unidos.	*I am from the United States.*
Estoy en Washington.	*I am in Washington.*

◆ Both are used as auxiliary verbs. **Ser** is used in the passive voice; **estar** helps conjugate the progressive forms (equivalent of *-ing* in English). The passive voice is treated in Unit 12.

El caso **fue estudiado** por las autoridades.	*The case **was studied** by the authorities.*
Estamos considerando tu propuesta.	*We **are considering** your proposal.*

But **ser** and **estar** are very different both in meaning and in usage.

Let's start with a key distinction: **ser** is used to describe permanent or more lasting situations, while **estar** indicates location and what are considered temporary situations.

Soy Graciela.	*I am Graciela.*
Ahora, **estoy** en Madrid.	*I am in Madrid now.*

28

Trying to reason out what is permanent and what is temporary will not help us in all situations where either **ser** or **estar** may be used. The initial, basic distinction between permanent and temporary conditions is not absolute, and, on occasion, may appear somewhat confusing. Sometimes the uses of these two verbs seem to defy logic.

¡**Está** muerto!   *He **is** dead!*

Is death not permanent? As you become familiar with their uses, it will be easier to choose which of these two verbs you will need to communicate your meaning.

When is **ser** used in Spanish?

Use **ser** to indicate

- the identity of the subject (person, thing, or event).

  Soy Pedro.   *I **am** Pedro.*
  Éste **es** el mercado.   *This **is** the market.*
  El 4 de julio **es** el Día de la   *The Fourth of July **is** Independence Day*
     Independencia de los Estados Unidos.   *in the United States.*

- someone's occupation or profession.

  Raúl **es** dentista.   *Raul **is** a dentist.*
  Somos estudiantes.   *We **are** students.*

  Note that the indefinite article **un**, **una**, **unos**, or **unas** is omitted in Spanish when stating a profession following the verb **ser**. The indefinite article is used if an adjective modifies the occupation.

  Eres **un buen** estudiante.   *You are **a good** student.*

- essential or inherent qualities not likely to change, such as nationality, moral attributes, and religion.

  El guacamole **es** un plato mexicano.   *Guacamole **is** a Mexican dish.*
  Felicia **es** cubana.   *Felicia **is** Cuban.*
  El señor Benigno **es** muy honrado. *Mr. Benigno **is** very honest.*
  La familia de Delia **es** católica. *Delia's family **is** Catholic.*

  Remember that adjectives and nouns of nationalities are not capitalized in Spanish.

- characteristics of physical appearance and personality. They may also be considered inherent. A person's appearance may change: one's hair may be colored, for instance, but the results are considered lasting if not permanent.

  Charley **es** alto, rubio y simpático.   *Charley **is** tall, blond, and pleasant.*
  Antes, Rosa **era** pelirroja. Ahora,   *Before, Rosa **used to be** a redhead. Now she*
    es rubia.   ***is** a blond.*

- relationships. Even after the death or dissolution of someone or something, a relationship is expressed with a form of **ser**. Relationships are examples of identity.

  Ellas **son** mis hermanas.   *They **are** my sisters.*
  John **es** su ex-marido.   *John **is** her ex-husband.*
  ¡Tú **eres** mi amigo!   *You **are** my friend!*

◆ time. The singular form **es** is used to refer to *it is* for *one o'clock*. Use the plural **son** for all other hours.

Es la una y media.	*It is half past one.*
Son las ocho y cuarto.	*It is eight fifteen.*

◆ place and date of an event.

Mañana **es** mi cumpleaños.	*Tomorrow is my birthday.*
Las reuniones **son** en el salón de conferencias.	*The meetings are in the conference room.*
Hoy **es** el primero de mayo.	*Today is May 1.*

◆ origin, possession, and the materials that objects are made of, with the preposition **de**.

Estos zapatos **son de** Italia.	*These shoes are from Italy.*
La casa **es de** Lucy.	*The house is Lucy's.*
Mi reloj no **es de** oro.	*My watch is not (made of) gold.*

◆ quantity and price.

Cuatro por tres **son** doce.	*Four times three is twelve.*
—¿Cuánto **es**?	*"How much is it?"*
—**Son** doce euros.	*"It is twelve euros."*

Ser is also used

◆ in the passive voice construction **ser** + participle (+ **por**).

Las playas **son admiradas por** los turistas.	*The beaches are admired by the tourists.*
El libro **será publicado** en San Juan.	*The book will be published in San Juan.*

Note that in the passive voice construction with **ser**, the past participle of the verb functions as an adjective and must agree in gender and number with the subject.

◆ in impersonal expressions.

¡**Es urgente** llamar a tu casa ahora!	*It is urgent to call your house now!*

EJERCICIO
3·1

¿Verdadero o falso?

_____ 1. La luna es un planeta.

_____ 2. Picasso es un científico famoso.

_____ 3. Cuatro por cinco son veinte.

_____ 4. La biología es una ciencia.

_____ 5. Buenos Aires es la capital de Ecuador.

_____ 6. Una hora es una medida de tiempo.

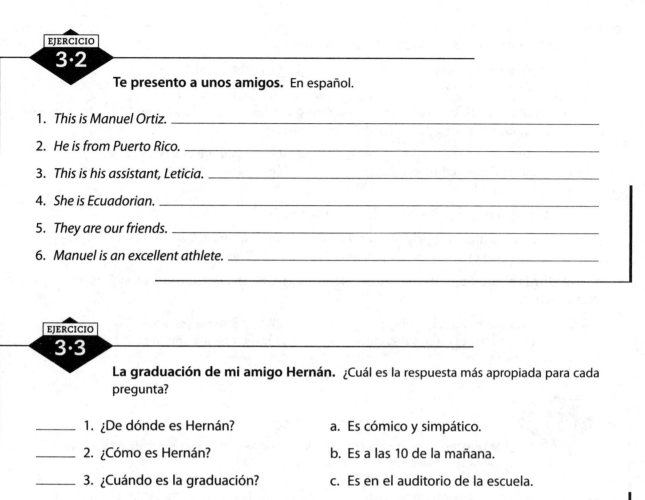

Te presento a unos amigos. En español.

1. *This is Manuel Ortiz.* _____

2. *He is from Puerto Rico.* _____

3. *This is his assistant, Leticia.* _____

4. *She is Ecuadorian.* _____

5. *They are our friends.* _____

6. *Manuel is an excellent athlete.* _____

La graduación de mi amigo Hernán. ¿Cuál es la respuesta más apropiada para cada pregunta?

_____ 1. ¿De dónde es Hernán?   a. Es cómico y simpático.

_____ 2. ¿Cómo es Hernán?   b. Es a las 10 de la mañana.

_____ 3. ¿Cuándo es la graduación?   c. Es en el auditorio de la escuela.

_____ 4. ¿A qué hora es?   d. Es gratis.

_____ 5. ¿Dónde es la ceremonia?   e. Es de San Diego, California.

_____ 6. ¿Cuánto es cada entrada?   f. Es el 25 de mayo.

When is **estar** used in Spanish?

You learned that **estar** is used mainly to indicate location and temporary situations or conditions. Use **estar** to express

◆ location—permanent, temporary, or short term, real or imaginary.

La ciudad de Miami **está** en la Florida.	*The city of Miami **is** in Florida.*
Estoy en la sala ahora.	*I **am** in the living room now.*
Estaré afuera en dos minutos.	*I **will be** outside in two minutes.*
Ella **está** en la luna.	*She **is** lost.*

◆ temporary physical conditions.

Los chicos **están** enfermos.	*The children **are** ill.*

Remember that temporary conditions are not characteristics. A temporary condition could indicate a short-lived state, as is the case with **están enfermos**. The condition described with **estar** could also indicate the result of a previous action.

La sesión **está cancelada**.	*The session **is canceled**.*

- temporary mental conditions and moods.

| ¡Yo **no estoy** loca! | *I **am not** crazy!* |
| ¡**Estás** deprimida! | ***You are** depressed!* |

- temporary traits or qualities. **Estar** emphasizes a short-term condition or a basis for a comparison with a previous state or condition.

| Hombre, **estás** delgado. | *Listen, **you are** (**you look**) thin.* |
| Para su edad, **están** muy maduros estos chicos. | *For their age, these kids **are** very mature.* |

- a temporary situation with the preposition **de**.

| Luisa **es** ingeniera pero ahora **está de** camarera en un restaurante muy fino. | *Luisa **is** an engineer, but now she **is** a server at a fancy restaurant.* |

Estar is also used with the **-ando, -iendo** forms of the **gerundio** in the present progressive construction.

| **Estamos buscando** trabajo. | *We **are looking for** work.* |
| Los bailarines **están saliendo** al escenario. | *The dancers **are coming out** to the stage.* |

EJERCICIO
3·4

¿Ser o estar? El entrenamiento. Lee las oraciones. De acuerdo al contexto, escribe la forma apropiada de **ser** o **estar**.

1. _____ las once de la mañana y Patricia _____ tomando el sol en su traje de baño.

2. Ella _____ lista para nadar una milla de estilo libre (*freestyle*).

3. Patricia _____ en muy buena forma (*good shape*).

4. Ella usa una crema y _____ muy buena para proteger la piel.

5. Los ejercicios de calentamiento (*warm-up*) _____ a las ocho de la mañana.

6. Patricia _____ una deportista dedicada.

EJERCICIO
3·5

¿Por qué? Vuelve al Ejercicio 3-4. Explica por qué escribiste **ser** o **estar** en cada oración.

1. _____

2. _____

3. _____

4. _____

5. _____

6. _____

Adjectives that change their meaning when used with either **ser** or **estar**

Ser and **estar** determine the meaning of some adjectives. The ideas they convey are different, as you can see in the following examples. Keep in mind that your choice of **ser** or **estar** will strongly affect your message.

ser		estar	
ser aburrido(a)	to be boring	**estar aburrido(a)**	to be bored
ser bueno(a)	to be good	**estar bueno(a)**	to be fine, tasty
ser listo(a)	to be clever	**estar listo(a)**	to be ready
ser malo(a)	to be bad	**estar malo(a)**	to be ill
ser orgulloso(a)	to be conceited, vain	**estar orgulloso(a)**	to be proud
ser pálido(a)	to be pale complexioned	**estar pálido(a)**	to be pale
ser rico(a)	to be rich	**estar rico(a)**	to be tasty
ser seguro(a)	to be safe	**estar seguro(a)**	to be sure, certain
ser viejo(a)	to be old	**estar viejo(a)**	to look old
ser vivo(a)	to be sharp	**estar vivo(a)**	to be alive

EJERCICIO 3·6

¿Ser o estar? Subraya (*underline*) la respuesta correcta.

1. Arturo quiere bailar. Él (es | está) listo para la fiesta.

2. ¡Ay! ¡Alicia tiene solamente treinta años pero en la foto (es | está) vieja!

3. Yo necesito saber la respuesta. Quiero (ser | estar) seguro.

4. Voy a comprar estos quesos. (Son | Están) frescos.

5. Los empleados (son | están) orgullosos de su trabajo.

6. Ella siempre ayuda a sus amigos. (Es | Está) atenta y servicial.

EJERCICIO 3·7

En español.

1. *I am depressed, but I am not crazy.* _____

2. *These are not my shoes.* _____

3. *Why are you (Uds.) here?* _____

4. *You (Uds.) are not sure!* _____

5. *Well, I am hungry and tired.* _____

6. *Are we ready to leave?* _____

7. *The game is at the university stadium.* _____

Expressions with estar

Estar appears in common expressions used in everyday communication in Spanish. Note the English equivalents of the examples.

estar a + date *to be a certain date*

Estamos a cuatro de mayo.	*It is May 4.*

estar a punto de + infinitive *to be just about to*

Estoy a punto de acabar.	*I am just about to finish.*

estar de acuerdo (con) *to agree with*

Estamos de acuerdo con María.	*We agree with María.*

estar para + infinitive *to be about to*

Estoy para salir.	*I am about to leave.*

estar por + a noun *to be in favor of*

Estoy por la reducción de los impuestos.	*I am in favor of cutting taxes.*

estar conforme (con) *to agree, be in agreement (with)*

¿**Están conformes con** nuestra decisión?	*Do you agree with our decision?*

estar de vacaciones *to be on vacation*

Eva López **está de vacaciones** en Los Ángeles.	*Eva López is on vacation in Los Angeles.*

estar de vuelta *to be back*

Todos **están de vuelta**.	*They are all back.*

EJERCICIO
3·8

Es lo mismo. Escoge la letra necesaria para traducir la frase.

_____ 1. *It's April 25.*   a. estar de vacaciones

_____ 2. *She is just about to finish.*   b. estar a punto de

_____ 3. *We are all for peace.*   c. estar a

_____ 4. *Do you (tú) agree with me?*   d. estar de acuerdo

_____ 5. *They are on vacation.*   e. estar de vuelta

_____ 6. *The boss is back.*   f. estar por

Te toca a ti. En español. *Go back to Ejercicio 3-8. Translate the numbered sentences into Spanish using the expressions you selected.*

1. _____

2. _____

3. _____

4. _____

5. _____

6. _____

Los deseos de un candidato y su familia. Traduce. Usa el **Vocabulario útil.**

Arturo Pérez, his wife, and his children are from Texas. Arturo's ancestors are from the Canary Islands, Spain. He is fifty-five years old, he is bilingual, and he is a lawyer. He is pleasant, tenacious, and very honest. Now, he is just about to start his campaign to be a judge. He thinks that he is the ideal candidate for this position. Melina, his wife, agrees with him, and she is ready to help Arturo in his campaign. She is very compassionate, and she is proud of her husband's professional success. Arturo's family hopes to celebrate his victory. Ángel, Arturo's grandson, believes that his grandfather can be the star of a new TV show on a Spanish station in San Antonio: "Judge Arturo." Ángel says that learning Spanish is in fashion.

Vocabulario útil

ancestor	**antepasado**	position	**el cargo; el puesto**
campaign	**la campaña**	tenacious	**tenaz**
Canary Islands	**las Islas Canarias**	that's why	**por eso**
compassionate	**compasivo(a)**	to be fashionable,	**estar a la moda,**
frank	**franco(a)**	to be in fashion	**estar de moda**
judge	**el juez, la juez(-a)**	to be just about to	**estar a punto de**
pleasant	**agradable**		

The preterit tense

Regular verbs in the preterit

The preterit (**el pretérito**) is one of several past tenses used in Spanish. As you study how to narrate and communicate in the past, you will be able to distinguish these past tenses by their endings and the specific functions they perform in context.

The preterit of regular verbs is formed by dropping the -**ar**, -**er**, and -**ir** of the infinitives and adding the following endings.

nadar (*to swim*)		**comer** (*to eat*)		**vivir** (*to live*)	
nad**é**	nad**amos**	com**í**	com**imos**	viv**í**	viv**imos**
nad**aste**	nad**asteis**	com**iste**	com**isteis**	viv**iste**	viv**isteis**
nad**ó**	nad**aron**	com**ió**	com**ieron**	viv**ió**	viv**ieron**

Note the following.

- The first- and third-person singular forms of the preterit have a written accent mark.

- The **nosotros** form of -**ar** and -**ir** verbs is the same in the preterit and the present.

The context (words surrounding the conjugated verb) will give you the clues necessary to identify and use the appropriate tense. In the examples that follow, each of the first two statements expresses an habitual action in the present with the help of the expressions **todos los días** (*every day*) and **siempre** (*always*). The present tense is appropriate in these examples.

| **Llegamos** a las doce **todos los días**. | *We arrive at noon every day.* |
| **Siempre viajamos** a California los veranos. | *We always travel to California in the summer.* |

On the other hand, the expressions of time **ayer... a la una y media** (*yesterday . . . at one thirty*) and **el año pasado** (*last year*) change the context of the statements, pointing to actions or events that took place at specific times in the past.

| **Ayer llegamos a la una y media.** | *Yesterday, we arrived at one thirty.* |
| **El año pasado viajamos** a Venezuela. | *Last year, we traveled to Venezuela.* |

These expressions of time provide context and help determine when the actions take or took place.

Noticias de ayer: un robo en una galería de arte. Escribe la forma apropiada del pretérito del verbo entre paréntesis.

1. Dos hombres _____ (robar) dos cuadros de Frida Kahlo en una galería.

2. La galería _____ (perder) sus pinturas más famosas.

3. Yo _____ (correr) detrás de un sospechoso (*suspect*) pero desapareció.

4. Los guardias de la galería no _____ (disparar) (*shoot*) las armas.

5. Marcelo y yo _____ (sospechar) que los guardias cooperaron con el robo (*robbery*).

6. ¿_____ (escuchar, tú) la noticia del robo por la radio?

7. Una agente de policía _____ (salir) en un carro de patrulla para buscar a los ladrones.

8. ¿_____ (comprar) ustedes el periódico para leer esa noticia?

When is the preterit used in Spanish?

Verb endings in Spanish indicate which noun or pronoun is doing the action. In addition, they provide details about the time and the circumstances under which the action takes place. As you describe experiences, events, or situations in the past, remember that different past tenses communicate different ideas. Thus, you must choose the tense that fits the message you want to convey. You have already seen some examples of uses of the preterit and expressions of time used with this tense.

The preterit is used to express

◆ an action that was totally completed in the past.

Ellos **viajaron** el mes pasado.　　　*They **traveled** last month.*

◆ an action completed at a definite, specific moment in the past.

Mi suegro **regresó** a las cuatro.　　　*My father-in-law **came back** at four o'clock.*

Key time expressions help us establish the meaning of each sentence. **El mes pasado** and **a las cuatro** point out the time the actions took place and signal the use of the preterit. Sometimes, these signals or expressions may not be stated literally. A single word such as **salí** is equivalent to *I left*, communicating a simple action completed in the past. Learn the following expressions, which indicate a specific or fixed point in the past, or when an action began or ended, so that you can use the preterit correctly.

Vocabulary

a esa hora	at that time	**el año pasado**	last year
anoche	last night	**el (lunes) pasado**	last (Monday)
anteanoche	the night before last	**el mes pasado**	last month
anteayer	the day before yesterday	**en ese momento**	at that moment
ayer al mediodía	yesterday at noon	**hace (diez) años**	(ten) years ago
ayer por la mañana	yesterday morning	**hoy por la mañana**	this morning
ayer por la noche	yesterday evening	**la semana pasada**	last week
ayer por la tarde	yesterday afternoon		

EJERCICIO 4·2

En español. Usa la lista de expresiones para escribir en español las oraciones siguientes.

1. *The night before last, Ana returned home.*

   _____

2. *This morning, Pilar sent three e-mails to the bank.*

   _____

3. *Roberto traveled to San Antonio last month.*

   _____

4. *Ten years ago, I moved to this building.*

   _____

5. *Detective Rojas and his assistant solved (**resolver**) the case last week.*

   _____

6. *At eight o'clock this morning, the doctor visited his new patient.*

   _____

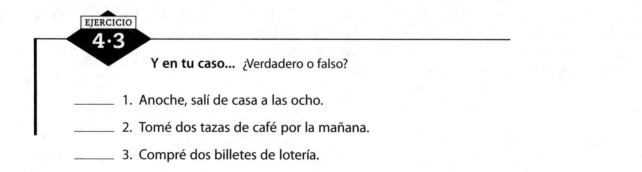

EJERCICIO 4·3

Y en tu caso... ¿Verdadero o falso?

_____ 1. Anoche, salí de casa a las ocho.

_____ 2. Tomé dos tazas de café por la mañana.

_____ 3. Compré dos billetes de lotería.

_____ 4. Visité un museo en la ciudad.

_____ 5. Regresé a casa por la tarde.

_____ 6. Leí mis mensajes en Internet.

Other uses of the preterit

The preterit is also used to communicate other actions in the past, such as

- ◆ an action or event that lasted for a specific period of time. If you can determine how long the action took place, use the preterit.

  Esperó dos horas en el consultorio del Dr. Bernal. | ***She waited two hours*** *at Dr. Bernal's office.*

- ◆ a series of actions or events completed in the past. Note that you may not be able to determine when these actions took place or for how long, yet you can identify a series of specific actions in the past.

  Yo llegué a la oficina, **preparé** un café, **me senté** y **llamé** a un cliente. | ***I arrived*** *at the office,* ***prepared*** *a cup of coffee,* ***sat down****, and* ***called*** *a client.*

- ◆ actions or events that are not usually repeated, using the following expressions.

cumplir años	to turn a specific age	**descubrir**	to discover
darse cuenta de	to realize	**graduarse**	to graduate
decidir	to decide	**morir**	to die

Usually, it is easy to establish that the action was completed at a certain point in the past or to determine the specific time it occurred, making the use of the preterit logical.

Mi hermano **cumplió** treinta años. | *My brother* ***turned*** *thirty.*
Los gemelos **se graduaron** hace varios años. | *The twins* ***graduated*** *a few years ago.*
Ella **murió** a los noventa años. | *She* ***died*** *at ninety years of age.*

EJERCICIO
4·4

Momentos importantes de la vida de Paco. Indica el orden de esos momentos con los números 1 a 5.

_____ 1. Estudió cuatro años en la escuela secundaria.

_____ 2. Trabajó en un proyecto de arquitectura por tres años.

_____ 3. Decidió cambiar de profesión.

_____ 4. Nació en una ciudad pequeña.

_____ 5. Se graduó de arquitecto de la Universidad de Madrid.

Carlos y yo pasamos el fin de semana juntos. En español.

Carlos y yo...

1. *bought a TV to watch movies.*

_____

2. *ate Mexican food, drank a soda, and washed the dishes.*

_____

3. *visited my aunt Matilde.*

_____

4. *arrived at 3:00 and chatted with my aunt.*

_____

5. *realized that Matilde's dog is very ugly.*

_____

¿Qué hiciste ayer? Escribe en español.

1. Por la mañana _____, _____ y _____.

2. Al mediodía, yo _____ y _____.

3. Por la tarde _____, _____ y también yo

_____.

4. Por la noche _____, _____ y _____.

Verbs with spelling changes in the preterit

Some verbs have spelling changes in the preterit tense. Technically, they are not irregular verbs, but the changes are required by Spanish spelling rules to preserve the hard sound of the consonants **c** and **g** with **-que** and **-gue**, as well as to maintain the soft sound before **i** and **e** with **c**. Note that in the preterit these changes apply to the **yo** form only.

- ◆ Verbs that end in **-car** change the **c** to **qu**: **explicar**, expli**qué**.
- ◆ Verbs that end in **-gar** change the **g** to **gu**: **llegar**, lle**gué**.
- ◆ Verbs that end in **-zar** change the **z** to **c**: **almorzar**, almor**cé**.

Study the following frequently used verbs that show these spelling changes.

-car		-gar		-zar	
atacar	to attack	**agregar**	to add	**abrazar**	to hug
buscar	to look for	**apagar**	to put out (*a light*)	**alcanzar**	to reach
chocar	to crash	**cargar**	to load	**almorzar**	to eat, have
colocar	to place	**castigar**	to punish		lunch
complicar	to complicate	**entregar**	to hand over	**cruzar**	to cross
explicar	to explain	**jugar**	to play (*a game*	**empezar**	to begin
pescar	to fish		*or sport*)	**gozar**	to enjoy
practicar	to practice	**negar**	to deny	**lanzar**	to throw
sacar	to take out	**pagar**	to pay	**rezar**	to pray
tocar	to touch; to play	**pegar**	to glue; to hit	**tranquilizar**	to calm
	(*music, an*			**tropezar**	to trip
	instrument)				

EJERCICIO
4·7

El sábado Marta estuvo muy ocupada. Subraya el verbo entre paréntesis que tiene sentido en la frase.

1. (Busqué | Indiqué) mi equipo de béisbol por toda la casa.

2. (Tranquilicé | Llegué) al parque a las ocho.

3. Entonces (lancé | abracé) la pelota unos minutos para calentar el brazo.

4. (Apagué | Jugué) un partido con mis amigos de la oficina.

5. Al mediodía (almorcé | cargué) con mis amigos.

6. Luego (crucé | saqué) unas fotos de mis colegas.

7. (Organicé | Castigué) una fiesta para mi jefe.

8. (Jugué | Toqué) el piano en la fiesta.

9. (Negué | Gocé) mucho ese día.

EJERCICIO
4·8

¿Qué hiciste tú? Busca el verbo que tiene sentido. Después, escribe la primera persona del pretérito.

abrazar	buscar	empezar	jugar	practicar
almorzar	colocar	explicar	pagar	tocar

1. _____ las cuentas a tiempo con mi tarjeta de crédito.

2. _____ una nueva dieta.

3. _____ un empleo en el periódico.

4. _____ el piano por dos horas.

5. _____ al tenis con un amigo.

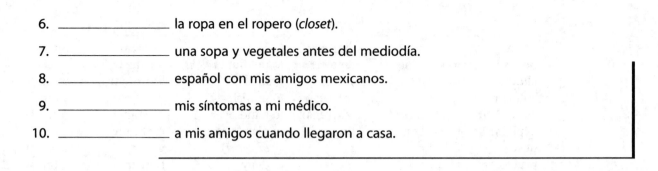

6. _____ la ropa en el ropero (*closet*).

7. _____ una sopa y vegetales antes del mediodía.

8. _____ español con mis amigos mexicanos.

9. _____ mis síntomas a mi médico.

10. _____ a mis amigos cuando llegaron a casa.

Other spelling changes in the preterit

Other verbs have spelling changes in the preterit. Observe the conjugations of **leer**, **oír**, and **construir**.

leer (*to read*)		oír (*to hear*)		construir (*to build*)	
leí	leímos	oí	oímos	construí	construimos
leíste	leísteis	oíste	oísteis	construiste	construisteis
leyó	leyeron	oyó	oyeron	construyó	construyeron

Observe that

◆ **leer**, **oír**, and **construir** change **i** to **y**, but only in the third-person singular and plural forms. All the forms of **leer** and **oír** have accent marks on the endings except the **ellos/ellas** form.

◆ other verbs frequently used in Spanish follow the patterns of **leer**, **oír**, and **construir**.

Read and study the following lists.

VERBS LIKE **leer**		VERBS LIKE **oír**		VERBS LIKE **construir**	
caer(se)	to fall	**desoír**	to ignore	**concluir**	to finish
creer	to believe			**contribuir**	to contribute
poseer	to own, possess			**distribuir**	to distribute
				huir	to flee
				incluir	to include
				intuir	to feel, have a sense

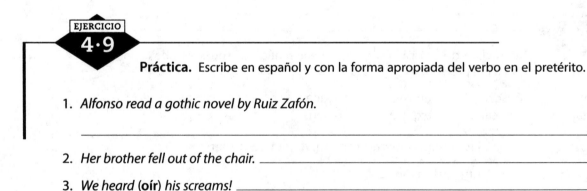

EJERCICIO
4·9

Práctica. Escribe en español y con la forma apropiada del verbo en el pretérito.

1. *Alfonso read a gothic novel by Ruiz Zafón.*

_____

2. *Her brother fell out of the chair.* _____

3. *We heard (**oír**) his screams!* _____

4. *Their dogs barked* (**ladrar**) *and contributed to the noise.*

_____

5. *The cat fled from the house.* _____

6. *Alfonso built this home many years ago.*

_____

7. *I had a feeling* (**intuir**) *that this family is crazy.*

_____

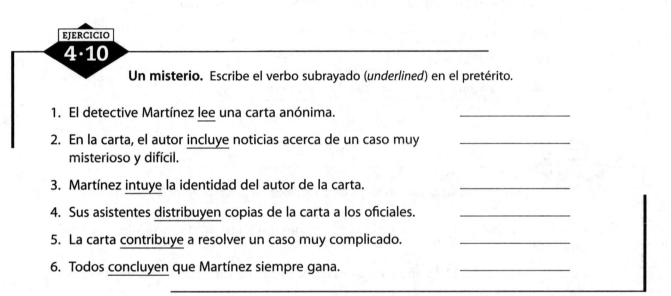

EJERCICIO
4·10

Un misterio. Escribe el verbo subrayado (*underlined*) en el pretérito.

1. El detective Martínez <u>lee</u> una carta anónima. _____

2. En la carta, el autor <u>incluye</u> noticias acerca de un caso muy _____
   misterioso y difícil.

3. Martínez <u>intuye</u> la identidad del autor de la carta. _____

4. Sus asistentes <u>distribuyen</u> copias de la carta a los oficiales. _____

5. La carta <u>contribuye</u> a resolver un caso muy complicado. _____

6. Todos <u>concluyen</u> que Martínez siempre gana. _____

Stem-changing verbs in the preterit

As in the present tense, there is a pattern of stem changes in the Spanish preterit. Remember that

- **-ar** verbs with stem changes in the present tense *do not* have stem changes in the preterit.

- **-ir** verbs with stem changes in the present tense also have stem changes in the preterit.

The changes in the preterit for **-ir** verbs are as follows: **e** changes to **i** and **o** changes to **u**, *only* in the third-person singular and plural forms.

pedir (*to ask for*)		**dormir** (*to sleep*)		**preferir** (*to prefer*)	
pedí	pedimos	dormí	dormimos	preferí	preferimos
pediste	pedisteis	dormiste	dormisteis	preferiste	preferisteis
p**i**dió	p**i**dieron	d**u**rmió	d**u**rmieron	pref**i**rió	pref**i**rieron

Study the following verbs conjugated like **pedir**, **dormir**, and **preferir**.

VERBS LIKE **pedir**		VERBS LIKE **dormir**		VERBS LIKE **preferir**	
conseguir	to get	**morir**	to die	**divertir**(se)	to have fun
convertir	to change			**mentir**	to lie (*tell a falsehood*)
reír	to laugh			**sentir**	to feel; to be sorry
repetir	to repeat				
seguir	to follow				
servir	to serve				
sonreír(se)	to smile				
vestir(se)	to get dressed				

Observe the conjugation of **reír** and **sonreír** in the preterit. All the forms except the third-person plural of **reír** and **sonreír** have a written accent mark.

reír (*to laugh*)		**sonreír** (*to smile*)	
reí	reímos	sonreí	sonreímos
reíste	reísteis	sonreíste	sonreísteis
rió	rieron	sonrió	sonrieron

EJERCICIO
4·11

Celebraron su aniversario en Cancún. Escribe la forma apropiada del pretérito.

1. Hace un mes, Mario y Pola _____ (conseguir) una oferta excelente en un hotel en Cancún.

2. Mario_____ (preferir) pagar más por una habitación con un balcón de cara a (*facing*) la playa.

3. Anoche, ellos _____ (dormir) en El Palacio de Cancún, un hotel de lujo.

4. Esta mañana el gerente del hotel les _____ (sonreír) y los saludó.

5. Entraron a la piscina y en el bar_____ (pedir) dos limonadas.

6. En pocos minutos, el camarero _____ (servir) la limonada.

7. Pola _____ (reírse) mucho con los comentarios y los chistes (*jokes*) del camarero.

8. Mario salió de la piscina y _____ (vestirse) para jugar minigolf.

9. Muchos de los visitantes _____ (pedir) una sombrilla para sentarse al frente de la playa.

10. En verdad, Mario y Pola _____ (divertirse) y _____ (disfrutar) mucho en Cancún.

¿Qué pasó? En español. Usa el pretérito.

1. *At the gym, Marisa managed (**conseguir**) to finish her exercises early.*

   _____

2. *She got dressed and arrived at the movies at 6:00 P.M.*

   _____

3. *She bought a ticket and ordered (**pedir**) a soda.*

   _____

4. *A young girl served her the drink and smiled.*

   _____

5. *In the theater, she sat and watched the commercials.*

   _____

6. *So many commercials! She paid to see a movie, not boring commercials!*

   _____

7. *Marisa slept for one hour.* _____

8. *She woke up twenty minutes before the end of the movie.*

   _____

Irregular verbs in the preterit

Many common verbs have irregular forms in the Spanish preterit. These verbs have irregular stems and are easy to group according to their patterns of stem changes and endings. Instead of the regular preterit verb endings, they have a distinctive set of endings. Note that they are without accent marks: **-e, -iste, -o, -imos, -isteis, -ieron.**

Study the following patterns of irregular verbs.

◆ Verbs with **uv** in the stem

andar (*to walk*)	**anduv-**	anduve, anduviste, anduvo, anduvimos, anduvisteis, anduvieron
estar (*to be*)	**estuv-**	estuve, estuviste, estuvo, estuvimos, estuvisteis, estuvieron
tener (*to have*)	**tuv-**	tuve, tuviste, tuvo, tuvimos, tuvisteis, tuvieron

◆ Verbs with **u** in the stem

caber (*to fit*)	**cup-**	cupe, cupiste, cupo, cupimos, cupisteis, cupieron
haber (*must, to be*)	**hub-**	hube, hubiste, hubo, hubimos, hubisteis, hubieron
poder (*to be able*)	**pud-**	pude, pudiste, pudo, pudimos, pudisteis, pudieron
poner (*to put*)	**pus-**	puse, pusiste, puso, pusimos, pusisteis, pusieron
saber (*to know*)	**sup-**	supe, supiste, supo, supimos, supisteis, supieron

Práctica. Usa el pretérito.

1. *Alberto could not.* _____

2. *Last night, Rita put the keys on the table.* _____

3. *The suitcase did not fit in the car trunk.* _____

4. *Yesterday, there was a meeting.* _____

5. *They were here.* _____

6. *I put the fork in the drawer (gaveta).* _____

7. *We had to go to the store.* _____

8. *Were you (Uds.) at the party?* _____

9. *My friends had an accident.* _____

◆ Verbs with **i** in the stem

hacer (*to do*)	**hic-**	hice, hiciste, hizo, hicimos, hicisteis, hicieron
querer (*to want*)	**quis-**	quise, quisiste, quiso, quisimos, quisisteis, quisieron
venir (*to come*)	**vin-**	vine, viniste, vino, vinimos, vinisteis, vinieron

Note that, because of a spelling change, the third-person form of **hacer** is **hizo**.

◆ Verbs that have **j** in the stem

atraer (*to attract*)	**atraj-**	atraje, atrajiste, atrajo, atrajimos, atrajisteis, atrajeron
decir (*to say*)	**dij-**	dije, dijiste, dijo, dijimos, dijisteis, dijeron
producir (*to produce*)	**produj-**	produje, produjiste, produjo, produjimos, produjisteis, produjeron
traer (*to bring*)	**traj-**	traje, trajiste, trajo, trajimos, trajisteis, trajeron
traducir (*to translate*)	**traduj-**	traduje, tradujiste, tradujo, tradujimos, tradujisteis, tradujeron

Note that the third-person plural ending of this last group of verbs is **-eron**.

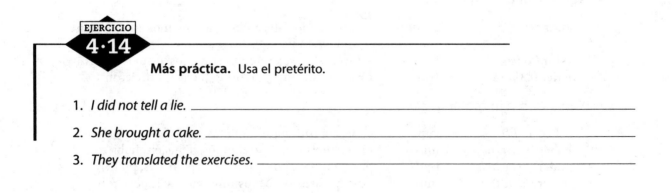

Más práctica. Usa el pretérito.

1. *I did not tell a lie.* _____

2. *She brought a cake.* _____

3. *They translated the exercises.* _____

4. *We did the work.* _____

5. *You (tú) came late.* _____

6. *Tim did the homework.* _____

7. *Did they come?* _____

Now that you have learned irregular verbs in the Spanish preterit, you will be able to conjugate and use compound verbs.

Many compound verbs are formed with a prefix plus an irregular verb. These compounds follow the conjugation patterns of the basic verbs. Here are some examples.

COMPOUNDS OF **poner**		COMPOUNDS OF **hacer** AND **venir**	
componer	to repair; to compose	**deshacer**	to undo
disponer	to arrange; to dispose	**rehacer**	to make over; to rebuild
suponer	to assume	**convenir**	to agree

COMPOUNDS OF **decir, producir,** AND **traer**	
desdecir	to disagree
predecir	to predict
reproducir	to reproduce
atraer	to attract
distraer	to distract

More irregular verbs in the preterit

Dar, ser, and **ir** are irregular.

dar (*to give*)		**ser** (*to be*) AND **ir** (*to go*)	
di	dimos	fui	fuimos
diste	disteis	fuiste	fuisteis
dio	dieron	fue	fueron

Note that

♦ **dar** takes the regular **-er**, **-ir** preterit endings.

♦ **ser** and **ir** forms in the preterit are the same for both verbs. The context (the words surrounding the verb) will help you guess their meaning.

Ellos **no fueron** a la playa el domingo.	*They **did not go** to the beach on Sunday.*
Ellos **fueron** los campeones del torneo de golf.	*They **were** the champions of the golf tournament.*

In the first example, **ir** is the logical guess because the preposition **a** follows: **a la playa**. In the second example, **fueron**, a preterit form of **ser**, links the pronoun **ellos** and the noun **campeones**. For better understanding, always try to read or listen to the entire sentence or meaningful group of words.

La semana pasada en la agencia. Escribe la forma del pretérito que corresponde.

1. El lunes, Ana _____ (hacer) todo su trabajo.

2. La Srta. Simpson _____ (traer) unos paquetes para las secretarias.

3. La secretaria le _____ (dar) un informe a su jefe.

4. Paula y yo _____ (ir) al departamento de finanzas.

5. El miércoles, yo _____ (poner) un aviso en el boletín (*newsletter*).

6. El vicepresidente de la compañía _____ (venir) a saludar a los trabajadores.

7. El jueves, los anuncios en la página de la Web _____ (producir) buenos resultados.

8. Ana y yo _____ (proponer) una campaña para la tele.

9. El viernes, yo no _____ (poder) ir a la oficina.

10. Mi jefe _____ (suponer) que yo estaba enfermo.

Verbs with a special meaning in the preterit

Some verbs change their basic meaning when conjugated in the preterit. Remember the following special meanings in the preterit.

- **conocer** (*to meet*)

    Conocí al director de la escuela ayer.   *I **met** the school principal yesterday.*

- **saber** (*to find out, discover*)

    Supo la verdad.   *He **found out** the truth.*

- **poder** (*to manage*)

    No pudieron terminar.   *They **did not manage** to finish.*

- **querer** (*to refuse* [*in negative sentences*])

    Yo no quise salir a tiempo.   *I **refused** to leave on time.*

- **querer** (*to try*)

    Marta **quiso** ayudarme.   *Marta **tried** to help me.*

- **tener** (*to receive, get*)

    Tuve noticias hoy.   *I **got** (**received**) news today.*

En español. Usa el pretérito en tus respuestas.

1. *Yesterday, I met Lily, the new secretary.*

   _____

2. *I found out she speaks three languages.*

   _____

3. *But she did not manage to finish her first task on time.*

   _____

4. *She refused to work after five o'clock.*

   _____

5. *Lily translated three documents.* _____

6. *She did a great job.* _____

7. *I read the documents.* _____

8. *We found out the news the next day.*

   _____

9. *Lily left before five and did not come back the next day.*

   _____

10. *I refused to believe it. We need a new secretary!*

    _____

¿Verdadero o falso? Un poco de historia.

_____ 1. John Glenn fue el primer hombre que alunizó en nuestro satélite, la Luna.

_____ 2. Los chinos enviaron el primer perro al espacio.

_____ 3. El muro de Berlín cayó en 1990.

_____ 4. La Copa del Mundial 2010 se celebró en España.

_____ 5. Los juegos olímpicos de 2008 fueron en China.

_____ 6. La ciudad de Albuquerque celebró el tercer centenario hace pocos años.

_____ 7. En 1947 Hawái se convirtió en el estado número 50 de los Estados Unidos.

_____ 8. El primer vuelo transatlántico sin escalas (*nonstop*) ocurrió en 1933.

EJERCICIO

4·18

Matemáticas, ¿dónde estás? Traduce. Usa el **Vocabulario útil**.

A bookstore is not just a place to buy printed books. Yesterday, I spent hours at my favorite bookstore. I sat on the floor and read a couple of magazines. With a copy of a new novel, I moved to a very comfortable chair near the café. I decided to drink a cup of green tea. Then, I listened to my favorite songs from my laptop. Later, I went to the Spanish book section and found out that Mathematics, where are you? is a real book! I never understood math, but I picked out the paperback book. I went to the cash register, but I refused to buy it at the store. I found a promotion online with a fifteen percent discount and free shipping. Of course, I had to do my math to find out the real price!

Vocabulario útil

bookstore	**la librería**	magazine	**la revista**
cash register	**la caja (registradora)**	paperback	**la edición de bolsillo**
comfortable	**cómodo(a)**	place	**el lugar**
couple	**un par**	printed	**impreso(a)**
discount	**el descuento**	real	**de verdad; real**
free shipping	**el envío gratis**	to do the math	**sacar cuentas**
laptop	**el ordenador portátil;**	to pick (out)	**elegir, coger, tomar**
	la computadora portátil		

The imperfect tense

The imperfect (**el pretérito imperfecto** or **el imperfecto**) is a tense used to communicate certain circumstances about actions occurring in the past. One of these circumstances is the unspecified duration or length of the action; another is how frequently the action took place.

When narrating in the past, we may want to recount what we used to do in earlier days, without setting specific times or the length of the actions. We may consider this an indeterminate duration. The beginning and ending of the action is neither specified nor necessary for your message.

> **Yo tenía** un perro.   *I used to have a dog.*

The message may also indicate the repeated nature of some actions while, again, not specifying the length of the action or the point at which it started or finished. In the next example, the imperfect communicates an action that was ongoing in the past.

> Mi perro Sultán y yo **jugábamos**   *My dog Sultan and I **played** almost*
> casi todos los días.   *every day.*

Regular verbs in the imperfect

The imperfect is formed by dropping the endings of the infinitive, **-ar**, **-er**, and **-ir**, and adding the following endings.

nadar (*to swim*)		**comer** (*to eat*)		**vivir** (*to live*)	
nad**aba**	nad**ábamos**	com**ía**	com**íamos**	viv**ía**	viv**íamos**
nad**abas**	nad**abais**	com**ías**	com**íais**	viv**ías**	viv**íais**
nad**aba**	nad**aban**	com**ía**	com**ían**	viv**ía**	viv**ían**

Note that in the imperfect

- ◆ **-er** and **-ir** verbs share the same endings and all forms have a written accent mark.

- ◆ the **nosotros** form is the only **-ar** verb form with a written accent mark.

Visita a Punta Cana. Usa la forma apropiada del imperfecto de los verbos entre paréntesis.

1. Todas las mañanas, Ignacio _____ (caminar) por la arena en la playa.

2. Por lo general Ignacio _____ (ponerse) su careta para bucear (*swim underwater*).

3. Generalmente él _____ (nadar) por un rato y luego _____ (dormir).

4. De vez en cuando nosotros dos _____ (jugar) al voleibol en la playa.

5. También yo _____ (correr) por la arena muchas veces.

6. Raras veces, yo _____ (volver) a mi habitación antes de las tres.

7. Todos los días, yo _____ (comer) platos dominicanos.

8. _____ (Querer, yo) visitar Fun-Fun, una cueva (*cave*) muy profunda cerca del hotel.

9. Ignacio _____ (preferir) un vuelo en helicóptero.

10. Él y yo _____ (soñar) con pescar barracudas en un barco grande.

¿Qué hacía Carlos? Usa el verbo más apropiado para cada frase. Escribe la forma correspondiente del imperfecto.

aprender	cantar	leer	recibir	tocar
arreglar	jugar	mirar	tener	vivir

1. _____ fútbol todos los días.

2. _____ en su clase mucho.

3. _____ su cama todas las mañanas.

4. _____ el piano a menudo.

5. _____ buenas notas.

6. _____ cuentos de fantasía.

7. _____ en San Antonio.

8. _____ la televisión por las noches.

9. _____ un perro y un gato.

10. _____ cuando se bañaba.

Irregular verbs in the imperfect

It is easy to remember that there are only three verbs with irregular conjugations in the imperfect: **ir**, **ser**, and **ver**.

ir *(to go)*		ser *(to be)*		ver *(to see)*	
iba	íbamos	era	éramos	veía	veíamos
ibas	ibais	eras	erais	veías	veíais
iba	iban	era	eran	veía	veían

EJERCICIO
5·3

Festivales de música caribeña. Usa la forma apropiada del imperfecto de **ir**, **ver** o **ser**, de acuerdo al contenido de la frase.

1. Todos los veranos, nosotros _____ a un festival de música del Caribe.

2. Los conciertos _____ en San Juan.

3. Los grupos de cantantes siempre _____ fantásticos.

4. Mis amigos y yo _____ muy jóvenes y animábamos (*cheer*) a los grupos.

5. Personas de todas las edades _____ los conciertos en una pantalla gigante en un parque.

6. El espectáculo _____ divertido y la gente bailaba y cantaba.

7. Carlos y Ana _____ a sus padres bailando y sacaban fotos.

8. Al final del festival los músicos y los cantantes _____ a saludar al público.

When is the imperfect used in Spanish?

The imperfect is one of the tenses used to narrate past actions. Unlike the preterit, the imperfect does not refer to the specific time an action took place or when the beginning or the end of an action occurred. The imperfect tense describes the ongoing duration of an action or how frequently the action took place. You will use the imperfect tense

◆ to describe continuing, ongoing actions in the past.

Elsa **tenía** muchos amigos y pocas preocupaciones.

*Elsa **had** many friends and few worries.*

The above example refers to a past time (**tenía**). It does not tell us exactly when or for how long Elsa was in these circumstances. The speaker's message (with **tenía**) includes the notion of a continuing action.

◆ to indicate actions that took place on a regular basis, that were repeated, or that were habitual or customary in the past.

Cuando Carlos **vivía** en Nueva York, **iba** al teatro con frecuencia.

*When Carlos **lived** in New York, **he used to go** to the theater frequently.*

In the previous example, the imperfect form **vivía** refers to a past, ongoing time when Carlos lived in New York. It does not tell us when specifically the action of **vivir** took place, nor for how long. The second part of the sentence, **iba** (*he used to go*), refers to a past action whose exact time or number of times is not specified, since it is not important to the message. Rather, the emphasis is on the repeated nature of Carlos's activity, reinforced by the expression **con frecuencia** (*frequently*).

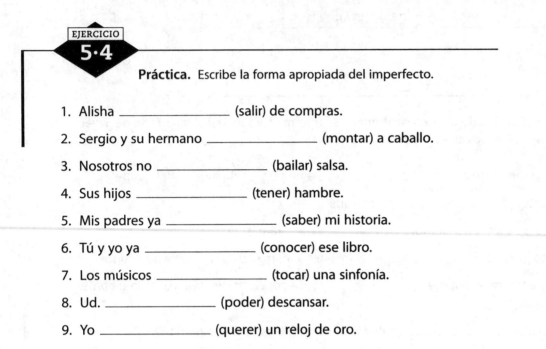

EJERCICIO
5·4

Práctica. Escribe la forma apropiada del imperfecto.

1. Alisha _____ (salir) de compras.
2. Sergio y su hermano _____ (montar) a caballo.
3. Nosotros no _____ (bailar) salsa.
4. Sus hijos _____ (tener) hambre.
5. Mis padres ya _____ (saber) mi historia.
6. Tú y yo ya _____ (conocer) ese libro.
7. Los músicos _____ (tocar) una sinfonía.
8. Ud. _____ (poder) descansar.
9. Yo _____ (querer) un reloj de oro.

Other uses of the imperfect

The imperfect tense is also used in other circumstances. Remember to use the imperfect

◆ to describe people or states of indefinite duration in the past.

> **Era** un político muy honrado.   ***He was** a very honest politician.*

In this example, **era** underscores the ongoing nature of the characteristic. Again, the description does not convey a specific time or times.

Keep in mind that **ser** is used to describe qualities or states of indefinite duration in the past.

> Marta **era** extremadamente   *Marta **was** extremely careful.*
> cuidadosa.

◆ to express the English equivalent of the construction *would* + verb, referring to actions that took place repeatedly or customarily in the past.

> **Yo pasaba** muchas horas allí.   ***I would** (**used to**) **spend** many hours there.*

Note that this use of *would* does not imply the conditional mood in English. There is no condition to be met. Compare the following examples and observe the context.

Compraría (*conditional*) el carro pero no tiene dinero.	*She would buy the car, but she does not have the money.*
Compraba (*imperfect*) un vestido nuevo todos los meses el día de cobro.	*She would buy (**used to buy**) a new dress every month on payday.*

In the first example, *would buy* is a clear use of the conditional in English and corresponds to the use of the conditional in Spanish; if a condition were met—having money—then *she would buy the car*. In the second example, *she would buy* is the same as *she used to buy*, a customary action, and the Spanish equivalent is **compraba**. The sentence includes an expression of time, **todos los meses**, indicating a repeated action and showing its habitual nature (**compraba**).

EJERCICIO
5·5

¿Qué hacían? En español.

1. *Ana would buy chocolates.* _____

2. *I used to write postcards.* _____

3. *She used to swim.* _____

4. *You (**Ud.**) would call often.* _____

5. *You (**Uds.**) and I would work.* _____

6. *They used to go to the library.* _____

7. *You (**tú**) would always help.* _____

8. *Louise and you (**tú**) would save money.* _____

Certain expressions of time stress the customary or repetitive nature of the actions in the imperfect tense. You learned some of these expressions in Ejercicio 5-1. The list that follows contains several more. Try to use these expressions when you use the imperfect to communicate repeated actions in the past.

Vocabulary

a menudo	often	**muchas veces**	many times
a veces	at times	**por lo general**	generally
algunas veces	sometimes	**rara vez**	rarely
casi nunca	hardly ever	**siempre**	always
casi siempre	almost always	**todas las mañanas**	every morning
de vez en cuando	from time to time	**todos los años**	every year
generalmente	generally	**todos los días**	every day
mientras	while		

En español. Usa la forma apropiada del imperfecto en tus respuestas.

1. *Every day, she would rest after lunch.* _____

2. *Almost always, they put sugar in their coffee.*

   _____

3. *At times, you (**Ud.**) would get up early.* _____

4. *From time to time, Sheila stayed at home.* _____

5. *Generally, the train arrived late in the morning.*

   _____

6. *Many times, I would miss the bus.* _____

7. *My mother would hardly ever sleep.* _____

More about the uses of the imperfect

The imperfect is also used

- ◆ to express age in the past.

  La actriz **tenía** treinta años.   *The actress **was** thirty years old.*

- ◆ to describe the background or circumstances of an action.

  Era un día hermoso, fresco.   *It **was** a beautiful, cool day.*

- ◆ to indicate the time of day in the past.

  Eran las cuatro de la tarde.   *It **was** four in the afternoon.*

Cuando Lucinda vivía en Ponce. Traduce las experiencias de Lucinda. Nota las frases que indican las costumbres y actividades usuales.

1. *When I was twenty years old, I used to live in Ponce, Puerto Rico.*

   _____

2. *Every morning, I went to my Spanish class.*

   _____

3. Usually, my class would end at midday.

_____

4. My friends and I wanted to stay in a nice city.

_____

5. I would often go to the market to talk to the local folks.

_____

6. Once in a while, I would miss my family.

_____

7. But hardly ever would I want to go back home.

_____

8. On Sundays, Carla and Jorge used to take me to have dinner at their home.

_____

9. Jorge would make jokes, but they were not funny.

_____

¿Por qué usamos el imperfecto? *Go back to your answers to the previous exercise (Ejercicio 5-7). For each statement, write down any key Spanish expression that signals a customary or repeated action. If no expression of time appears in a given statement, leave a blank.*

1. _____

2. _____

3. _____

4. _____

5. _____

6. _____

7. _____

8. _____

9. _____

The imperfect is also used to express the past

◆ to indicate a mental state, a mental action, or a state of indefinite duration with verbs such as **sentir**, **creer**, **conocer**, **pensar**, **querer**, and **saber**. Mental states are considered ongoing conditions.

Él pensaba en mí.	*He thought about me.*
Nos conocíamos desde que **éramos** pequeños.	*We have known each other since we were little.*
Me gustaba caminar por las calles.	*I used to like walking down the streets.*

◆ in the Spanish equivalent of the English *-ing* forms, referring to past actions. Usually, they refer to *simultaneous* actions, and there is no mention of a specific time in the past.

Ella trabajaba y yo **descansaba**.	*She was working and I was resting.*
El ladrón salía mientras **nosotras entrábamos** a la habitación.	*The thief was leaving while we were going into the room.*

EJERCICIO
5·9

Y el verbo es... Completa las frases con la forma apropiada de uno de los verbos. Usa el imperfecto.

comprar   estar   salir
decir   pensar   sentir

1. Siempre _____ en ti.

2. Yo no _____ mentiras (*lies*).

3. Sus amigos _____ mucho dolor.

4. En el cine tú _____ las entradas.

5. El día _____ espectacular.

6. Llovía cuando tú _____ de la tienda.

The imperfect and the preterit in the same sentence

Often, more than one tense will be needed in a sentence: the imperfect to point out ongoing actions or background information and the preterit to express actions seen as "interrupting" the actions in the imperfect.

Llovía y de momento **salió el sol**.	*It was raining, and all of a sudden the sun came out.*

In the previous example, note the description in the past. The verb **llovía** appears in the imperfect. While this action is taking place, a different action is expressed in the preterit (**salió**). **De momento** (*suddenly*) points to the specific time that action took place. The preterit is the appropriate tense to express the "interrupting" action.

> Mientras **caminaba** por la calle me **saludó Juan**.

> *While **I was walking** down the street, **Juan greeted** me.*

The ongoing action in the second example above is **caminaba**, expressed with reference to **saludó**, an action completed in the past. Again, the preterit is used to describe the "interrupting" action.

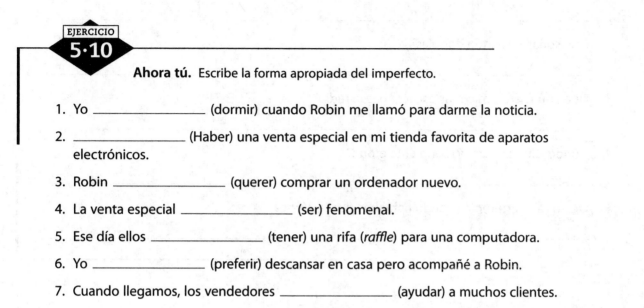

EJERCICIO 5·10

Ahora tú. Escribe la forma apropiada del imperfecto.

1. Yo _____ (dormir) cuando Robin me llamó para darme la noticia.

2. _____ (Haber) una venta especial en mi tienda favorita de aparatos electrónicos.

3. Robin _____ (querer) comprar un ordenador nuevo.

4. La venta especial _____ (ser) fenomenal.

5. Ese día ellos _____ (tener) una rifa (*raffle*) para una computadora.

6. Yo _____ (preferir) descansar en casa pero acompañé a Robin.

7. Cuando llegamos, los vendedores _____ (ayudar) a muchos clientes.

EJERCICIO 5·11

¿Qué pasó mientras Luis...? Escribe la forma apropiada del imperfecto del verbo que corresponde a cada oración.

bañarse	entrar	leer	regresar
dormir	hablar	mirar	ser

1. _____ cuando sonó el despertador.

2. _____ cuando tú llamaste por teléfono.

3. _____ el periódico y entonces el perro quiso salir al patio.

4. Salía de casa cuando _____ las ocho.

5. _____ en el mercado cuando empezó a llover.

6. _____ la televisión cuando empezó su película favorita.

7. Mientras _____ con un cliente, el jefe lo interrumpió.

8. _____ a casa cuando descubrieron al ladrón.

Preguntas personales.

1. ¿Qué hacías ayer mientras trabajabas?

   _____

2. ¿Qué soñaste cuando dormías?

   _____

3. ¿Qué anunciaron mientras escuchabas la radio?

   _____

4. ¿Dónde estabas cuando sonó el teléfono?

   _____

5. ¿Quién te interrumpió cuando hablabas por teléfono?

   _____

EJERCICIO
5·13

Un viaje a las aguas del Caribe. Traduce. Usa el **Vocabulario útil**.

Charlotte travels frequently. When she was a girl, she would visit her aunt in Alaska. They would take guided tours to watch the whales. When she was a student at a university, she wanted to be a marine biologist. In those days, she would prefer to travel to the Caribbean. In the spring, she would book a round-trip ticket. She always traveled on a nonstop flight to Punta Cana, in the Dominican Republic. As usual, she would check her luggage and walk to the gate. Upon landing, she would pick up her suitcase and go through customs. Her suitcase was heavy, because she would pack her diving gear. From the airport, she would go on a bus to a hotel in the Bay of Samaná. The next day, she was ready for an exciting experience: whale watching in a warm climate. Charlotte was able to watch and study more whales in the Caribbean than in Alaska!

Vocabulario útil

as usual	**como de costumbre**	suitcase	**la maleta**
bay	**la bahía**	ticket	**el boleto, el billete**
Bay of Samaná	**la Bahía de Samaná**	to book (a trip)	**hacer la reserva de**
customs	**la aduana**		**(un viaje)**
gate	**la puerta de embarque**	to check luggage	**facturar el equipaje**
guided tour	**la excursión con guía**	to dive	**bucear**
luggage	**el equipaje**	upon landing	**al aterrizar**
nonstop flight	**el vuelo directo**	whale	**la ballena**
round-trip ticket	**el billete, el boleto de**	whale watching	**observar las ballenas**
	ida y vuelta		

More about the preterit and the imperfect

Summary and contrast of the preterit and the imperfect

Continue to review and contrast the uses of the preterit and the imperfect, keeping in mind the ideas you want to communicate when narrating in the past. In English, the context often communicates the meanings conveyed by Spanish verb tenses alone, since Spanish verb endings give the subject of the verb and also the time (present, past, future, etc.). Contrast *She used to smoke* with **Fumaba**, where a single word indicates a habitual action repeated in the past.

This unit will help you review and practice the preterit and the imperfect and their specific messages. As you work with the exercises, you may wish to go back to the previous units (Units 4 and 5) on the preterit and the imperfect to review the explanations.

The following sections summarize the uses of the preterit and the imperfect tenses.

Preterit

Use the preterit when you wish

◆ to indicate an action that took place in the past.

Ellos se casaron el mes pasado.   *They got married last month.*

◆ to express an action completed at a definite moment in the past.

Los Ortega **regresaron** anoche.   *The Ortegas returned last night.*
Yo estuve en su casa por tres horas.   *I was in their house for three hours.*

◆ to express a series of actions or events completed in the past.

Tú entraste, miraste a Felipe y le   *You entered, looked at Felipe, and*
diste la mano.   *shook his hand.*

◆ to express actions that, because of their nature, are not usually repeated, such as *to get married* (**casarse**), *to turn a specific age* (**cumplir años**), *to realize (something)* (**darse cuenta de**), *to decide* (**decidir**), *to graduate* (**graduarse**), *to die* (**morir**), etc.

El hijo de Antonio **nació** en ese   *Antonio's son was born in that*
hospital.   *hospital.*

Here are some expressions associated with the use of the preterit.

anoche	last night	**entonces**	then
anteanoche	the night before last	**finalmente**	finally
anteayer	the day before yesterday	**la semana pasada**	last week
ayer	yesterday	**por fin**	finally
de pronto	suddenly	**por primera vez**	for the first time
de repente	suddenly	**un día**	one day
el mes pasado	last month	**una noche**	one night
en ese (aquel) instante	at that moment	**una vez**	once
en ese (aquel) momento	at that moment		

Imperfect

Use the imperfect tense

- ◆ to describe actions that took place on a regular basis, that were repeated, or that were habitual or customary in the past.

  Yo veía a mis primos todas las semanas.   *I used to see my cousins every week.*

- ◆ to describe continuing or ongoing conditions or actions in the past.

  El teatro **tenía** tres salidas.   *The theater **had** three exits.*

- ◆ to describe people or states of indefinite duration in the past with no reference to its beginning or end.

  Su esposo **era** alto.   *Her husband **was** tall.*
  Nosotros **estábamos** muy nerviosos.   *We **were** very nervous.*

- ◆ to express age in the past.

  Mis abuelos **tenían** sesenta años.   *My grandparents **were** sixty years old.*

- ◆ to express time in the past.

  Eran las diez.   *It **was** ten o'clock.*

- ◆ to express a mental state or a mental action.

  Ellas pensaban en sus parientes.   *They **were thinking** (**used to think**) about their relatives.*

Here are some expressions associated with the use of the imperfect.

a menudo	often, frequently	**mientras**	while
a veces	at times	**muchas veces**	many times
algunas veces	sometimes	**normalmente**	normally
cada día, cada noche	each day, each night	**por lo general**	generally
con frecuencia	frequently, often	**siempre**	always
constantemente	constantly	**todas las mañanas, tardes...**	every morning, afternoon . . .
de costumbre	usually		
de vez en cuando	from time to time	**todos los meses, años...**	every month, year . . .
frecuentemente	frequently		
generalmente	generally		

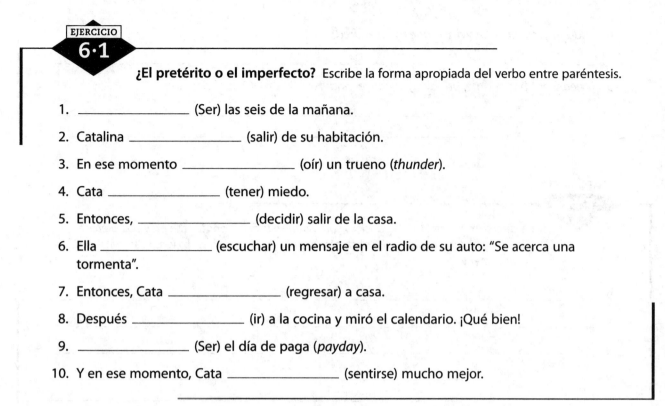

EJERCICIO

6·1

¿El pretérito o el imperfecto? Escribe la forma apropiada del verbo entre paréntesis.

1. _____ (Ser) las seis de la mañana.

2. Catalina _____ (salir) de su habitación.

3. En ese momento _____ (oír) un trueno (*thunder*).

4. Cata _____ (tener) miedo.

5. Entonces, _____ (decidir) salir de la casa.

6. Ella _____ (escuchar) un mensaje en el radio de su auto: "Se acerca una tormenta".

7. Entonces, Cata _____ (regresar) a casa.

8. Después _____ (ir) a la cocina y miró el calendario. ¡Qué bien!

9. _____ (Ser) el día de paga (*payday*).

10. Y en ese momento, Cata _____ (sentirse) mucho mejor.

EJERCICIO

6·2

Los domingos. En español. El domingo, ¿es tu día favorito también? Usa el pretérito para los verbos subrayados.

1. *Sunday was my favorite day of the week. I would wake up late and read the newspaper in bed.*

_____

2. *That Sunday was different.* _____

3. *I got up early, got dressed quickly, and left to ride my bike around the neighborhood* (**el barrio**).

_____

4. *It was a beautiful morning. It was chilly, too.*

_____

5. *While I rode my bicycle, there were many active people in the park.*

_____

6. *Two young women were jogging while a dog followed them.*

_____

7. *An older gentleman exercised in the park, and two children played.*

_____

8. *Suddenly, so much activity <u>made</u> me feel tired.*

_____

9. *I then <u>went</u> back home, <u>put away</u> the bike, and <u>fixed</u> a cup of hot chocolate.*

_____

_____

EJERCICIO
6·3

La decisión correcta. *Go back to your Spanish translations for the previous exercise (Ejercicio 6-2), and explain why each of the underlined English verbs was best translated by the preterit.*

2. _____

3. _____

8. _____

9. _____

More uses of the preterit and the imperfect

The following reference list contains a few more uses of these two tenses.

◆ The preterit is used to "interrupt" an ongoing action or the background information surrounding an action in the past.

Hacía un día hermoso y de repente **empezó** a llover.	*It was a beautiful day, and suddenly it started to rain.*
El reportero **salía** de la tienda cuando **ocurrió** el accidente.	*The reporter was leaving the store when the accident occurred.*

◆ The imperfect is used to indicate simultaneous actions.

Ana **cocinaba** mientras yo **preparaba** la mesa.	*Ana cooked while I set the table.*

◆ If you want to express an action that went on for a period of time in the past, you may use the following constructions: (1) **hacía** + expression of time + **que** + verb in the imperfect, or (2) verb in the imperfect + **desde hacía** + expression of time.

Hacía tres meses **que trabajaba** en la oficina de turismo.	*I had been working in the tourist office for three months.*
Trabajaba en la oficina de turismo **desde hacía** tres meses.	

To ask a question using this construction, use either of the following models.

¿**Cuánto (tiempo) hacía que** + verb in the imperfect?
¿**Hacía cuánto (tiempo) que** + verb in the imperfect?

Study the following three examples of these constructions and their single English equivalent.

¿Cuánto tiempo hacía que trabajabas
    en la oficina de turismo?
¿Hacía cuánto tiempo que trabajabas
    en la oficina de turismo?   *How long had you been working in the*
¿Desde cuándo trabajabas en la oficina   *tourist office?*
    de turismo?

If you want to express a past action that took place at a specific time (*ago*), use the preterit in the following construction.

Hace + expression of time + **que** + verb in the preterit

    Hace dos meses **que vi** a Ricardo.   *I saw Ricardo two months **ago**.*

EJERCICIO 6·4

En español.

1. *While I was doing my work, a patient called me on the phone.*

    _____

2. *She was talking, and all of a sudden she hung up (**colgar**) the phone.*

    _____

3. *I was looking for a document when someone knocked on the door.*

    _____

4. *My assistant opened the window (**la ventanilla**) while I filled out the form (**el formulario**).*

    _____

EJERCICIO 6·5

¿Qué hacías tú? Traduce la expresión entre paréntesis. Usa la expresión para completar la frase, según el ejemplo.

EJEMPLO   iba a la playa (*once in a while*)   *yo iba a la playa de vez en cuando.*

Cuando yo era más joven...

1. leía novelas de ciencia-ficción (*often*) _____
2. salía con mis amigos (*every weekend*) _____
3. ponía la mesa para la cena (*every night*) _____
4. no me preocupaba mucho (*never*) _____
5. era muy impaciente (*always*) _____

EJERCICIO

6·6

En español. Escribe en español la expresión entre paréntesis.

1. (*On Monday*) compré una novela de ciencia-ficción. _____

2. (*Last weekend*) salí con mis amigos. _____

3. (*Last night*) puse la mesa para la cena. _____

4. (*Two months ago*) estuve preocupado por mi situación económica. _____

5. (*Yesterday*) estaba muy impaciente. _____

6. (*This morning*) pensé en mis padres. _____

EJERCICIO

6·7

¿Cuál es la respuesta correcta? Decide si el pretérito o el imperfecto es la respuesta correcta y subráyala. *Remember that the message in an isolated sentence must rely on the words surrounding the verb. You may find that both tenses are acceptable in some of your answers.*

1. Julio (salía | salió) a las ocho en punto.

2. (Hacía | Hizo) buen tiempo cuando empezó el partido de tenis.

3. (Veíamos | Vimos) la película el mes pasado.

4. Los vendedores (ganaban | ganaron) el 20% de comisión ese día.

5. Los niños (creían | creyeron) el cuento.

6. Ustedes (eran | fueron) imparciales.

7. Mientras tú cantabas yo (tocaba | toqué) el piano.

EJERCICIO

6·8

¿Por qué es la respuesta correcta? *For each of the sentences in the previous exercise (Ejercicio 6-7), write the reason you chose the preterit or the imperfect. If a key expression gives you a clue, include it in your answer.*

1. _____

2. _____

3. _____

4. _____

5. _____

Verbs with a special meaning: ponerse, volverse, and hacerse

Some verbs are used more frequently in the past than in other tenses. One example in English is *to become*. **Poner(se)**, **volver(se)**, and **hacer(se)** are all reflexive verbs (used with the corresponding reflexive pronouns) that express *to become* in English. For a more detailed explanation of reflexive constructions in Spanish, consult Unit 8 in this book.

Note the use of the preterit in the following examples. Keep in mind that in different contexts these verbs communicate different ideas. These examples are narrations in the past, but you will also see these verbs in other tenses.

◆ Use **ponerse** + adjective to express changes of an emotional or physical nature.

   Él se puso enojado.   *He became angry.*

◆ Use **volverse** + adjective to express an involuntary or sudden change.

   Carlos se volvió loco.   *Carlos became crazy.*

The message intended here implies a sudden expression of rage that may suggest true insanity.

◆ Use **hacerse** + noun or adjective or **llegar a ser** + adjective (not reflexive) to express a profession or social status that required effort, dedication, and time.

   Yo me hice contable.   *I became an accountant.*
   Nosotros llegamos a ser mejores que   *We became better than the other players.*
   los otros jugadores.

EJERCICIO
6·9

Y en tu caso... ¿Verdadero o falso?

_____ 1. Después de estudiar mucho, me hice ingeniero(a).

_____ 2. Cuando me aumentaron el sueldo me puse muy contento(a).

_____ 3. De tanto pensar en mi problema, me volví loco(a).

_____ 4. Practiqué mucho y llegué a ser un(-a) gran tenista.

_____ 5. Cuando vi los resultados de la bolsa de valores (*the stock market*), me puse triste.

¿Cuál es la respuesta correcta? Subraya la respuesta apropiada para cada una de las siguientes oraciones.

1. Después de asistir a la universidad por cuatro años, Julio (se volvió | se hizo) maestro.

2. Cuando su novia le dijo que no quería salir más con él, (se hizo | se puso) triste.

3. Me robaron la cartera en el metro y cuando me di cuenta, (me volví | me puse) nerviosa.

4. Después de trabajar mucho, nosotros (nos hicimos | nos pusimos) ricos.

5. Te dije una mentira y (te pusiste | te hiciste) histérica.

6. Julieta encontró un billete de $100.00 y (se volvió | se hizo) loca de alegría.

Una boda magnífica. Traduce. Usa el **Vocabulario útil**.

Five years ago, María Luisa married Jacobo. He studied five years in Miami and became an engineer. The ceremony was in the evening in a beautiful chapel in Santo Domingo. After the wedding, the reception started at nine o'clock at night in an old mansion. While the guests waited for the bride and groom, they chatted and had a drink. Suddenly, they heard music and they realized the newlyweds were there. The guests were waiting to see María Luisa and her father dance. All of a sudden, they heard a "merengue," a typical dance from the Dominican Republic. This is a Dominican tradition, and the guests enjoyed the dance. Then, Jacobo danced with María Luisa. Everyone joined them on the floor and danced all night. No one wanted to stop dancing. Jacobo and María Luisa sneaked out around one thirty in the morning. The next day, they left on a cruise from Florida to the British Isles for their honeymoon.

Vocabulario útil

around	**a eso de**	newlywed	**el/la recién casado(a)**
bride	**la novia**	orchestra	**la orquesta**
chapel	**la capilla**	to enjoy	**disfrutar**
despite	**a pesar de**	to join	**acompañar**
Dominican	**dominicano(a)**	to marry	**casarse con**
engineer	**el/la ingeniero(a)**	to realize	**darse cuenta de**
groom	**el novio**	to sneak away	**escabullirse; escaparse**
guest	**el/la invitado(a)**	wedding	**la boda**
honeymoon	**la luna de miel**		

The future
and the conditional

The future tense

The future tense is used to indicate actions that will take place at some point later on, viewed from the present. In Spanish, **el futuro** is the equivalent of English *will* or *shall* followed by a verb. Although you will find the future tense in written Spanish, spoken Spanish, like spoken English, frequently conveys the future with a **perífrasis**. **Perífrasis** literally means the use of a *group of words* to express an idea, a concept, or an action. The future tense is used less frequently in Spanish than in English. Note in the second example below how the same idea is expressed with the future tense and then with periphrasis in both languages.

Compraremos el auto mañana.	*We will buy* the car tomorrow.
Vamos a comprar el auto mañana.	*We are going to buy* the car tomorrow.

Both English and Spanish use the "to go" verb: *going to (buy, run, work, etc.)* = **ir a** + infinitive to express the future.

Regular verbs in the future

The future tense in Spanish is formed by attaching the appropriate future endings to the (entire) infinitive of a verb. Use the following conjugations as models for all regular verbs in the future tense.

arreglar (*to fix*)		**devolver** (*to return*)		**pedir** (*to ask for*)	
arreglaré	arreglar**emos**	devolveré	devolver**emos**	pediré	pedir**emos**
arreglar**ás**	arreglar**éis**	devolver**ás**	devolver**éis**	pedir**ás**	pedir**éis**
arreglar**á**	arreglar**án**	devolver**á**	devolver**án**	pedir**á**	pedir**án**

Note that

- all future forms have an accent mark, except the **nosotros** form.

- the three conjugations have the same endings.

- the future tense in Spanish is expressed by a single word. (The auxiliaries *shall* or *will* are needed to conjugate the equivalent tense in English.)

Marta **leerá** las noticias.	*Marta **will read** the news.*
Mañana **será** martes.	*Tomorrow **will be** Tuesday.*

Conjugación. Escribe el futuro de los siguientes verbos entre paréntesis.

1. yo _____ (bajar)

2. sus padres _____ (viajar)

3. nosotras no _____ (cocinar)

4. tus amigos _____ (pedir)

5. nosotros _____ (leer)

6. ustedes _____ (decidir)

7. mis hermanos _____ (recibir)

8. las chicas _____ (bailar)

9. ellos _____ (cooperar)

10. tú _____ (vender)

11. Ud. _____ (temer)

12. los norteamericanos _____ (elegir)

¿Qué harán? Escribe la forma apropiada del futuro del verbo entre paréntesis.

1. Mañana, Alicia _____ (estar) ocupada.

2. Primero, ella _____ (llevar) su carro al mecánico temprano por la mañana.

3. Yo la _____ (recoger) allí a las nueve.

4. Después nosotros _____ (ir) al consulado de Chile.

5. Alicia y su hermana _____ (pasar) dos meses en Suramérica este verano.

6. Sus padres _____ (mudarse) a Chile en unas semanas.

En español.

1. *You* (**tú**) *will prepare dinner.* _____

2. *The children will not play video games.*

_____

3. *The sales clerk will add up the bill* (**la cuenta**).

_____

4. *Carly's mother will not talk to her neighbor.*

_____

5. *My friends will eat at La Valentina.* _____

6. *My sister and I will wait.* _____

Irregular verbs in the future tense

There are relatively few irregular verbs in the future tense. They follow one of three patterns: **poner** (*to put*), **poder** (*to be able*), and **decir** (*to tell*).

♦ Verbs like **poner** drop the **e** or **i** of the infinitive and add the consonant **d: pon(e)dré.**

poner (*to put*)   pondré, pondrás, pondrá, pondremos, pondréis, pondrán

VERBS LIKE **poner**

salir	to leave, go out	**saldré**	I will/shall go out
tener	to have	**tendré**	I will/shall have
valer	to be worth	**valdré**	I will/shall be worth
venir	to come	**vendré**	I will/shall come

♦ Verbs like **poder** drop the vowel of the infinitive entirely: **pod(e)ré.**

poder (*to be able*)   podré, podrás, podrá, podremos, podréis, podrán

VERBS LIKE **poder**

caber	to fit	**cabré**	I will/shall fit
haber	to have	**habré**	I will/shall have
querer	to want	**querré**	I will/shall want
saber	to know	**sabré**	I will/shall know

Haber is conjugated fully when it is used as an auxiliary verb in a perfect tense.

♦ The verbs **decir** and **hacer** have irregular stems: **diré** and **haré.**

decir (*to tell*)   diré, dirás, dirá, diremos, diréis, dirán
hacer (*to do*)   haré, harás, hará, haremos, haréis, harán

Remember that these irregularities occur only in the radical (or stem). Compounds of these verbs are also irregular. The endings are the same for regular and irregular verbs in the future tense.

The future of **haber**, when not used as an auxiliary verb in a perfect tense, translates *there will be* and is used in the third-person singular only.

Habrá muchas sorpresas en la fiesta.   ***There will be** many surprises at the party.*

COMPOUND VERBS

componer	to fix	**compondré**		**oponer(se)**	to oppose	**(me) opondré**	
deshacer	to undo	**desharé**		**proponer**	to propose	**propondré**	
detener	to detain	**detendré**		**rehacer**	to do again	**reharé**	
disponer	to dispose	**dispondré**		**reponer**	to replace	**repondré**	
exponer	to expose	**expondré**		**retener**	to retain	**retendré**	
imponer	to impose	**impondré**		**satisfacer**	to satisfy	**satisfaré**	
mantener	to maintain	**mantendré**		**suponer**	to suppose	**supondré**	
obtener	to obtain	**obtendré**					

Note: The verb **satisfacer** is a compound of **hacer**. The **f** is an indication of the old spelling and pronunciation of **facer** (which later became **hacer**) and has remained in this compound.

Práctica. Cambia los verbos subrayados y escribe la forma apropiada del futuro.

1. <u>Salimos</u> de la ciudad para ir al campo.   _____

2. En la ciudad <u>hay</u> mucho ruido.   _____

3. En el campo <u>encuentras</u> tranquilidad y paz.   _____

4. ¿No <u>quieres</u> ir al campo con nosotros?   _____

5. Ud. <u>puede</u> viajar en el auto con nosotros   _____ / _____
   porque <u>tenemos</u> espacio.

6. Los chicos no <u>vienen</u> esta vez con nosotros.   _____

La bola de cristal. Usa la forma apropiada del futuro para indicar las predicciones siguientes.

1. Mañana, tu hermano _____ (recibir) una oferta de trabajo.

2. Esta semana tú _____ (poder) solucionar tus problemas económicos.

3. Tus padres _____ (salir) de viaje para visitarte en tu casa.

4. Tus amigos _____ (ir) a tu casa para llevarte un regalo de cumpleaños.

5. Una persona te _____ (invitar) a una fiesta el fin de semana.

6. Tú _____ (saber) quiénes son tus verdaderos amigos.

When is the future tense used in Spanish?

The future tense is used to indicate actions that will take place in the future. However, the future tense in Spanish communicates other messages as well. Here is a summary of its uses.

◆ To indicate an action or event that will happen or is likely to happen at a future time.

Mañana, **veré** a Ada.	*Tomorrow, **I will see** Ada.*
La fiesta **será** el viernes.	*The party **will be** on Friday.*

The key expressions **mañana** and **el viernes** in the examples above give the time the action is supposed to take place. Here are some frequently used time expressions that indicate the future.

a la una, a las dos de la tarde	at one, at two in the afternoon	**esta primavera**	this spring
de aquí a dos (tres, etc.) días	in two (three, etc.) days	**esta tarde**	this afternoon
		este verano	this summer
el año que viene	next year	**la semana que viene**	next week
el lunes que viene	next Monday	**luego**	later
el martes	on Tuesday	**mañana**	tomorrow
el mes que viene	next month	**mañana por la mañana**	tomorrow morning
en un mes	in a month		
en una semana	in one week	**mañana por la noche**	tomorrow night
esta noche	tonight	**mañana por la tarde**	tomorrow afternoon
		pasado mañana	the day after tomorrow

◆ To express a conjecture, supposition, or probability in the present. This use is the equivalent of some English expressions: *can*, *I wonder*, *must be*, and *probably*.

La chica que viene, ¿**será** María?   *The girl who is coming, **can it be** María?*
Estaremos a diez millas de Madrid.   *We **must be** ten miles away from Madrid.*
¿Cuánto **costará** ese bolso tan bonito?   *I **wonder** how much that beautiful bag **costs**.*

Note, in the last example, that the English equivalent is an indirect question preceded by *I wonder*.

EJERCICIO
7·6

¿Qué planes tienes tú para mañana? Usa el futuro en tus respuestas.

1. ¿A qué hora te despertarás mañana? _____

2. ¿Qué sección leerás en el periódico? _____

3. ¿Qué ropas llevarás? _____

4. ¿Adónde irás? ¿Al mercado? _____

5. ¿Qué comprarás? _____

6. ¿Cuántos ejercicios harás en tu cuaderno de español?

_____

7. ¿Cuántas horas trabajarás? _____

EJERCICIO
7·7

Conjeturas. Completa cada pregunta con una conjetura, según el ejemplo. Usa el futuro del verbo subrayado.

EJEMPLO   No <u>conocemos</u> al nuevo jefe. ¿Quién ___*conocerá*___ al nuevo jefe?

1. <u>Es</u> una mujer famosa. ¿Quién _____?

2. Ahora <u>va</u> a un lugar secreto. ¿Adónde _____?

3. Sé que <u>hay</u> una fiesta en su honor. ¿Dónde _____ una fiesta?

4. ¿Sabes a qué hora <u>llega</u> su limosina? ¿Cuándo _____ su limosina?

5. <u>Vienen</u> muchos a la fiesta. ¿Quiénes _____?

EJERCICIO
7·8

Predicciones. ¿Verdadero o falso? ¿Eres pesimista u optimista?

_____ 1. Habrá paz en el mundo.

_____ 2. Existirá una crema mágica para eliminar las arrugas (*wrinkles*).

_____ 3. Tendremos menos corrupción en la política.

_____ 4. Los científicos encontrarán la cura para muchas enfermedades.

_____ 5. Consumiremos más productos saludables (*healthful*).

_____ 6. Comeremos menos carne.

De 6 respuestas con **V**, eres muy optimista.
De 4 a 5, eres optimista.
De 2 a 3, eres algo pesimista.
De 1, ¡sin comentarios!

EJERCICIO
7·9

En español. En tu traducción usa el futuro del verbo entre paréntesis.

1. *Tonight, it will not rain* (llover) *in Las Vegas.*

_____

2. *The probability of showers* (**aguaceros**) *will increase* (aumentar) *on Monday in Southern California.*

_____

3. *A cold front* (**frente frío**) *will arrive* (llegar) *in Santa Fe this weekend.*

_____

4. *There will be* (haber) *scattered showers* (**chubascos**) *in San Marcos.*

_____

5. *In Albuquerque, the temperature will drop* (bajar) *to forty-five degrees.*

_____

6. *Three inches of snow will accumulate* (acumularse) *in Chicago.*

_____

Other ways of expressing the future in Spanish

Several other Spanish constructions indicate future actions or events. A reference to a future time will often appear in the context along with these constructions. In this unit, review the earlier list of expressions of time that refer to the future. The time expressions are also used in sentences with the following future constructions. Use

◆ a form of **ir a** + an infinitive to indicate an action or event that will take place in the near future.

> Luego, **voy a comprar** peras en la frutería.
> *Later, **I will buy** pears at the fruit stand.*

◆ the present indicative to describe events that will take place in a not-too-distant future.

> Mañana **discuto** el plan en la reunión.
> *Tomorrow, **I'll discuss** the plan at the meeting.*
>
> Este verano, **viajo** a Alemania.
> *I will travel to Germany this summer.*

Note that the English use of the future (*will, shall*) does not always correspond to the use of the future tense in Spanish. Use

◆ a form of the Spanish present instead of the future to request instructions or permission. (The equivalent English situations translate with *will* or *shall*.)

> ¿**Bebes** agua o vino?
> ***Will you drink** wine or water?*
>
> ¿**Abro** la puerta?
> ***Shall I open** the door?*

◆ a form of the Spanish present (not the future) in conditional *if*-clause sentences to state the condition in the present. The verb in the main clause, also called the *result clause*, may be either in the present or the future.

> Si **tienes** dinero, **puedes** comprar las golosinas.
> *If **you have** money, **you can** buy the candy.*
>
> Si **tienes** dinero, **podrás** comprar las golosinas.
> *If **you have** money, **you will be able** to buy the candy.*

EJERCICIO
7·10

Situaciones. Escribe el resultado de las situaciones siguientes. Usa la forma apropiada de **ir a** + infinitivo de acuerdo a lo que aparece entre paréntesis.

1. Si no llega el cheque por correo, yo _____ (ir a + exigir) una explicación.

2. Marta _____ (ir a + venir) a mi casa si yo necesito su ayuda.

3. Si tú no trabajas, ¡ellos no _____ (ir a + hacer) nada!

4. Lucía y Ali _____ (ir a + pagar) las entradas del concierto si ustedes las acompañan.

5. Si convences al vendedor, nosotros _____ (ir a + recibir) una rebaja del precio.

6. Yo me _____ (ir a + levantar) temprano si suena mi despertador.

7. Si llevo mi paraguas, ¡no _____ (ir a + llover)!

Un minuto de fama: ¿quién ganará? Traduce. Usa el **Vocabulario útil**.

Next month, my friend Rosa will go to a competition at a local TV station. Until then, Rosa will practice her favorite song every day. She has the willpower to win. Rosa will get up early in the morning, she will play the piano, and she will sing her favorite song in front of a mirror. Her neighbor, Manuel, tells me that he needs earplugs. Why? Manuel will hear the same song again and again every day! Rosa will try to change her appearance. She will run five miles every evening and she will eat less. She will change the color of her hair or she will wear a wig, and she will buy a red dress. Rosa thinks that she will be the best contestant and will win first place. She will have a minute of fame. Rosa thinks that she will have an audition for a show. Will she win? Will there be a totally unexpected and surprising finale? Who knows!

Vocabulario útil

again and again	**una y otra vez**	first place	**el primer lugar**
appearance	**el aspecto; la apariencia**	mirror	**el espejo**
		neighbor	**el/la vecino(a)**
contest	**el concurso**	show	**el espectáculo de variedades; el show**
contestant	**el/la concursante**		
earplugs	**los tapones para los oídos**	to try	**intentar, tratar de**
		willpower	**la fuerza de voluntad**

The conditional mood

The future and the conditional are used to indicate different circumstances at a future time. The formation of the future and the conditional are similar. Both use the infinitive, including the endings -**ar**, -**er**, or -**ir**, as the base of each conjugation. In addition, the same verbs have the same irregular stems in the future and the conditional.

First, let us look at the forms of the conditional, called the **condicional** or **potencial** in Spanish. The conditional is formed by attaching the following endings to the infinitive.

sacar (*to take out*)		**perder** (*to lose*)		**servir** (*to serve*)	
sacaría	sacaríamos	perdería	perderíamos	serviría	serviríamos
sacarías	sacaríais	perderías	perderíais	servirías	serviríais
sacaría	sacarían	perdería	perderían	serviría	servirían

Study the endings and remember that

- all conditional forms have an accent mark on the **í**.

- the three conjugations (-**ar**, -**er**, and -**ir**) have the same endings.

- the conditional in Spanish is a single-word construction. (The word *would* is needed to conjugate the equivalent in English.)

Yo no compraría esta silla.	*I would not buy this chair.*
Tocan a la puerta. ¿Qué **harías**?	*They knock on the door. What **would you do**?*

Conjugación. Escribe el condicional de los verbos que aparecen entre paréntesis.

1. yo _____ (subir)

2. su padre _____ (comprar)

3. las chicas no _____ (planchar)

4. Wilma _____ (investigar)

5. ustedes _____ (leer)

6. vosotros _____ (comer)

Problemas con el auto. ¿Qué sugerirían estas personas? Escribe la forma apropiada del condicional del verbo entre paréntesis.

1. Alberto y Lilly _____ (llamar) al servicio de grúas (*tow-truck service*).

2. Marcos _____ (esperar) a sus amigos que tienen un coche nuevo.

3. Nosotros _____ (ofrecer) ayuda a nuestros amigos.

4. Mis hijos me _____ (llevar) al centro comercial.

5. Bertha _____ (tomar) un autobús.

6. Fred no _____ (ayudar) a nadie.

En español.

1. *Would you (**Uds.**) eat the tortillas?* _____

2. *The children would not play with this toy.*

   _____

3. *Who would bring the beer?* _____

4. *Pedro would not laugh (**reírse**).* _____

5. *I would not read this novel.* _____

6. *The mail carrier would bring (**traer**) the magazines.*

   _____

Irregular verbs in the conditional

The irregular verbs in the conditional are the same verbs that have irregular stems in the future tense. Study these groups and their corresponding patterns.

◆ Verbs like **poner** drop the **e** or **i** of the infinitive and add the consonant **d**: **pon(e)dría**.

poner (*to put*)   pondría, pondrías, pondría, pondríamos, pondríais, pondrían

VERBS LIKE **poner**

salir	**saldría**	I would go out
tener	**tendría**	I would have
valer	**valdría**	I would be worth
venir	**vendría**	I would come

◆ Verbs like **poder** drop the vowel of the infinitive entirely: **pod(e)ría**.

poder (*to be able*)   podría, podrías, podría, podríamos, podríais, podrían

VERBS LIKE **poder**

caber	**cabría**	I would fit
haber	**habría**	I would have
querer	**querría**	I would want
saber	**sabría**	I would know

Haber is conjugated fully when it is used as an auxiliary verb in a perfect tense. The conditional of **haber**, when not used as an auxiliary verb in a perfect tense, translates *there would be* and is used in the third-person singular only.

◆ The verbs **decir** and **hacer** show a change in their base or radical: **diría**, **haría**.

decir (*to tell*)   diría, dirías, diría, diríamos, diríais, dirían
hacer (*to do*)   haría, harías, haría, haríamos, haríais, harían

Remember that in the irregular forms, only the stem (radical or base) of the verb changes. All endings for regular and irregular verbs are the same. Compounds of these verbs are also irregular. Consult the list of compound verbs in the section *Irregular verbs in the future tense*, which appears earlier in this unit.

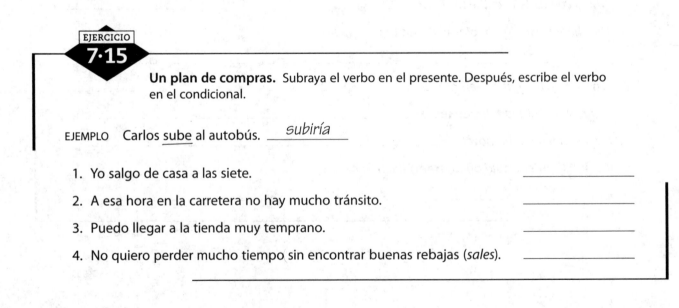

EJERCICIO
7·15

Un plan de compras. Subraya el verbo en el presente. Después, escribe el verbo en el condicional.

EJEMPLO   Carlos <u>sube</u> al autobús. ___*subiría*___

1. Yo salgo de casa a las siete. _____

2. A esa hora en la carretera no hay mucho tránsito. _____

3. Puedo llegar a la tienda muy temprano. _____

4. No quiero perder mucho tiempo sin encontrar buenas rebajas (*sales*). _____

En español. Usa la forma apropiada del condicional en tus respuestas.

1. *There would be too much noise.* _____

2. *Would they go, too?* _____

3. *Carlos would smile.* _____

4. *Who would come?* _____

En cada situación, ¿qué harías? *Write an affirmative or negative sentence using the appropriate form of the conditional of the infinitive that appears after the sentence.*

1. La fregadora de platos no funciona. (fregar) _____

2. El auto no tiene gasolina. (ir) _____

3. No hay un programa interesante en la tele. (salir) _____

4. ¡Pablo quema la cena! (cenar) _____

When is the conditional used in Spanish?

Both in English and Spanish, the conditional is used to communicate several different messages. As you have seen in the previous examples and exercises, it expresses probability. The conditional is also used

- ◆ to indicate the probability of a future action from the perspective of a previous action in the past.

  Mona dijo que **vendría**.   *Mona said **she would come**.*

- ◆ to indicate hypothetical actions or events that may or may not happen in the future.

  Claro que **iríamos** a Roma.   *Of course, **we would go** to Rome.*
  Valdría la pena preguntar cuándo es   ***It would be worth it*** *to ask when the conference*
  la conferencia.   *is (takes place).*

In the first example above, the speaker expresses the possibility of traveling to Rome, **iríamos**, but there is no certainty about the time the action will take place, or even if the action will happen at all.

- ◆ to express hypothetical actions or events that may or may not happen in the present.

  Ahora mismo, **me tomaría** una copa   *Now, **I would drink** a glass of wine.*
  de vino.
  Sería conveniente salir pronto.   ***It would be*** *convenient to go out soon.*

The use of the conditional indicates the action is not happening at the present moment. **Me tomaría una copa de vino** tells us the speaker is willing, but is currently not yet drinking a glass of wine.

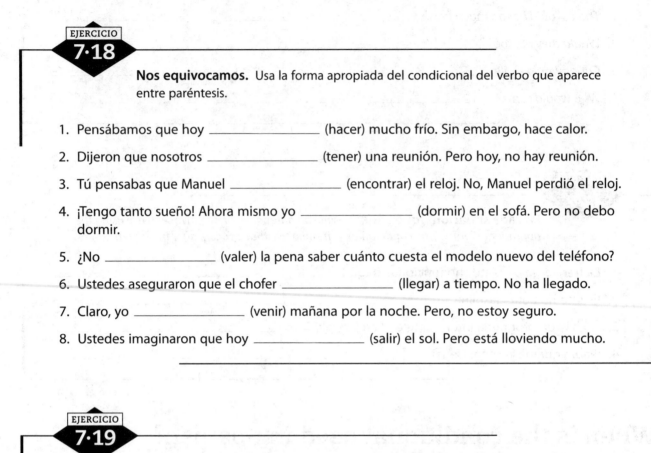

EJERCICIO
7·18

Nos equivocamos. Usa la forma apropiada del condicional del verbo que aparece entre paréntesis.

1. Pensábamos que hoy _____ (hacer) mucho frío. Sin embargo, hace calor.

2. Dijeron que nosotros _____ (tener) una reunión. Pero hoy, no hay reunión.

3. Tú pensabas que Manuel _____ (encontrar) el reloj. No, Manuel perdió el reloj.

4. ¡Tengo tanto sueño! Ahora mismo yo _____ (dormir) en el sofá. Pero no debo dormir.

5. ¿No _____ (valer) la pena saber cuánto cuesta el modelo nuevo del teléfono?

6. Ustedes aseguraron que el chofer _____ (llegar) a tiempo. No ha llegado.

7. Claro, yo _____ (venir) mañana por la noche. Pero, no estoy seguro.

8. Ustedes imaginaron que hoy _____ (salir) el sol. Pero está lloviendo mucho.

EJERCICIO
7·19

Conexiones. ¿Qué les gustaría hacer a estas personas? *Choose the letter of the statement that indicates why these people would like to do these things.*

_____ 1. Alina comería una paella.

_____ 2. Iría a Hawái.

_____ 3. Beberían una cerveza.

_____ 4. Cerrarían la ventana.

_____ 5. Comprarían un auto.

_____ 6. Podría dormir.

a. Está de vacaciones.

b. Tengo sueño.

c. Tienen frío.

d. Tienen sed.

e. Tiene hambre.

f. No les gusta ir en autobús.

Other uses of the conditional
Conjecture in the past

In some situations, you will need to consider the context to determine the message conveyed by the conditional. The conditional is used

- to communicate probability or conjecture referring to a past time or activity with verbs such as **decir**, **estar**, **haber**, **ser**, and **tener**. The English equivalents *approximately*, *probably*, *must have*, *could*, *I wonder*, etc., are used to express the sense of wondering or conjecture.

Estaríamos ocupados cuando llamaste.	*We were probably busy when you called.*
Habría unos veinte autos.	*There were approximately twenty cars.*
¿Cuánto **costaría** el traje que compró Ricardo?	*I wonder how much the suit Ricardo bought cost.*

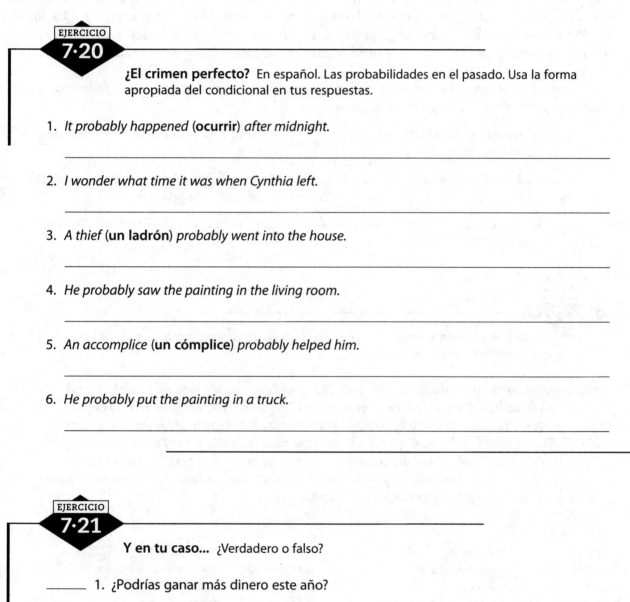

EJERCICIO
7·20

¿El crimen perfecto? En español. Las probabilidades en el pasado. Usa la forma apropiada del condicional en tus respuestas.

1. *It probably happened (**ocurrir**) after midnight.*

_____

2. *I wonder what time it was when Cynthia left.*

_____

3. *A thief (**un ladrón**) probably went into the house.*

_____

4. *He probably saw the painting in the living room.*

_____

5. *An accomplice (**un cómplice**) probably helped him.*

_____

6. *He probably put the painting in a truck.*

_____

EJERCICIO
7·21

Y en tu caso... ¿Verdadero o falso?

_____ 1. ¿Podrías ganar más dinero este año?

_____ 2. ¿Aprenderías alemán y francés?

_____ 3. ¿Viajarías a Europa este verano?

_____ 4. ¿Comprarías una casa en la playa?

_____ 5. ¿Aprenderías a tocar la guitarra?

_____ 6. ¿Dormirías más cada mañana?

The conditional in contrary-to-fact *if*-clauses

The conditional is used in other hypothetical situations. As its name suggests, the conditional is linked to explicit or implicit conditions for an action or event to be completed, if the conditions can be met. Use the conditional to express hypothetical situations in conditional clauses.

Si pudiera, **compraría** este brazalete de perlas.   *If I could, **I would buy** this pearl bracelet.*

The speaker is talking about his or her wish to buy the pearl bracelet using the conditional form **compraría**. It is unlikely that this wish will become a reality. This type of sentence is known as *contrary-to-fact* because the actions are hypothetical, not real. Note that the tense appearing in the *if*-clause is the past subjunctive: **si pudiera**. The unlikely outcome appears in the *result clause*, where you find the conditional. To study contrary-to-fact sentences, you may also review the unit on the subjunctive (Unit 16).

Note that the imperfect tense of **deber** in the expression **deber de** plus an infinitive is also used to communicate probability in the past.

Debían de ser las ocho cuando llegó Carmen.   ***It was probably*** *eight o'clock when Carmen arrived.*

Remember that in English, *would* is also used to express habitual actions in the past. When *would* is used in the sense of *used to*, use the imperfect indicative in Spanish.

Los chicos **iban** a la playa todos los veranos.   *The kids **would go** to the beach every summer.*

EJERCICIO
7·22

Salud y turismo. Traduce. Usa el **Vocabulario útil**. *Use the conditional or the future as needed in each situation.*

Josefina would like to visit Ecuador in December. She would exercise, she would lose weight, and then she will be able to climb one of the volcanoes near Quito. She will not spend money on junk food, and she will prepare her lunch every day. I think that she would be healthier, too. Josefina will open a savings account at the bank. She would save one hundred dollars every week. But who knows? Josefina is not thrifty. She will need discipline and a plan to reach her goal. I would travel with her to Ecuador! I would love to see the Avenue of the Volcanoes and enjoy a vacation. We would explore many interesting places and enjoy the Ecuadorian cuisine.

Vocabulario útil

cuisine	**la cocina**	to climb	**escalar; subir**
Ecuadorian	**ecuatoriano(a)**	to lose weight	**perder (e > ie) peso**
goal	**la meta**	to reach	**alcanzar; lograr**
junk food	**la comida chatarra**	to save	**ahorrar**
savings account	**la cuenta de ahorros**	vacation	**las vacaciones**
thrifty	**ahorrativo(a), económico(a)**	volcano	**el volcán**
		who knows	**quién sabe**
to be healthy	**estar, ser saludable**		

Reflexive verbs and reflexive constructions

Reflexive verbs are used in reflexive constructions, which consist of a verb + a reflexive pronoun. The subject of the verb, a person or thing, performs and receives the action expressed by the verb. A verb is reflexive if the action the subject does is directed back to the subject. Study the following examples.

Nos duchamos por la mañana.	*We **shower** in the morning.*
Siempre **te miras** al espejo.	*You always **look at yourself** in the mirror.*

The first example literally says *we shower ourselves*. The ending in the present-tense form **duchamos** indicates the person **nosotros** as the subject, as does the reflexive pronoun **nos** preceding the verb. The same is true for the second example and the person **tú**, indicated by the ending -**as** in **miras** and the reflexive pronoun **te**, the object of the action. In other words, the subject and the object receiving the action are the same.

Me afeito todos los días.	*I **shave (myself)** every day.*

In the previous example, the person **yo** does the action, **afeito**. The subject **yo** receives the action; the pronoun **me** indicates the subject, that is, the receiver of the action.

Reflexive verbs in English are not quite as common as in Spanish. However, one use of reflexive pronouns in English is indeed equivalent to the reflexive pronouns in Spanish.

Leo **se defendió**.	*Leo **defended himself**.*

In English, reflexive pronouns are often used to emphasize an action. In those cases, they are equivalent to Spanish emphatic forms of the subject pronouns with **mismo(a)**, **mismos(as)** (*myself, yourself, him/herself,* etc.). Reflexive pronouns in Spanish are also used to emphasize something a person does for himself or herself. The first example that follows shows the subject pronoun and **mismo(a)** used *without* a reflexive construction; the second example, with similar meaning, is instead expressed with a reflexive verb.

Yo mismo(a) escogí el número ganador.	*I **myself chose** the winning number.*
Ellos se compran los billetes en la Internet.	*They **themselves purchase** the tickets on the Internet.*

Spanish has numerous reflexive verbs. Practically any verb that takes a direct object may be used with a reflexive pronoun. Because they are used with their corresponding reflexive pronouns, textbooks and dictionaries usually list them with the pronoun **se** attached to the infinitive: **lavar(se)**, **afeitar(se)**, **vestir(se)**, etc. Remember that their English equivalents may *not* necessarily be used reflexively (that is, with *-self, -selves*).

Reflexive verbs and pronouns

To conjugate a reflexive verb, use the corresponding reflexive pronoun. Use the following model to form reflexive verbs in the present tense.

bañar(se) *(to bathe, take a bath)*	
me baño	**nos** bañamos
te bañas	**os** bañáis
se baña	**se** bañan

Study the pronouns, and remember that

◆ the forms of the reflexive pronouns are as follows.

me	myself	**nos**	ourselves
te	yourself	**os**	yourselves
se	yourself/himself/herself	**se**	yourselves/themselves

◆ persons **Ud.**, **Uds.**, **él/ella**, and **ellos/ellas** have the same reflexive pronoun, **se**.

◆ reflexive pronouns are placed immediately before a conjugated verb.

Some commonly used regular reflexive verbs appear in the lists that follow. Remember the type of situation where reflexive verbs are likely to appear in Spanish: verbs that express actions related to personal care and daily routine or habits are often reflexive, because the subject receives the action he or she does to or on himself or herself.

afeitarse	to shave	mirarse	to look at oneself
cepillarse	to brush	ponerse	to put on
desayunarse	to have breakfast	quitarse	to take off
ducharse	to shower	secarse	to dry oneself, dry off

EJERCICIO
8·1

Mi rutina diaria. *Choose one of the reflexive verbs from the previous list to complete the thought in each sentence. Use the* **yo** *form.*

1. Generalmente no _____ hasta las ocho.

2. Voy al baño y _____ en el espejo.

3. Entonces, _____ la barba con cuidado.

4. _____ el pijama y entro en la ducha.

5. Con agua caliente, _____ y canto bajo el agua.

6. Cuando termino, _____ con la toalla.

7. Después _____ los dientes.

More reflexive verbs

When expressing actions regarding personal care, Spanish reflexive verbs are used with a definite article preceding parts of the body. In English, the possessive adjective is used instead.

Nos lavamos **la cara**.	*We wash **our faces**.*
Se cepillan **los dientes**.	*They brush **their teeth**.*

Note that **la cara**, the noun referring to a part of the body, is singular, despite the fact that more than one person is washing his or her face. In Spanish, it is understood that each one washes his or her own face. The same use of the singular applies to individual items of clothing with reflexive verbs. Of course, if the noun refers to more than one item, the plural of the noun is used.

Se quitan **el sombrero** para saludar.	*They take off **their hats** to greet you.*
Estos chicos no se limpian **las uñas**.	*These kids do not clean **their nails**.*

TYPICAL VERBS

bañarse	to bathe, take a bath	**maquillarse**	to put on makeup
cortarse	to cut	**peinarse**	to comb one's hair
destaparse	to uncover, take off	**pintarse (los labios)**	to put on lipstick
lavarse	to wash	**taparse**	to cover
limarse (las uñas)	to file (one's nails)		

EJERCICIO
8·2

En español. Escribe la forma apropiada del verbo y el pronombre reflexivo.

1. *I cut my nails.* _____

2. *Lana combs her hair.* _____

3. *We wash our hands.* _____

4. *The clowns (**payasos**) put makeup on.* _____

5. *I cover myself with a blanket.* _____

6. *The receptionist is filing her nails.* _____

Reflexive constructions with stem-changing and irregular verbs

Stem-changing verbs in reflexive constructions

The following list contains several reflexive verbs with stem changes in the present. Review them before doing the next exercise. If necessary, consult the unit on verbs with stem changes (Unit 2) for a more extensive review.

acostarse (o > ue)	to go to bed	me acuesto
despedirse (e > i)	to say good-bye	me despido
despertarse (e > ie)	to wake up	me despierto
desvestirse (e > i)	to get undressed	me desvisto
dormirse (o > ue)	to go to sleep	me duermo
probarse (o > ue)	to try on (clothing)	me pruebo
sentarse (e > ie)	to sit down	me siento
torcerse (o > ue)	to twist	me tuerzo
vestirse (e > i)	to get dressed	me visto

EJERCICIO 8·3

¿Qué hacen? Escribe la forma apropiada del presente del verbo reflexivo entre paréntesis.

1. Hace calor y Marcela _____ (vestirse) con ropa ligera (light).

2. En la tienda, las señoras _____ (probarse) unos sombreros muy elegantes.

3. Antes de darse un baño, Ana _____ (desvestirse).

4. Todos los días, los chicos _____ (despedirse) de sus amigos antes de regresar a casa.

5. Casi todas las noches yo _____ (acostarse) a las 11 de la noche.

6. Tom nunca _____ (dormirse) antes de la medianoche.

Irregular reflexive verbs

Many irregular verbs are used in reflexive constructions.

Me pongo el abrigo.   ***I put on** my coat.*

Here are a few irregular verbs used in reflexive constructions. Examples are given in the present and with the **yo** form.

distraerse	to distract oneself	me distraigo
irse	to leave	me voy
reponerse	to get better	me repongo
sostenerse	to support, sustain oneself	me sostengo

Note: Many of these verbs are compounds of irregular verbs like **tener**, **traer**, etc., and are conjugated like the basic verb. Not all the English equivalents are expressed with *-self* or *-selves*.

The use of reflexive verbs in Spanish

Reflexive verbs and pronouns are used

♦ to describe actions related to personal care and habitual routines.

Se lavan los dientes.	**They brush/clean** their teeth.
Por la noche, **me siento** para ver mi telenovela en español.	At night, **I sit down** to watch my soap opera in Spanish.

♦ to express feelings and emotions or changes in conditions, moods, and emotional states. In English, the verbs *to get*, *to become*, or a nonreflexive construction communicate these ideas.

Vi la película y **me enamoré** de Benedict Cumberbatch.	I saw the movie and **I fell in love** with Benedict Cumberbatch.
Nos divertimos mucho con estos chistes.	**We have fun** (**enjoy ourselves**) with these jokes.
Allan **se enferma** cada vez que **se moja**.	Allan **gets sick** every time **he gets wet**.
Bella **se enoja** con su contable si tiene que pagar más impuestos.	Bella **gets upset** with her accountant if she has to pay more taxes.

Review the following list of verbs. Note that some are used with or without certain prepositions. Some of the English equivalents require corresponding prepositions, while others do not.

aburrirse (de)	to get bored (with)
acordarse (de)	to remember
alegrarse (de)	to be glad, rejoice (about)
convertirse (en)	to become
disgustarse (de, con)	to become upset (over, about, with)
divertirse (con)	to enjoy oneself (with)
enfermarse	to become ill, get sick
enloquecerse	to drive oneself crazy; to go crazy
enojarse (con)	to get mad, angry (about, with)
olvidarse (de)	to forget
volverse	to become

EJERCICIO
8·4

En español.

1. *I get upset.* _____

2. *She gets sick easily.* _____

3. *We get bored in this class.* _____

4. *You (**Ud.**) forget the rules.* _____

5. *Inés is glad.* _____

6. *He becomes (**volverse**) an animal!* _____

7. *How do you (**Uds.**) remember?* _____

8. *They become upset.* _____

9. *I enjoy the movies.* _____

10. *Marcos goes crazy.* _____

¿Eres sensible (*sensitive***)?** Indica sí o **no**.

_____ 1. ¿Te enojas cuando los vecinos hacen ruido por la noche?

_____ 2. ¿Te disgustas si llegas tarde a tu trabajo?

_____ 3. ¿Te olvidas del cumpleaños de tu supervisor?

_____ 4. ¿Te alegras cuando tu rival pierde a su novio(a)?

_____ 5. ¿Te enfermas de los nervios si tu jefe te regaña?

_____ 6. ¿Te acuerdas de las fechas más importantes para tus familiares?

_____ 7. ¿Te niegas a cooperar con los trabajos de la casa?

_____ 8. ¿Te aburres en el trabajo todos los días?

_____ 9. ¿Te arrepientes inmediatamente después de pelear con un amigo?

_____ 10. ¿Te muerdes las uñas cuando ves una película de horror?

Verbs that change meaning when used as reflexive verbs

Numerous verbs may be used as reflexive or nonreflexive. In many cases, the basic meaning of the verb changes in the reflexive form.

Lavamos el coche.	*We **wash** the car.*
Nos lavamos las manos.	*We **wash** our hands.*

The meaning in these two examples changes slightly. In the reflexive form (the second example), the action is directed to the subject; in the first, the car receives the action. However, note the more significant change in meaning in the next two examples.

Los soldados **acuerdan** no pelear más.	*The soldiers **agree** not to fight any longer.*
Nos acordamos de traer el dinero.	*We **remember** to bring the money.*

Compare the change in meaning of the following verbs, nonreflexive versus reflexive. This is of course a select list; almost any Spanish verb may be used in both a nonreflexive and a reflexive construction.

BASIC MEANING		REFLEXIVE MEANING	
acercar	to bring near	acercarse	to get closer
acordar (o > ue)	to agree	acordarse	to remember
acostar (o > ue)	to put to bed	acostarse	to go to bed
colocar	to place	colocarse	to get a job
dormir (o > ue)	to sleep	dormirse	to fall asleep
enfermar	to make ill/sick	enfermarse	to become ill, get sick
engañar	to deceive	engañarse	to deceive oneself
esconder	to hide (*someone or something*)	esconderse	to hide
llamar	to call	llamarse	to be called/named
llevar	to take	llevarse con	to get along with (*someone*)
negar (e > ie)	to deny	negarse	to refuse
parecer	to appear	parecerse a	to look like (*someone*)
preparar	to prepare	prepararse	to get ready
probar (o > ue)	to try, test; to taste	probarse	to try on
quitar	to take away	quitarse	to take off
sentir (e > ie)	to feel	sentirse	to feel (*emotionally or physically*)
volver (o > ue)	to return	volverse	to become

EJERCICIO
8·6

¿Reflexivo o no? *Choose the verb with the basic or the reflexive meaning that fits the sentence. Then write the appropriate form of the verb in the present tense.*

1. Ahora, Ted _____ (preparar/prepararse) la sopa para nosotros.

2. Ted también _____ (preparar/prepararse) para una fiesta.

3. Si tú tomas la sopa de Ted, tú _____ (enfermar/enfermarse).

4. ¡Esa sopa _____ (enfermar/enfermarse) a cualquiera!

5. Elisa _____ (probar/probarse) la sopa.

6. Ahora ella _____ (probar/probarse) un vestido nuevo para ir a la fiesta.

7. Luisa _____ (quitar/quitarse) los zapatos.

8. Nancy _____ (quitar/quitarse) los platos de la mesa.

9. Yo _____ (llevar/llevarse) bien con todos mis parientes.

10. Nosotros _____ (llevar/llevarse) los platos a los invitados.

11. Luis _____ (acostar/acostarse) a los niños a las ocho.

12. Berta _____ (acostar/acostarse) en el sofá.

The commands in reflexive constructions

In the previous examples and exercises, you have seen reflexive pronouns precede the conjugated verb in simple tenses. Reflexive pronouns precede perfect (compound) tenses as well.

Los gimnastas **se han preparado** para las olimpiadas.	*The gymnasts **have prepared themselves** for the Olympic Games.*
No se habían engañado.	***They had not fooled themselves.***

Reflexive verbs and reflexive constructions are also used in commands (imperative forms; see Unit 16). Before creating a command with a reflexive pronoun, note whether the command is negative or affirmative.

◆ With affirmative commands, attach the pronoun to the command.

Cepíllense los dientes antes de acostarse.	***Brush your teeth** before you go to bed.*
Llévese Ud. estos papeles.	***Take** these papers **with you**.*

◆ In the case of two object pronouns, place the reflexive pronoun (indirect object) *before* any direct object pronoun that may appear in the same sentence. Note that both pronouns are attached to the command in that order.

¡Mesero! Este pescado no huele bien. **¡Lléveselo!**	*Waiter! This fish does not smell good.* ***Take it away (with you)!***

Remember to place an accent mark on the stressed vowel of the affirmative command if a reflexive pronoun is followed by another pronoun.

La cena está lista. ¡Sírvansela!	*Dinner is ready. Serve it (to yourselves)!*
¿Por qué llevas los zapatos mojados? ¡Quítatelos!	*Why are you wearing wet shoes? Take them off!*

◆ With negative commands, follow the general rule for sentences and place the pronoun before the verb.

No se lave Ud. el pelo con ese jabón.	***Do not wash** your hair with that soap.*
¡No os olvidéis de enviarme la carta!	***Do not forget** to send me the letter!*

EJERCICIO
8·7

¡Practica! Escribe la forma del mandato del verbo entre paréntesis. Escribe el acento si es necesario.

1. No _____. (levantarse/tú)

2. ¡_____! (subirse/Ud.)

3. No _____. (asustarse/tú)

4. ¡_____! (acostarse/vosotros)

5. ¡_____ los zapatos! (quitarse/Uds.)

6. No _____. (dormirse/tú)

7. Vengan y _____ el abrigo. (quitarse/Uds.)

8. Marta, _____. (prepararse/tú)

¿Cuál es la traducción apropiada? Subraya la respuesta para cada oración.

1. *Try them* [m.] *on!* (**Uds.**) ¡Pruébenselos! | ¡Pruébenselas!

2. *Carlos, put it* [m.] *on.* (**tú**) Carlos, póntela | póntelo.

3. *Do not shave here.* (**Uds.**) No te afeites aquí. | No se afeiten aquí.

4. *Cut it* [m.], *Laura.* (**tú**) Córtelo | Córtalo, Laura.

5. *Dry it* [f.] *up!* (**Ud.**) ¡Séquela! | ¡Sécala!

6. *Get closer.* (**Uds.**) Acércate. | Acérquense.

7. *Prepare them* [m.] *now.* (**Uds.**) Prepárenlos | Prepáralos ahora.

8. *Please, take them* [m.] *with you.* (**tú**) Por favor, llévatelas | llévatelos.

The infinitive and present participle in reflexive constructions

As a rule, reflexive pronouns precede both the simple and compound tenses of conjugated verbs. With a present participle (**gerundio** in Spanish), the verb forms that end in **-ando**, **-iendo** (equivalents of *-ing* in English), or with an infinitive, two options are possible.

◆ Reflexive pronouns may be attached to either verbal form.

Estoy durmi**éndome**.	*I am falling asleep.*
Quiero acostar**me**.	*I want to go to bed.*

◆ Or pronouns may precede conjugated forms that end with an infinitive or a **gerundio**.

Me estoy durmiendo.	*I am falling asleep.*
Me quiero acostar.	*I want to go to bed.*

Remember to place the reflexive pronoun before any direct object pronoun that may appear in the construction.

¿Dónde está mi sombrero? Quiero poné**rmelo**.	*Where is my hat? I want **to put it on**.*
¿Y mis guantes? **Me los** quiero poner.	*And my gloves? I want **to put them on**.*

Notice the added accent mark on the original stressed vowel when the attached pronoun(s) add one or more syllables to a multisyllable **gerundio** or infinitive, as is the case in **durmiéndome** and **ponérmelo** in the above examples. There is no accent mark if the verb form with pronouns naturally maintains its stressed vowel (**levantarme**, **dormirse**, etc.).

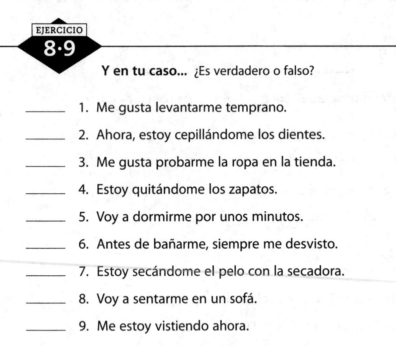

EJERCICIO
8·9

Y en tu caso... ¿Es verdadero o falso?

_____ 1. Me gusta levantarme temprano.

_____ 2. Ahora, estoy cepillándome los dientes.

_____ 3. Me gusta probarme la ropa en la tienda.

_____ 4. Estoy quitándome los zapatos.

_____ 5. Voy a dormirme por unos minutos.

_____ 6. Antes de bañarme, siempre me desvisto.

_____ 7. Estoy secándome el pelo con la secadora.

_____ 8. Voy a sentarme en un sofá.

_____ 9. Me estoy vistiendo ahora.

_____ 10. Voy a ponerme el pijama esta noche.

_____ 11. ¡Estoy volviéndome loco(a) con este capítulo!

EJERCICIO
8·10

Consejos y mandatos. Escribe la letra de la frase que indica un consejo (*advice*) o mandato apropiado.

_____ 1. ¿Tienes frío y tienes un abrigo?   a. Cálmate.

_____ 2. ¿Te gustan estos zapatos?   b. Duérmete.

_____ 3. Tienes el pelo muy largo.   c. Quítatelos.

_____ 4. Estás muy nerviosa.   d. ¡Póntelo!

_____ 5. ¿Estás muy aburrida?   e. Despídete.

_____ 6. Tienes la cara sucia.   f. Escóndete.

_____ 7. ¿No quieres que te vean?   g. Lávatela.

_____ 8. ¿Tienes calor con esos guantes?   h. Córtatelo.

_____ 9. ¿Tienes mucho sueño?   i. Pruébatelos.

_____ 10. ¿Vas a salir ahora?   j. ¡Diviértete!

En la tienda. Traduce. Usa el **Vocabulario útil**.

Carlos and Alexandra go shopping frequently. Alex tries on expensive dresses at the store, but Carlos does not get angry. Usually, she does not spend a lot of money, but she takes a long time shopping. Alex goes to the fitting room, she undresses, she tries on several dresses of famous designers, she looks at herself in the mirror, and she forgets about Carlos. He gets tired of waiting, sits on a sofa, and falls asleep. While Carlos sleeps, Alex goes to the shoe department and puts on several pairs of shoes. Then, she goes to the perfume and makeup section, and she buys herself several beauty products. She knows Carlos does not get upset, because she does not spend too much money. Later, Alex says good-bye to the saleslady, and she meets Carlos. He wakes up. He is surprised, because Alex is carrying many packages, and he worries a bit. Alex says she does not spend too much money, and Carlos calms down. They go to the cafeteria, and they have an afternoon snack. As usual, it is late, and they decide it is not worth it to go to the men's department.

Vocabulario útil

as usual	**como siempre**	to be surprised	**sorprenderse**
beauty product	**el producto de belleza**	to be worried	**preocuparse**
designer	**el/la diseñador(-a)**	to be worth it	**valer la pena**
fitting room	**el probador**	to calm oneself	**tranquilizarse**
makeup	**el maquillaje**	to get tired	**cansarse**
men's department	**el departamento de caballeros**	to have an afternoon snack	**merendar (e > ie)**
pair of shoes	**el par de zapatos**	to meet (*someone*)	**reunirse**
shoe department	**la zapatería**	to say good-bye	**despedirse (e > i)**

Reflexive constructions in reciprocal actions

The plural forms of the reflexive constructions in Spanish are also used to indicate reciprocal actions between or among people, animals, or objects. Note the English and Spanish equivalents. Use a reflexive construction to indicate

- mutual actions with the plural forms of reflexive verbs and the corresponding pronouns. The equivalent in English is the phrase *each other*.

Pedro y yo **nos ayudamos**.	*Pedro and I **help each other**.*
Mi gato y mi perro **se pelean** todos los días.	*My cat and my dog **fight with each other** every day.*

- Use the phrases **el uno al otro, la una a la otra, los unos a los otros, las unas a las otras,** or the adverb **mutuamente** to point out the reciprocal use of the reflexive pronouns when the context is not sufficiently clear.

Nunca nos enfadamos **el uno con el otro**.	*We never get angry **with each other**.*
Ellos se ven en el espejo.	*They see themselves in the mirror.*
Ellos se ven mutuamente en el espejo.	*They see **each other** in the mirror.*

In the first example, without any added clarification, **nos enfadamos** could mean either *we get angry* or *we get angry with each other*. If we add the adverb **mutuamente** to the second example, we clarify the message (as in the third example), and we understand *they see each other* (or *one another*) *in the mirror*.

EJERCICIO
8·12

En español.

1. *Amanda and I hug (**abrazarse**) each other.* _____

2. *You (**Uds.**) see yourselves in the mirror.* _____

3. *The two teams admire each other.* _____

4. *The children always quarrel (**pelearse**) with each other.*

   _____

5. *Do you (**Uds.**) know one another?* _____

6. *We help each other.* _____

7. *My husband and I respect one another.* _____

8. *Carlos and his brother talk to each other every day.*

   _____

9. *Do you (**vosotros**) see each other very often?* _____

10. *My friends greet (**saludarse**) each other.* _____

11. *We understand each other.* _____

12. *Julia and Jena brush their hair.* _____

How to express *to become* in Spanish

In Unit 6, you studied how to express *to become* in Spanish and how to use it in the preterit. Remember that **poner(se)**, **volver(se)**, and **hacer(se)** are reflexive verbs used with reflexive pronouns to communicate equivalents of *to become*. In Spanish, each of these constructions suggests a specific idea and offers a subtle distinction not present in the other two.

The following constructions express *to become* in Spanish.

- Use **ponerse** + adjective to express changes of an emotional or physical nature, which do not require a conscious effort.

Él se pone pálido cuando su jefe le habla.	*He becomes pale when his boss speaks to him.*
Él se puso triste.	*He became sad.*

* Use **volverse** + adjective to express an involuntary sudden change.

    Carlos **se volvió loco.**   *Carlos **became** (**went**) **crazy**.*

* Use **hacerse** + noun or adjective to express the attainment of a profession or social status that requires a considerable effort.

    Puedes hacerte contable, si estudias.   ***You can become** an accountant if you study.*
    Juan **se hizo** una persona respetable.   *Juan **became** a respectable person.*

EJERCICIO
8·13

¿Verdadero o falso?

_____ 1. Si piensas mucho puedes volverte loco(a).

_____ 2. Nos ponemos furiosos(as) si se ríen de nosotros(as).

_____ 3. Nos ponemos contentos(as) cuando nos critican.

_____ 4. Si estudias sicología, puedes hacerte ingeniero(a).

_____ 5. Te haces un(-a) tenista famoso(a) si practicas todos los días.

_____ 6. Cuando pierdo mis llaves me vuelvo loco(a).

_____ 7. Podemos hacernos ricos(as) si ahorramos disciplinadamente.

_____ 8. Cuando nuestro equipo no gana, nos ponemos tristes.

_____ 9. Si comes demasiado te pones flaco(a) (*thin*).

EJERCICIO
8·14

¿Qué pasa en estas circunstancias? Subraya la forma apropiada de **hacerse**, **volverse** o **ponerse** de acuerdo al contexto de las oraciones siguientes.

1. Emilio (se hace | se pone | se vuelve) nervioso cuando tiene que hablar en público.

2. Tú no (te haces | te pones | te vuelves) rico porque no tienes metas (*goals*).

3. Nosotros (nos hacemos | nos ponemos | nos volvemos) felices cuando llegan las vacaciones.

4. Si el jefe envía un e-mail a Felipe, ¡él (se hace | se pone | se vuelve) loco!

5. Cuando llega el invierno, tú (te haces | te pones | te vuelves) triste.

6. ¡Los niños (se hacen | se ponen | se vuelven) contentos cuando les llevamos regalos!

7. Nadie (se hace | se pone | se vuelve) millonario sin trabajar mucho.

8. Nosotros (nos hacemos | nos ponemos | nos volvemos) histéricos con esta mala noticia.

En español.

1. *Lina gets angry when she works too much.*

_____

2. *I become very nervous when you (**tú**) shout!*

_____

3. *People (**la gente**, singular) become crazy when there is a party.*

_____

4. (**Tú**) *Do not get angry!* _____

5. *Who becomes an expert without experience?*

_____

The reflexive construction in other tenses

In this unit, you have practiced reflexive constructions mostly in the present tense, along with infinitives and commands. Reflexive constructions are used in all tenses (present, past, and future), as well as in all moods (indicative, subjunctive, conditional, and imperative). As always, the appropriate reflexive pronouns are required.

Los chicos se acostaron a las ocho.	*The children went to bed at eight.*
Mientras **se reían, nosotros nos divertíamos** también.	*While **they laughed, we were having fun**, too.*
Me bañaré antes de acostarme.	*I will take a bath before going to bed.*
Ellos se acostarían.	*They would go to bed.*

As usual, the context will help you determine the tense or mood you need. If necessary, review certain units on verb tenses or moods in this book.

Las almas gemelas. Traduce. Usa el **Vocabulario útil**.

One day, Ariela woke up early. She looked at herself in the mirror. She washed her face. She put on her new lipstick and she combed her hair. She had a new hairstyle, a ponytail. She was happy with her new look. Then, she got dressed. She put on her new outfit. She walked out of her house and she saw her new neighbor, Zoe. Ariela and Zoe looked at each other. They greeted each other, and then they laughed. They had the same hairdo and the same outfit! Ariela took out her camera, they smiled, and now they have the picture. Since then, Ariela and Zoe speak to each other every day. They are soul mates.

Vocabulario útil

hairdo	**el peinado**	ponytail	**la cola de caballo**
lipstick	**el lápiz / la barra de labios**	since then	**desde entonces**
new look	**el nuevo look**	soul mate	**el alma gemela**
outfit	**el conjunto**	to put on lipstick	**pintarse los labios**

 **·9·**

The progressive tenses

The progressive tenses are formed with the present participle (**gerundio** in Spanish). They express an action in progress in the present, the past, or the future. The English equivalent of these constructions consists of a form of the auxiliary verb *to be* followed by a present participle, the *-ing* form of the verb.

> *The detective **is searching** for the victim.*
> *She **was singing** when I came in.*
> *I **will be waiting** before you get to the station.*

In the three examples above, the action is in progress, not yet completed, and it is taking place at that moment, whether in the present, the past, or the future. In Spanish, it is made up of a form of **estar** plus **el gerundio** (**Estoy leyendo**, *I am reading*).

The forms of the present participle in regular, irregular, and stem-changing verbs

With their **-ndo** ending, the Spanish **gerundio** forms are easy to spot.

Regular verbs

For regular verbs, you will drop the **-ar**, **-er**, or **-ir** from the infinitive, and add the corresponding ending, **-ando** for **-ar** verbs and **-iendo** for **-er** and **-ir** verbs.

sacar	to take out	**sacando**
beber	to drink	**bebiendo**
sufrir	to suffer	**sufriendo**

Remember that **-er** and **-ir** verbs have the same ending.

El autobús **está llegando** a la estación.	*The bus **is arriving** at the station.*
Estoy aprendiendo a cocinar con Hernán.	*I am **learning** to cook with Hernán.*
Ahora **ellos están escribiendo** el contrato.	*Now, **they are writing** the contract.*

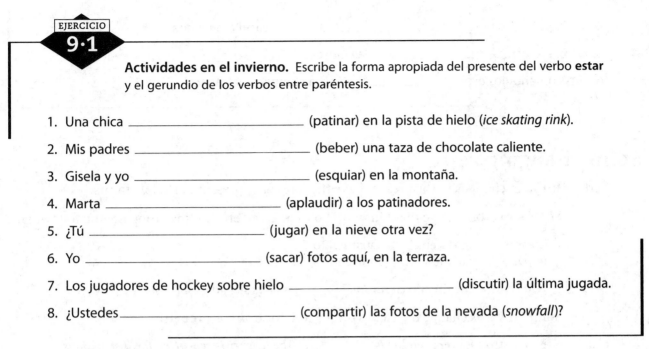

Actividades en el invierno. Escribe la forma apropiada del presente del verbo **estar** y el gerundio de los verbos entre paréntesis.

1. Una chica _____ (patinar) en la pista de hielo (*ice skating rink*).

2. Mis padres _____ (beber) una taza de chocolate caliente.

3. Gisela y yo _____ (esquiar) en la montaña.

4. Marta _____ (aplaudir) a los patinadores.

5. ¿Tú _____ (jugar) en la nieve otra vez?

6. Yo _____ (sacar) fotos aquí, en la terraza.

7. Los jugadores de hockey sobre hielo _____ (discutir) la última jugada.

8. ¿Ustedes_____ (compartir) las fotos de la nevada (*snowfall*)?

Present participles ending in -*yendo*

Verbs with stems that end in a vowel have slightly different present participle forms.

- For -**er** and -**ir** verbs with stems ending in a vowel, add -**yendo**.

  Lara **está leyendo** las instrucciones en la receta.   *Lara **is reading** the instructions in the recipe.*

The following is a list of commonly used present participles that end in -**yendo**.

VERBS ENDING IN -er			VERBS ENDING IN -ir		
atraer	to attract	**atrayendo**	**construir**	to build	**construyendo**
caer	to fall	**cayendo**	**contribuir**	to contribute	**contribuyendo**
contraer	to contract	**contrayendo**	**destruir**	to destroy	**destruyendo**
creer	to believe	**creyendo**	**huir**	to flee	**huyendo**
leer	to read	**leyendo**	**incluir**	to include	**incluyendo**
traer	to bring	**trayendo**	**influir**	to influence	**influyendo**
			oír	to hear	**oyendo**

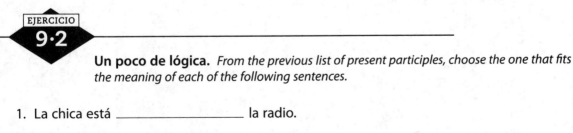

Un poco de lógica. *From the previous list of present participles, choose the one that fits the meaning of each of the following sentences.*

1. La chica está _____ la radio.

2. El criminal está _____ de la policía.

3. El huracán está _____ los árboles.

4. En la playa, los niños están _____ un castillo de arena.

5. ¡El pastel está _____ las moscas!

6. Tus comentarios están _____ a complicar la situación.

Stem-changing verbs

Verbs with stem changes in the present have the following present participle forms.

◆ Some -**ir** verbs change the stem vowel **o** to **u**. Two verbs in this group are the following.

dormir	to sleep	**durmiendo**
morir	to die	**muriendo**

¿Quién **está durmiendo** en mi sofá?   *Who **is sleeping** on my sofa?*

◆ Some -**ir** verbs change the stem vowel **e** to **i**, for example, **repetir**.

El maestro **está repitiendo** las   *The teacher **is repeating** the instructions*
instrucciones a los alumnos.   *to the students.*

Here is a list of commonly used verbs with the **e** to **i** change in the gerund.

advertir	to warn	**advirtiendo**	**reír**	to laugh	**riendo**
competir	to compete	**compitiendo**	**reñir**	to fight	**riñendo**
conseguir	to get	**consiguiendo**	**repetir**	to repeat	**repitiendo**
consentir	to agree	**consintiendo**	**seguir**	to follow	**siguiendo**
convertir	to convert	**convirtiendo**	**sentir**	to feel	**sintiendo**
decir	to say	**diciendo**	**servir**	to serve	**sirviendo**
hervir	to boil	**hirviendo**	**sugerir**	to suggest	**sugiriendo**
mentir	to lie	**mintiendo**	**venir**	to come	**viniendo**
pedir	to ask for	**pidiendo**			

Note: We suggest that you review stem-changing verbs in the third-person singular of the preterit tense (Unit 4). They mirror the changes in the present participle.

Irregular present participles

The verbs **ir** and **poder** have irregular gerund forms.

ir	to go	**yendo**
poder	to be able	**pudiendo**

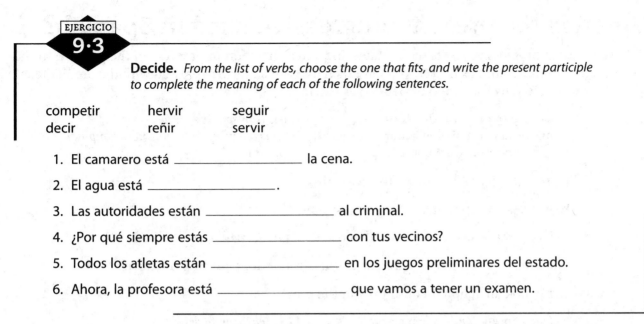

Decide. *From the list of verbs, choose the one that fits, and write the present participle to complete the meaning of each of the following sentences.*

competir	hervir	seguir
decir	reñir	servir

1. El camarero está _____ la cena.

2. El agua está _____.

3. Las autoridades están _____ al criminal.

4. ¿Por qué siempre estás _____ con tus vecinos?

5. Todos los atletas están _____ en los juegos preliminares del estado.

6. Ahora, la profesora está _____ que vamos a tener un examen.

Placement of reflexive pronouns and other object pronouns with the present participle

As a rule, reflexive pronouns precede the conjugated forms of verbs. The pronouns may be attached to the end of the present participle, however. An alternate Spanish form has the pronoun *preceding* the conjugated form of **estar** in the progressive construction. Both constructions are equally common. Observe the placement of the reflexive pronouns in the examples that follow.

El gato **no está despertándose**.
El gato **no se está despertando**. } *The cat is not waking up.*

The same rules apply to direct or indirect object pronouns.

¿Quién **está vendiéndolo**?
¿Quién *lo* **está vendiendo**? } *Who is selling it?*

Note the accent marks on **despertándose** and **vendiéndolo**. When a pronoun is added to the Spanish present participle, the accent mark indicates the original stressed vowel.

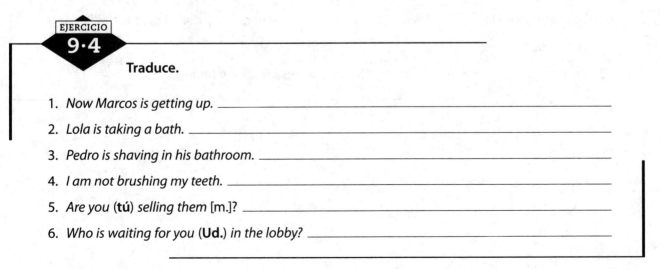

Traduce.

1. *Now Marcos is getting up.* _____

2. *Lola is taking a bath.* _____

3. *Pedro is shaving in his bathroom.* _____

4. *I am not brushing my teeth.* _____

5. *Are you (**tú**) selling them [m.]?* _____

6. *Who is waiting for you (**Ud.**) in the lobby?* _____

When is the present progressive used in Spanish?

The present progressive, as its name states, indicates an action in progress in the present. In the previous exercises and examples, you have seen its Spanish form expressed with the present tense of **estar** followed by the -**ando** or -**iendo** verb forms.

Chris **está preparando** la cena.	Chris **is preparing** dinner.
Juan **está aprendiendo** a usar el nuevo programa de la computadora.	Juan **is learning** to use the new computer program.

The present progressive in Spanish is used

◆ to express an action that is in progress now.

Laura **está leyendo** una novela ahora.	Laura **is reading** a novel now.

Note that the action is not finished: Laura is not done reading the novel.

◆ to say that an action is continuing in the present.

Estoy aprendiendo a manejar.	**I am learning** to drive.

This example also indicates an action in progress, but the process is gradual. It takes time to learn to drive.

The present progressive is not used in Spanish as frequently as it is in English. Spanish normally uses the present tense—*not* the present progressive—to describe an action happening now. However, the English equivalent of the simple Spanish present is often a progressive form.

Traigo las manzanas en la bolsa.	**I am bringing** the apples in my bag.

EJERCICIO
9·5

¿Qué están haciendo ahora? Escribe la forma apropiada del presente de **estar** y el gerundio de los verbos entre paréntesis.

1. El ladrón _____ (esconder) la evidencia del robo (*robbery*).

2. El reloj _____ (dar) las ocho.

3. ¿Quiénes _____ (gritar) en el pasillo (*corridor*)?

4. Los hermanos Díaz _____ (esperar) el autobús para ir a Málaga.

5. ¿Y Marlo? ¿_____ (dormir) la siesta?

6. Andy _____ (vivir) una pesadilla (*nightmare*).

En español. Usa el verbo **estar** + el gerundio.

1. *The fans (**fanáticos**) are watching a good game.*

_____

2. *It is not raining now.* _____

3. *The team is playing well.* _____

4. *The trainer (**entrenador**) is encouraging (**animar**) his players (**jugadores**).*

_____

5. *A beer vendor (**vendedor**) is climbing up the stairs.*

_____

6. *He is yelling: "Peanuts, beer!"* _____

7. *Now, the band is playing music.* _____

8. *The fans are having fun.* _____

9. *The other team is losing the game.* _____

The progressive forms in other tenses

In Spanish, as in English, there are progressive forms in all tenses and moods. Here are some examples.

El reportero **estaba investigando** el incidente.	*The reporter **was investigating** the incident.*
Pedro **estuvo buscándote** ayer por la mañana.	*Pedro **was looking for you** yesterday morning.*
Estaríamos durmiendo.	*We **might have been sleeping.***

Note: A continuing action in the past can be expressed with the imperfect tense *or* with the imperfect of **estar** + **gerundio**.

Yo dormía.	
Yo estaba durmiendo.	*I was sleeping.*

Both examples above communicate the same idea: the action was in the process of taking place, and it was of unspecific duration.

En el banco. Practiquemos un poco. Describe la escena en el banco ayer. Usa el verbo **estar** en el imperfecto de indicativo (**estaba, estabas, estaba...**) + el gerundio.

1. Carlos (buscar) una silla para sentarse. _____

2. Marta y Raúl (rellenar) una planilla (*form*). _____

3. La secretaria (escribir) una nota. _____

4. Las telefonistas (responder) a los clientes por teléfono. _____

5. El cajero (*teller*) (recibir) los depósitos de los clientes. _____

6. Dos señoras (hacer) unas preguntas en el pasillo. _____

7. Yo (cambiar) euros por dólares. _____

8. El director de finanzas (tomar) un café. _____

9. Marta (leer) un libro en la fila (*line*). _____

Preguntas personales. Contesta en español.

1. ¿Qué estás haciendo ahora? _____

2. ¿Quién está gobernando los Estados Unidos ahora?

_____

3. ¿Qué libro estás leyendo? _____

4. ¿Con quién estabas hablando ayer por teléfono?

_____

5. ¿Qué estabas haciendo anoche a las diez?

_____

Verbs of motion in progressive tenses

The progressive tenses formed with the present participle (-**ando**, -**iendo** forms) are used with the verbs **seguir** and **continuar** and with verbs of motion such as **andar**, **ir**, and **venir**. As with **estar**, they emphasize an action that continues, is repeated, or is not finished.

Sigue trabajando para la misma compañía chilena.	*He/She is still working for the same Chilean company.*
Ando buscando trabajo.	*I am looking for a job.*
Van diciendo que somos una pareja.	*They are going around saying we are a couple.*
Vienen caminando.	*They come walking.*

These forms are also used in other tenses and moods. The following examples are in the past, future, and conditional.

Thomas **andaba buscando** a su hermana.	*Thomas **was looking for** his sister.*
¿**Irás caminando** o en auto?	*Will you **go walking** or by car?*
¿**Continuarías viendo** esta película?	*Would you **continue watching** this movie?*

EJERCICIO
9·9

En español. Usa el verbo entre paréntesis para traducir el verbo subrayado.

1. *Miriam <u>continues</u> singing the same song.* (seguir)

   _____

2. *My son <u>is</u> looking for a job.* (andar) _____

3. *Who <u>continues</u> making noise (**ruido**)?* (continuar)

   _____

4. *We'll <u>go</u> searching for an answer.* (ir) _____

5. *They will not <u>continue</u> lying.* (seguir) _____

6. *She <u>is</u> losing hope.* (estar) _____

7. *He will <u>go on</u> supporting (**apoyar**) his friends.* (continuar)

   _____

8. *<u>Were</u> you (**tú**) working in this office yesterday?* (estar)

   _____

Present participle: Spanish compared to English

We have studied **-ando, -iendo** forms in uses equivalent to the English progressive tenses. In that role, the **gerundio** is equivalent to the English present participle.

There are three other considerations regarding the present participle.

◆ Used in a phrase *without* an auxiliary verb such as **estar**, the **gerundio** is the equivalent of the English present participle.

Meneando la cola, el gato se sentó en el sofá.	*Swaying its tail, the cat sat down on the sofa.*
Los huéspedes, **esperando** pacientemente en la fila, hablan del tiempo.	*The guests, **waiting** patiently in line, talk about the weather.*

Note the phrases above followed or enclosed by commas. In English, these are called participial phrases.

The Spanish infinitive, and not **el gerundio**, is used in sentences as a noun.

Bailar es divertido.	*Dancing is fun.*

In the example above, literal translation into the **-ando, -iendo** Spanish forms is not possible.

◆ In Spanish, always use the infinitive after prepositions.

Después de desayunar, ya estaba corriendo por el barrio.	***After having breakfast**, he/she was running around the neighborhood.*

◆ **Al** + infinitive is equivalent to *upon* + present participle in English.

Al escuchar sonar el teléfono, se levantaron.	***Upon hearing** the phone ring, they got up.*

EJERCICIO
9·10

En la piscina. ¿El gerundio o el infinitivo? Escribe la forma apropiada del gerundio o el infinitivo del verbo entre paréntesis, de acuerdo a la frase.

1. Ando _____ (buscar) a mis amigos.

2. Quiero encontrarlos para _____ (ir) a la piscina.

3. _____ (nadar) es un ejercicio excelente y muy relajante.

4. Por fin, después de _____ (encontrar) a Marcos, estamos ya en la piscina.

5. ¡Hay mucha gente _____ (disfrutar) esta mañana aquí!

6. Delia está _____ (broncearse) al sol.

7. Pedro está _____ (flotar) en el agua.

8. Alina y Tony siguen _____ (dormir).

EJERCICIO
9·11

La robótica. Traduce. Usa el **Vocabulario útil**.

*What am I doing? Right now, I am writing a research paper for my robotics class. At the same time, I am watching a video from a university in Japan. A young man who is studying dentistry is drilling a female patient's tooth. Now, tears are coming out of her eyes. She is also waving her hands. The patient is not smiling, she is screaming, because she feels a lot of pain. Poor thing! Perhaps she needs anesthesia for this procedure. Upon hearing her cries, the student is nervous. Ha, an assistant is bringing the student a glass of water! I think you (**tú**) are going to laugh. The patient is not real. The student is practicing with a robot. At least the student is not torturing a patient.*

Vocabulario útil

dentistry	**la odontología**	research paper	**el reporte**
drill	**el taladro**	robotics	**la robótica**
ha	**ja**	to drill	**taladrar**
Japan	**(el) Japón**	to torture	**torturar**
patient	**el/la paciente**	to wave (a hand)	**agitar (la mano)**
poor thing	**pobrecito(a)**	tooth	**el diente; la muela**
procedure	**el procedimiento**		

Compound tenses: the present perfect and the past perfect

10

Compound tense forms (**formas compuestas**), as their name indicates, consist of more than one verb element. These tenses are conjugated with a basic form of a verb called a past participle (**participio**), preceded by an auxiliary verb.

Reminder: Knowing to which of the three conjugations (-**ar**, -**er**, or -**ir**) a verb infinitive (such as **cantar**, **beber**, or **vivir**) belongs helps us conjugate both simple and compound tenses.

> Elisa canta bien, bebe té y vive aquí.   *Elisa sings well, drinks tea, and lives here.*

In Spanish, past participles (equivalents of *-ed* forms or regular past participles in English) are also based on the infinitive. They end in -**ado** or -**ido**. The following example shows two verbs in the present perfect.

> Elisa **ha terminado** pero **no ha salido**.   *Elisa **has finished** but **has not left**.*

Notice the similarities in the formation of the English and Spanish present perfect (**ha terminado**, *has finished*). Note also that in the present perfect, **haber** rather than **tener** is used as the auxiliary verb.

The present perfect

The present perfect (**pretérito perfecto**) is one of several compound tenses used in Spanish and English. In Spanish, it uses a form of the auxiliary **haber**, a verb not commonly used in simple tenses, except for the impersonal forms **hay** (*there is, there are*), **había** (*there was, there were*), etc. Here are the present tense forms of **haber**, used to form the present perfect.

yo	**he**	nosotros/nosotras	**hemos**
tú	**has**	vosotros/vosotras	**habéis**
él/ella/Ud.	**ha**	ellos/ellas/Uds.	**han**

As you know, the past participle is the second component of a compound tense. To form regular past participles in Spanish, take the infinitive,

- drop the -**ar** ending, and add -**ado**: bail(**ar**) → bail**ado**.

- drop the -**er** or -**ir** ending, and add -**ido**: ten(**er**) → ten**ido**, sal(**ir**) → sal**ido**.

107

The present perfect is formed with a present form of **haber** followed by the past participle of the verb you wish to conjugate.

pintar (to paint)		perder (to lose)		salir (to leave, go out)	
he pintado	hemos pintado	he perdido	hemos perdido	he salido	hemos salido
has pintado	habéis pintado	has perdido	habéis perdido	has salido	habéis salido
ha pintado	han pintado	ha perdido	han perdido	ha salido	han salido

Gabriela **ha pintado** retratos magníficos.   *Gabriela **has painted** magnificent portraits.*
¡**He perdido** mi reloj de oro!   *I **lost** my gold watch!*
Lisa y Frank **han recibido** buenas   *Lisa and Frank **have received** good news.*
  noticias.

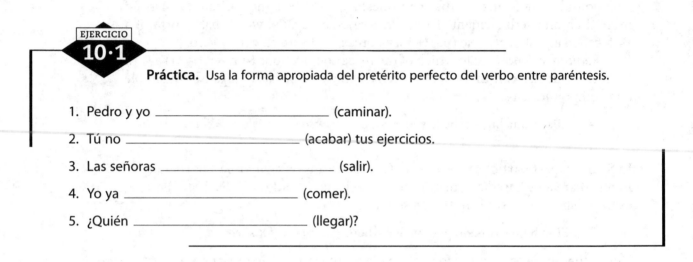

EJERCICIO
10·1

Práctica. Usa la forma apropiada del pretérito perfecto del verbo entre paréntesis.

1. Pedro y yo _____ (caminar).

2. Tú no _____ (acabar) tus ejercicios.

3. Las señoras _____ (salir).

4. Yo ya _____ (comer).

5. ¿Quién _____ (llegar)?

EJERCICIO
10·2

Tu lista. ¿Has estado muy activo(a) hoy? Indica **sí** o **no**.

_____ 1. Me he despertado antes de la siete.   _____ 4. He trabajado en casa.

_____ 2. He tomado un baño.   _____ 5. He tomado un café.

_____ 3. Me he cepillado los dientes.   _____ 6. He pagado tres cuentas.

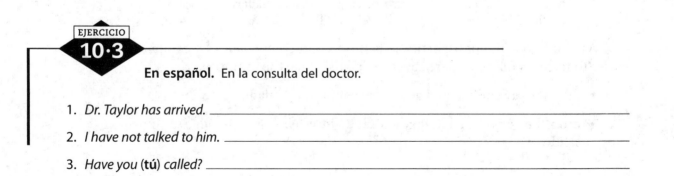

EJERCICIO
10·3

En español. En la consulta del doctor.

1. *Dr. Taylor has arrived.* _____

2. *I have not talked to him.* _____

3. *Have you (**tú**) called?* _____

4. *Lola has turned on the TV in the waiting room.*

_____

5. *The nurse has not come out.* _____

6. *Who has taken (**llevarse**) my magazine?* _____

7. *The examination (**examen** [m.]) has ended.* _____

Past participles ending in **-ído** and irregular past participles

Two groups of commonly used verbs form their past participles in slightly different ways. **-Er** or **-ir** verbs with stem vowels **a**, **e**, or **o** immediately preceding the infinitive ending require a written accent mark over the **-í** of the participle form. Here are some examples.

atraer	to attract	**atraído**	**oír**	to hear	**oído**
caer	to fall	**caído**	**reír**	to laugh	**reído**
creer	to believe	**creído**	**sonreír**	to smile	**sonreído**
leer	to read	**leído**	**traer**	to bring	**traído**

EJERCICIO
10·4

En la fiesta. De acuerdo al significado, usa uno de los verbos irregulares de la lista anterior. Completa la frase con la forma apropiada del pretérito perfecto.

1. Yo _____ la invitación para esta fiesta.

2. El camarero _____ unas copas de vino.

3. ¿_____ Ud. esta canción antes?

4. El público _____ con los chistes.

5. Las chicas _____ al fotógrafo.

6. ¡Pobre Carlos! Se _____ en el salón.

7. Ellos no _____ tus mentiras (*lies*).

IRREGULAR PAST PARTICIPLES IN SPANISH

abrir	to open	**abierto**	**morir**	to die	**muerto**
cubrir	to cover	**cubierto**	**poner**	to put	**puesto**
decir	to tell	**dicho**	**resolver**	to resolve	**resuelto**
disolver(se)	to dissolve	**disuelto**	**romper**	to break	**roto**
escribir	to write	**escrito**	**ver**	to see	**visto**
hacer	to make	**hecho**	**volver**	to return	**vuelto**
imprimir	to print	**impreso**			

Otra vez. De acuerdo al significado, usa uno de los verbos irregulares de la lista anterior. Completa la frase con la forma apropiada del pretérito perfecto.

1. El azúcar se _____ en el café.

2. ¿Quién _____ los zapatos encima de la mesa?

3. Lana me _____ una carta de recomendación.

4. Berta no _____ la ventana.

5. ¿_____ tú ese problema ya?

6. Yo no _____ la tarea.

7. Los chicos no _____ de Perú.

Compounds of the verbs with irregular past participles in the list above also have irregular past participles.

componer	to mend; to compose	**compuesto**	**imponer**	to impose	**impuesto**	
			oponer(se)	to oppose	**opuesto**	
describir	to describe	**descrito**	**predecir**	to predict	**predicho**	
descubrir	to find, discover	**descubierto**	**proponer**	to propose	**propuesto**	
deshacer	to undo, break	**deshecho**	**reponer**(se)	to get better, recover	**repuesto**	
devolver	to return (*something*)	**devuelto**	**revolver**	to stir	**revuelto**	
disponer	to dispose	**dispuesto**	**suponer**	to suppose	**supuesto**	
freír	to fry	**frito**				

¿Qué ha pasado? En español. Usa el pretérito perfecto.

1. *I have discovered there is a mouse (**ratón** [m.]) in my room.*

_____

2. *I have not recovered from the experience.*

_____

3. *I have described the scene to my neighbor Rosa.*

_____

4. *She has proposed to call an exterminator (**fumigador**).*

_____

5. *She has predicted the end of my problem.*

_____

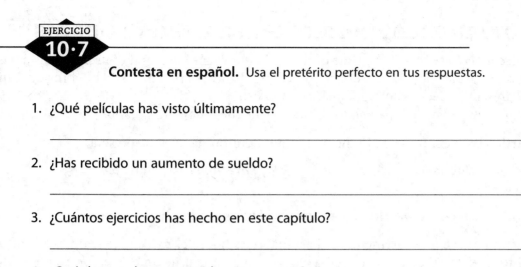

Contesta en español. Usa el pretérito perfecto en tus respuestas.

1. ¿Qué películas has visto últimamente?

   _____

2. ¿Has recibido un aumento de sueldo?

   _____

3. ¿Cuántos ejercicios has hecho en este capítulo?

   _____

4. ¿Qué deporte has practicado esta semana?

   _____

5. ¿Qué noticias has escuchado hoy?

   _____

6. ¿Te has levantado hoy de buen humor?

   _____

7. ¿Te has cepillado los dientes más de tres veces?

   _____

¿Cuál es la respuesta? Indica la letra de la respuesta apropiada para cada pregunta.

_____	1. ¿Han pedido un vino tinto (*red*)?	a.	No, no ha sonado en todo el día.
_____	2. ¿Has decidido qué vas a hacer mañana?	b.	Han llegado Julio y su hermana.
_____	3. ¿Ha llamado alguien por teléfono?	c.	No, hemos decidido beber una cerveza.
_____	4. ¿Has incluido la propina (*tip*)?	d.	No, no he pensado mucho en eso.
_____	5. ¿No han oído esta canción nueva?	e.	No, él no ha pasado por aquí.
_____	6. ¿Quién ha roto los vasos?	f.	La he dejado en el auto.
_____	7. ¿Has probado las papas fritas?	g.	Sí, ¡están muy picantes!
_____	8. ¿Qué has hecho con tu chaqueta?	h.	Un camarero.
_____	9. ¿Han visto Uds. a Don Francisco?	i.	La hemos escuchado varias veces.
_____	10. ¿Quiénes han entrado?	j.	He añadido (*add*) el quince por ciento.

When is the present perfect tense used in Spanish?

The name *present perfect* hints at the time of the action or event in several of its uses. It is a past tense, yet we refer to it as the *present* perfect, indicating that the action may still be going on. This is true of the present perfect in both Spanish and English.

Use the present perfect in Spanish to communicate the following situations.

- An action or event initiated in the past that is continuing into the present.

    Hemos vivido aquí por más de diez años.   *We have lived here for over ten years.*

    The message says we *have lived* here and we continue to live here.

- An action or event occurring in the past that does not refer to a concrete time. It is often used to refer to an action completed at a recent moment in time. See, for example, the second example below.

    Elly nos **ha esperado** en recepción.   *Elly has waited for us in the reception area.*
    El correo **ha llegado**.   *The mail has arrived.*

    Remember that you can also express an action recently completed with the present of **acabar** + **de** + infinitive (*to have just*).

    El correo **acaba de llegar**.   *The mail has just arrived.*

The form of **haber** always begins the present perfect. Object pronouns are placed immediately before the auxiliary **haber**: first, indirect or reflexive object pronouns, and then direct object pronouns, in that order. Adverbs cannot be placed between the form of **haber** and the present participle; the two elements are never separated in Spanish.

Sabrina **se ha comido** tres chocolates.   *Sabrina has eaten three chocolates.*
Ella **ha respondido rápidamente** a mis preguntas.   *She has quickly answered my questions.*

EJERCICIO
10·9

¿Verdadero o falso?

_____ 1. Los Estados Unidos han participado en todos los juegos olímpicos.

_____ 2. El béisbol ha sido el deporte más popular en el mundo entero.

_____ 3. Los japoneses han creado automóviles más económicos.

_____ 4. El Óscar ha consistido en el premio más prestigioso de la música.

_____ 5. Desde hace más de cien años ha existido el arte de la fotografía.

_____ 6. La ciencia médica ha alargado (*prolonged*) la vida del ser humano.

_____ 7. Los insectos han sobrevivido (*survived*) por miles de años.

La mudanza. Traduce. Usa el **Vocabulario útil**.

I have always wanted a new home. We have finally moved to our new house. We have discovered a few surprises. I have written a list of the repairs. We have fixed a leak in the roof. We have bought new tools, and I have learned to use a hammer. I have repaired a wall and changed many light bulbs! Luckily, I have not broken my nails or fractured a finger. And we have laughed, too. We've invited many friends. They have come to help us, and they have brought food and gifts. I have heard many times that friends are like family. I have discovered this is true.

Vocabulario útil

finger	**el dedo**	lightbulb	**un bombillo, una bombilla**
(finger)nail	**la uña**	to fracture	**fracturar**
gift	**el regalo**	to move (house)	**mudar(se)**
hammer	**el martillo**	to repair	**arreglar**
it is true	**es verdad**	tool	**la herramienta**
leak	**una gotera**	wall	**la pared**

The past perfect or pluperfect

The past perfect or pluperfect (**el pretérito pluscuamperfecto**) is another compound tense that is similar in Spanish and English. As usual, in Spanish two components are needed: a form of the auxiliary verb **haber** plus the past participle of the verb to be conjugated. In English, the auxiliary form *had* is used for every person of this tense. The forms of the Spanish imperfect (**el imperfecto**) of **haber** are used in the past perfect, followed by the past participle of the verb to be conjugated.

bailar (*to dance*)

había bailado	habíamos bailado
habías bailado	habíais bailado
había bailado	habían bailado

ser (*to be*)		**ir** (*to go*)	
había sido	habíamos sido	había ido	habíamos ido
habías sido	habíais sido	habías ido	habíais ido
había sido	habían sido	había ido	habían ido

Note that

- the first- and third-person singular of the past perfect forms are the same.

- there are written accent marks on the **í** of all the imperfect forms of **haber**.

Practica. Usa el pluscuamperfecto del verbo entre paréntesis.

1. Ellos no _____ (salir).

2. ¿Por qué Ud. no _____ (empezar) los ejercicios?

3. Las actrices _____ (entrar) al teatro.

4. Pedro _____ (devolver) el libro a la biblioteca.

5. ¿Quiénes _____ (vivir) aquí antes que tú?

6. ¡Berta y yo _____ (sacar) esas fotos!

En español. ¿Qué habían hecho Uds.?

1. We had finished three exercises from this chapter.

_____

2. We had called my sister before going to the market.

_____

3. We had prepared our breakfast. _____

4. We had opened the windows in your (**tú**) room.

_____

5. We had not finished our work until eleven o'clock in the morning.

_____

6. We had made an appointment for a haircut (**un corte de pelo**).

_____

When is the past perfect used in Spanish?

The past perfect tenses in English and Spanish are formed similarly, and their uses are practically the same in both languages.

Use the past perfect to express an event or an action completed in the past before other actions or events.

La fiesta **había comenzado**.	*The party **had begun**.*
Marta **había salido** cuando yo entré.	*Marta **had left** when I arrived.*

In the first of the two examples, there is no indication when the action took place other than at a distant point in the past: **había comenzado**. This isolated sentence does not give any other clues about time. But, in the second example, we know that **Marta** was already gone, **había salido**, prior to a past action indicated by **yo entré**.

Before you do the following exercises, you may wish to review the presentation of irregular past participles and participles with added accent marks earlier in this unit.

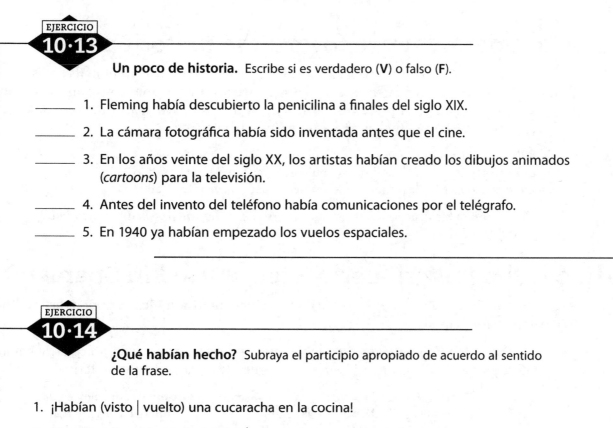

EJERCICIO
10·13

Un poco de historia. Escribe si es verdadero (**V**) o falso (**F**).

_____ 1. Fleming había descubierto la penicilina a finales del siglo XIX.

_____ 2. La cámara fotográfica había sido inventada antes que el cine.

_____ 3. En los años veinte del siglo XX, los artistas habían creado los dibujos animados (*cartoons*) para la televisión.

_____ 4. Antes del invento del teléfono había comunicaciones por el telégrafo.

_____ 5. En 1940 ya habían empezado los vuelos espaciales.

EJERCICIO
10·14

¿Qué habían hecho? Subraya el participio apropiado de acuerdo al sentido de la frase.

1. ¡Habían (visto | vuelto) una cucaracha en la cocina!

2. El meteorólogo había (predicho | opuesto) una tormenta de nieve.

3. Mi hermano no había (dispuesto | disuelto) el azúcar en el café.

4. No te conocieron porque no te habías (revuelto | repuesto) de tu accidente.

5. El gobierno había (impreso | impuesto) nuevas regulaciones para la importación de frutas.

6. Mi gato se había (creído | caído) del techo varias veces.

¿Qué habías hecho el año pasado? *What had you done or not before the New Year? You may use the following list of verbs and expressions to talk about your accomplishments or unfinished plans.*

Vocabulario

aprender otra lengua	to learn another language	**dejar de fumar**	to quit smoking
		empezar un negocio	to start a business
bajar de peso	to lose weight	**liquidar las deudas**	to pay off debts
casarse	to get married	**pagar la hipoteca**	to pay off the mortgage
comprar un auto nuevo	to buy a new car		
conseguir un empleo mejor	to find a better job	**publicar un libro**	to publish a book

Other compound tense forms: the preterit perfect

The preterit perfect (**el pretérito anterior**) is included here mainly for recognition. Its use is practically limited to formal or literary style; nowadays, it is hardly used in everyday communication. It is formed with the preterit (**el pretérito**) of **haber** and the past participle of the verb. Like the pluperfect, it is translated into English as *had* + past participle.

hube pagado, vendido, salido	**hubimos** pagado, vendido, salido
hubiste pagado, vendido, salido	**hubisteis** pagado, vendido, salido
hubo pagado, vendido, salido	**hubieron** pagado, vendido, salido

Cuando **hubo terminado**, fuimos a su despacho.	*As soon as **he had finished**, we went into his office.*

When is the preterit perfect tense used in Spanish?

Note the name of this tense in Spanish: **pretérito anterior**. **Anterior** indicates prior or before. The preterit perfect tense is used

- when the action or event expressed in the preterit perfect happened immediately before another past action. The preterit perfect is frequently replaced by the preterit.

En cuanto **hubo empezado** la película, Ángela se sentó. En cuanto **empezó** la película, Ángela se sentó.	*As soon as the movie **had started**, Angela sat down.*

- after adverbs and phrases such as **cuando, después de que, en cuanto, tan pronto como**, and others that point to a recently completed action.

Tan pronto como el general **hubo desertado**, llamó a sus parientes.	*As soon as the general **had deserted**, he called his relatives.*

Haber + a participle: the Spanish equivalent of the perfect infinitive

The perfect infinitive in English is expressed with the construction *having* + a past participle (see examples below). In Spanish, this construction is rendered by the infinitive of the auxiliary verb **haber** + a past participle. The Spanish form has a noun function and is used after certain prepositions or as a complement of verbs.

No pude votar en las elecciones **después de haber llegado** tarde.	*After having arrived late, I could not vote in the election.*
Por haber comido tanto, tienes dolor de estómago.	*For having eaten so much, you have a stomachache.*

When is the infinitive of haber + a participle used in Spanish?

As in English, this compound form is used to indicate an action or event that happened prior to another action or event.

Al haber cruzado la calle, vimos a Lola.　*Upon having crossed the street, we saw Lola.*

Al haber cruzado happened prior to **vimos**. Keep in mind that the infinitive and *not* the **gerundio** (-**ando** or -**iendo** form) follows a preposition in Spanish.

EJERCICIO
10·16

En español.

1. *After having won first prize, Marcela is very proud.*

   _____

2. *Upon having a conversation with us, Mirta decided to accept our invitation.*

   _____

3. *After having met Carmela, Marcos found out (**saber**) the truth.*

   _____

4. *For having left so late, we missed (**perder**) the flight.*

   _____

5. *After having worked the whole week, we deserved a vacation.*

   _____

6. *For not having checked the price, we paid too much.*

   _____

7. *Upon having finished your work before the deadline (la fecha de entrega), you (tú) deserve a rest.*

_____

8. *For having done all the exercises in this chapter, now I write better in Spanish.*

_____

EJERCICIO
10·17

¡Qué sorpresa! Traduce. Usa el **Vocabulario útil**.

A few weeks ago, Beni and Celia had organized a day trip to San Diego. They had lived there several years. Beni always likes to play jokes. He had decided to surprise his friend, Pablo. Beni and Celia parked their car in front of Pablo's house. Celia had taken her video camera to film their visit. They knocked on the door, but no one answered. They went back to their car and saw a police car. The police officer had given them a fine for parking too close to a fire hydrant. Who had called the police? Pablo! He has always suspected other people's intentions. He had seen a car parked in front of his house. He thought they were trespassers. Celia filmed the scene when Pablo and Beni finally hugged each other.

Vocabulario útil

day trip	**la excursión**	to hug	**abrazarse**
fine	**la multa**	to park	**aparcar, estacionar**
fire hydrant	**el hidrante (de incendios)**	to play a joke	**hacer bromas**
police car	**la patrulla**	to suspect	**sospechar**
to film	**grabar**	trespasser	**el/la intruso(a)**

Compound tenses: the future perfect and the conditional perfect

The future perfect

In English, the future perfect tense describes an action or event that will be completed at a moment in the future, *before* some other action or event takes place. As with other compound tenses, the future perfect consists of two elements: an auxiliary verb plus a past participle. In the sentence ***I will have waited*** *at least an hour by the time* ***you arrive*** *at the airport*, the action of *waiting* will have taken place before the action expressed in *you arrive*. Note that in the English sentence, *you arrive* is expressed in the present tense, not in the future.

In Spanish, the equivalent tense is **el futuro perfecto**.

As usual, the forms of the future tense of **haber** are used as the auxiliary verb of the future perfect. The past participle follows the auxiliary.

Here are examples of the three conjugations with **pagar**, **vender**, and **salir** in the future perfect.

> **habré** pagado, vendido, salido
> **habrás** pagado, vendido, salido
> **habrá** pagado, vendido, salido
>
> **habremos** pagado, vendido, salido
> **habréis** pagado, vendido, salido
> **habrán** pagado, vendido, salido

Remember that

- all auxiliary (**haber**) future forms have an accent mark on the last syllable, except the **nosotros** form.

- the elements of a compound tense cannot be separated in Spanish.

> El paciente seguramente **se habrá recuperado**.
> *The patient **will** surely **have recovered**.*
> Mañana a las ocho, ya **habremos terminado** este capítulo.
> *Tomorrow at eight, **we will have** this chapter **finished**.*

Práctica. ¿Qué habrá pasado? Usa el futuro perfecto.

1. Las hijas de Verónica _____ (salir) ya. No las veo aquí.

2. ¿Quién no _____ (comer) hoy? Hay mucha carne y arroz aquí.

3. Hace mucho calor. María Elena _____ (cerrar) las ventanas.

4. Tienes mal aspecto. Tú no _____ (dormir) mucho anoche.

5. Jorge no ha llegado. Tal vez _____ (recibir) una visita en su casa.

6. Luis y tú están gastando mucho dinero. Uds. _____ (sacarse) la lotería.

7. Juan no está en el hospital; él _____ (recuperarse) de su operación.

8. Yo _____ (olvidar) los boletos en casa. No los tengo.

¿Cuáles son tus planes? Indica **sí** o **no**. *Will you have done these things a few years from now?*

_____ 1. Habré viajado a varios países de Hispanoamérica.

_____ 2. Habré llegado a ser un ejecutivo en una empresa (*company*).

_____ 3. Habré cambiado mi estilo de vida.

_____ 4. Habré terminado varios nuevos cursos en línea (*online*).

_____ 5. Habré logrado todas mis metas (*goals*).

_____ 6. Habré terminado los pagos de mi hipoteca (*mortgage*).

_____ 7. Habré subido de peso.

La duda. Escribe la forma apropiada del futuro perfecto. *Some of the participles are irregular or have spelling changes.*

1. ¿Quién _____ (creer) que Susie tiene treinta y nueve años?

2. ¿Por qué ella _____ (cubrirse) la cara con tanto maquillaje?

3. Uds. _____ (oír) que ella es más joven que yo.

4. Todos nosotros _____ (hacer) la misma pregunta.

5. Yo no _____ (resolver) el misterio de la edad de Susie.

6. Pero todos Uds. _____ (ver) que ella no revela su edad.

En español. Estaremos listos para el fin de semana. Usa el futuro perfecto en tus respuestas.

1. *The weather will have improved tomorrow.*

_____

2. *The mechanic will have fixed the car.*

_____

3. *I will have filled the gas tank.*

_____

4. *Will you (tú) have picked up the clothes from the laundry (la lavandería)?*

_____

5. *I will have bought the fruit at the market.*

_____

6. *We will have paid the bills for this month.*

_____

When is the future perfect used in Spanish?

In Spanish, the future perfect is used

- to express an action that will take place in the future before another action or event.

A estas horas mañana ya ellos **habrán salido** del país.	*At this time tomorrow, they **will have left** the country.*

- to express conjecture or probability in the past.

¿Quién **habrá tocado** a la puerta?	*Who **could have knocked** at the door?*
Larry no respondió. **Se habrá ido.**	*Larry did not answer. **He must have left.***

- to express reservations or to question the reality of an action in the past.

Lucy **habrá bajado de peso** pero no se nota.	*Lucy **might have lost weight**, but it is not noticeable.*

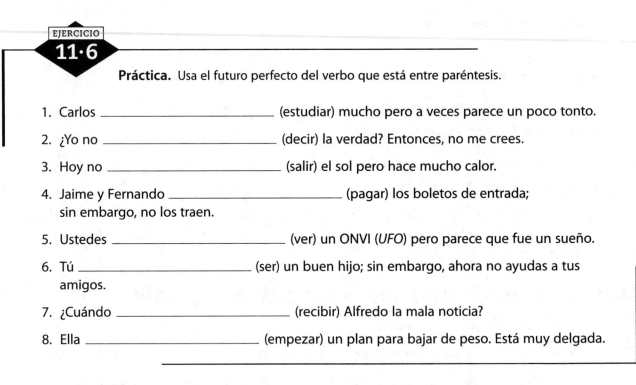

Y en tu opinión... ¿Verdadero o falso? En diez años... ¿qué habrá pasado?

_____ 1. Habremos logrado (*achieved*) la paz en el mundo.

_____ 2. Habremos evitado (*avoided*) la corrupción en la política.

_____ 3. Los científicos habrán descubierto una píldora para curar todas las enfermedades.

_____ 4. Habremos reducido el consumo de gasolina en un cincuenta por ciento.

_____ 5. La violencia en la televisión habrá disminuido considerablemente.

_____ 6. El gobierno habrá reducido muchos de los impuestos (*taxes*).

_____ 7. Los profesores habrán eliminado las tareas en las escuelas.

_____ 8. Los científicos habrán encontrado sustitutos para la gasolina.

Práctica. Usa el futuro perfecto del verbo que está entre paréntesis.

1. Carlos _____ (estudiar) mucho pero a veces parece un poco tonto.

2. ¿Yo no _____ (decir) la verdad? Entonces, no me crees.

3. Hoy no _____ (salir) el sol pero hace mucho calor.

4. Jaime y Fernando _____ (pagar) los boletos de entrada;
   sin embargo, no los traen.

5. Ustedes _____ (ver) un ONVI (*UFO*) pero parece que fue un sueño.

6. Tú _____ (ser) un buen hijo; sin embargo, ahora no ayudas a tus
   amigos.

7. ¿Cuándo _____ (recibir) Alfredo la mala noticia?

8. Ella _____ (empezar) un plan para bajar de peso. Está muy delgada.

Conjeturas. Traduce. Usa el **Vocabulario útil**.

Today, I must have received fifteen messages from strangers: three credit card offers, two advertisements about a miraculous pill that cures all illnesses, six dishonest propositions, two jokes, and two letters I must forward to other users. Who could have sent so many e-mails? How many people could have received this information? Who could have found the addresses of so many people? Cyberspace might have created infinite possibilities of communication at great speed, but it has not foreseen the great number of ridiculous and suspicious messages we receive every day. This message says that if I mail this letter to ten people, in three days I will have received a pleasant surprise. And these people will have returned the same messages ten more times! But if I do not send the message, in one week I will have seen an unfavorable change in my life. What will I find out three days from today? I will drive carefully . . . just in case.

Vocabulario útil

advertisement	**el anuncio**	speed	**la velocidad**
cyberspace	**el espacio cibernético**	stranger	**el/la desconocido(a)**
dishonest	**deshonesto(a)**	suspicious	**sospechoso(a)**
illness	**la enfermedad, el padecimiento**	to foresee	**prever**
joke	**el chiste**	to forward	**reenviar**
just in case	**por si acaso**	unfavorable	**desfavorable**
miraculous	**milagroso(a)**	user	**el/la usuario(a)**
proposition	**la proposición**		

The conditional perfect

Consider an action or event that *would have* happened but did not, because some conditions, specified by the speaker or not, were not met, or other events prevented the action from taking place. In other words, the event or actions expressed with the conditional perfect did not really happen. This is the message in an English utterance such as "They would have come." What prevented the subject *they* from completing the action? When explained, *if* or *but* is usually included in the statement (". . . if they'd been free").

The conditional perfect (**el condicional perfecto**) in Spanish is a compound tense. The forms of the conditional (**el condicional simple**) of **haber** are used as the auxiliary verb for the conditional perfect. The past participle of the verb being conjugated is added to the auxiliary to create the compound tense.

Note: Remember that the verb **haber** is also commonly used in the impersonal forms **hay** (*there is, there are*), **había** (*there was, there were*), etc.

Here are examples of the three conjugations with **pagar**, **vender**, and **salir** in the conditional perfect.

habría pagado, vendido, salido	**habríamos** pagado, vendido, salido
habrías pagado, vendido, salido	**habríais** pagado, vendido, salido
habría pagado, vendido, salido	**habrían** pagado, vendido, salido

Remember that

- ◆ all conditional forms of **haber**, the auxiliary verb, have an accent mark on the **í**.
- ◆ the elements of a compound tense cannot be separated.

Rosa **habría comprado** un diamante.	*Rosa **would have bought** a diamond.*
¡Yo te **habría ayudado**!	*I **would have helped** you!*

En la playa. Práctica. Usa la forma apropiada del condicional perfecto del verbo entre paréntesis.

1. Yo no _____ (tomar) sol.

2. ¿_____ (Llevar) tú tu cuaderno de español?

3. Las chicas nunca _____ (ponerse) esos trajes de baño.

4. Nosotras _____ (sacar) muchas fotos.

5. ¿Quiénes no _____ (caminar) por la playa?

6. ¡Clara y su hermana _____ (comprar) el bronceador (*suntan lotion*)!

En caso de una tormenta. Estudia los participios irregulares si es necesario. Escribe la forma apropiada del condicional perfecto.

1. El viento _____ (romper) los cristales.

2. El Canal 1 de televisión _____ (cubrir) el desastre de la tormenta.

3. Los vecinos _____ (volver) a sus casas después del huracán.

4. Todos nosotros _____ (oír) el viento.

5. Yo _____ (poner) el auto en el garaje.

6. Varios árboles _____ (caerse) en el barrio.

Durante tus vacaciones. ¿Habrías hecho estas cosas? Indica **sí** o **no**.

_____ 1. Habría ido a México.

_____ 2. Me habría despertado tarde todos los días.

_____ 3. Habría ido en un crucero (*cruise*).

_____ 4. Habría visitado lugares remotos.

_____ 5. Habría viajado con unos amigos.

_____ 6. Habría probado platos mexicanos auténticos.

_____ 7. Habría pedido un préstamo (*loan*) para pagar mi viaje.

El periódico del domingo. Traduce al español.

1. *We would have read the whole newspaper.*

_____

2. *I would have looked for the crossword puzzle (**crucigrama** [m.]).*

_____

3. *Lisa would have asked for the sports section.*

_____

4. *The children would have fought for the comics (**comiquitas**).*

_____

5. *Fernando would have examined (**revisar**) the classifieds (**anuncios clasificados**).*

_____

6. *My mother would have cut out the coupons.*

_____

When is the conditional perfect used in Spanish?

Use the conditional perfect in Spanish to indicate

◆ an action or event that *would have* happened if certain conditions, expressed or not, were met in the past.

Habríamos comprado los regalos.	*We would have bought the gifts.*
Habríamos comprado los regalos **pero** no tuvimos tiempo.	*We would have bought the gifts, **but** we had no time.*
Luis **habría terminado** la carrera **pero** estaba agotado.	*Luis **would have finished** the race, **but** he was exhausted.*

Note that the condition expressed in the second example above is introduced with **pero** followed by **no tuvimos tiempo**, in the preterit indicative. In the last example above, the verb following **pero** is in the imperfect, also an indicative tense.

♦ an action or event that *did not* happen, followed by an *if*-clause. The *if*-clause expresses the situation that prevented the action from taking place.

La fiesta habría terminado más tarde **si tú hubieras tocado** la guitarra.

The party would have ended *later **if you had played** the guitar.*

In this contrary-to-fact sentence, a form of the *imperfect subjunctive* follows **si** (*if*). The uncertainty and improbability implied in the message of the *if*-clause requires the use of the subjunctive. Note that the *if*-clause may also begin this type of sentence.

Si tú hubieras tocado la guitarra, **la fiesta habría terminado** más tarde.

For a more detailed explanation of *if*-clauses, turn to the unit on the subjunctive tenses in the past (Unit 15).

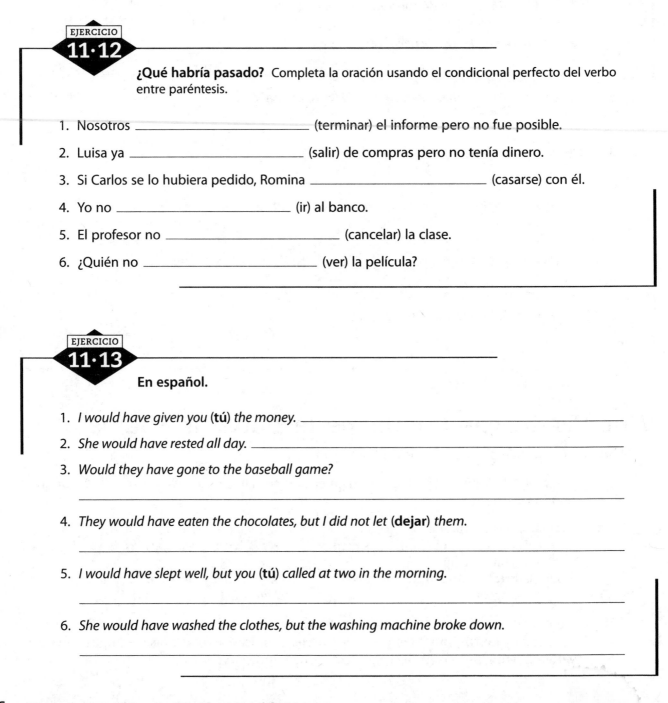

EJERCICIO
11·12

¿Qué habría pasado? Completa la oración usando el condicional perfecto del verbo entre paréntesis.

1. Nosotros _____ (terminar) el informe pero no fue posible.

2. Luisa ya _____ (salir) de compras pero no tenía dinero.

3. Si Carlos se lo hubiera pedido, Romina _____ (casarse) con él.

4. Yo no _____ (ir) al banco.

5. El profesor no _____ (cancelar) la clase.

6. ¿Quién no _____ (ver) la película?

EJERCICIO
11·13

En español.

1. *I would have given you (**tú**) the money.* _____

2. *She would have rested all day.* _____

3. *Would they have gone to the baseball game?*

_____

4. *They would have eaten the chocolates, but I did not let (**dejar**) them.*

_____

5. *I would have slept well, but you (**tú**) called at two in the morning.*

_____

6. *She would have washed the clothes, but the washing machine broke down.*

_____

One more use of the conditional perfect

Probability or conjecture in the past is expressed with the conditional perfect. In this case, the equivalent phrases in English are *I wonder*, *could . . . ?*, or *probably*.

Habríamos caminado unas diez cuadras.

We had probably walked ten blocks.

¿Habrían depositado el dinero?

I wonder if they had deposited the money.

EJERCICIO
11·14

Una pequeña prueba. ¿Qué habrías hecho tú en estas circunstancias?

Vas a leer cinco situaciones que ocurrieron en una tienda. ¿Qué habrías hecho tú en esas situaciones? Escribe la letra de tu respuesta. Después, lee los resultados de esta prueba.

_____ 1. En una tienda, la vendedora (*saleslady*) le entregó diez dólares extra a un cliente.
   a. Habría devuelto el dinero.
   b. No habría dicho nada.

_____ 2. Una niña rompió una lámpara en la sección de muebles (*furniture*).
   a. Habría avisado al gerente.
   b. Habría ido a otro departamento.

_____ 3. Una clienta devolvió los zapatos después de usarlos una semana. Eran incómodos (*uncomfortable*).
   a. Me habría quedado (*to keep*) con los zapatos viejos.
   b. Habría pedido un par de zapatos nuevos.

_____ 4. Un participante ganó un premio de cinco mil dólares para hacer compras en la tienda.
   a. Habría donado una cantidad a la Cruz Roja.
   b. Habría gastado todo el dinero.

_____ 5. Un cliente vio a un ladrón salir de una joyería.
   a. Habría cooperado con la policía.
   b. No habría dicho nada a nadie.

Resultados

De 3 a 5 respuestas **a**: eres un(-a) ciudadano(a) responsable, generoso(a) y honesto(a).
De 1 a 2 respuestas **a**: tienes dudas en cuanto a tus responsabilidades como ciudadano(a).
0 respuestas **a**: sin comentarios.

¿Qué habría pasado? Traduce. Usa el **Vocabulario útil**.

Last Wednesday, I was waiting for Rafael at the entrance of an amusement park. Rafael is always very punctual. It was five thirty, and he had not arrived. I wondered if Rafa had forgotten our date. Impossible! He probably had an accident. I would have called him, but I did not have my cell phone. I wondered if Rafa had gone to the movies instead of the park. No way! He would have called me. Finally, I saw Rafael. He said he would have arrived on time, but it was impossible. He did not know that he needed to fill up the tank with gas. Rafael got stuck in the middle of the turnpike. That is silly!

Vocabulario útil

amusement park	**el parque de atracciones/ diversiones**	tank	**el tanque**
		That is silly!	**¡Qué tontería!**
		to fill up	**llenar**
instead	**en vez de**	to get stuck	**quedar(se) varado**
No way!	**¡Qué va!**	turnpike	**la autopista de peaje**

The passive voice and passive constructions

In English and Spanish, we use both the active and the passive voices. In the active voice, the subject of the sentence performs the action. In the passive voice, the subject of the sentence receives the action. An agent accomplishes the action in the passive voice. If the agent is expressed, it is introduced with the preposition *by* in English and with the preposition **por** in Spanish.

Los mecánicos repararon el auto. (active voice, subject: **los mecánicos**)	*The mechanics repaired the car.*
El auto fue reparado por dos mecánicos. (passive voice, subject: **el auto**; agent: **dos mecánicos**)	*The car was fixed by two mechanics.*

Think of the passive verb form **fue reparado** as an action performed *upon* the subject. The car *was fixed* by the agent, in this case *two mechanics*. Remember that in the passive voice, the agent does not need to be named.

Los votos **fueron contados**.	*The votes were counted.*

In English, grammar texts and computerized grammar checkers advise against the overuse of the passive voice. Its use is recommended in two types of situations: to express an action whose subject is unknown or when it is tactful or advantageous not to make the subject known. Note that the agent is omitted in the following two examples.

*The books **were delivered** yesterday.*
*Bad taste **was shown** in this decision.*

In the first sentence, who delivered the books is probably not known or is irrelevant. In the second, the speaker has chosen not to disclose who had bad taste.

The passive voice in Spanish

The use of the passive voice (**la voz pasiva**) in Spanish is similar to its use in English. Consider the following statement in the active voice: **Diego Velázquez pintó el cuadro *Las Meninas*.**

Now, note the passive version of this sentence: **El cuadro *Las Meninas* fue pintado por Diego Velázquez.** In the passive voice, **el cuadro *Las Meninas*** becomes the subject receiving the action from the agent **Diego Velázquez**.

In forming sentences in the passive voice in Spanish,

- always use a form of **ser** + a past participle.

El elefante **fue atacado** por un león.　　The elephant **was attacked** by a lion.
Las mariposas **serán dibujadas**.　　The butterflies **will be sketched**.

- the agent may be expressed as follows.

subject + a form of **ser** + a past participle + **por** + the agent

La película fue filmada **por un director**　　The movie was filmed **by a British director**.
británico.

- or the agent may be omitted.

subject + a form of **ser** + a past participle

Después, el director **fue aclamado** en　　Later, the director **was acclaimed** at the film
el festival de cine.　　festival.

In Spanish, the past participle in the passive voice functions as an adjective and must agree in gender and number with the subject of the sentence. In the examples above, the participles **dibujadas** and **filmada** agree with **las mariposas** and **la película**, the subjects of the sentences. In the last example, **aclamado** agrees with **el director**. Note that in the last example, the agent is not named.

In the above examples, the speaker uses the preterit tense (**fue**, a form of **ser**). The passive voice with **ser** may be used in any tense, but it appears most frequently in the past. You may wish to review the other tenses of the irregular verb **ser** and the irregular past participles in Units 3, 4, 5, 7, 10, and 13, and the Verb tables.

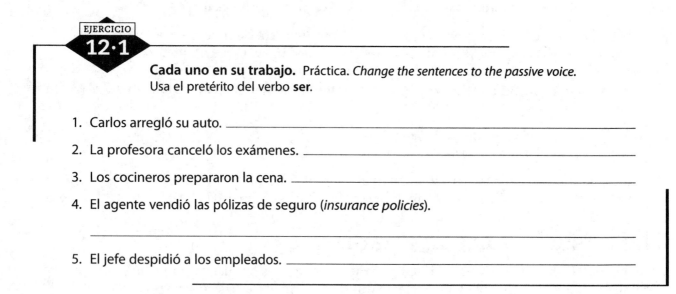

EJERCICIO
12·1

Cada uno en su trabajo. Práctica. *Change the sentences to the passive voice.*
Usa el pretérito del verbo **ser**.

1. Carlos arregló su auto. _____

2. La profesora canceló los exámenes. _____

3. Los cocineros prepararon la cena. _____

4. El agente vendió las pólizas de seguro (*insurance policies*).

_____

5. El jefe despidió a los empleados. _____

Un proyecto para celebrar una feria. En español. Usa la forma pasiva del futuro del verbo **ser**.

1. *The project will be approved by a commission.*

   _____

2. *The equipment will be installed by a local company.*

   _____

3. *All volunteers will be trained by our manager.*

   _____

4. *Many raffle prizes (**el premio de [la] rifa**) will be donated by several families.*

   _____

5. *The inauguration ribbon (**el lazo**) will be cut by the fair queen.*

   _____

6. *The tickets will be sold at the gate.* _____

7. *All children will be greeted by a clown.* _____

8. *The last day will be celebrated with fireworks (**fuegos artificiales**).*

   _____

When is the passive voice used in Spanish?

Spanish, in general, prefers the use of the active voice, especially in everyday communication. However, newscasters use the passive voice, and it appears frequently in written communication, especially in newspaper and magazine articles. The passive voice construction with **ser**

 ◆ is used to underscore the agent who performs the action.

   Los ciudadanos **fueron recibidos por el presidente** de la República de Chile.   *The citizens **were welcomed by the president** of the Republic of Chile.*

 ◆ is used in written language, especially journalistic style. The agent is usually expressed.

   Los manifestantes **fueron detenidos por la policía**.   *The protesters **were detained by the police**.*

 ◆ appears most frequently in the past and future tenses.

   El poema **fue escrito** por Pablo Neruda.   *The poem **was written** by Pablo Neruda.*
   La boda **será celebrada** en el salón Primavera.   *The wedding **will be celebrated** at the Primavera Ballroom.*

EJERCICIO
12·3

Un poco de historia. ¿Verdadero o falso?

_____ 1. La radio fue inventada por Marconi.

_____ 2. El básquetbol fue popularizado en los Estados Unidos.

_____ 3. *La Mona Lisa* fue pintada por Picasso.

_____ 4. El programa de televisión *¿Quién quiere ser millonario?* fue creado en Inglaterra.

_____ 5. La frase famosa "Ser o no ser" fue pronunciada por Don Quijote.

_____ 6. El primer semáforo (*traffic light*) fue instalado en el siglo XIX.

_____ 7. El telescopio Hubble fue lanzado al espacio a principios del siglo XXI.

_____ 8. La ciudad de San Agustín fue fundada por los españoles.

_____ 9. El teléfono fue inventado por A. Graham Bell.

EJERCICIO
12·4

Una noticia curiosa. Traduce. Usa el **Vocabulario útil**.

Last-minute news. A car with a peculiar passenger was discovered on the Avenida Simón Bolívar. A lion was seen in the backseat. The authorities were called immediately. The driver was detained by the police. The car was driven by a mysterious woman whose identity still is not known. The woman and the lion were finally identified as members of the Circo Moderno. When she was interviewed, the extravagant woman introduced her lion, Bebé. The mystery woman offered a lot of information to the press. It was revealed that Bebé wears a leash with diamonds. The incident has been considered a publicity stunt.

Vocabulario útil

authorities	**las autoridades**	press	**la prensa**
backseat	**el asiento trasero**	stunt	**el truco**
extravagant	**extravagante**	to call	**avisar**
identity	**la identidad**	to detain	**detener**
last-minute	**de última hora**	to interview	**entrevistar**
leash	**la correa**	to reveal	**revelar**
passenger	**el/la pasajero(a)**	whose	**cuyo/cuya**

The passive construction with the pronoun se

Spanish has another passive construction that is actually used more frequently than **ser** + past participle. It is called the **pasiva pronominal** or **pasiva refleja**, because one of its components is the reflexive pronoun **se**. This construction consists of the pronoun **se** + the third person of the verb, singular or plural. The verb agrees with the subject receiving the action.

Se habla inglés.	*English **is spoken** (here).*
Se cierran las puertas a las ocho.	*The doors **are closed** at eight.*

The passive construction with **se** is also an impersonal construction, because the agent is never named.

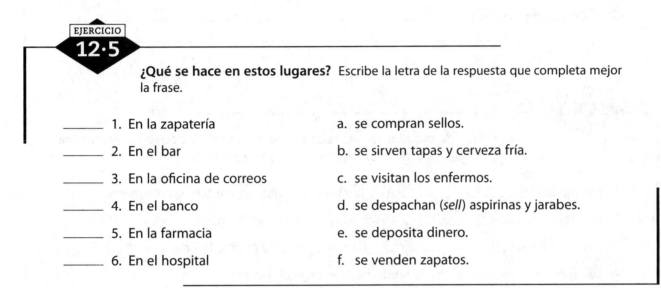

EJERCICIO

12·5

¿Qué se hace en estos lugares? Escribe la letra de la respuesta que completa mejor la frase.

_____ 1. En la zapatería   a. se compran sellos.

_____ 2. En el bar   b. se sirven tapas y cerveza fría.

_____ 3. En la oficina de correos   c. se visitan los enfermos.

_____ 4. En el banco   d. se despachan (*sell*) aspirinas y jarabes.

_____ 5. En la farmacia   e. se deposita dinero.

_____ 6. En el hospital   f. se venden zapatos.

When is the passive construction with se used in Spanish?

Use this passive construction

- in everyday communication.

Se dice que la gasolina va a subir de precio.	*It **is said** that the price of gas is going up.*

- if the subject is not a person.

Se alquila casa amueblada.	*Furnished house **(is) for rent**.*

- when the agent or "doer" is deliberately omitted.

Se cometieron muchos errores.	*Many mistakes **were made**.*

- to underscore an impersonal construction.

Se pueden visitar los lugares históricos.	*Historical places **can be visited**.*

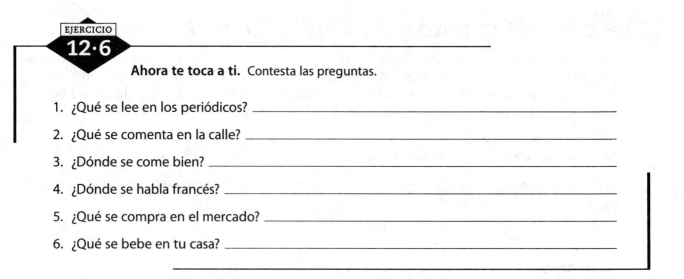

Ahora te toca a ti. Contesta las preguntas.

1. ¿Qué se lee en los periódicos? _____

2. ¿Qué se comenta en la calle? _____

3. ¿Dónde se come bien? _____

4. ¿Dónde se habla francés? _____

5. ¿Qué se compra en el mercado? _____

6. ¿Qué se bebe en tu casa? _____

En una tienda de caballeros. Usa la pasiva refleja, la construcción con el pronombre
se y la forma apropiada del presente del verbo entre paréntesis.

1. Los maniquíes _____ (vestir) con camisas y pantalones elegantes.

2. Los trajes _____ (colocar) en las perchas (*hangers*).

3. Los vestidores _____ (limpiar) antes de abrir la tienda.

4. La caja _____ (abrir) cuando llega el gerente.

5. Los regalos _____ (envolver) en el segundo piso.

6. Las puertas _____ (cerrar) a las siete de la tarde.

¿Verdadero o falso?

_____ 1. Se habla español en Guinea Ecuatorial.

_____ 2. El euro se ha convertido en la moneda oficial de Argentina.

_____ 3. Recientemente se han descubierto nuevas galaxias en el universo.

_____ 4. Se han publicado muchos libros digitales en los últimos años.

_____ 5. Ya no se usan los escáners en los aeropuertos para la seguridad de los viajeros.

_____ 6. Durante las tormentas tropicales se evitan problemas con las evacuaciones
de la población.

En español. Usa la pasiva refleja (con **se**). Observa si el verbo está en el presente, pasado o futuro.

1. *Used cars are sold here.* _____

2. *It is said that crime does not pay.* _____

3. *Credit cards will not be accepted.* _____

4. *English and Spanish are spoken here.* _____

5. *The museum will be inaugurated (inaugurar) tomorrow.*

_____

Impersonal constructions used to substitute for passive constructions

There are other Spanish constructions in which the agent or "doer" is omitted. These include a variety of impersonal constructions. The translations below will remind you that the equivalent constructions are also very common in English. Other constructions include

- **se** + intransitive Spanish verbs. (Intransitive verbs have no direct object.)

  ¿Cómo **se sale** de este laberinto? *How does **one leave** (**get out of**) this labyrinth?*
  Se está muy mal en la cárcel. ***One feels** bad in jail.*

- the **tú** form with the pronoun **te**.

  Te matas a trabajar y nadie te ayuda. ***You kill yourself working**, and no one helps you.*

- **uno** as the subject of the sentence.

  ¡**Uno no sabe** qué hacer! ***One does not know** what to do!*

- the third-person plural form of the verb.

  Cuentan que ella no tiene dinero. ***They say** she has no money.*

En busca de un tesoro. Traduce. Usa el **Vocabulario útil** y la pasiva refleja.

"One gets information, prepares oneself, and looks for lost treasures at the bottom of the sea. It is known that in the waters of the Caribbean Sea many sunken treasures are found. The Spanish ship Santa Margarita *was discovered by divers looking for treasure. More than two million dollars in gold and jewels were recovered from that ship! And from the ship* Atocha *almost fifty tons of silver and thousands of emeralds the size of a walnut! But you have to prepare yourself. You buy yourself the best diving equipment, you find an ideal spot for your adventure, and you go find your treasure."* *These words were said by an expert treasure hunter. You believe these words, you buy your equipment with your credit card, you go looking for treasure, you forget about reality, you spend your life under the ocean, and you go bankrupt before you find your sunken treasure at the bottom of the sea.*

Vocabulario útil

bottom	**el fondo**	silver	**la plata**
Caribbean Sea	**el Mar Caribe**	size	**el tamaño**
diver	**el buzo**	sunken	**hundido(a), enterrado(a)**
diving	**el buceo**	to go bankrupt	**arruinar(se)**
emerald	**la esmeralda**	to recover	**recuperar**
hunter	**el cazador / la cazadora**	ton	**la tonelada**
jewel	**la joya**	treasure	**el tesoro**
lost	**perdido(a)**	walnut	**la nuez**
ship	**el barco, el buque**		

The subjunctive mood: the present and the present perfect subjunctive tenses in noun clauses

The subjunctive mood: the present subjunctive

When you study the indicative mood tenses (**el indicativo**) in Spanish, you learn that the speaker is talking about actions, events, or states that he or she perceives as facts or truths. When studying the subjunctive mood (**el subjuntivo**), you will see that the attitude of the speaker determines the mood that will convey the message. Note the attitude or point of view of the subject in the following examples.

> Mario **confirmó** su reservación.   *Mario **confirmed** his reservation.*
> Mario **recibirá** su billete por correo   *Mario **will receive** his ticket by*
> electrónico.   *e-mail.*

Both **confirmó** in the preterit and **recibirá** in the future are actions expressed in the indicative mood. The speaker perceives these actions as real—facts or actual events that happened in the past or will happen in the future. The description of Mario's activities directly expresses that reality. On the other hand, if the perspective of the subject conveys doubt or uncertainty, the *subjunctive mood* is necessary. Study the following example.

> **Mario duda que** el agente de viajes   *Mario **doubts** (**that**) the travel agent*
> **confirme** su reservación.   *will **confirm** his reservation.*

Note that there are two parts or clauses (**cláusulas**) in the preceding example. The first clause (**Mario duda**) is in the indicative mood, and it reflects Mario's own feelings (doubt) about the action or future action of a different subject, *the travel agent*. In the second clause, **confirme** is in the subjunctive mood, because this action is not likely to be true or may not be completed at the time the action in the first clause takes place. Mario is uncertain about the outcome of the action performed by the agent; it may not even take place! The two clauses in this sentence are linked by the conjunction **que**. Note that the subject of the second or dependent clause (**el agente de viajes**) is different from the subject expressing doubt (**Mario**).

    The clause in the indicative mood is called the main or independent clause. The clause containing the verb in the subjunctive mood is the dependent clause. In grammatical terms, these dependent clauses are known as noun clauses, because they have a function similar to that of a noun in a simple sentence.

The subjunctive mood communicates the personal feelings or emotions of the subject in the main clause; these include wishes, hopes, and preferences. Verbs such as **esperar** (*to hope*), **querer** (*to wish*), **desear** (*to desire*), **preferir** (*to prefer*), **permitir** (*to allow*), and others are used in the main clause, followed by **que** introducing a different subject. Later, we will study in more detail the uses of the subjunctive in Spanish. For now, note its use in the following examples.

Marta **quiere que** Ana **mande** la carta.	*Marta **wants** Ana **to send** the letter.*
Espero que tu hermana **acepte** mi oferta.	*I **hope** your sister **accepts** my offer.*
Preferimos que los miembros del equipo **viajen** en tren.	*We **prefer** (**that**) the members of the team **travel** by train.*

The English clauses do not necessarily include a literal translation of **que**, as you can see in the above English equivalents. Both the English infinitive form and the English future tense are often used to translate the Spanish subjunctive. **Que** *always* links the two clauses in Spanish. The dependent clause may also contain indicative forms. The perspective of the verb in the main clause determines which mood is used in the dependent clause.

El aviso **dice que** la sesión **termina** por la tarde. (**termina**, indicative)	*The notice **says** (**that**) the session **ends** in the afternoon.*
El investigador **duda que** el interrogatorio **termine** antes de la seis. (**termine**, subjunctive)	*The investigator **doubts** the interrogation **will end** before six.*

In the first example, the verb **decir** (**dice**) does not convey an attitude of doubt (uncertainty, hope, desire, need, etc.) in the main clause and therefore does not require the use of the subjunctive in the dependent clause. In that sentence, **termina** is in the present indicative. In the second example, the verb **dudar** (**duda**) communicates doubt and therefore requires the subjunctive (**termine**) in the dependent clause. Later, you will see that the dependent clauses in the subjunctive can be present or past forms. The subjunctive is used more frequently in Spanish than in English. Determining when to use it will require some skill and experience.

There are six subjunctive tenses in Spanish; four are frequently used: the present, the present perfect, the imperfect, and the pluperfect subjunctive. Two are presented in this unit: the present and the present perfect subjunctive.

The present subjunctive

To conjugate the present subjunctive of most verbs, refer to the present indicative forms, and follow these steps.

♦ Drop the **-o** of the **yo** form as shown in the models **cant-o**, **com-o**, and **recib-o**.

♦ Add the corresponding endings for each person in the three conjugations, as follows.

cantar (*to sing*)		**comer** (*to eat*)		**recibir** (*to receive*)	
cante	cantemos	coma	comamos	reciba	recibamos
cantes	cantéis	comas	comáis	recibas	recibáis
cante	canten	coma	coman	reciba	reciban

Observe that

- the first- and third-person singular present subjunctive forms have the same endings.

- -er and -ir regular verbs have the same endings.

    Note that this rule applies to most verbs. Verbs with spelling changes in the present indicative preserve the spelling change in the present subjunctive. (Review the lists in Unit 1.)

- verbs ending in -ger and -gir change the g of the stem to j, keeping the j in the stem of the present subjunctive.

escoger (to choose)		exigir (to demand)	
escoja	escojamos	exija	exijamos
escojas	escojáis	exijas	exijáis
escoja	escojan	exija	exijan

Escojo mi vestido en este catálogo. Quiero que tú **escojas** tus zapatos también.	*I choose* my dress from this catalog. I want you *to choose* your shoes, too.
Exijo mis derechos. Quiero que todos **exijan** sus derechos también.	*I demand* my rights. I want everyone *to demand* their rights, too.

- verbs that end in -guir change gu to g in the present subjunctive.

extinguir (to extinguish)	
extinga	extingamos
extingas	extingáis
extinga	extingan

- verbs that end in -cer change the c to z in the yo form: convencer, convenzo.

El candidato **no convence** a los trabajadores. La oposición duda que **convenza** a los maestros.	*The candidate **does not convince** the workers. The opposition doubts that **he convinces** the teachers.*

EJERCICIO
13·1

Decide. Observa los verbos entre paréntesis. Después, subraya la respuesta apropiada: el presente de indicativo o el presente de subjuntivo.

1. Yo sé que tú (lees | leas) el periódico todos los días en tu oficina.

2. Arturo quiere que su esposa (compra | compre) más vegetales.

3. Rodrigo prefiere que nosotros no (cantamos | cantemos) en su fiesta.

4. Tu hermano asegura (*assures*) que ahora (comes | comas) platos saludables.

5. Miguel sabe que su novia (escribe | escriba) poemas a sus amigos.

6. Mis padres anuncian que Lucía y Marcos (se casan | se casen) en mayo.

Práctica. Usa la forma apropiada del presente de subjuntivo del verbo entre paréntesis.

1. Maira duda que la paella _____ (estar) cocinada antes de las siete de la noche.

2. Marcos prefiere que Maira _____ (ayudar) a los niños a terminar la tarea.

3. Carla y Martina quieren que los niños _____ (preparar) la merienda.

4. La nutricionista prefiere que tú _____ (beber) agua y no un refresco.

5. Mis padres desean que nosotros _____ (recibir) una invitación para el almuerzo.

6. Nosotros dudamos que la sirvienta _____ (comprender) tu letra (*handwriting*).

Verbs with spelling changes in the present subjunctive

In Unit 4, review the preterit indicative verbs with spelling changes (that is, verbs that end in **-car**, **-gar**, and **-zar**) to learn spelling changes in the present subjunctive forms. For the present subjunctive, use the spelling changes that occur in the **yo** form of the preterit indicative. Note the change applies to all the forms of the present subjunctive.

- **-Car** changes to **qu**.

    Ayer **expliqué** mis propuestas. Hoy, quiero que tú **expliques** el problema.

    Yesterday, I explained my proposal. Now, I want you to explain the problem.

- **-Gar** changes to **gu**.

    Llegué a tiempo. Espero que **llegues** a tiempo también.

    I arrived on time. I hope that you arrive on time also.

- **-Zar** changes to **c**.

    Ya **empecé** a investigar el caso Smith. Quiero que **empecemos** a revisar los resultados.

    I began to research the Smith case. I want us to start (that we start) to review the results.

Refer to the lists of frequently used verbs with spelling changes in Unit 4.

En español. Usa el presente de subjuntivo para traducir las palabras subrayadas en cada oración.

1. *I want you (**tú**) to practice the tango and salsa.*

_____

2. *Marcos wants us to have lunch (**almorzar**) at this restaurant.*

_____

3. *They prefer that we explain our plan.*

_____

4. *We want you (**Ud.**) to look for the answer.*

_____

5. *The cashier [f.] doubts that you'll (**Uds.**) pay cash (**en efectivo**).*

_____

6. *The public prefers that Lamas play the guitar.*

_____

7. *Marta and I doubt that he'll take out the money.*

_____

Verbs with stem changes in the present subjunctive

To conjugate the present subjunctive of stem-changing verbs, refer to the stem changes that occur in the present indicative. You may want to review Unit 2.

Stem-changing verbs ending in -ar and -er

-Ar and **-er** verbs that change the stem vowel **e** to **ie** in the present indicative show the same changes in the present subjunctive. As in the present indicative, this change affects all forms except the plurals **nosotros** and **vosotros**.

pensar (*to think*)		**entender** (*to understand*)	
piense	pensemos	entienda	entendamos
pienses	penséis	entiendas	entendáis
piense	piensen	entienda	entiendan

Quiero que **pienses** en tu problema.	*I want **you to think** about your problem.*
Dudo que **entiendan** mis explicaciones.	*I doubt **they understand** my explanations.*

Refer to the lists of frequently used verbs with changes in the preterit (indicative) in Unit 4.

En español. En el partido de tenis. Usa el presente de subjuntivo del verbo subrayado.

1. *The coach wants the match to <u>start</u> on time tomorrow.*

_____

2. *She prefers that all the players <u>wake up</u> earlier.*

_____

3. *I doubt that all of you (**Uds.**) <u>understand</u> the rules to play tennis.*

_____

4. *Our rivals want us to <u>lose</u> the match tomorrow.*

_____

5. *I prefer that you (**Ud.**) <u>sit</u> in the second row, close to the turf (**el césped**).*

_____

6. *The assistant to the coach doubts that Bernardo <u>defends</u> his title with dignity.*

_____

-**Ar** and -**er** verbs that change the stem vowel **o** to **ue** in the present indicative show the same changes in the present subjunctive. As in the present indicative, this change affects all forms except the plurals **nosotros** and **vosotros**.

volar (*to fly*)		**devolver** (*to return [something]*)	
vuele	volemos	devuelva	devolvamos
vueles	voléis	devuelvas	devolváis
vuele	vuelen	devuelva	devuelvan

Y en tu opinión... ¿Verdadero o falso?

_____ 1. Muchos jóvenes desean que sus padres resuelvan sus problemas.

_____ 2. Los jugadores de tenis prefieren que llueva durante el partido.

_____ 3. Algunos empleados prefieren que su jefe encuentre una excusa para ir de vacaciones.

_____ 4. Muchos padres permiten que sus hijos se acuesten muy tarde.

_____ 5. Los espectadores desean que los actores demuestren sinceridad.

Stem-changing verbs ending in -ir

-Ir stem-changing verbs show the following changes in the stem vowel in the present subjunctive: **e** to **ie**, **o** to **ue**, and **e** to **i**.

e > ie		o > ue		e > i	
sentir (to feel)		*dormir (to sleep)*		*pedir (to ask for, request)*	
sienta	sintamos	duerma	durmamos	pida	pidamos
sientas	sintáis	duermas	durmáis	pidas	pidáis
sienta	sientan	duerma	duerman	pida	pidan

Note that changes occur in all forms of these verbs and that a different change affects the **nosotros** and **vosotros** forms: **e** changes to **i**, and **o** changes to **u**.

Los meteorólogos dudan que **sintamos** los efectos de la tormenta aquí.	*The meteorologists doubt that **we'll feel** the effects of the storm here.*
El gerente del hotel prefiere que **los perros no duerman** en el lobby.	*The hotel manager prefers that **dogs (do) not sleep** in the lobby.*
Dudo que **él pida** un descuento.	*I doubt that **he asks for** a discount.*

EJERCICIO
13·6

La alerta de un ciclón. Usa el presente de subjuntivo de los verbos entre paréntesis.

La comunidad espera que el centro de huracanes...

1. _____ (seguir) la ruta de la tormenta.

2. _____ (advertir) los peligros.

3. _____ (pedir) ayuda a otras comunidades.

4. _____ (sugerir) soluciones.

5. no _____ (consentir) (*to allow*) rumores alarmantes.

Verbs ending in **-uir** add a **y** following the **u** in all forms of the present subjunctive.

incluir *(to include)*	
incluya	incluyamos
incluyas	incluyáis
incluya	incluyan

-Iar and **-uar** verbs in the present subjunctive have an accent mark on the **í** or **ú**, except in the **nosotros** and **vosotros** forms. (Note the usual accent mark on the **é** of the second-person plural.)

enviar *(to send)*		situar *(to place)*	
envíe	enviemos	sitúe	situemos
envíes	enviéis	sitúes	situéis
envíe	envíen	sitúe	sitúen

Una nueva serie de televisión: Los malos nunca ganan. Usa el presente de subjuntivo del verbo que aparece entre paréntesis.

1. El público quiere que la serie _____ (continuar) todo el año.

2. Todos prefieren que los personajes malos _____ (influir) mucho en la novela.

3. Yo no quiero que el productor _____ (sustituir) a mi personaje favorito.

4. Los televidentes sugieren que cada capítulo _____ (concluir) con una sorpresa.

5. ¿Quién prefiere que los personajes malos _____ (destruir) a los buenos?

6. Mi abuelo quiere que tú _____ (enviar) flores a la protagonista.

Irregular verbs in the present indicative and in the present subjunctive

Refer to the forms of irregular verbs in the indicative (Unit 1 and Verb tables) to conjugate the corresponding forms of the present subjunctive. The following list includes -**er** and -**ir** verbs that have an irregular **yo** form only in the present indicative. To conjugate the present subjunctive of these verbs, follow the general rule: drop the -**o** and add -**a** to the first person. For the rest of the forms, use this "subjunctive" stem, and add the set of endings you have already learned for -**er** and -**ir** regular present subjunctive conjugations.

INFINITIVE		INDICATIVE	SUBJUNCTIVE
caber	to fit	quep-**o**	quep**a**
caer	to fall	caig-**o**	caig**a**
hacer	to do	hag-**o**	hag**a**
parecer	to look like	parezc-**o**	parezc**a**
poner	to put	pong-**o**	pong**a**
salir	to go out	salg-**o**	salg**a**
traer	to bring	traig-**o**	traig**a**
valer	to be worth	valg-**o**	valg**a**
ver	to see	ve-**o**	ve**a**

En español.

1. *Pedro wants them to bring the new CDs.*

_____

2. *My mother prefers that you (**tú**) do the list.*

_____

3. *They want you (**Ud.**) to see the results.*

_____

4. *She prefers that you (**Uds.**) leave at once.*

_____

5. *I doubt the movie is worth it (**valer la pena**).*

_____

6. *Sheila hopes her suitcase fits in the car.*

_____

Irregular verbs in the present subjunctive

Six verbs do not follow the regular rule for the formation of the present subjunctive. The irregular present subjunctives follow.

dar	to give	dé, des, dé, demos, deis, den
estar	to be	esté, estés, esté, estemos, estéis, estén
haber	to have (*auxiliary*)	haya, hayas, haya, hayamos, hayáis, hayan
ir	to go	vaya, vayas, vayas, vayamos, vayáis, vayan
saber	to know	sepa, sepas, sepa, sepamos, sepáis, sepan
ser	to be	sea, seas, sea, seamos, seáis, sean

EJERCICIO

13·9

En español. Usa el subjuntivo.

El gerente quiere que...

1. *the secretary to bring the papers.* _____

2. *the assistant to go out.* _____

3. *the accountant to see the documents.* _____

4. *the president to know his wishes to earn more money.*

_____

5. *his employees to be courteous.* _____

Pareados. Escribe la letra de la respuesta apropiada para completar cada oración.

_____ 1. Margarita prefiere que tú   a. es más saludable que la carne.

_____ 2. Juan quiere que Uds.   b. sea peligrosa para esta área.

_____ 3. El juez prohíbe que el ladrón   c. salga de la cárcel.

_____ 4. Aseguran que el pescado   d. salgas a las cuatro con ella.

_____ 5. Nosotros no queremos que Luisa   e. den más dinero a su iglesia.

_____ 6. Pablo no cree que la tormenta   f. vaya a la reunión sola.

When is the present subjunctive used in Spanish?
The present subjunctive in noun clauses

You have learned how to conjugate the present subjunctive and have seen examples of its uses. They include complex (two-clause) sentences in which the subject expresses doubt, a wish, or a preference in the main clause about the outcome of a course of action by a different subject in the dependent clause. In the dependent clause, the conjunction **que** introduces the second subject + a verb in the present subjunctive. Here is a more detailed look at the uses of the subjunctive.

It is used

◆ in the dependent clause to reflect denial, doubt, disbelief, or uncertainty about the reality or the outcome of actions or events of a different subject. The verbal expression of "uncertainty" occurs in the main clause.

No creo que llueva.   *I do not believe that it will rain.*
Samuel duda que tú lo ayudes.   *Samuel doubts that you (will) help him.*

dudar (que)	to doubt (that)
negar (que)	to deny (that)
no creer (que)	not to believe (that)
no estar seguro(a) de (que)	not to be sure (that)
no pensar (que)	not to think (that)

◆ in the dependent clause following verbs that express advice, command, or suggestion.

Te **aconsejo que** salgas.   *I advise you to leave.*
Mi padre **no deja que** Bertha vaya   *My father does not let Bertha go to the party.*
    a la fiesta.

aconsejar (que)	to advise (that)	**hacer** (que)	to make (that)
decir (que)	to tell (*with the intention of giving a command*) (that)	**ordenar** (que)	to order (that)
		recomendar (que)	to recommend (that)
dejar (que)	to allow (that)	**sugerir** (que)	to suggest (that)
exigir (que)	to demand (that)		

Práctica. Todos están muy ocupados hablando de otras personas. Escribe la forma apropiada del subjuntivo en las siguientes oraciones para comprender el mensaje.

1. La madre no está segura de que su hija _____ (buscar) un libro interesante para leer.

2. Yo no creo que los científicos _____ (llegar) a otras galaxias muy pronto.

3. Le exigimos a Lola que _____ (medir) sus palabras.

4. Mi jefe sugiere que nosotros _____ (acabar) este informe.

5. El agente le aconseja a Julia que no _____ (firmar) este contrato.

Use the subjunctive

◆ to communicate attitudes, feelings, or emotions in dependent clauses about a subject different from the one in the main clause.

Sentimos que ustedes no puedan venir a cenar.	*We regret that you cannot come to dinner.*
Teme que yo gane.	*He fears that I'll win.*

The following verbs express feelings and emotions.

alegrar(se) de (que)	to be glad (that)
enojarse de (que)	to be angry (that)
estar contento(a) de (que)	to be glad (that)
molestar(se) (que)	to get annoyed (that)
sentir (que)	to regret (that)
temer (que)	to fear (that)

◆ to express hope, wish, or preference about the actions of subjects in the dependent clause.

Los empleados **esperan que** el jefe apruebe el aumento de sueldo.	*The employees **hope that** their boss will approve a raise.*
Preferimos que tú trabajes.	*We **prefer that** you work.*

Here are some verbs of hope, wish, or preference.

desear (que)	to wish (that)
esperar (que)	to hope (that)
insistir en (que)	to insist (that)
preferir (que)	to prefer (that)
querer (que)	to want (that)

◆ to ask permission or to make a request.

Pide que devuelvas el libro a tiempo.	*She **asks that** you return the book on time.*

Here are some verbs of permission or requesting.

pedir (que)	to ask (that)
rogar (que)	to beg (that)
suplicar (que)	to plead (that)

The subjunctive mood: the present and the present perfect subjunctive tenses in noun clauses   **147**

◆ to communicate surprise and disbelief.

Nos sorprende que el presidente no reciba la aprobación del Senado.

We are surprised (It is surprising to us) that the president does not have the approval of the Senate.

Here are some verbs of surprise.

maravillar(se) de (que)   to marvel (that)
sorprender(se) de (que)   to be surprised (that)

Note: **Sorprender** can be used in an impersonal construction (**nos sorprende de que**, *it surprises us that*) or a reflexive one (**nos sorprendemos de que**, *we are surprised that*).

In the above examples, the subject expressing emotions, feelings, suggestions, wishes, etc., tries to influence or sway someone else's actions.

Important: In all the example sentences above, the verb in the main clause is in the indicative and the verb following **que** in the dependent clause is in the subjunctive. If the subjects of the main clause and the dependent clause are the *same*, the *infinitive* is used, not the subjunctive, and **que** is omitted.

Me sorprende recibir su regalo.   *I am surprised to receive his gift.*
Quieren ir al cine.   *They want to go to the movies.*

EJERCICIO
13·12

Y en tu opinión... ¿Verdadero o falso?

_____ 1. La gente se alegra de que baje la bolsa de valores de Nueva York.

_____ 2. Los norteamericanos prefieren que el café sea de Colombia.

_____ 3. Deseamos que nuestros vecinos sean amables.

_____ 4. Preferimos que las fiestas sean aburridas.

_____ 5. Insistimos en que nuestros colegas no abusen de nuestra generosidad.

EJERCICIO
13·13

En español. *Use the present subjunctive where you see an underlined verb. Note that if the verb is not underlined, you may choose the present indicative or the infinitive form.*

1. *We doubt that the boys will arrive before eight.*

_____

2. *He tells me to open the window now.* _____

3. *Who wishes to tell a story?* _____

4. *I want you (**Uds.**) to understand my point of view.*

_____

5. *The inspector sees that the road needs work.*

_____

6. *She suggests that we work on her project.*

_____

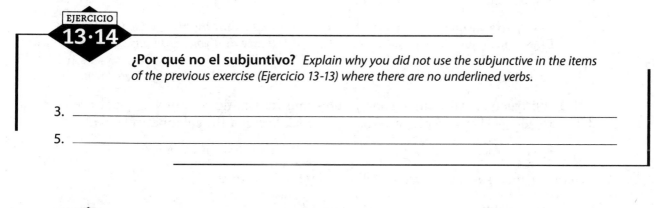

EJERCICIO

13·14

¿Por qué no el subjuntivo? *Explain why you did not use the subjunctive in the items of the previous exercise (Ejercicio 13-13) where there are no underlined verbs.*

3. _____

5. _____

EJERCICIO

13·15

Mi nueva compañera de cuarto. Traduce. Usa el **Vocabulario útil**.

I think my new roommate is not very nice. I want her to know that I am upset. I prefer that we discuss the matter soon. She does not want me to feel comfortable in our apartment. Our lease forbids us to have (that we have) pets in the apartment, but she wants to keep her parrot, Tonto. Well, the truth is, Tonto wakes up at 5:30 every morning and I prefer to sleep late on weekends. I am going to ask her to find a new apartment.

Vocabulario útil

comfortable	**cómodo(a)**	pet	**la mascota**
lease	**el contrato**	roommate	**el/la compañero(a) de cuarto**
matter	**el asunto**	to keep	**quedarse con**
parrot	**el loro**	upset	**disgustado(a), enojado(a)**

Other uses of the present subjunctive

The subjunctive is also used after impersonal expressions followed by **que**. These impersonal expressions indicate disbelief, doubt, uncertainty, necessity, emotion, denial, etc. They are called impersonal expressions, because they do not have a specific subject. Most impersonal expressions are formed with the third-person singular of the verb **ser**.

Es probable que lleguen tarde.	*It is probable that they'll arrive late.*
Es necesario que estudies.	*It is necessary that you study.*

Here are some common impersonal expressions that require the subjunctive in the dependent clause. Note that adjectives in impersonal expressions (**dudoso**, **seguro**) are in the masculine singular form.

conviene que	it is advisable that	**es necesario que**	it is necessary that
es dudoso que	it is doubtful that	**es posible que**	it is possible that
es importante que,	it is important that	**es probable que**	it is probable that
es preciso que		**es una pena que**	it is a pity that
es imposible que	it is impossible that	**es útil que**	it is useful that
es increíble que	it is unbelievable that	**más vale que**	it is better that
es inútil que	it is useless that	**ojalá (que)**	I wish, if only (that)
es lástima que	it is a pity that	**parece mentira que**	it seems unreal that
es mejor que	it is better that	**parece que**	it seems that

Es importante que vengas a ayudarnos.   *It is important that you come to help us.*

Es una pena que pierdas esta oportunidad.   *It is a pity that you're missing this opportunity.*

Es dudoso que bajen los precios.   *It is doubtful that prices will go down.*

Note that constructions with impersonal expressions indicating certainty or that leave no room for doubt are followed by **que** plus a verb in the *indicative*, not the subjunctive, mood.

Es cierto que somos felices.   *It is true that we are happy.*

Here are impersonal expressions followed by the *indicative*.

es cierto que	it is certain/true that
es verdad que	it is true that
está comprobado que	it's proven that
no hay duda que	there's no doubt that

EJERCICIO
13·16

En tu opinión, ¿cómo es la mascota ideal? Indica **sí** o **no** si estás de acuerdo o no con estas ideas.

_____ 1. Es necesario que sea cariñoso(a) con los vecinos.

_____ 2. Es indispensable que demuestre mucho afecto.

_____ 3. Es necesario que siga mis órdenes.

_____ 4. Más vale que no muerda las patas (*legs*) de los muebles.

_____ 5. Es imprescindible (*indispensable*) que no haga mucho ruido.

_____ 6. Es mejor que no pelee con los perros y gatos de los vecinos.

_____ 7. Es posible que tenga pulgas (*fleas*).

_____ 8. Es improbable que duerma mucho.

EJERCICIO
13·17

Una carta. Escribe la forma apropiada de los verbos entre paréntesis. Decide si necesitas usar el indicativo o el subjuntivo.

Querida Elena:

1. Deseo que (tú) _____ (estar) bien.

2. Quiero que _____ (saber) que voy a abrir otra oficina en el centro comercial La Reina.

3. Espero que muchas personas _____ (venir) a la inauguración el martes 15 de marzo.

4. Necesito que (tú) les _____ (recomendar) mis servicios a tus amistades.

5. Estoy segura de que (tú) _____ (conocer) a muchos de mis clientes.

6. Ojalá tú y tus amigos _____ (poder) pasar por la oficina y conocer a nuestro personal.

7. Es conveniente que ustedes _____ (llegar) temprano para participar de una rifa (*raffle*).

8. Es necesario que los participantes _____ (recoger) un boleto en la entrada.

9. Te recomiendo que _____ (subir) a mi oficina antes de las once para tomar un café.

EJERCICIO
13·18

El nuevo gerente. Traduce. Usa el **Vocabulario útil**.

Today, the Telemast Company announces the arrival of its new general manager. Bob hopes the new manager is a nice and flexible man. It is better that the new boss understand that Bob arrives late at the office once in a while. Bob wants to create a good first impression, and today he arrives on time. He wishes the new manager will understand that employees need more time for lunch. It is important that he allow his employees to make personal calls from the office. He wishes the new manager to be very patient and not too demanding. However, it is very probable that Bob will receive a big surprise. The individual who now occupies the position of general manager has just arrived at Telemast. She is Mrs. Almagro. She is well known among her friends as "The Iron Lady."

Vocabulario útil

arrival	**la llegada**	Iron Lady	**la Dama de hierro**
demanding	**exigente**	it is better	**más vale** (*requires the subjunctive*)
general manager	**el/la gerente general**	on time	**a tiempo**
I wish, I wish that, if only	**ojalá, ojalá que**		

The present perfect subjunctive

The present perfect subjunctive (**pretérito perfecto compuesto de subjuntivo**) is another subjunctive tense used in Spanish. The word **compuesto** refers to compound tenses, which as you know are formed with **haber**. Although it is called a **pretérito**, the present perfect subjunctive usually refers to an action completed in the immediate or recent past.

The present perfect subjunctive is formed with the present subjunctive of **haber** plus the past participle of the verb you wish to conjugate.

bailar (*to sing*)	
haya bailado	**hayamos** bailado
hayas bailado	**hayáis** bailado
haya bailado	**hayan** bailado

Observe that

- the first- and third-person singular forms of this tense are the same.

- the only form of **haber** with a written accent mark is the **vosotros** form.

When is the present perfect subjunctive used in Spanish?

You remember that the subjunctive is used when the subject of the main clause expresses doubt or uncertainty, a command, a piece of advice, a suggestion, feelings, or emotions about the actions or events of a different subject in the dependent clause.

The use of the present perfect subjunctive requires an appropriate sequence of tenses. The present perfect subjunctive is used when the action in the dependent clause happened *before* the action in the main clause.

Ellos se sorprenden de que **yo haya entregado** los papeles **ayer**.	*They are surprised (that)* **I turned in** *the papers* ***yesterday***.

In the main clause, the action of the subject(s) (**se sorprenden**) is happening now, in the present; however, **haya entregado**, expressed with the present perfect subjunctive, happened in the past, before the action in the main clause takes place. Certain clues may help you determine the time of the action in the dependent clause. For example, the adverb **ayer** in the sentence above is an expression of time pointing to the past. Now, consider a different situation.

Saldrá **cuando tú hayas terminado**.	*He/She will go out (will leave)* **when you have finished**.

In this example, **saldrá** refers to an action in the future; **hayas terminado** says that the action of "finishing" will have happened by the time the subject of the main clause "goes out." Therefore, **hayas terminado**, expressed with the present perfect subjunctive, is also a future action. Depending on the context, the present perfect subjunctive may express an action that takes place in the past or in the future.

Las reacciones de la gente. Práctica. Usa el pretérito perfecto de subjuntivo del verbo entre paréntesis para expresar las emociones de estas personas.

1. El hombre duda que su esposa _____ (seguir) las instrucciones.

2. El capitán siente que tu madre _____ (tener) un accidente.

3. Yo dudo que el avión _____ (despegar) (*to take off*).

4. Lisa teme que ustedes _____ (perder) el partido.

5. El escritor espera que la editorial (*publisher*) _____ (aceptar) su novela.

6. Pedro se sorprende de que Dora _____ (romper) su compromiso (*engagement*).

7. Es dudoso que las autoridades _____ (permitir) la manifestación (*demonstration*).

8. No es probable que los actores _____ (terminar) el ensayo (*rehearsal*).

9. Dudo que tú _____ (entregar) tu trabajo antes del lunes.

En español. Usa el pretérito perfecto de subjuntivo de los verbos subrayados.

1. *We are sorry Ana has arrived.* _____

2. *I hope they have delivered the package.* _____

3. *It will be necessary that you* (**tú**) *read the books before the meeting.*

   _____

4. *Her husband hopes she has returned the new hat to the store.*

   _____

5. *The travelers are glad the plane has left* (**salir**) *on time.*

   _____

6. *The agent will demand that the director pay the actors before the weekend.*

   _____

The subjunctive mood: the present and the present perfect subjunctive tenses in noun clauses   **153**

EJERCICIO
13·21

Los inversionistas están contentos. Usa el pretérito perfecto de subjuntivo en tus respuestas.

Los inversionistas se alegran de que...

1. el precio de las acciones _____ (subir).

2. el congreso _____ (reducir) los impuestos.

3. los ejecutivos _____ (disminuir) los gastos en la empresa.

4. los vendedores _____ (vender) mucho más este año.

5. el presidente _____ (rebajar) el salario de los ejecutivos.

6. la campaña publicitaria _____ (ser) un éxito (*a success*).

EJERCICIO
13·22

Los cambios en la formación profesional. Traduce. Usa el **Vocabulario útil**.

I am happy that Pamela learned new techniques at work. It is unbelievable that she took so many courses in computer science. I wish her parents helped her to pay the costs of the virtual classes! It seems unreal that Pam took all long-distance learning classes. It is probable that she shared all her answers with her professor through the screen of her computer, at home, in her comfortable pajamas! It is amazing that in the last decades many careers have changed so much.

Vocabulario útil

amazing	**sorprendente**	pajamas	**el pijama; la payama**
career	**la carrera, la profesión**	screen	**la pantalla electrónica**
computer science	**la informática**	technique	**la técnica**
decade	**la década**	through	**a través de**
long-distance learning	**la clase a distancia**	virtual class	**la clase virtual**

More uses of the subjunctive: adverb and relative clauses

·14·

The subjunctive in adverb clauses

In Unit 13, you learned that the speaker uses the subjunctive in noun clauses to communicate doubt, wish, denial, etc., about the actions of other subjects in dependent noun clauses. The subjunctive mood is also used in other situations of doubt, uncertainty, purpose, and condition following certain conjunctions, connecting phrases, and adverbs.

A conjunction (**conjunción**) is a word or expression used to link sentences or clauses within a sentence. Many conjunctions are really connecting phrases usually ending in **que**: **antes (de) que** (*before*) or **para que** (*in order that*), for example.

These connecting expressions link the main clause to dependent clauses or adverb clauses because they function as an adverb, modifying or specifying the manner, place, time, etc., in which the action of the main clause takes place.

> Puedo terminar el informe **antes de que** Alina llegue.
>
> *I can finish the report **before** Alina arrives.*

Note the circumstances surrounding the verb in the main clause with respect to the information in the dependent clause, **antes de que Alina llegue**. The dependent clause functions as an adverb of time for **puedo terminar**, indicating when the action of the main clause is taking place. In this example, the action in the main clause will take place before the action expressed in the dependent clause.

Other conjunctions or connecting phrases with **que** introduce a dependent clause + subjunctive to express a purpose, condition, proviso, etc., with regard to the verb in the main clause.

> Leo el cuento de hadas **para que** los niños **se diviertan**.
>
> *I read the fairy tale **in order that** (**so that**) the children **might have fun**.*

The conjunction **para que** introduces a dependent clause indicating the purpose or reason for **leo**, the verb in the main clause.

When is the subjunctive used in dependent adverb clauses in Spanish?

If anticipation, doubt, purpose, or a condition concerning the outcome of an action or event is implied, certain conjunctions and phrases are used followed by the subjunctive.

Use the subjunctive in dependent clauses that may include information related to questions such as *how? when? where?* or *why?*

Escribo la nota **para que** la leas.   *I write the letter **so that** you might read it.*

Here are some expressions that introduce the subjunctive in dependent clauses.

a condición de que	provided that	**con tal que**	provided that
a fin de que	in order that, so that	**en caso de que**	in case
a menos que	unless	**para que**	in order that
antes (de) que	before	**sin que**	without

Corre más rápido **a fin de que ganes** la apuesta.

A menos que tú no quieras, iremos al museo mañana.

El tren sale **antes de que tú llegues** a la estación.

Desayunen Uds. **antes de que yo vaya** de compras.

Te cuento mi problema **con tal que guardes** el secreto.

En caso de que llueva, Juan lleva el paraguas.

*Run faster **so that you win** the bet.*

*We will go to the museum tomorrow **unless you do not want to**.*

*The train leaves **before you arrive** at the station.*

*Eat breakfast **before I go** shopping.*

*I will tell you my problem **provided you keep** the secret.*

In case it rains, Juan takes his umbrella.

The adverb clause may also precede the main clause, as we see in the last example above. Remember: The *infinitive*, not the subjunctive, is used in Spanish if the subject of the main clause and the subject of the dependent clause are the *same*. Note the preposition (**para**) that precedes the infinitive in the following example.

Hago ejercicio **para estar** en forma.   *I exercise **in order to stay** in shape.*

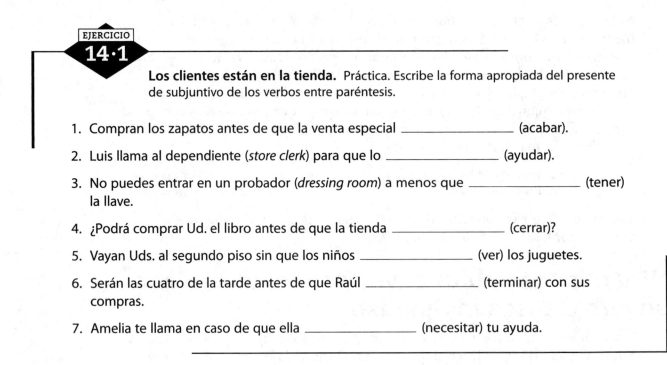

EJERCICIO
14·1

Los clientes están en la tienda. Práctica. Escribe la forma apropiada del presente de subjuntivo de los verbos entre paréntesis.

1. Compran los zapatos antes de que la venta especial _____ (acabar).

2. Luis llama al dependiente (*store clerk*) para que lo _____ (ayudar).

3. No puedes entrar en un probador (*dressing room*) a menos que _____ (tener) la llave.

4. ¿Podrá comprar Ud. el libro antes de que la tienda _____ (cerrar)?

5. Vayan Uds. al segundo piso sin que los niños _____ (ver) los juguetes.

6. Serán las cuatro de la tarde antes de que Raúl _____ (terminar) con sus compras.

7. Amelia te llama en caso de que ella _____ (necesitar) tu ayuda.

Preparamos una fiesta. ¿Cuál es la conjunción apropiada? Escoge la conjunción y escríbela en el espacio en blanco. *You may use the choices more than once.*

a menos que   en caso de que   sin que
antes (de) que   para que

1. Hoy tenemos una fiesta sorpresa _____ Gloria celebre su cumpleaños.

2. Tenemos que preparar la fiesta _____ ella regrese a casa.

3. Vamos a decorar la casa _____ Gloria descubra que hay una fiesta.

4. Compraremos mucha comida _____ los invitados tengan hambre.

5. No veremos la televisión _____ haya un programa muy cómico.

6. Voy a llevar mis discos de salsa _____ la gente baile.

7. María va a traer su guitarra _____ los invitados quieran oírla tocar.

La cultura de Argentina. Escribe las frases en español. Usa el presente de subjuntivo.

1. *Diego invites his colleagues to a restaurant in Miami so that they taste (**probar**) typical dishes from Argentina.*

   _____

2. *Diego does not go to a restaurant unless it has a good menu.*

   _____

3. *He suggests a pasta dish in case his friends do not want to eat churrasco, a dish of grilled beef (**a la parrilla**).*

   _____

4. *The waiters always serve a dish with appetizers before the customers decide their entrée (**plato fuerte**).*

   _____

5. *There is a big screen in the terrace so that the customers watch TV programs and videos from Argentina.*

   _____

6. *A video shows a recent tango competition in order that the clients know that the winners are from Japan and Colombia.*

   _____

Pareados. Luis y Ana compran una casa nueva y tienen planes. Escribe la letra de la respuesta más lógica para completar la oración.

_____ 1. Van a pintar la casa para que

_____ 2. ¿Van a comprar un piano para que

_____ 3. No pueden comprar la casa sin que

_____ 4. ¿Van a invitar a la mamá de Ana para que

_____ 5. Un agente acepta ayudarlos con tal que

_____ 6. Van a comprar una computadora para que

_____ 7. No pueden gastar más dinero a menos que

_____ 8. El banco aprueba la hipoteca (*mortgage*) con tal que

_____ 9. ¿Se mudan a su nueva casa antes de que

a. paguen su comisión exagerada.

b. llegue la primavera?

c. ganen la lotería.

d. vaya a vivir con ellos?

e. Ana trabaje desde la casa.

f. ellos paguen el 7% de interés.

g. esté más bonita.

h. el banco apruebe un préstamo.

i. sus hijos practiquen todos los días?

Expressions that may or may not require the subjunctive

As you have seen, there are many conjunctions and expressions with **que** that convey the time of the action in the dependent clause. The expressions of time include the following.

así que	as soon as	**hasta que**	until
cada vez que	each time that	**luego que**	as soon as
cuando	when	**mientras que**	while
después (de) que	after	**tan pronto como**	as soon as
en cuanto	as soon as	**una vez que**	once

Other conjunctions express purpose.

a fin de que	in order that, so that	**de manera que**	so, so that
aunque	although, even though, even if	**de modo que**	so, so that
		para que	in order that, so that

◆ The subjunctive is used after these conjunctions and expressions of time *if the action or event has not yet occurred*. The actions expressed in dependent clauses generally occur or are expected to occur *after* the action of the verb in the main clause.

Nosotros esperamos el autobús **hasta que llegue**.

*We wait for the bus **until it arrives**.*

Carlos comprará los billetes **después de que decidamos** la fecha de salida.

*Carlos will buy the tickets **after we decide** the date of departure.*

Traiga Ud. los papeles **en cuanto estén** listos.

*Bring the papers **as soon as they are** ready.*

Note that each of the main clauses in the three examples above uses a different tense or mood: **esperamos**, the present, **comprará**, the future, and finally, **traiga**, an imperative. In each instance, the action in the dependent clause has yet to occur.

◆ Use the subjunctive when there is uncertainty or lack of evidence that the action or event will actually take place. **Aunque** (*even if*) is used to introduce a clause referring to hypothetical circumstances or events, either unknown or not clear.

> **Aunque sea** difícil, voy a ahorrar dinero todos los meses.
> *Even if it is (**may be**) difficult, I will save money every month.*

With **aunque** followed by the subjunctive **sea**, the speaker reveals an uncertain situation: saving money every month may or may not be difficult for him or her. Such hypothetical situations or events require the subjunctive after the conjunction.

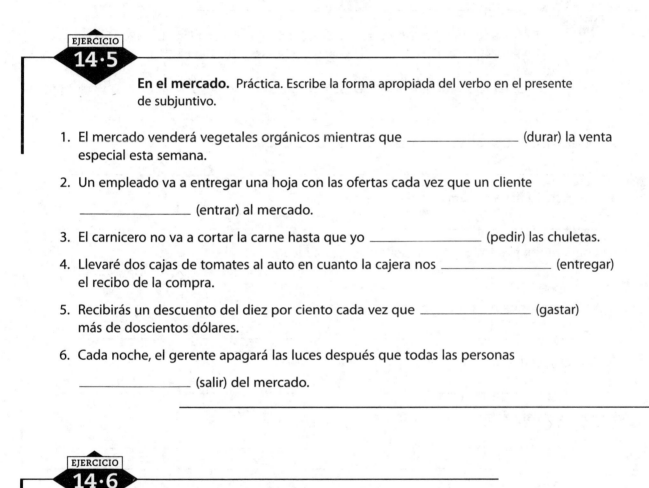

EJERCICIO
14·5

En el mercado. Práctica. Escribe la forma apropiada del verbo en el presente de subjuntivo.

1. El mercado venderá vegetales orgánicos mientras que _____ (durar) la venta especial esta semana.

2. Un empleado va a entregar una hoja con las ofertas cada vez que un cliente

   _____ (entrar) al mercado.

3. El carnicero no va a cortar la carne hasta que yo _____ (pedir) las chuletas.

4. Llevaré dos cajas de tomates al auto en cuanto la cajera nos _____ (entregar) el recibo de la compra.

5. Recibirás un descuento del diez por ciento cada vez que _____ (gastar) más de doscientos dólares.

6. Cada noche, el gerente apagará las luces después que todas las personas

   _____ (salir) del mercado.

EJERCICIO
14·6

En la oficina, todos ayudan. En español. Usa el subjuntivo en tus respuestas.

1. *I will read the message as soon as I can.*

   _____

2. *She brings the magazine so that you (**tú**) read the article.*

   _____

3. *We will finish the report (**el informe**) in order that you (**Uds.**) find the information.*

   _____

4. *Each time the phone rings, Marsha will answer.*

_____

5. *You (**Uds.**) will work even if you are tired.*

_____

6. *The receptionist will call the clients after the meeting ends.*

_____

Expresa tus ideas. Usa el presente de subjuntivo para completar las oraciones con tus propias ideas. Puedes usar el verbo que aparece entre paréntesis.

1. Voy a hacer los ejercicios de este libro de español aunque... (ser)

_____

2. Quiero que mi trabajo sea interesante de modo que... (poder)

_____

3. Me gusta llamar a mis amigos para que ellos... (salir)

_____

4. Coopero con mis amigos de modo que ellos... (ayudar)

_____

5. Voy a ahorrar dinero cada vez que mi jefe... (pagar)

_____

6. No voy a poder descansar hasta que... (llegar)

_____

7. Voy a cocinar mientras que tú... (ir)

_____

When is the subjunctive *not* used in dependent adverb clauses in Spanish?

Dependent adverb clauses do not always require the subjunctive. Use the indicative

- if the action in the dependent clause has occurred *prior to* the action happening in the main clause.

Las chicas vieron las fotos **después que nosotras las revelamos**.	*The girls saw the pictures **after we developed them**.*

- when the adverb clause indicates *habitual actions*.

Leemos las revistas **cuando las compro**.	*We read the magazines **when I buy them**.*
Solamente bebe vino **cuando come** en un restaurante.	*He/She only drinks wine **when he/she eats** at a restaurant.*

- when we refer to actions that are *real* or perceived as being real.

Aunque tiene mucho dinero, ella compra ropa barata.	***Although she has** a lot of money, she buys inexpensive clothes.*
Aunque es muy difícil, voy a hacer esta tarea.	***Although it is** difficult, I am going to do this assignment.*

When followed by an indicative tense, as in the preceding examples, **aunque** means *even though* or *although*. In those sentences, the context indicates a known fact.

Now, compare the following example.

Aunque pague poco, voy a aceptar el puesto.	***Even if it pays** little, I am going to accept the position.*

When the expression **aunque** (*even if*) indicates that uncertainty surrounds this action, it requires the use of the subjunctive: the job may or may not pay well.

EJERCICIO
14·8

¿Subjuntivo o indicativo? Subraya la forma correcta del verbo en las siguientes oraciones.

1. Bebemos agua cuando (tengamos | tenemos) sed.

2. Leila nos llamará en cuanto (llega | llegue) a su oficina.

3. No quieren tener hijos hasta que (tienen | tengan) una posición económica cómoda.

4. Aunque es rico no (gasta | gaste) mucho dinero.

5. Cuando Ramón (tiene | tenga) problemas, ¿lo ayudan siempre sus amigos?

6. Después de que (duermo | duerma) la siesta, me siento mejor.

7. Ana promete visitar a la Tía Carmela cada vez que (puede | pueda).

8. Cuando (es | sea) mi cumpleaños, siempre espero regalos de mis amigos.

9. Los agentes secretos saben cuando (sale | salga) el avión del campo enemigo.

10. Siempre comen en esta cafetería aunque saben que la comida no (es | sea) muy buena.

Explica por qué usaste el indicativo o el subjuntivo. *Go back to Ejercicio 14-8. Explain why you chose the indicative or the subjunctive in the following sentences.*

1. Bebemos agua cuando... _____

3. No quieren tener hijos hasta que... _____

5. Cuando Ramón... _____

7. Ana promete visitar a la Tía Carmela... _____

8. Cuando... mi cumpleaños... _____

Las finanzas y mis planes para el futuro. Traduce. Usa el **Vocabulario útil**.

*I want to retire early, as early as possible. I want to stop working when I am (**cumplir**) fifty-five years old. I have twenty-five years to earn money. That is why I listen to my friends' advice. My friend Pete is extremely conservative, and he suggests that I put my money in the bank. He says that as soon as I receive my paycheck this month, I should save twenty-five percent of my salary. Marcia is a manager at a bank, and she believes I should buy a property so that the price goes up and I make a lot of money! Mark is more aggressive. He says that if I do not invest my money in the stock market, I am not going to stop working until I am seventy years old. What if the market goes down and I lose all my money? Just in case, I buy lottery tickets every once in a while.*

Vocabulario útil

advice	**el consejo**	property	**la propiedad**
aggressive	**agresivo(a)**	salary	**el salario, el sueldo**
conservative	**conservador(-a)**	(stock) market	**la bolsa (de valores)**
extremely	**extremadamente**	to earn money	**ganar dinero**
just in case	**por si acaso**	to invest	**invertir (e > ie)**
lottery ticket	**el billete de lotería**	to retire	**jubilarse**
manager	**el/la gerente**		

More uses of the subjunctive: the subjunctive in adjective clauses

Remember that a subordinate (dependent) clause may function as a noun, adverb, or adjective clause. Just as the subjunctive appears in noun and adverb clauses, it may be used in adjective clauses. An adjective modifies a noun or pronoun; an adjective clause modifies a noun or pronoun in the main clause. Adjective clauses are usually introduced by a relative pronoun (**que, quien, quienes**, or the adverb **donde**), and for this reason they are called relative clauses.

Elard quiere conocer **un periodista**
   que sea imparcial.

*Elard wants to meet **a journalist who is** unbiased.*

Busco **un lugar donde haya** silencio.

*I am looking for **a place where there is** quiet.*

In the first example above, the relative pronoun **que** refers to the noun preceding it, **un perio-dista**. This noun preceding the relative pronoun is called the antecedent (**el antecedente**). The dependent clause, **que sea imparcial**, modifies **un periodista**, and it describes a quality "Elard" wants to find in a journalist. Finally, in the second example, **donde** refers to a place that is sought after; it does not confirm the existence of such a place.

When is the subjunctive used in adjective clauses?

Both the subjunctive and the indicative may be used in dependent adjective (or relative) clauses. The antecedent will help you determine whether the subjunctive or the indicative is used.

◆ Use the subjunctive after a relative pronoun in a relative clause when the antecedent (a person, place, or thing) is vague or indefinite, desired but not realized. Remember that the subjunctive is generally associated with uncertainty, indefiniteness, or doubt.

Buscamos una oficina **que tenga** una
   vista al mar.

*We are looking for an office **with** (**that has**)
   an ocean view.*

Necesita un gerente **que hable** árabe.

*He/She needs a manager **who speaks** Arabic.*

In **buscamos una oficina**, the message allows for the possibility that such an office may not be found. In **necesita un gerente**, the existence of this individual is uncertain.

Note: There is *no* personal **a** before the direct object in the main clause of the second example above. The antecedent is the subject of a search; he does not yet exist. Compare with **Invité *a* nuestro gerente**. (*I invited our manager.*)

If the antecedent is real, concrete, or not in doubt, use the indicative in the relative clause (after **que**).

Conocemos a una chica **que habla**
   tres idiomas.

*We know a girl **who speaks** three languages.*

Visitamos un restaurante **donde puedes
   llevar** tu propia botella de vino.

*We visit a restaurant **where you can take** your
   own bottle of wine.*

In the first example above, the personal **a** in the phrase **Conocemos *a* una chica** indicates that the person definitely exists.

◆ Use the subjunctive after a negative antecedent (**nada**, **nadie**, **ninguno[a]**) pointing to a nonexistent person, place, or thing.

Matthew no necesita a **nadie que lo
   ayude** a traducir los documentos.

*Matthew does not need **anyone to help him**
   translate the documents.*

No hay **nada que sea** más importante.

*There isn't **anything that's** more important.*

No hay **ninguna persona que pueda**
   ayudar.

*There is **no one who can** help.*

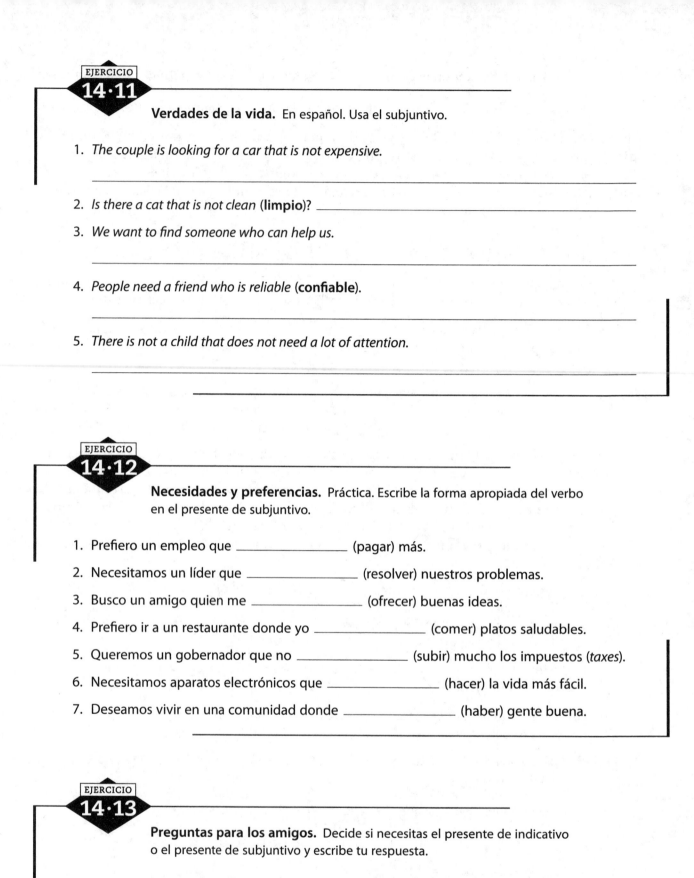

Verdades de la vida. En español. Usa el subjuntivo.

1. *The couple is looking for a car that is not expensive.*

   _____

2. *Is there a cat that is not clean (**limpio**)?* _____

3. *We want to find someone who can help us.*

   _____

4. *People need a friend who is reliable (**confiable**).*

   _____

5. *There is not a child that does not need a lot of attention.*

   _____

Necesidades y preferencias. Práctica. Escribe la forma apropiada del verbo en el presente de subjuntivo.

1. Prefiero un empleo que _____ (pagar) más.

2. Necesitamos un líder que _____ (resolver) nuestros problemas.

3. Busco un amigo quien me _____ (ofrecer) buenas ideas.

4. Prefiero ir a un restaurante donde yo _____ (comer) platos saludables.

5. Queremos un gobernador que no _____ (subir) mucho los impuestos (*taxes*).

6. Necesitamos aparatos electrónicos que _____ (hacer) la vida más fácil.

7. Deseamos vivir en una comunidad donde _____ (haber) gente buena.

Preguntas para los amigos. Decide si necesitas el presente de indicativo o el presente de subjuntivo y escribe tu respuesta.

1. ¿Hay por aquí una tienda que _____ (vender) disfraces para niños?

2. ¿Conoces al presidente que _____ (estar) a cargo (*in charge*) de esta compañía?

3. ¿Sabes si hay alguien que _____ (saber) las respuestas para la tarea de mañana?

4. ¿Han visto Uds. una película que _____ (ser) adecuada para niños?

5. ¿Vas a ver la competencia de tango que _____ (empezar) a las ocho?

6. ¿Sabes el nombre de la señora que _____ (vivir) en el segundo piso?

7. ¿No han encontrado Uds. a nadie que _____ (poder) arreglar su auto hoy?

EJERCICIO
14·14

Y en tu caso... ¿Es verdadero o falso?

_____ 1. Busco una persona que me haga feliz.

_____ 2. Cualquier persona que mienta (*tells lies*) no es mi amigo.

_____ 3. Conozco a un joven que pinta como Picasso.

_____ 4. Necesito un trabajo que pague más.

_____ 5. Prefiero un gimnasio donde tengan equipo muy moderno.

_____ 6. No conozco a nadie que sea famoso.

EJERCICIO
14·15

En español.

1. *Marcos is looking for a tennis player who can win the match.*

_____

2. *Do you (**Uds.**) know a store that sells Mexican products?*

_____

3. *We need an office that is big and inexpensive.*

_____

4. *There isn't anything you (**tú**) can do to solve this problem.*

_____

5. *I prefer a friend who is honest.* _____

6. *There isn't anyone who can understand this message!*

_____

- ◆ Use the subjunctive when the antecedent is one of the following compound words with -**quiera**, when they involve uncertain or improbable situations.

adondequiera	wherever
como quiera que	however
cualquier/cualquiera (singular), **cualesquiera** (plural)	any
cuando quiera	whenever
dondequiera	wherever
quienquiera (singular), **quienesquiera** (plural)	whoever

Quienquiera que venga recibirá las entradas.	*Whoever comes will receive the tickets.*
Saludaré a Manuel **dondequiera que lo vea**.	*I will greet Manuel wherever I see him.*

-**Quiera** is a form of the subjunctive of **querer** (*to wish, want*). It suggests that these words refer to a person, place, or thing that is not concrete or real. Use the form **cualquier** before a noun.

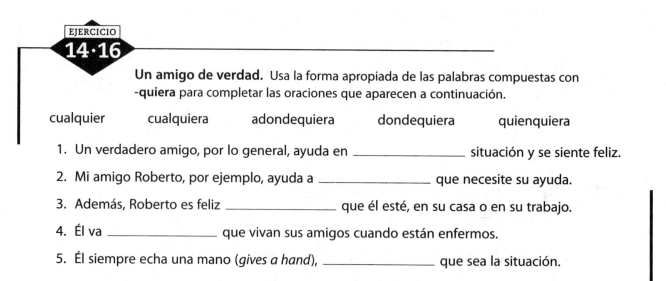

EJERCICIO
14·16

Un amigo de verdad. Usa la forma apropiada de las palabras compuestas con -**quiera** para completar las oraciones que aparecen a continuación.

cualquier	cualquiera	adondequiera	dondequiera	quienquiera

1. Un verdadero amigo, por lo general, ayuda en _____ situación y se siente feliz.

2. Mi amigo Roberto, por ejemplo, ayuda a _____ que necesite su ayuda.

3. Además, Roberto es feliz _____ que él esté, en su casa o en su trabajo.

4. Él va _____ que vivan sus amigos cuando están enfermos.

5. Él siempre echa una mano (*gives a hand*), _____ que sea la situación.

Other uses of the subjunctive

- ◆ Use the subjunctive in constructions with **por** + adjective or adverb + **que** + subjunctive. Study these examples.

Por distraído que sea podrá responder estas preguntas fáciles.	*No matter how absentminded he may be, he will be able to answer these easy questions.*
Por duro que yo trabaje, no puedo terminar este informe a tiempo.	*No matter how hard I work, I cannot finish this report on time.*

- ◆ The subjunctive is also used in the following constructions: (1) subjunctive + **lo que** + subjunctive, which translates to *no matter how . . .* , and (2) subjunctive + **como**, **cuando**, or **donde** + subjunctive.

    These constructions point out uncertain or improbable situations, reasons that call for the use of the subjunctive.

| Gasten lo que gasten no van a ser felices nunca. | *No matter how much they spend*, *they will never be happy.* |
| Vayas donde vayas te seguiré. | *Wherever you go*, *I will follow you.* |

◆ The subjunctive is used following the expressions **acaso**, **a lo mejor**, **tal vez**, **puede (ser) que**, and **quizás** or **quizá**. All these expressions mean *perhaps* or *maybe*. They are followed by the subjunctive when the speaker wants to stress uncertainty or doubt.

Tal vez tengamos suerte.	*Maybe we'll be lucky.*
Acaso él no regrese a Madrid.	*Perhaps he won't come back to Madrid.*
Quizás Marta no haya visto la última película de Penélope Cruz.	*Maybe Marta has not seen Penelope Cruz's latest movie.*

The adverbs **posiblemente** (*possibly*) and **probablemente** (*probably*) communicate a similar degree of uncertainty. Usually, these are preceded by an idea previously expressed or understood and followed by a subjunctive form: **Posiblemente él no regrese a Madrid.**

However, if the statement is considered somewhat more *probable* than improbable, the speaker will use these expressions (see the preceding list) with an indicative tense. The choice of mood requires a certain degree of judgment.

| Tal vez llego a la cita a tiempo. | *Perhaps I'll be on time for my appointment.* |
| ¡A lo mejor tu padre compra el auto nuevo! | *Maybe your father will buy the new car!* |

◆ Use the subjunctive in constructions such as **que ella recuerde**, **que yo sepa**, etc., that stress some doubt or limits to the speaker's knowledge about what is happening (or not).

| —¿Viene el alcalde? | *"Is the mayor coming?"* |
| —No, **que yo sepa**. | *"Not **that I know**."* |

EJERCICIO
14·17

Más práctica. Escribe la forma apropiada del subjuntivo.

1. Marta no va a encontrar un libro interesante por más que lo _____ (buscar) en la biblioteca.

2. Juanita no gana peso (*weight*) por mucho que _____ (comer).

3. Que yo _____ (saber), Uds. tienen que asumir las responsabilidades.

4. Puede ser que la mujer o el hombre ideal nunca _____ (llegar).

5. No quiere ver la película española porque _____ (pensar) que es mala.

6. ¿Aceptas su decisión, aunque ella _____ (decir) lo que diga?

7. Posiblemente nosotros _____ (aceptar) las sugerencias (*suggestions*) del delegado.

8. Que ella _____ (recordar), nunca encuentra nada bueno en las subastas (*auctions*).

EJERCICIO
14·18

En español. ¡Tania es muy lista y muy buena vendedora!

1. *Tania is very clever no matter what people may say.*

   _____

2. *Maybe we'll be lucky today if we sell as many products as she sold yesterday.*

   _____

3. *Probably Tania will arrive before eight o'clock to decorate the showcase (**la vitrina**).*

   _____

4. *Perhaps Tania will receive a raise soon.*

   _____

5. *Even though you (**tú**) don't believe it, she wants to have her own business.*

   _____

6. *Wherever she works, she will be successful (**tener éxito**).*

   _____

EJERCICIO
14·19

Frases que conectan ideas de una manera lógica. Escoge la frase para conectar el mensaje con sentido lógico.

cuando quiera que vayan	por mucho que llames	sea como sea
cuesten lo que cuesten	por muy barato que sea	tal vez

1. Marcos es mentiroso. _____ nunca diga la verdad.

2. A Lucy no le gusta este sombrero. _____ no quiere comprarlo.

3. Marta detesta contestar el teléfono. _____ no va a contestar.

4. Los chicos quieren ver el show de Broadway. _____, van a comprar las entradas.

5. Prefieren ver el partido aunque pierda su equipo. _____, verán el partido por televisión.

6. Quieren ir a España con unos amigos pero no saben cuándo.

   _____ se divertirán con ellos.

El 15 de abril: la carrera contra el tiempo. Traduce. Usa el **Vocabulario útil**.

I am not going to see Daniela until after April 15. She does not answer my calls even if I leave ten messages on her answering machine. She is lazy and does not make decisions until the last minute. Even if she does not want to, she has to fill out her tax return forms and look for all the receipts she needs to declare her expenses. She gets sick and will not rest until she completes her tax return. She is going to suffer a hysteria attack unless someone solves her problem. She needs an accountant who wants to help her on such short notice. Maybe she finds this exciting! Daniela must change. As a Spanish proverb says: "Don't leave for tomorrow what you can do today."

Vocabulario útil

accountant	**el/la contable**	short notice	**en poco tiempo**
answering machine	**la contestadora (automática)**	tax	**el impuesto**
		tax return	**la declaración de impuestos**
exciting	**emocionante**		
expense	**el gasto**	to fill out	**rellenar**
form	**el formulario**	to get sick	**enfermar(se)**
receipt	**el recibo**		

The subjunctive mood past tenses: the imperfect and the pluperfect subjunctive

Before learning the subjunctive past tenses, you may wish to review the general rules of the use of the subjunctive mood (Units 13 and 14). The same basic rules are used to narrate in the past with the past subjunctive tenses. The more experience you have with the present and the present perfect subjunctive forms, the better prepared you will be to understand and use the past subjunctive tenses.

You will need to identify the tense that appears in the main clause of each sentence in order to determine the subjunctive tense required in the dependent clause. This is called the *sequence of tenses*. It can be observed in the following examples. Compare each tense in the main clause of the sentence and its relationship to the verb in the dependent clause.

<table>
<tr><td>**Es necesario que tengas** tus documentos.</td><td>*It is necessary that you have your documents.*</td></tr>
</table>

Es, a present tense indicative form in the main clause, is part of the impersonal expression **es necesario**. The dependent clause introduced by **que** follows with a different subject and a present subjunctive verb, **tengas**. In the next example below, the past tense in the impersonal expression (**era necesario**) in the main clause is followed by the imperfect subjunctive **tuvieras** to complete the dependent clause.

<table>
<tr><td>**Era necesario que tuvieras** tus documentos.</td><td>*It was necessary that you have* (*It was necessary to have*) *your documents.*</td></tr>
</table>

The imperfect subjunctive

From your study of Spanish verbs, you probably associate the *imperfect* with the indicative tense used when verbs describe the duration of time in the past. The differences in the uses of the imperfect and the preterit indicative tenses are based on when the actions took place, how often they occurred, and so on. These distinctions *do not* apply to the imperfect (past) subjunctive or any other subjunctive past tense. The time of the action in the main clause determines the tense you will use in the dependent clause. Some patterns ask for the use of the imperfect subjunctive.

To form the imperfect subjunctive (**imperfecto de subjuntivo**) in Spanish, use the third-person plural (**ellos/ellas**) form of the preterit tense of the indicative mood. Then,

◆ drop the -**ron** ending of the third-person plural of the preterit (**habla**-ron, **pudie**-ron, **sintie**-ron)

◆ and add the corresponding endings according to the models that follow.

hablar (*to talk*)		**poder** (*to be able*)		**sentir** (*to feel*)	
hablara	habláramos	pudiera	pudiéramos	sintiera	sintiéramos
hablaras	hablarais	pudieras	pudierais	sintieras	sintierais
hablara	hablaran	pudiera	pudieran	sintiera	sintieran

El director **quería que yo hablara** a la asamblea.
*The principal **wanted me to speak** to the assembly.*
No fue posible que el guía acompañara al grupo.
It was not possible for the guide to accompany the group.

A second or alternate set of endings of the imperfect subjunctive, referred to as the **-se** endings, has the same meanings. These endings are less frequently seen.

viajar (*to travel*)		**traer** (*to bring*)		**pedir** (*to ask, request*)	
viajase	viajásemos	trajese	trajésemos	pidiese	pidiésemos
viajases	viajaseis	trajeses	trajeseis	pidieses	pidieseis
viajase	viajasen	trajese	trajesen	pidiese	pidiesen

El director **quería que yo hablase** a la asamblea.
*The principal **wanted me to speak** to the assembly.*
No fue posible que el guía acompañase al grupo.
It was not possible for the guide to accompany the group.

Note that

◆ these models apply to all regular and irregular verbs, verbs with stem changes, and verbs with spelling changes.

◆ the first- and third-person singular forms are exactly the same.

◆ the **nosotros** forms have a written accent mark on the vowel preceding the **r** (or the **s**) of the endings.

EJERCICIO
15·1

La conjugación. Observa las formas del pretérito de indicativo. Escribe el imperfecto de subjuntivo de los verbos. Usa la forma que termina en **-ra**.

1. ellos caminaron _____

2. la joven y su amiga vivieron _____

3. tu hermano salió _____

4. mi loro (*parrot*) durmió _____

5. yo canté _____

6. tú fuiste _____

7. Uds. se cayeron _____

8. la cena costó _____

9. el camarero sirvió _____

10. Uds. trajeron _____

Práctica. Escribe las dos formas del imperfecto de subjuntivo: la forma en **-ra** y la forma en **-se**.

1. Yo quería que Lola _____/_____ (venir).

2. Preferíamos que tú _____/_____ (tocar) la guitarra.

3. No recuperaría mi collar de perlas aunque la policía _____/_____ (encontrar) al ladrón.

4. Antes de que la reunión _____/_____ (terminar), Marta y Luisa se fueron.

5. ¿Por qué insistieron en que Uds. _____/_____ (pagar) la cuenta?

6. Fue indispensable que los colegios _____/_____ (cerrar) sus puertas.

7. Buscaban un asistente que _____/_____ (saber) usar el equipo de sonido.

8. No fue posible que los delegados _____/_____ (hablar) a la asamblea.

En el cine. En español. Usa la forma **-ra** del imperfecto de subjuntivo.

1. *It was necessary (that) they wait twenty minutes to buy the tickets.*

_____

2. *Joe asked Mary to buy chocolates.*

_____

3. *Mary bought sodas in case they were thirsty.*

_____

4. *Ann and Mary wanted seats that were close to the screen (**la pantalla**).*

_____

5. *They did not want to watch the commercials before the movie started.*

_____

6. *Jack left (**irse**) the movie theater before the film ended.*

_____

When is the imperfect subjunctive used in Spanish?

Here is a summary of the uses of the imperfect subjunctive.

Use the imperfect subjunctive in a noun, adverb, or relative clause to express what was happening, if the verb in the main clause is in the imperfect, preterit, pluperfect indicative, or conditional. As you read the following examples, note the tenses that appear in the main clause.

Los agentes **no permitían que** los ciudadanos **protestasen** en el parque. (imperfect)	*The officers **didn't allow** the citizens **to protest** in the park.*
La policía **arrestó** a tres de los manifestantes **antes de que llegaran** a la ONU. (preterit)	*The police **arrested** three of the demonstrators **before they arrived** at the U.N.*
La mujer **había exigido que** la congresista la **escuchase**. (pluperfect)	*The woman **had demanded that** the congresswoman **hear** her.*
Yo preferiría que tú leyeras el periódico después. (conditional)	*I **would prefer that you read** the newspaper later.*

Note that the English equivalents do not need to show the same sorts of distinctions Spanish displays with its sequence of tenses. English equivalents often use the infinitive (*to protest*), the simple past (*they arrived*), and the simple English subjunctive (*that the congresswoman hear, that you read*). Remember that in Spanish, the infinitive, not the imperfect subjunctive, is used if the subject of the main clause and the subject of the dependent clause are the *same*. Compare the following examples.

Deseaban **que tú llegaras** a tiempo.	*They hoped **that you would arrive** on time.*
Deseabas **llegar** a tiempo.	*You hoped **to arrive** on time.*

The second example above lacks a dependent clause introduced by **que**, and so the infinitive follows the principal verb.

EJERCICIO
15·4

La cena. Te toca a ti. Usa la forma apropiada del imperfecto de subjuntivo del verbo entre paréntesis. *Add your own words to each sentence to complete the meaning.*

1. Mis amigos me habían llevado a un restaurante para que todos nosotros

   _____ (divertirse).

2. La propietaria nos trajo el menú de modo que lo _____ (leer).

3. El camarero sugirió que nosotros _____ (probar).

4. No queríamos gastar mucho dinero a menos que la comida _____ (ser).

5. Después de comer, le pedimos al camarero que _____ (traer).

Ana tiene ahora una viña (*vineyard*) **en California.** Escribe la forma apropiada del imperfecto de subjuntivo (**-ra**) del verbo entre paréntesis.

1. Los padres de Ana tenían una viña en Chile para que su familia _____ (trabajar) en esa industria.

2. Ana quería comprar una viña en Sonoma, California, de modo que ella _____ (poder) vivir en los Estados Unidos.

3. Ana quería que los visitantes _____ (conocer) los vinos de Sonoma.

4. Ella preparó y decoró la tienda de su viña sin que nadie le _____ (dar) consejos.

5. Después, instalaron equipos de refrigeración antes de que los trabajadores _____ (recoger) la primera cosecha (*harvest*) de uvas.

6. Los técnicos le recomendaron que la nevera _____ (mantener) los vinos a una temperatura baja y seca.

7. Había muchas ofertas para viajes económicos de modo que los turistas _____ (visitar) las bodegas (*cellars*).

8. Era necesario poner avisos en la tienda para que los turistas _____ (tener) cuidado con las leyes de tránsito en California.

En la peluquería. Traduce. Usa el **Vocabulario útil**.

*Sabrina had long, brown, straight hair. She went to the hair salon and told her hairdresser to cut her hair. Pete, the hairdresser, suggested she change the color of her hair. Sabrina always wanted her hair to be different. She decided she wanted to be a blonde. Pete looked for a color (that) Sabrina liked. She preferred (**prefería**) a color that was light. Three and a half hours after he changed the color of her hair, Pete started using his scissors. When Pete finished, Sabrina looked at her face in the mirror. And she saw a very different woman! When Sabrina returned home, she came in and her husband did not say much. He seemed confused. Before Sabrina asked for his opinion, her husband said: "Why not a permanent, too?"*

Vocabulario útil

blonde	**rubio(a)**	mirror	**el espejo**
confused	**confundido(a), confuso(a)**	permanent	**el permanente**
hair salon	**la peluquería**	scissors	**las tijeras**
hairdresser	**el/la peluquero(a)**		

Other uses of the imperfect subjunctive

You have learned that the imperfect subjunctive appears mostly in dependent clauses connecting thoughts to a past tense or to a conditional expressing conjecture in the main clause. Remember that the English equivalent of the subjunctive in the dependent clause is very often expressed with an infinitive.

No me gustaría que tú fueses al cine con Carla.	*I would not like you to go to the movies with Carla.*

The imperfect subjunctive is also used in some independent clauses to express a wish in the present or to underscore a situation unlikely to happen in the present.

Use the imperfect subjunctive

◆ after **qué, quién** to express a wish in the present.

¡Quién supiera la verdad!	*If only we knew the truth! (If only the truth were known!)*

◆ after **ni que** in negative constructions to accentuate an improbable or uncertain situation in the present.

—Llevo estas botas, un abrigo, una gorra y guantes.	*"I am wearing boots, a coat, a cap, and gloves."*
—¡**Ni que estuviera** nevando!	*"As if it were snowing!"*

◆ after **ojalá** (**que**) to express a wish in the present.

¡Ojalá ganaras el concurso!	*I hope (that) you win the contest!*

◆ in polite requests with **deber** (*should, ought*), **querer** (*to wish, like*), and **poder** (*to be able*), where the **-ra** forms of the imperfect subjunctive may be used instead of the conditional.

Quisiera pedirle un favor, señor.	*Sir, I would like to ask you a favor.*
¿Pudieran Uds. enviar la medicina inmediatamente?	*Could you send the medicine immediately?*
Ud. debiera salir del edificio ahora.	*You should (ought to) leave the building now.*

EJERCICIO

15·7

¡Qué amable! En español. Usa el imperfecto de subjuntivo de los verbos **poder**, **querer** y **deber** que aparecen en inglés en las siguientes oraciones.

1. *Could you (**Ud.**) open the door, please?* _____

2. *I would like to come in.* _____

3. *You (**Ud.**) should finish now.* _____

4. *You (**Ud.**) should close the door now.* _____

5. *I would not like to buy this tie.* _____

6. *I should apologize (**pedir perdón**) for my mistakes.*

_____

Reacciones. Escribe la letra de la frase que conecta y completa la frase de una manera lógica.

_____ 1. *I am lonely.*

_____ 2. *This restaurant is expensive.*

_____ 3. *The exam is so hard.*

_____ 4. *Luis is buying a luxury car.*

_____ 5. *Why are you running to class?*

_____ 6. *I want to ski.*

_____ 7. *I am sleepy.*

a. ¡Ojalá pudiera dormir una siesta!

b. Ni que fuera millonario.

c. ¡Ojalá nevara!

d. Ni que fuera tan bueno.

e. ¡Ojalá tuviera un buen amigo!

f. Ni que fuera tarde.

g. ¡Quién supiera las respuestas!

The pluperfect subjunctive

Another subjunctive past tense is the pluperfect (past perfect) subjunctive (**el pluscuamperfecto de subjuntivo**), a compound tense. Remember that in Spanish all compound tenses need a form of the auxiliary verb **haber** preceding the past participle of the verb being conjugated.

Take the **ellos** form of the preterit indicative of **haber** and follow these steps.

- ◆ Drop the -**ron** ending of the third-person plural **hubie**ron.

- ◆ Add the corresponding ending of the imperfect subjunctive -**ra** or -**se** forms. See the model that follows.

- ◆ Add the past participle of the verb you want to conjugate: -**ado** ending for -**ar** verbs and -**ido** ending for -**er** and -**ir** verbs.

- ◆ Remember that frequently used verbs may have irregular past participles, such as **dicho** (**decir**, *to tell*), **visto** (**ver**, *to see*), and **escrito** (**escribir**, *to write*). See Unit 10 and the Verb tables in this book for review of irregular forms.

hub**iera** (hub**iese**) **sacado**	hub**iéramos** (hub**iésemos**) **dicho**
hub**ieras** (hub**ieses**) **vendido**	hub**ierais** (hub**ieseis**) **visto**
hub**iera** (hub**iese**) **pedido**	hub**ieran** (hub**iesen**) **venido**

Note that the first- and third-person singular forms are the same.

Even though the -**ra** form appears to be the more widely used in the Hispanic world, in most instances, either form is acceptable.

Su padre esperaba **que hubiese ido** al médico.	*His father hoped **(that) he had gone** to the doctor.*
El director dudó **que yo hubiera convencido** a la asamblea.	*The principal doubted **(that) I had convinced** the assembly.*

Conjugación. Cambia la forma del presente del verbo al pluscuamperfecto de subjuntivo. Usa las dos formas que terminan en **-ra** y en **-se**.

1. los jóvenes salen _____/_____

2. mi madre permite _____/_____

3. Betsy y yo queremos _____/_____

4. yo no puedo _____/_____

5. tú escribes _____/_____

Un caso difícil. Escribe la forma apropiada del pluscuamperfecto de subjuntivo de los verbos entre paréntesis. Usa la forma que termina en **-ra**.

1. La recepcionista no cerró la puerta hasta que todos _____ (pasar) al salón.

2. ¿Quién no _____ (creer) que Uds. habían dicho la verdad?

3. El abogado nunca pensó que su cliente _____ (mentir) (*to lie*).

4. El juez esperó hasta que los testigos (*witnesses*) _____ (sentarse).

5. La acusada negó que ella _____ (cometer) el crimen.

6. Pero en ese momento nadie _____ (afirmar) su inocencia.

When is the pluperfect subjunctive used in Spanish?

The pluperfect subjunctive tells what was happening in the past, in a noun, adverb, or relative clause. The verb in the main clause must be in a past tense: the imperfect, the preterit, the pluperfect, or the conditional perfect. Observe the following examples.

Los meteorólogos no creyeron **que hubiera nevado** por tanto tiempo.	*The meteorologists did not think **it would have snowed** for so long.*
Silvia había comprado los televisores **antes de que la venta especial hubiera acabado**.	*Silvia bought the televisions **before the special sale had ended**.*
Yo habría exigido **que el servicio hubiera sido incluido** en la cuenta.	*I would have demanded **that the service be included** in the bill.*

Note that the action in the pluperfect subjunctive (after **que**) happens *before* the action in the main clause. Remember: If the subject of the main clause and the subject of the dependent clause are the *same*, the infinitive is used in the dependent clause.

Una campaña publicitaria. Termina la frase en español. *Write the italicized portion of the sentence in Spanish. Use the pluperfect subjunctive* **-ra** *form.*

1. Melissa envió un fax antes de que _____
   they had left their office.

2. Nosotras habíamos dudado que _____
   Elías had created a new campaign.

3. Elías habría preferido que _____
   everyone had listened to his suggestions.

4. No había ninguna persona quien _____
   had seen the name "Bubbles" (**burbuja**) *on a bottle of shampoo* (**champú**).

5. Sus colegas reaccionaron como si _____
   they had seen an extraterrestrial.

Other uses of the pluperfect subjunctive

You have seen the pluperfect subjunctive in dependent clauses connecting to a past tense in the main clause. The pluperfect subjunctive is also used in some independent clauses to express a wish in the past or to emphasize a possible or unlikely situation in the past.

Use the pluperfect subjunctive

- after **qué, quién** to express a wish in the past.

   ¡Quién hubiera ganado ese partido!   *If only (I, we) had won that match!*

- after **ojalá (que)** to express a wish in the past.

   ¡Ojalá lo hubiera sabido entonces!   *I wish I had known it then!*

- in negative constructions after **ni que** to accentuate improbable or doubtful situations in the past.

   —El vendedor quería que yo comprara   *"The salesman wanted me to buy a watch,*
   un reloj, un brazalete de oro, un   *a gold bracelet, a diamond . . ."*
   diamante...
   —**¡Ni que tú hubieras necesitado** todo   *"As if you had needed all those things!"*
   eso!

Y en tu caso... ¿Es verdadero o falso?

_____ 1. Mi familia quería que hubiera elegido una buena ocupación para tener un buen empleo.

_____ 2. ¡Ojalá yo hubiera escuchado esos consejos!

_____ 3. Mi contable dudaba que yo hubiera pagado mis impuestos antes del 15 de abril.

_____ 4. ¡Ojalá hubiera tomado varios cursos de economía!

_____ 5. He recibido muchas ofertas de nuevas tarjetas de crédito por correo sin que yo las hubiera solicitado.

_____ 6. ¡Ojalá yo hubiera resistido la tentación!

_____ 7. El mes pasado llegó la cuenta del mes de agosto antes de que yo hubiera pagado la cuenta de julio.

_____ 8. ¡Ojalá hubiera tomado decisiones más prácticas en mi vida!

The imperfect and pluperfect subjunctive in contrary-to-fact conditional clauses

Hypothetical situations require the use of the subjunctive. These hypotheses appear frequently in contrary-to-fact situations, sentences requiring a conditional clause introduced with the conjunction _if_.

> **If you were** nice, **you would bring** me a cup of hot tea now.

The message implies "you are not nice" and that the likelihood of getting that cup of tea is rather remote.

On the other hand, there are real conditions, likely to happen, that also require an _if_-clause. The word "real" suggests that the subjunctive is not used in this case. The likely or unlikely result of the condition appears in the _result clause_, again indicating the use of the indicative. Note the present indicative in the _if_-clauses that follow and the present or future indicative in the main clause of the sentences.

Si ganas más dinero, **puedes** ahorrar más.	**If you earn** more money, **you are able to** (**can**) save more.
Si ganas más dinero, **podrás** ahorrar más.	**If you earn** more money, **you will be able to** save more.

"Real condition" clauses followed by result clauses may also refer to past actions.

Si ganabas más dinero, **podías** ahorrar más.	**If you earned** more money, **you were able to** (**could**) save more.

In the sentence above, the speaker is sure that the result clause was a reality, **podías ahorrar más**, as long as the _if_-clause did take place: **si ganabas más dinero**. Both clauses are expressed in the indicative mood.

Contrary-to-fact conditions express hypothetical situations. This uncertainty and improbability require the use of the subjunctive.

Si ganaras (**ganases**) más dinero, **podrías** ahorrar más.	**If you earned** more money, **you could** save more.

In this example, the _if_-clause expresses a contrary-to-fact condition, one that is not true because "you" are not earning more money. Since it is not real, the contrary-to-fact condition is expressed in the imperfect subjunctive (even though the speaker is talking about the present).

Unlikely or hypothetical *if*-clauses can refer to past actions or events as well. In that case, the pluperfect subjunctive tense is used.

Si hubieras ganado más dinero, **habrías ahorrado** más.	*If you had earned more money, you would have saved more.*

The uses of the subjunctive in *if*-clauses can be summarized as follows.

◆ Use the imperfect subjunctive in hypothetical, contrary-to-fact *if*-clauses that refer to situations in the present or future.

Si no tuviera un despertador, **llegaría** tarde al trabajo.	*If I did not have an alarm clock, I would get to work late.*

This can refer to an everyday situation—"in order for me to get to work on time, I need the alarm clock"—or it can refer to a hypothetical situation in the future.

◆ Use the pluperfect subjunctive to describe contrary-to-fact situations in the past.

Si no hubiera tenido un despertador, **habría llegado** tarde al trabajo.	*If I had not had an alarm clock, I would have arrived at work late.*

Note that the **-ra** form of the imperfect and pluperfect subjunctive can be used instead of the conditional (**potencial**) and conditional perfect indicative (**potencial compuesto**) in result clauses.

Si practicaras más a menudo, **jugaras** mejor al tenis.	*If you practiced more often, you would play tennis better.*

Note that the result clause does not necessarily follow the **si** (*if*)-clause.

Nosotros hubiéramos venido si hubiéramos sabido que nos necesitabas.	*We would have come if we had known you needed us.*

In real and contrary-to-fact sentences in Spanish, it is necessary to maintain the sequence of tenses.

if-CLAUSE (REAL)	RESULT CLAUSE	*if*-CLAUSE (HYPOTHETICAL, CONTRARY-TO-FACT)	RESULT CLAUSE
present indicative	present indicative	imperfect subjunctive	conditional indicative (simple tense) imperfect subjunctive, **-ra** form only
present indicative	future indicative	pluperfect subjunctive	conditional perfect (compound tense) pluperfect subjunctive, **-ra** form only

◆ Use the imperfect or pluperfect subjunctive in **como si** constructions.

Rick me miró **como si yo estuviera** loco.	*Rick looked at me as if I were crazy.*

The message in **si yo estuviera loco** is hypothetical. (I know I am not crazy.)

Los candidatos actuaban **como si hubieran ganado** las elecciones.	*The candidates acted as if they had won the election.*

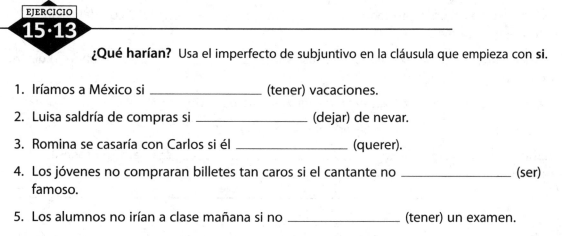

EJERCICIO 15·13

¿Qué harían? Usa el imperfecto de subjuntivo en la cláusula que empieza con **si**.

1. Iríamos a México si _____ (tener) vacaciones.

2. Luisa saldría de compras si _____ (dejar) de nevar.

3. Romina se casaría con Carlos si él _____ (querer).

4. Los jóvenes no compraran billetes tan caros si el cantante no _____ (ser) famoso.

5. Los alumnos no irían a clase mañana si no _____ (tener) un examen.

6. Yo iría hoy al cine si la película _____ (ser) buena.

EJERCICIO 15·14

Si pudiéramos vivir una fantasía. ¿Subjuntivo o indicativo? Subraya la respuesta correcta.

1. Carlos haría películas en Hollywood si (puede | pudiera).

2. Luisa será reina de belleza si (compite | compitiera) en el concurso (*pageant*).

3. Yo compraría un equipo de sonido nuevo si (tengo | tuviera) más dinero.

4. Cenicienta no se habría casado con el príncipe si no (pierde | hubiese perdido) la zapatilla de cristal.

5. El atleta corría como si (podía | pudiera) ganar la carrera.

6. Nosotros ganaremos el premio si (compramos | compráramos) unos boletos.

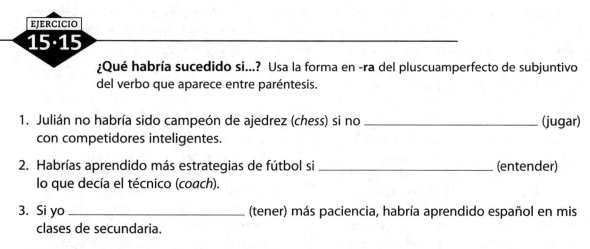

EJERCICIO 15·15

¿Qué habría sucedido si...? Usa la forma en **-ra** del pluscuamperfecto de subjuntivo del verbo que aparece entre paréntesis.

1. Julián no habría sido campeón de ajedrez (*chess*) si no _____ (jugar) con competidores inteligentes.

2. Habrías aprendido más estrategias de fútbol si _____ (entender) lo que decía el técnico (*coach*).

3. Si yo _____ (tener) más paciencia, habría aprendido español en mis clases de secundaria.

4. Habríamos sido más tolerantes con Raúl si nosotros _____ (escuchar) sus comentarios a tiempo.

The subjunctive mood past tenses: the imperfect and the pluperfect subjunctive **181**

5. Habría estado Ud. más informado si _____ (leer) con detalle el informe que le envié ayer.

6. Obviamente, yo habría comprado esta casa si _____ (ahorrar) dinero en mi cuenta de banco.

7. Habrían podido descansar más el fin de semana pasado si Uds. _____ (hacer) todo su trabajo.

8. Habrías sido más ágil y flexible si _____ (salir) a correr todas las mañanas.

EJERCICIO
15·16

Y en tu caso... ¿Es verdadero o falso?

_____ 1. No iría al cine si subieran los precios de las entradas.

_____ 2. Entendería mejor el uso del subjuntivo en español si estudiara más.

_____ 3. Sería feliz si tuviera la oportunidad de trabajar en un circo.

_____ 4. Si fuera más alto(a), jugaría al baloncesto profesionalmente.

_____ 5. Si ahorro el 10% de mi sueldo podría comprar una motocicleta nueva.

EJERCICIO
15·17

Si prestáramos atención protegeríamos el medio ambiente. Traduce. Usa el **Vocabulario útil**.

It is necessary to keep the balance of nature to preserve human and animal life. Had we not destroyed many natural resources, we would have been able to maintain a better economic and social situation in our world. Had we not ignored the consequences, we would have saved many tropical forests. We consume too much energy, and that is a problem. Yet we all want to drive a car, have electric appliances at home, and live a comfortable life. If we used more solar energy, wind energy, and other renewable energy, we would protect the environment. And if we protected endangered species in a park, we would promote ecotourism. We would help our planet if we took measures to protect the environment.

Vocabulario útil

balance of nature	**el equilibrio de la naturaleza**	to consume	**consumir**
		to pay attention	**prestar atención**
endangered species	**la especie en peligro de extinción**	to promote	**fomentar, promover**
		to save	**salvar**
environment	**el medio ambiente**	to take measures	**tomar medidas**
natural resource	**el recurso natural**	tropical forest	**la selva tropical**
renewable energy	**la energía renovable**	wind energy	**la energía eólica**
to conserve	**preservar**		

The commands

Commands (**los mandatos**) in the imperative mood (**el imperativo**) are used to give direct orders, instructions, or advice. A command can only be given directly to the second-person *you*, singular or plural. Review the subject pronouns used in Spanish to designate the second person.

◆ Familiar singular: **tú** Familiar plural: **vosotros/vosotras**

◆ Formal (polite) singular: Formal (polite) plural: **ustedes (Uds.)**
  usted (Ud.)

All four are the equivalent of *you* in English. As in English, the subject pronoun is generally *not* used in the Spanish imperative. When used in Spanish, the subject pronoun usually follows the imperative form. In formal commands, it signals extra politeness. Occasionally, the subject pronoun is used with familiar commands; there it emphasizes or clarifies the subject.

Entre Ud., ¡por favor!	***Come in**, please!*
Estudia tú y pasarás el examen.	***Study** and you'll pass the exam.*

Actions in the imperative mood are always in the present. Adverbial expressions of time may be used to stress the urgency of the message or to direct the listener to follow the command at a certain time.

Abre la puerta.	***Open** the door.*
Contesta el teléfono **ahora**.	***Answer** the phone **now**.*

If the speaker expects the action to be carried out later, he or she may indicate the time with appropriate adverbs or adverbial phrases.

Paga la cuenta **la semana que viene**.	***Pay** the bill **next week**.*
Trae el dinero **mañana**.	***Bring** the money **tomorrow**.*

With affirmative or negative commands, the speaker tells another person or persons to do or not do an action.

Guarden los libros ya.	***Put** the books **away** immediately.*
No bailen ahora.	***Don't dance** now.*

We may encourage or admonish ourselves to do or not do something by using the second-person *you* (**tú**).

Y me digo a mí mismo: "Alberto, **toca** el piano de una vez".	*And I say to myself: "Alberto, once and for all, (**go**) **play** the piano."*

Under special conditions, the infinitive is an alternative to the use of the imperative forms. An infinitive may be used instead of a command

♦ with instructions or recipes.

Ver las notas de la página 25.   *Look at the notes on page 25.*

♦ on public signs.

No fumar.   *No smoking.*

All languages have a system or set of rules based on social status, age, etiquette, degree of familiarity, etc., to properly address your interlocutor. You must consider all these factors before giving a direct command. In Spanish, remember to follow these rules as you choose whether to address a listener with a formal or a familiar command.

Formal or polite commands

Forms of the present subjunctive in Spanish echo many of the forms of the imperative. (If you have not yet studied the subjunctive, you will use your knowledge of the imperative when you tackle the subjunctive.) Thus in this unit, we present the formation of the imperative in two ways: (1) based on the present subjunctive forms, and (2) based on the present indicative **yo** form.

To form an *affirmative or negative formal (polite) command*, use the present subjunctive **usted** form for the singular and the **ustedes** form for the plural. These forms are the same in the present subjunctive and the imperative in all regular verbs, in most irregular verbs, and in verbs with stem and spelling changes (**mire**, **diga**, **no se vaya**).

If you have not yet studied the subjunctive, you can use the **yo** form of the present indicative and follow these steps.

♦ Drop the **-o** of the **yo** form.

♦ Add the corresponding ending according to each person, as follows.

cantar (*to sing*) (cant-o)	comer (*to eat*) (com-o)	recibir (*to receive*) (recib-o)
cant**e** Ud. cant**en** Uds.	com**a** Ud. com**an** Uds.	recib**a** Ud. recib**an** Uds.

Observe that in the formal (polite) imperative,

♦ **-er** and **-ir** regular verbs have the same endings.

♦ the plural form **ustedes** is formed by adding **-n** to the singular **Ud.** form.

♦ if used, the pronouns **Ud.** and **Uds.** usually follow the imperative forms and indicate politeness.

♦ negative commands add **no** before the affirmative command.

♦ the **yo** present indicative form will help you remember the imperative forms of all verbs.

♦ exclamation points may be used to indicate the speaker's voice modulation.

Escuche Ud. las instrucciones antes de empezar el examen.   *Listen to the instructions before starting the exam.*
¡**No abra Ud.** el cuaderno todavía!   *Do not open the booklet yet!*

En el correo. Usa la forma **Ud.** del imperativo del verbo que aparece entre paréntesis.

1. _____ (abrir) Ud. la puerta de la oficina.

2. _____ (pasar) Ud. al mostrador (*counter*).

3. _____ (escribir) Ud. la dirección claramente.

4. _____ (leer) las instrucciones del formulario.

5. _____ (depositar) la carta en el buzón.

6. _____ (comprar) las estampillas nuevas para su colección de sellos.

The same endings appear in the formal commands of all verbs: regular, irregular, and those with spelling and stem changes in the present indicative. A quick review of verbs with spelling changes follows. For a more detailed study of verbs with spelling changes, review the unit on the present indicative (Unit 1).

- ◆ Verbs ending in **-gar** change **g** to **gu** before the **-e** ending.

  pagar (*to pay*)   pa**gu**e Ud., pa**gu**en Uds.

- ◆ Verbs ending in **-ger** or **-gir** change **g** to **j** before the **-a** ending.

  escoger (*to choose*)   esco**j**a Ud., esco**j**an Uds.

- ◆ Verbs ending in **-guir** change **gu** to **g** before the **-a** ending.

  extinguir (*to extinguish*)   extin**g**a Ud., extin**g**an Uds.

- ◆ Verbs ending in **-cer** and **-cir** change **c** to **z** before the **-a** ending.

  convencer (*to convince*)   conven**z**a Ud., conven**z**an Uds.

- ◆ Verbs ending in **-car** change **c** to **qu** before the **-e** ending.

  tocar (*to touch*)   to**qu**e Ud., to**qu**en Uds.

- ◆ Verbs ending in **-zar** change **z** to **c** before the **-e** ending.

  comenzar (*to begin*)   comien**c**e Ud., comien**c**en Uds.

You may wish to review the conjugation of regular verbs, as well as verbs with stem and spelling changes, in the present indicative (Units 1, 2, and 3).

EJERCICIO
16·2

En el aeropuerto. Los viajeros escuchan las instrucciones antes de subir al avión. Usa la forma **ustedes** del imperativo del verbo entre paréntesis.

1. Por favor, _____ (seguir) las instrucciones.

2. _____ (escoger) sus asientos en el avión.

3. _____ (obtener) su tarjeta de embarque (*boarding pass*).

4. _____ (mostrar) su documentación al guardia de seguridad.

5. _____ (recoger) sus objetos personales.

6. No _____ (llegar) tarde a la puerta de embarque (*gate*).

EJERCICIO
16·3

En español. Instrucciones a los empleados del hotel La Gaviota. Usa la forma **ustedes** del imperativo.

1. *Do not arrive late to work.* _____

2. *Greet the guest* (**el huésped**). _____

3. *Take the luggage to the room.* _____

4. *Turn on the lights in the room.* _____

5. *Do not ask* (**hacer preguntas**) *indiscreet questions.*

_____

6. *Close the door and go back to the front desk* (**la recepción**).

_____

Irregular forms of formal commands

The following verbs have an irregular first-person form in the present indicative. The corresponding formal commands are as follows.

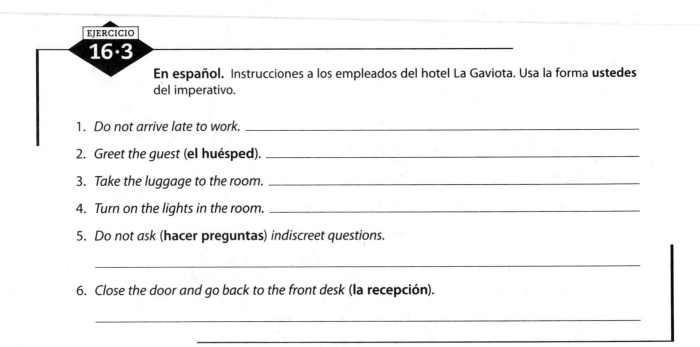

INFINITIVE	PRESENT INDICATIVE	FORMAL SINGULAR	FORMAL PLURAL
dar (*to give*)	yo **doy**	**dé** Ud.	**den** Uds.
estar (*to be*)	yo **estoy**	**esté** Ud.	**estén** Uds.
ir (*to go*)	yo **voy**	**vaya** Ud.	**vayan** Uds.
saber (*to know*)	yo **sé**	**sepa** Ud.	**sepan** Uds.
ser (*to be*)	yo **soy**	**sea** Ud.	**sean** Uds.

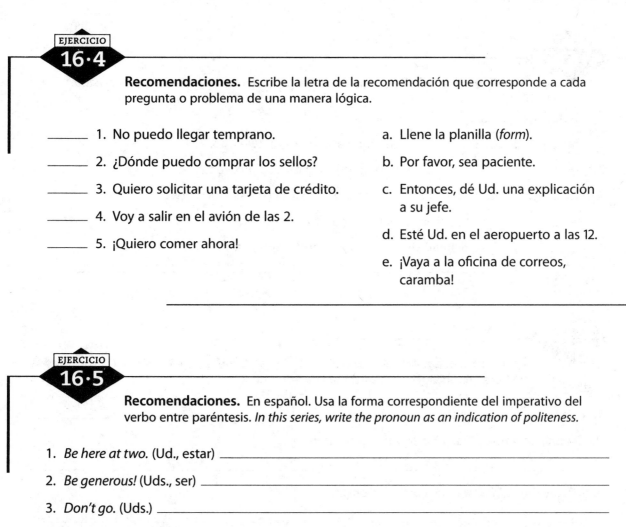

EJERCICIO 16·4

Recomendaciones. Escribe la letra de la recomendación que corresponde a cada pregunta o problema de una manera lógica.

_____ 1. No puedo llegar temprano.

_____ 2. ¿Dónde puedo comprar los sellos?

_____ 3. Quiero solicitar una tarjeta de crédito.

_____ 4. Voy a salir en el avión de las 2.

_____ 5. ¡Quiero comer ahora!

a. Llene la planilla (*form*).

b. Por favor, sea paciente.

c. Entonces, dé Ud. una explicación a su jefe.

d. Esté Ud. en el aeropuerto a las 12.

e. ¡Vaya a la oficina de correos, caramba!

EJERCICIO 16·5

Recomendaciones. En español. Usa la forma correspondiente del imperativo del verbo entre paréntesis. *In this series, write the pronoun as an indication of politeness.*

1. *Be here at two.* (Ud., estar) _____

2. *Be generous!* (Uds., ser) _____

3. *Don't go.* (Uds.) _____

4. *Know the truth.* (Ud.) _____

5. *Don't give money.* (Uds.) _____

When are formal commands used in Spanish?

As customs become more relaxed, addressing a listener or an audience in an informal tone is more prevalent in many areas of the Spanish-speaking world. However, it is still customary to use the formal commands when giving a direct command to a person or persons

- to whom you owe respect because of title, rank, or age.

- whom you are meeting for the first time or whom you consider unfamiliar. (Children and teenagers generally use the familiar forms among themselves, even at first meeting.)

- whom you are unsure how to address.

- whom you encounter in business, commercial, or professional settings. (It is generally safer for travelers, tourists, and other nonnative speakers to adhere to the formal form until they have made some native-speaker friends who suggest switching to the familiar form.)

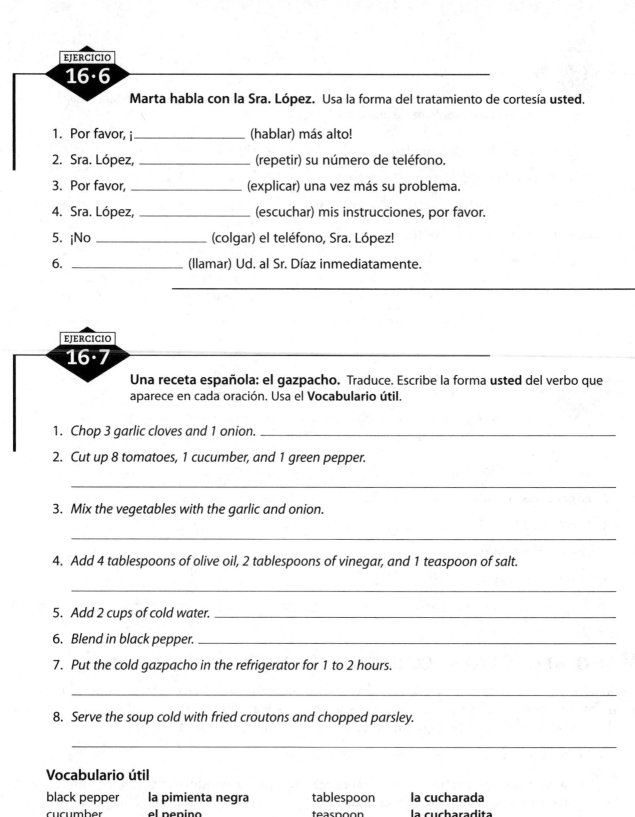

EJERCICIO 16·6

Marta habla con la Sra. López. Usa la forma del tratamiento de cortesía **usted**.

1. Por favor, ¡_____ (hablar) más alto!

2. Sra. López, _____ (repetir) su número de teléfono.

3. Por favor, _____ (explicar) una vez más su problema.

4. Sra. López, _____ (escuchar) mis instrucciones, por favor.

5. ¡No _____ (colgar) el teléfono, Sra. López!

6. _____ (llamar) Ud. al Sr. Díaz inmediatamente.

EJERCICIO 16·7

Una receta española: el gazpacho. Traduce. Escribe la forma **usted** del verbo que aparece en cada oración. Usa el **Vocabulario útil**.

1. *Chop 3 garlic cloves and 1 onion.* _____

2. *Cut up 8 tomatoes, 1 cucumber, and 1 green pepper.*

_____

3. *Mix the vegetables with the garlic and onion.*

_____

4. *Add 4 tablespoons of olive oil, 2 tablespoons of vinegar, and 1 teaspoon of salt.*

_____

5. *Add 2 cups of cold water.* _____

6. *Blend in black pepper.* _____

7. *Put the cold gazpacho in the refrigerator for 1 to 2 hours.*

_____

8. *Serve the soup cold with fried croutons and chopped parsley.*

_____

Vocabulario útil

black pepper	**la pimienta negra**	tablespoon	**la cucharada**
cucumber	**el pepino**	teaspoon	**la cucharadita**
fried croutons	**el pan frito**	to add	**añadir**
garlic clove	**el diente de ajo**	to blend, mix	**mezclar**
green pepper	**el pimiento verde**	to chop	**picar**
olive oil	**el aceite de oliva**	to cut up	**cortar**
onion	**la cebolla**	to fry	**freír (e > i)**
parsley	**el perejil**	to serve	**servir (e > i)**
salt	**la sal**	tomato	**el tomate**

En español. Delia escucha las instrucciones para dejar el auto en el aeropuerto. Usa la forma **usted**.

1. *Arrive (**llegar**) at the first stop sign.* _____

2. *Turn left at the corner.* _____

3. *Drive five blocks and turn right.* _____

4. *Pay the toll (**el peaje**) at the tollbooth (**la caseta**).*

   _____

5. *Park the car in our garage.* _____

6. *Leave your keys in the car.* _____

Informal (tú) affirmative command forms

Refer to the conjugations of the present indicative (Units 1, 2, and 3) to learn the familiar affirmative **tú** command forms of regular and irregular verbs, as well as verbs with stem and spelling changes.

For the familiar affirmative commands, use the third-person singular form of the present indicative. That is, drop the infinitive ending **-ar**, **-er**, or **-ir** from the radical and add the corresponding ending for **él/ella**. This form and the imperative **tú** form are the same.

comprar (*to buy*)	aprender (*to learn*)	escribir (*to write*)
compr**a**	aprend**e**	escrib**e**

Compra los lápices.   ***Buy** the pencils.*
¡Aprende las reglas!   ***Learn** the rules!*
¡Escribe la carta ahora!   ***Write** the letter now!*

Note that

- **tú** affirmative commands of **-er** and **-ir** verbs have the same endings.

- exclamation points (inverted before the sentence, and normal after the sentence) may be used to indicate the speaker's urgency.

- context and punctuation will help you distinguish the third-person singular present indicative from the imperative forms. For example, a comma tells you the speaker is addressing a person with the imperative.

  Alicia, trae la botella.   ***Alicia, bring** the bottle.*
  Alicia trae la botella.   ***Alicia brings** the bottle.*

- the speaker's tone and inflection will also tell you that an utterance such as the first of the next two examples is a command.

  ¡Lee el mensaje!   ***Read** the message!*
  Lee el mensaje.   *He/She reads the message.*

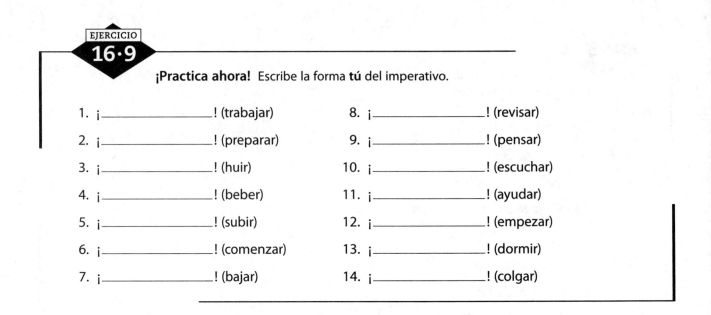

¡Practica ahora! Escribe la forma **tú** del imperativo.

1. ¡_____! (trabajar)   8. ¡_____! (revisar)

2. ¡_____! (preparar)   9. ¡_____! (pensar)

3. ¡_____! (huir)   10. ¡_____! (escuchar)

4. ¡_____! (beber)   11. ¡_____! (ayudar)

5. ¡_____! (subir)   12. ¡_____! (empezar)

6. ¡_____! (comenzar)   13. ¡_____! (dormir)

7. ¡_____! (bajar)   14. ¡_____! (colgar)

Irregular forms of familiar (tú) affirmative commands

Some frequently used verbs have irregular familiar (**tú**) forms for the affirmative commands.

INFINITIVE	FAMILIAR (**tú**) AFFIRMATIVE COMMAND
decir	**di**
hacer	**haz**
ir	**ve**
poner	**pon**
salir	**sal**
ser	**sé**
tener	**ten**
venir	**ven**

Consejos. Escoge el verbo apropiado para cada oración. Usa la forma **tú** del imperativo de la lista para completar la oración.

hacer   poner   venir   decir   ir

1. _____ siempre la verdad.

2. _____ un favor a quien lo necesite.

3. _____ a visitar a un amigo si está triste.

4. _____ todo tu esfuerzo en tu educación.

5. _____ a mi casa cuando me necesites.

Luisa da consejos a su hija. En español. Usa la forma **tú** del imperativo.

1. *Put your books here.* _____

2. *Do the homework.* _____

3. *Tell the truth.* _____

4. *Be careful* (**tener**). _____

5. *Go to school now.* _____

6. *Be good.* _____

Tú negative command forms

Negative familiar (**tú**) command forms are different from the affirmative familiar commands. They are identical to the **tú** form of the present subjunctive of each verb. Another way to create these forms is to add **-s** to the formal **Ud.** command of each verb.

INFINITIVE	FORMAL (**Ud.**) NEGATIVE COMMAND	FAMILIAR (**tú**) NEGATIVE COMMAND
pesc**ar** (*to fish*)	no pesque Ud.	no pesques
cos**er** (*to sew*)	no cosa Ud.	no cosas
sufr**ir** (*to suffer*)	no sufra Ud.	no sufras

Note that there are no irregular **tú** negative command forms. The above rule holds for the entire verb system.

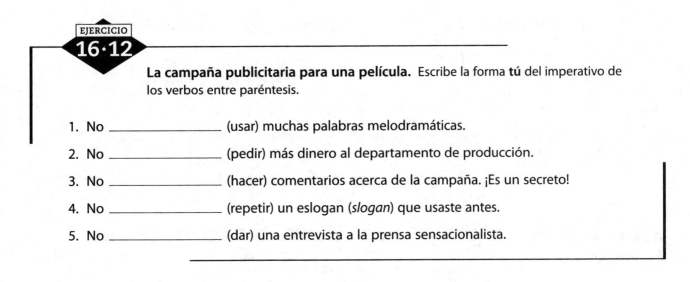

La campaña publicitaria para una película. Escribe la forma **tú** del imperativo de los verbos entre paréntesis.

1. No _____ (usar) muchas palabras melodramáticas.

2. No _____ (pedir) más dinero al departamento de producción.

3. No _____ (hacer) comentarios acerca de la campaña. ¡Es un secreto!

4. No _____ (repetir) un eslogan (*slogan*) que usaste antes.

5. No _____ (dar) una entrevista a la prensa sensacionalista.

Dora ayuda a su abuelo. Escribe la forma apropiada del imperativo de los verbos entre paréntesis. Usa la persona **tú**.

1. _____ (Venir) a la cocina. No _____ (ir) a tu casa antes de ayudarme.

2. _____ (Escribir) la lista de mis medicinas. No _____ (olvidar) la aspirina.

3. _____ (Sacar) el dinero del cajón. No _____ (perder) el recibo.

4. _____ (Devolver) este jarabe. No _____ (comprar) este producto otra vez.

5. _____ (Leer) las etiquetas con cuidado. No _____ (traer) pasta de dientes.

6. _____ (Salir) ahora. ¡No _____ (demorar) mucho!

Consejos para la salud. Usa la forma **tú** de los mandatos del verbo entre paréntesis.

1. ¿Tienes alto el colesterol? No _____ (comer) mucha carne y _____ (consumir) más vegetales.

2. ¿Quieres bajar de peso? _____ (Hacer) ejercicio o _____ (correr) tres veces a la semana.

3. ¿Estás muy cansado? _____ (Dormir) por lo menos ocho horas cada día y no _____ (beber) café.

4. ¿Deseas hacer otras actividades? _____ (Jugar) al tenis conmigo o _____ (ir) al cine con tu novia.

5. ¿Te sientes agitado? _____ (Respirar) profundo y _____ (pensar) en tu deporte favorito.

Plural familiar (**vosotros**) affirmative command forms

Vosotros is the plural familiar pronoun, used in Spain. To form the plural familiar affirmative command of each verb, drop the **-r** of the infinitive and add **-d**.

INFINITIVE	vosotros AFFIRMATIVE COMMAND
bailar (*to dance*)	bailad
saber (*to know*)	sabed
huir (*to flee*)	huid

¡Chicos, **comed** la tortilla!   *Boys, **eat** the omelet!*

This form is used primarily in Spain (except in the Canary Islands, off the coast of West Africa).

EJERCICIO
16·15

En un concierto. Escribid las respuestas. Usad la forma **vosotros** del imperativo.

1. _____ (comprar) las entradas.

2. _____ (leer) el programa.

3. _____ (escuchar) los gritos de los fanáticos.

4. _____ (despertar) a Luis, que está dormido.

5. _____ (aplaudir) al guitarrista.

Vosotros negative command forms

The **vosotros** negative command and the second-person plural of the present subjunctive forms are the same.

INFINITIVE	vosotros NEGATIVE COMMAND
pintar (*to paint*)	No pint**éis**
beber (*to drink*)	No beb**áis**
salir (*to go out*)	No salg**áis**

◆ To create the **vosotros** negative command without reference to the subjunctive, first note that it is based on the **yo** form of the present indicative of any verb. Drop the -**o** and add the corresponding ending.

remar (*to row*) (**rem**-o)	**vender** (*to sell*) (**vend**-o)	**recibir** (*to receive*) (**recib**-o)
No rem**éis**	No vend**áis**	No recib**áis**

◆ -**Er** and -**ir** verb endings are the same in the **vosotros** negative commands.

◆ All the forms in all conjugations have an accent mark.

◆ The **yo** form, minus the -**o** ending, is the stem for all regular verbs, verbs with spelling changes, and some irregular verbs or those with stem changes.

No sirváis la cerveza si no está fría.   ***Don't serve** the beer if it is not cold.*
¡**No conduzcáis** tan de prisa!   ***Do not drive** so fast!*

Irregular forms of **vosotros** negative commands

The **vosotros** negative command forms of **ir**, **saber**, and **ser** have the same stem as the **usted** command.

INFINITIVE	**Ud.** COMMAND	**vosotros** NEGATIVE COMMAND
ir (*to go*)	**vaya** Ud.	No **vayáis**
saber (*to know*)	**sepa** Ud.	No **sepáis**
ser (*to be*)	**sea** Ud.	No **seáis**

EJERCICIO
16·16

En español. Usa la forma **vosotros**.

1. *Don't play ball! Play* (**tocar**) *the piano.*

   _____

2. *Do not close the envelopes! Write the address first.*

   _____

3. *Do not go now! Wait ten minutes more.*

   _____

4. *Do not pay the bill yet! Add the tip* (**propina**).

   _____

5. *Don't cut the tomatoes! Peel* (**pelar**) *the cucumbers* (**pepinos**).

   _____

When are informal (tú) commands used in Spanish?

Use informal (**tú**) commands in all familiar situations

   ◆ among family members, established colleagues, friends, classmates, etc.

   ◆ when addressing children and adolescents and pets.

   ◆ if a familiar relationship has already been established between two or more people.

Commands and the position of reflexive and object pronouns

In Spanish, reflexive and direct and indirect object pronouns usually precede the verb in a sentence. If a verb has two object pronouns, the indirect precedes the direct object pronoun. In the command forms, before placing the object pronouns, you need to know whether the command is negative or affirmative.

With *negative* commands, follow these general rules.

- Place the pronouns before the command.

No te levantes antes de terminar.	*Do not get up before you finish.*
Llama a Juan. **No lo dejes pasar.**	*Call Juan. **Do not let him go.***
No le digas la verdad.	*Do not tell her/him the truth.*

- With double object pronouns, place the indirect pronoun *before* the direct object pronoun.

No te pongas el sombrero. **¡No te lo pongas!**	*Do not put on your hat. **Don't put it on!***

  Remember that indirect object pronouns **le** and **les** change to **se** if followed by the direct object pronouns **lo, la, los,** or **las.**

No le des el dinero a ese hombre. **¡No se lo des!**	*Do not give the money to that man. **Do not give it to him!***

With *affirmative* commands, the pronouns follow different rules.

- Attach the pronoun to the command form of the verb.

Dale el paraguas.	*Give him/her the umbrella.*
Levántate.	*Get up.*
Diles la verdad. **¡Dísela!**	*Tell them the truth. **Tell it to them!***

  Note that a written accent mark appears on the stressed syllable of these commands if the syllable is next to last (minus the attached pronoun) (**levántate**). There is no accent mark when a single pronoun is added to a one-syllable command (**diles**).

- Drop the **-d** of the affirmative **vosotros** command before adding a reflexive pronoun.

¡Callaos, por favor!	*Be quiet, please!*

En el garaje. ¡Practica! Sustituye los sustantivos subrayados con los pronombres correspondientes. *Attach the pronouns to the verb.*

EJEMPLO   Compra la revista aquí. _____ *Cómprala.* _____

1. Cambia el aceite del auto.   _____

2. Lava el auto.   _____

3. Llena el tanque de gasolina.   _____

4. Limpia las ventanillas.   _____

5. Revisa las llantas.   _____

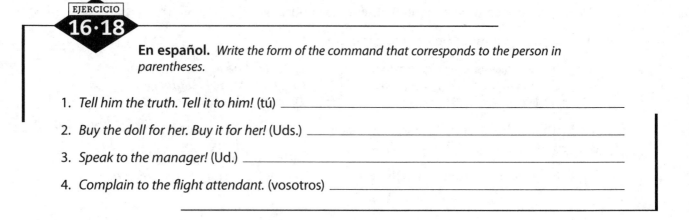

En español. *Write the form of the command that corresponds to the person in parentheses.*

1. *Tell him the truth. Tell it to him!* (tú) _____

2. *Buy the doll for her. Buy it for her!* (Uds.) _____

3. *Speak to the manager!* (Ud.) _____

4. *Complain to the flight attendant.* (vosotros) _____

Other ways of expressing a command (nosotros)

The **nosotros** commands are not actually a form of the imperative. They are, in fact, the **nosotros** form of the present subjunctive. *Let us* or *Let's* is used in English to express this idea. This form is used to invite or urge others to do or not do something, often when we ourselves may play a part. You may often find it in slogans, commercials, and so on.

Hablemos con los clientes ahora.	*Let us speak to the clients now.*
Toquemos la guitarra y **bailemos**.	*Let's play the guitar and let's dance.*
¡No volvamos aquí jamás!	*Let's not come back here ever again!*

The **nosotros** command form can also be derived from the present indicative. To form the **nosotros** commands of regular verbs, use the **yo** form of the present indicative.

- Drop the **-o** or **-oy** of the ending.

- Add the corresponding endings, as follows.

INFINITIVE	**nosotros** COMMAND
levant**ar** (*to raise*)	levant**emos**
le**er** (*to read*)	le**amos**
recib**ir** (*to receive*)	recib**amos**

- Add **no** before the verb to make a negative command.

No leamos esta revista.	*Let's not read this magazine.*

Un ensayo (rehearsal) **en el teatro.** ¡Practiquemos! Escribe la forma **nosotros** de los mandatos de los verbos entre paréntesis.

1. _____ (cambiar) los papeles.

2. _____ (recitar) las líneas.

3. _____ (hablar) en voz alta.

4. _____ (repasar) el final.

5. _____ (tomar) fotos.

6. No _____ (enojar) al director.

7. _____ (comprar) disfraces.

8. No _____ (olvidar) nada.

Remember the following rules regarding the **nosotros** command form.

◆ Spelling changes affect verbs ending in **-car**, **-gar**, **-zar**; as in other forms, they change to **qu**, **gu**, and **c**, respectively.

Eduquemos a nuestros jóvenes.	*Let us educate our youth.*
Carguemos estos paquetes.	*Let's pick up these packages.*
Comencemos este capítulo.	*Let us begin this chapter.*

◆ Only **-ir** stem-changing verbs show the following changes in the **nosotros** command form.

Verbs like **dormir** change **o** to **u**: durmamos.
Verbs like **mentir** change **e** to **i**: mintamos.
Verbs like **seguir** change **e** to **i**: sigamos.

Durmamos aquí esta noche.	*Let's sleep here tonight.*
No mintamos acerca de este asunto.	*Let's not lie about this matter.*
Sigamos este camino.	*Let's follow this road.*

◆ Attach pronouns as you would with other affirmative commands. Note that reflexive verbs drop the **-s** from the ending **-mos** of the verb before adding the reflexive pronoun **nos** to it: **probemos nos** (*let us try on*) turns into **probémonos**.

Levantémonos.	*Let's get up.*
Sirvámonos la cena.	*Let us serve ourselves dinner.*

◆ The verb **ir** and the reflexive **irse** are irregular in the affirmative command. Here are the forms.

¡Vamos! ¡Vámonos!	*Let's go! Let's go!*

The negative form is **No vayamos**.

◆ Frequently, **ir a** (in the **nosotros** form of the present indicative) + the infinitive substitutes for the affirmative command.

¡Vamos a nadar!	*Let's swim! (**Let's go swimming!**)*

EJERCICIO
16·20

Para estar más informados. Usa la forma **nosotros** de los mandatos de los infinitivos entre paréntesis.

1. _____ (navegar) (*surf*) en la Web.

2. _____ (investigar) esta noticia.

3. _____ (empezar) a trabajar.

4. _____ (buscar) las respuestas.

5. No _____ (hacer) comentarios ridículos.

Preparémonos para el concierto. *Replace the underlined direct objects with object pronouns and attach them to the verb.*

1. Alquilemos el teatro. _____

2. Dibujemos los carteles. _____

3. Compongamos nuevas canciones. _____

4. Incluyamos mi canción favorita. _____

5. Vendamos las entradas. _____

En la agencia de autos. Traduce. Usa el **Vocabulario útil**.

*I don't want to hear the ad again! "Visit (**Ud.**) us! Drive one of our new models! Leave us your old car and leave (depart) in your new car! Buy today and pay later! Compare our prices! Do not be fooled by other agencies! Take advantage of our end-of-the-year offer! Don't forget we have low-interest loans!" And then the voices of a couple who say: "Let's go now and let's buy the car of our dreams!" And I would tell them: "Don't be fooled! Don't pay an arm and a leg! Don't sign a contract for five years! Listen to this fool, and save money and headaches!"*

Vocabulario útil

ad	**el anuncio publicitario**	loan	**el préstamo**
agency	**la agencia**	to be fooled	**engañarse; dejarse engañar**
an arm and a leg	**un ojo de la cara**	to fool	**engañar**
auto dealer	**la agencia de autos**	to save	**ahorrar**
couple	**la pareja**	to take advantage	**aprovechar(se)**
end-of-the-year	**(el) final de año**		

Nouns and articles

Gender of nouns in Spanish: endings of nouns

Nouns (**los sustantivos**) designate people, places, actions, things, events, concrete or abstract ideas, and so on. In Spanish, nouns are either *feminine* or *masculine*, grammatically speaking. Sometimes, this classification will not make sense to the English-speaking learner of Spanish. **La mesa** (*table*) is not viewed as an object with a "feminine" nature, but as an inanimate object that is feminine because the ending (**la terminación**) in **-a** is an indication of grammatical gender: most nouns that end in **-a** are feminine in Spanish.

In Spanish, there are some general rules, which are not absolute, about the gender of nouns. In the examples that follow, the masculine article **el** and the feminine article **la** are placed before the nouns to indicate the gender. **El** and **la** are equivalent to the English definite article *the*.

Masculine nouns and their endings in Spanish

The general rule states that all nouns in Spanish are **sustantivos masculinos** or **sustantivos femeninos**. The gender is associated with specific word endings. The following endings generally indicate the masculine gender.

◆ Nouns that designate male beings generally (but not always) end in **-o**.

el cartero	mailman, mail carrier (masc.)
el general	general (*military*) (masc.)
el hombre	man
el profesor	(male) professor or teacher

◆ Most nouns ending in **-o** referring to animals, things, or ideas are masculine.

el año	year	**el queso**	cheese
el caballo	horse	**el zapato**	shoe
el catálogo	catalogue		

◆ However, some nouns that end in **-a** are masculine. Note that the following groups with the endings **-ía**, **-ma**, **-ama**, **-ema**, and **-oma** include many nouns that are cognates, that is, words that have similar spelling and meaning in English and Spanish.

el anagrama	anagram	**el idioma**	language
el aroma	aroma, fragrance	**el pentagrama**	pentagram
el clima	weather, climate	**el poema**	poem
el crucigrama	crossword puzzle	**el problema**	problem
el día	day	**el programa**	program
el dilema	dilemma	**el sistema**	system
el diploma	diploma	**el telegrama**	telegram
el emblema	emblem	**el tema**	theme
el fantasma	ghost, phantom	**el tranvía**	trolley (car)

Other groups of masculine nouns are

◆ nouns with the endings **-ambre** and **-aje**.

el alambre	wire	**el paisaje**	landscape
el calambre	cramp	**el pasaje**	passage, (train, bus) fare
el enjambre	swarm of bees	**el personaje**	character
el equipaje	luggage	**el salvaje**	savage
el montaje	setting		

◆ nouns that end in **-or** and **-án**.

el amor	love	**el refrán**	saying, proverb
el calor	heat	**el rencor**	hate
el diván	couch	**el sudor**	sweat
el imán	magnet	**el volcán**	volcano

Spanish has two contractions: **al** and **del**. They are combinations of the preposition **a** or **de** + the article **el**. **El** is the only form of the article that contracts with **a** or **de**. The contractions are not used if the article **el** is part of a proper noun.

No vamos **al cine** los lunes por la noche.   *We do not go **to the movies** on Monday nights.*
Éste es el juguete **del niño.**   *This is the **child's** toy.*

Notice the absence of the contraction in the next example; the article is part of the noun.

Le escribieron **de El Pardo**, una   *They wrote to him/her **from El Pardo**,*
población cerca de Madrid.   *a community near Madrid.*

EJERCICIO
17·1

Práctica. Con una **M**, indica los nombres que tienen una terminación (*ending*) masculina. Si no es masculina, escribe una **X**.

_____ 1. dolor (*pain*)

_____ 2. avión (*plane*)

_____ 3. maquillaje (*makeup*)

_____ 4. suspiro (*sigh*)

_____ 5. cabeza (*head*)

_____ 6. viaje (*trip*)

_____ 7. rumor (*rumor*)

_____ 8. visión (*vision*)

_____ 9. mensaje (*message*)

_____ 10. virtud (*virtue*)

_____ 11. síntoma (*symptom*)

_____ 12. belleza (*beauty*)

Feminine nouns and their endings in Spanish

The following endings generally identify feminine nouns.

◆ Nouns that identify female beings generally end in **-a**.

la enfermera	(female) nurse	**la profesora**	(female) professor
la hija	daughter	**la yegua**	mare (*horse*)

◆ Nearly all other nouns ending in **-a** are also feminine.

la cocina	kitchen	**la pelota**	ball
la guitarra	guitar	**la piscina**	pool
la maleta	suitcase		

◆ A few nouns ending in **-o** are feminine. With the exception of **la mano**, the other examples in this list are abbreviations of compound feminine nouns.

la foto (la fotografía)	photo, photograph
la mano	hand
la moto (la motocicleta)	motorcycle

◆ Nouns that end in **-ción** and **-sión** are feminine. These are often near cognates with English; note the similarities in spelling and meaning with the English equivalents.

la canción	song	**la exposición**	exposition, exhibit
la dirección	address; direction	**la inyección**	injection
la división	division	**la misión**	mission
la estación	station; season	**la pasión**	passion

◆ Nouns that have endings **-dad** and **-tad** are usually feminine. Many English equivalents are nouns ending in *-ty*.

la amistad	friendship	**la dignidad**	dignity
la ciudad	city	**la libertad**	liberty, freedom
la dificultad	difficulty	**la voluntad**	will

◆ Endings **-ie**, **-eza**, **-sis**, and **-itis** are generally feminine.

la crisis	crisis	**la serie**	series
la dermatitis	dermatitis	**la sinusitis**	sinusitis
la dosis	dosage, dose	**la tesis**	thesis
la especie	species	**la tristeza**	sadness
la riqueza	richness, riches		

◆ Nouns that end in **-tud** and **-umbre** are feminine. Many of these nouns designate abstract ideas. Most abstract nouns are feminine in Spanish.

la certidumbre	certainty	**la esclavitud**	slavery
la costumbre	custom, tradition	**la exactitud**	exactness, precision
la cumbre	summit, mountaintop	**la virtud**	virtue

EJERCICIO
17·2

El artículo y el género apropiado. Escribe la forma **el** o **la** del artículo para indicar si la palabra es del género femenino o masculino.

1. _____ enfermedad (*illness*)   5. _____ holograma   9. _____ temor (*fear*)

2. _____ pureza (*purity*)   6. _____ sociedad   10. _____ tranvía

3. _____ distracción   7. _____ leona   11. _____ eternidad

4. _____ pereza (*laziness*)   8. _____ explosión   12. _____ decencia

EJERCICIO
17·3

Vocabulario. Usa el sustantivo apropiado para cada oración.

el equipaje   la fealdad   la estación
el tenor   la dermatitis la dosis

1. _____ es una inflamación de la piel.

2. Debo tomar _____ apropiada de este medicamento.

3. _____ espera una ovación después del concierto.

4. Debes colocar _____ en el baúl (*trunk*) del auto.

5. El tren llega a _____ a las siete en punto.

6. _____ es lo opuesto de la belleza.

Other endings to consider for the gender of nouns

Some nouns do not fit into any of the previous groups. Memorization and frequent practice will help you learn their gender.

◆ Nouns ending in **-e** or in consonants not included in previous lists of noun endings may be either feminine or masculine.

el antifaz	mask		**la clase**	class
el cine	movies, movie house		**la cruz**	cross
el examen	exam		**la mente**	mind
el lápiz	pencil		**la miel**	honey
el merengue	meringue (*baked egg white*); merengue (*dance*)		**la vejez**	old age
el mes	month		**la vez**	turn; time

◆ Nouns designating professions and individuals may end in **-a**, **-ante**, **-e**, or **-ista**, and in general they may designate either a male or a female person. The article and adjectives, if expressed, normally agree in gender and number with the noun.

el/la atleta	athlete	**el/la pediatra**	pediatrician
el/la cantante	singer	**el/la periodista**	journalist
el/la gerente	manager	**el/la poeta**	poet
el/la intérprete	interpreter	**el/la turista**	tourist

◆ Nouns of professions, of people in general, and names of some animals that end in **-és**, **-n**, **-ón**, and **-or** are masculine. They add **-a** to create the feminine form and drop the accent mark (in the cases of **-és** and **-ón**).

el campeón / la campeona	champion
el director / la directora	principal, director
el león / la leona	lion
el profesor / la profesora	professor, teacher
el francés / la francesa	Frenchman, Frenchwoman

◆ Some nouns are spelled the same for the masculine and feminine, and only the article changes.

el joven / la joven	young man / young woman
el modelo / la modelo	male model / female model
el testigo / la testigo	(male) witness / (female) witness
el turista / la turista	(male) tourist / (female) tourist

El juez interrogó a **la testigo**.   *The judge interrogated the (female) witness*.

In English, the gender of this type of noun would be clarified by the context.

◆ Other nouns referring to people have different endings and articles for the masculine and feminine forms.

el muchacho / la muchacha	boy/girl
el niño / la niña	boy/girl/child
el novio / la novia	fiancé/fiancée

◆ Some nouns are *invariable*; that is, they designate both male and female individuals. Some of these end in **-a**, **-ente**, and **-ista**. The article *does not* change with invariable nouns. "Invariable" or "inv." will be noted in dictionary entries.

el ángel	angel	**la estrella**	star
el personaje	character	**la víctima**	victim
el ser	being		

Tu hermana es **un ángel**.   *Your sister is **an angel**.*
Bob es **la estrella** de este espectáculo.   *Bob is **the star** of this show.*

◆ Feminine nouns that begin with a stressed **a-** or **ha-** are feminine but, for purposes of pronunciation, take a masculine definite article in the singular form. Because they are feminine nouns, the feminine form of adjectives is used to modify them.

el agua (fem.)	water	**el arpa** (fem.)	harp
el águila (fem.)	eagle	**el aula** (fem.)	classroom
el alma (fem.)	soul	**el hacha** (fem.)	ax
el arma (fem.)	weapon	**el hambre** (fem.)	hunger

El agua fría es refrescante.   *Cold water is refreshing.*

Más vocabulario. Escribe la palabra y el artículo para completar la definición.

el águila	el arpa	el marqués	el hacha
la gerente	la campeona	la estrella	el mes

1. _____: instrumento musical de cuerdas.

2. _____: herramienta (*tool*) para cortar árboles.

3. _____: deportista que gana en las olimpiadas.

4. _____: persona que dirige una empresa.

5. _____: símbolo de los Estados Unidos.

6. _____: cuerpo celestial que brilla por la noche.

7. _____: título aristocrático.

8. _____: cada una de las doce partes en que se divide el año.

Other nouns and their gender

Certain groups of nouns are *masculine*.

- ◆ Days of the week and months of the year. Note that they are not capitalized in Spanish.

  El martes es mi cumpleaños.   *Tuesday is my birthday.*
  Éste ha sido **un diciembre** muy frío.   *This has been **a very cold December**.*

- ◆ Compound nouns. Note that these compounds usually consist of a verb + a noun. They end with an **-s** but are singular nouns.

el abrelatas	can opener	**el paraguas**	umbrella
el lavaplatos	dishwasher	**el sacacorchos**	corkscrew
el parabrisas	windshield	**el salvavidas**	lifeguard

- ◆ Nouns that name colors.

el amarillo	yellow	**el naranja**	orange
el azul	blue	**el negro**	black
el blanco	white	**el rojo**	red
el lila	lilac	**el rosado**	pink
el morado	purple	**el verde**	green

- ◆ Infinitives used as nouns. English equivalents are usually in the *-ing* form.

  El comer y **beber** mucho no son   *Eating and drinking a lot is not advisable.*
  recomendables.

Names of rivers, seas, and oceans.

El río Mississippi está en los Estados Unidos.

The Mississippi River is in the United States.

El mar Mediterráneo tiene playas fabulosas.

The Mediterranean Sea has fabulous beaches.

Note: The names of islands are *feminine*.

Las Malvinas están en el Atlántico y **las Galápagos** en el Pacífico.

The Malvinas are in the Atlantic and the Galápagos in the Pacific.

The names of many trees. However, the names of the fruit of these trees may be feminine.

los árboles de frutas (*fruit trees*)		las frutas (*fruits*)	
el cerezo	cherry tree	**la cereza**	cherry
el limonero	lemon tree	**el limón**	lemon
el manzano	apple tree	**la manzana**	apple
el naranjo	orange tree	**la naranja**	orange
el peral	pear tree	**la pera**	pear

Languages. Note that the names for languages are not capitalized in Spanish.

el alemán	German	**el inglés**	English
el árabe	Arabic	**el italiano**	Italian
el español	Spanish	**el japonés**	Japanese
el francés	French	**el portugués**	Portuguese

EJERCICIO 17·5

La respuesta apropiada. Repasa el vocabulario de los grupos de sustantivos en esta Unidad 17. Escribe el sustantivo y el artículo apropiado (**el, la**) para completar cada oración.

1. El árbol que da limón es _____.

2. El idioma oficial de Brasil es _____.

3. _____, _____ y _____ son los colores de la bandera de los Estados Unidos.

4. _____ es el árbol que da peras.

5. _____ es el primer día laboral de cada semana.

6. Necesitas _____ para limpiar los vasos y los cubiertos.

7. Para abrir la botella necesitas _____.

8. Cuando llueve, debes llevar _____ para protegerte de la lluvia.

9. _____ se habla en Austria, en parte de Suiza y en Alemania.

10. _____ Canarias están al noroeste de la costa de África.

One useful strategy to learn the gender of Spanish nouns is to study them in two ways: first, nouns with specific endings that indicate either feminine or masculine, and second, whole groups of nouns that are either masculine or feminine.

Two more groups deserve attention, especially because they include some very common words. These lists show words selected from these categories. Use them as a reference tool.

◆ Some nouns referring to people or animals may have different forms for the masculine and feminine. The articles, of course, change with the gender. Note the similarities of some of the English equivalents.

el actor / la actriz	actor/actress
el caballo / la yegua	horse/mare
el conde / la condesa	count/countess
el emperador / la emperatriz	emperor/empress
el héroe / la heroína	hero/heroine
el hombre / la mujer	man/woman
el marido, esposo / la esposa	husband/wife
el padre / la madre	father/mother
el príncipe / la princesa	prince/princess
el rey / la reina	king/queen
el varón / la hembra	male/female
el yerno / la nuera	son-in-law/daughter-in-law

◆ Some nouns have a different meaning if used with the masculine or the feminine article. Grammatical gender changes the meaning even though the word is spelled the same.

el capital / la capital	capital (*money*)/capital (*city*)
el cometa / la cometa	comet/kite
el corte / la corte	cut/court
el cura / la cura	priest/cure
el editorial / la editorial	newspaper editorial / publishing house
el frente / la frente	front/forehead
el guía / la guía	guide / female guide, telephone guide, or guidebook
el orden / la orden	order (*in a sequence*)/order (*command*)
el Papa / la papa	the Pope / potato
el policía / la policía	police officer / the police force

Note: The masculine or feminine article in Spanish may indicate a difference in size as in **el cesto / la cesta**, where the feminine indicates a larger basket. For certain words, albeit rare, the gender may be a matter of preference—as in **el mar / la mar**. Seamen tend to prefer **la mar** when they refer to the sea.

Note: Political correctness penetrates and affects language usage. The changes in the use of the gender of nouns show social evolution and preference for certain terms, for example, changes in the names of professions that formerly excluded women. In some areas of the Hispanic world, a woman appointed to a president's cabinet is called **la ministro** and in others, **la ministra**. Similarly, we see **la presidente** or **la presidenta**, as well as **la médica**, currently preferred as the feminine form of **el médico**. You will learn these preferences as you read up-to-date newspapers and magazines and listen to native speakers from different regions.

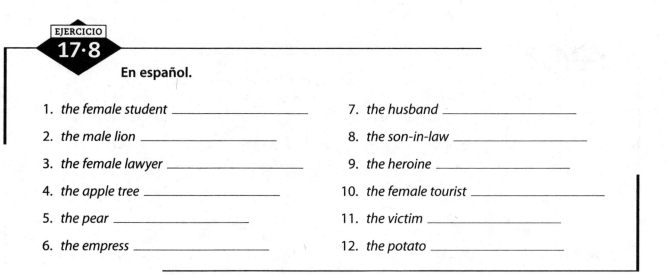

EJERCICIO 17·6

Más vocabulario. Escribe la forma femenina del sustantivo y el artículo.

1. el profesor _____

2. el maestro _____

3. el periodista _____

4. el rey _____

5. el pintor _____

6. el actor _____

7. el padre _____

8. el gerente _____

9. el caballo _____

10. el comandante _____

11. el artista _____

12. el bailarín _____

EJERCICIO 17·7

¿Verdadero o falso?

_____ 1. La médica probablemente trabaja en el hospital.

_____ 2. Muchos turistas necesitan una guía.

_____ 3. El francés es la lengua oficial de Alemania.

_____ 4. El orden es lo opuesto al desorden.

_____ 5. Las guerras son conflictos.

_____ 6. La papa es un vegetal.

EJERCICIO 17·8

En español.

1. *the female student* _____

2. *the male lion* _____

3. *the female lawyer* _____

4. *the apple tree* _____

5. *the pear* _____

6. *the empress* _____

7. *the husband* _____

8. *the son-in-law* _____

9. *the heroine* _____

10. *the female tourist* _____

11. *the victim* _____

12. *the potato* _____

Plural of nouns

The plural of nouns in Spanish is formed by adding the plural ending -**s** or -**es**. A definite article, **los** before masculine nouns and **las** before feminine nouns, indicates the plural of nouns. Follow these guidelines.

- For nouns that end in a vowel, add -**s**.

el café / los cafés	café/cafés	**la casa / las casas**	house/houses
el caso / los casos	case/cases	**la fruta / las frutas**	fruit/fruits
el vino / los vinos	wine/wines	**la niña / las niñas**	girl/girls

- For nouns that end in a consonant, add -**es**.

el papel / los papeles	paper/papers; role/roles
el reloj / los relojes	clock/clocks

Some spelling changes need to be observed.

- Singular nouns ending in -**z** change to -**ces** in the plural.

el lápiz / los lápices	pencil/pencils
la matriz / las matrices	matrix/matrices

- Nouns ending in -**í** and -**ú** add -**s** or -**es** and keep the accent mark in the plural. There are only a few nouns in this group.

el manatí / los manatís / los manatíes	manatee/manatees
el rubí / los rubís / los rubíes	ruby/rubies
el tabú / los tabús / los tabúes	taboo/taboos

- Nouns with accent marks on the last syllable lose the accent mark in the plural.

el camión / los camiones	truck/trucks
el francés / los franceses	Frenchman/Frenchmen
el león / los leones	lion/lions
el marqués / los marqueses	marquis/marquises

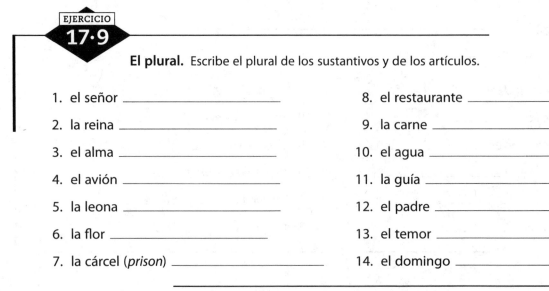

EJERCICIO
17·9

El plural. Escribe el plural de los sustantivos y de los artículos.

1. el señor _____

2. la reina _____

3. el alma _____

4. el avión _____

5. la leona _____

6. la flor _____

7. la cárcel (*prison*) _____

8. el restaurante _____

9. la carne _____

10. el agua _____

11. la guía _____

12. el padre _____

13. el temor _____

14. el domingo _____

Escribe el plural. Incluye la forma **los** o **las** del artículo en tu respuesta.

1. sopa _____
2. residencia _____
3. pasaje _____
4. mujer _____
5. reloj _____
6. española _____

7. bebé _____
8. mantel _____
9. rubí _____
10. canción _____
11. luz _____
12. región _____

More about the plural of nouns in Spanish

Some groups of nouns and their corresponding plurals are exceptions to the rules we have just studied. Note the plural of the following nouns.

◆ Nouns that end in **-s** do not change their spelling in the plural, if the final syllable is not stressed.

el miércoles / los miércoles	Wednesday/Wednesdays
el paraguas / los paraguas	umbrella/umbrellas
la tesis / las tesis	thesis/theses

All days of the week except **sábado** and **domingo** end in **-s**. The **los** form of the article identifies the plural form of **lunes**, **martes**, **miércoles**, etc.

Los lunes son siempre largos.   ***Mondays*** *are always long.*

◆ For compound words formed with two nouns, add the plural ending to the first element only.

el coche cama / los coches cama	sleeping car / sleeping cars
el hombre rana / los hombres rana	(deep-sea) diver/divers (*frogmen*)

◆ Some nouns are always plural in Spanish.

las afueras	the outskirts	**las vacaciones**	vacation
las cosquillas	tickling	**los binoculares**	binoculars
las gafas	eyeglasses	**los gemelos**	twins; cuff links
las tijeras	scissors	**los lentes**	eyeglasses; lenses

◆ Use the singular form of a noun when referring to parts of the body, items of personal hygiene, and clothing in statements such as the following.

Se lavan **la cara**.   *They wash **their faces**.*
Se ponen **el abrigo**.   *They put on **their coats**.*

En español.

1. *My vacation ends on Sunday.* _____

2. *I'm going to see the panthers (**panteras**) at the zoo tomorrow.*

_____

3. *Now, Lina and I put on our sunglasses.*

_____

4. *This hotel is on the outskirts of Madrid.*

_____

5. *We travel at night and rest in a sleeping car.*

_____

6. *Lina never brings her umbrella.* _____

Escoge. Usa la palabra apropiada de acuerdo al contexto.

las gafas	las tijeras	los domingos
las tesis	los binoculares	los gemelos

1. Pablo compra _____ de rubí para su camisa elegante.

2. Muchas personas no trabajan _____.

3. Desde su casa, Berta puede espiar a sus vecinos con _____.

4. No me gustan _____ que defienden mis enemigos.

5. Necesito _____ para cortar los papeles.

6. ¿Dónde están _____? No veo bien.

Definite articles

The definite articles (**artículos definidos**) have appeared in most of the examples and exercises in this unit. You are already familiar with their gender and number forms. The definite article introduces the noun it precedes and it agrees with it in gender and number. In English, *the* is the equivalent of four different forms in Spanish. English equivalents of Spanish nouns in context do not always include *the*.

◆ Feminine forms

la   las

> **La** luna es un satélite.   *The moon is a satellite.*
> **¡Las** vacaciones son siempre agradables!   *Vacations are always pleasant!*

◆ Masculine forms

el   los

> **El amor** es maravilloso.   *Love is wonderful.*
> **Los tigres** están en la jaula.   *The tigers are in the cage.*

EJERCICIO
17·13

¿Qué hacen estas personas? Escribe la forma apropiada del articulo definido: **el, los, la, las.**

1. _____ músicos prefieren _____ música pop.

2. _____ niños no piden _____ espárragos.

3. _____ orangutanes duermen en _____ árboles.

4. _____ senador enfrenta _____ crítica de sus opositores.

5. _____ meteorólogos estudian _____ tormentas.

6. _____ investigadoras escriben _____ reportajes.

7. _____ bailarines interpretan _____ ballet.

When are definite articles used in Spanish?

As we have already noted, in many instances where the definite article is necessary in Spanish, it is omitted in English.

> **Las mujeres** están presentes aquí.   *Women are present here.*

Using Spanish articles will take practice, since quite a few situations require their use in Spanish, but not in English. At times, it may appear that the use or omission of these articles is contrary to their use in the other language.

Use the definite articles in Spanish

◆ with nouns used in a general sense.

> **La comida española** es deliciosa.   *Spanish cuisine is delicious.*

◆ with days of the week. The English equivalent in this case is the preposition *on*.

> **El martes** tenemos un examen.   *On Tuesday, we have an exam.*
> No trabajamos **los domingos**.   *We do not work on Sundays.*

◆ with names of languages, except after **hablar**. Names of languages are not capitalized.

El alemán y **el inglés** no son lenguas romances.	*German* and *English* are not Romance languages.
No hablo **alemán**.	*I do not speak **German**.*

◆ with parts of the body, items of personal hygiene, and clothing. In English, the possessive adjective is used in these situations.

Me duele **la muela**.	*My tooth hurts.*

◆ to tell time.

Es **la una**.	*It is **one o'clock**.*
Son **las diez y media**.	*It is **ten thirty**.*

EJERCICIO
17·14

Un mensaje. Completa las oraciones con el artículo apropiado (**el, la, los, las**), solamente si es necesario.

1. _____ sección "Salud es vida", publicada todos 2. _____ martes, dice que

3. _____ espárragos son saludables. Si no hablas 4. _____ español, puedes leer

5. _____ artículos traducidos en la página escrita en 6. _____ inglés. ¿Te duele

7. _____ cabeza? Descansa, ya son 8. _____ seis de la tarde. ¿Te molesta

9. _____ luz? Cierra 10. _____ persianas y descansa en 11. _____ sofá de la sala.

EJERCICIO
17·15

En español.

1. *Today, I have an appointment at nine thirty in the morning.*

   _____

2. *I put on my coat and my gloves now before I leave.*

   _____

3. *The assistant to the dentist speaks Portuguese and Spanish.*

   _____

4. *My wisdom tooth (**la muela del juicio**) hurts.*

   _____

5. *Cavities may cause pain.* _____

6. *On Friday, I always get home late.* _____

7. *However, today I will go home around (**a eso de**) eleven thirty.*

_____

8. *I need to rest! My head is going to hurt, too.*

_____

More about the uses of definite articles in Spanish

The definite articles in Spanish are also required

- with names and titles.

El doctor Perdomo va a presentar a los invitados.	**Dr. Perdomo** *will introduce the guests.*
El director cerrará la sesión.	**The director** *will close the session.*

- with nouns that refer to weights and measurements. Note that the English equivalent takes the *indefinite* article.

Los huevos cuestan a un dólar **la docena**.	*Eggs cost one dollar **a dozen**.*
Y la harina se vende a cincuenta centavos **la libra**.	*And flour is sold at fifty cents **a pound**.*

- with nouns designating specific people and things.

Vi **el programa** que me recomendaste.	*I saw **the program** you recommended.*

- with last names referring to the members of a family in the plural, or referring to people who possess qualities associated with the people who bear those last names. Note that the proper names in this construction remain singular, while the articles are pluralized.

Los Martínez y **los López** no vienen a la fiesta.	*The **Martínezes** and the **Lópezes** are not coming to the party.*
Estos artistas son **los Dalí** y **Miró** del futuro.	*These artists are **the Dalís** and **the Mirós** of the future.*

- with nouns that refer to geographic places like rivers, mountains, bays, some cities, and regions.

El Amazonas está en Suramérica.	*The **Amazon River** is in South America.*
Los Pirineos son las montañas en la frontera entre Francia y España.	*The **Pyrenees** are mountains on the border between France and Spain.*
La Bahía de Cochinos está en el sur de Cuba.	*The **Bay of Pigs** is in the south of Cuba.*
La Mancha es famosa por el personaje Don Quijote.	*La **Mancha** is famous for the character Don Quixote.*

- with an infinitive functioning as a noun. The English equivalent is the present participle, with its *-ing* ending. The infinitive is usually used alone, but the definite article may be added for emphasis or style.

Dormir (**El dormir**) mucho no es bueno.	***Sleeping** a lot is not good.*

Frases en español. Si necesitas el artículo definido (**el, la, los, las**), escríbelo.

1. *a dime a dozen* _____

2. *the Goyas of today* _____

3. *the Lopezes* _____

4. *the United States* _____

5. *twelve dollars a yard* _____

6. *working hard* _____

7. *the Galapagos Islands* _____

8. *President Roosevelt* _____

9. *eating and drinking* _____

When are definite articles omitted in Spanish?

In a very few cases, the Spanish definite article is not used. Omit the definite article

◆ with titles when addressing the person, or with **San, Santo, Santa, Don**, and **Doña**.

Sra. Almendro, pase por favor.	*Mrs. Almendro, please come in.*
Santo Domingo es una ciudad caribeña.	*Santo Domingo is a Caribbean city.*
Aquí viene **Don Pedro**.	*Here comes Don Pedro.*

◆ with nouns that refer to academic subjects.

Estudia **matemáticas** y **sicología**.	*He/She studies mathematics and psychology.*

◆ with ordinal numbers used in titles.

Felipe **II** (**Segundo**)	*Philip the Second*

◆ when stating someone's occupation following a form of the verb **ser**.

Paulina **es terapeuta**.	*Paulina is a therapist.*
José **era maestro**.	*José was a teacher.*

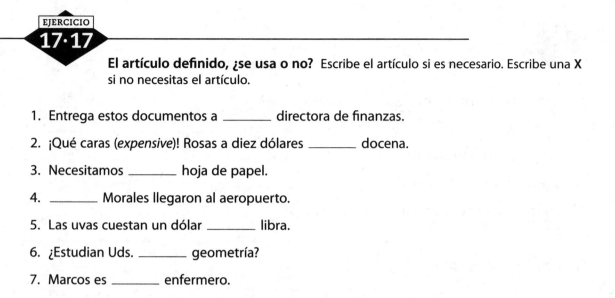

El artículo definido, ¿se usa o no? Escribe el artículo si es necesario. Escribe una **X** si no necesitas el artículo.

1. Entrega estos documentos a _____ directora de finanzas.

2. ¡Qué caras (*expensive*)! Rosas a diez dólares _____ docena.

3. Necesitamos _____ hoja de papel.

4. _____ Morales llegaron al aeropuerto.

5. Las uvas cuestan un dólar _____ libra.

6. ¿Estudian Uds. _____ geometría?

7. Marcos es _____ enfermero.

8. ¿Las galletas (*cookies*) cuestan tres dólares _____ docena?

Lo, the neuter article

In addition to the feminine and masculine gender forms, Spanish has a third "gender": the neuter. This form of the article is invariable. It is used in the following specific situations.

◆ Use **lo** + an adjective to communicate a quality or an abstract idea.

Siempre ves **lo malo** de las cosas.	*You always see **the bad side** of things.*

◆ Use **lo** + adjective or adverb + **que** to underscore the quality expressed by the adjective or adverb.

¿No ves **lo difícil** que está la vida?	*Don't you see **how difficult** life is?*
Veo **lo rápido** que trabajas.	*I see **how quickly** you work.*

Y en tu caso... ¿Es verdadero o falso?

_____ 1. Leer es mi pasatiempo favorito.

_____ 2. Estudio alemán y español.

_____ 3. El presidente de mi país es demócrata.

_____ 4. Lo bueno es lo rápido que aprendo español.

_____ 5. Ahorrar no es mi actividad preferida.

_____ 6. Voy al cine todos los martes.

_____ 7. Lo bueno es que no trabajo los fines de semana.

_____ 8. Ver los partidos de fútbol en televisión es mi pasión.

Preguntas personales. Contesta las preguntas en español.

1. ¿Prefieres lo romántico o lo emocionante? ¿Por qué?

_____

2. ¿Qué es lo aburrido para ti? _____

3. ¿Qué es lo curioso de la vida? _____

4. ¿Prefieres lo cómico o lo dramático en el teatro?

_____

5. ¿Y qué es lo mejor de la vida para ti?

_____

En español.

1. *Read the phrase "the good, the bad, and the ugly."*

_____

2. *The important thing is to study.* _____

3. *Swimming is the best exercise.* _____

4. *Carlos I is also Carlos V.* _____

5. *Look for the eagle in the picture.* _____

6. *This is Mr. Gómez's book.* _____

7. *We are not going to La Mancha.* _____

8. *Who does not want to visit the museum?*

_____

9. *The best thing is to sleep after the trip.*

_____

10. *See how easy this is!* _____

Indefinite articles

The indefinite article refers to one individual out of a general group. English has two forms: *a* and *an*. (*A* is used before words beginning with a consonant, and *an* before words beginning with a vowel sound.) In Spanish, indefinite articles have the same function but have two genders.

◆ Feminine forms

una   *a, an*   **unas**   *a few, some*

> **Una** pera es **una** fruta.   *A pear is **a** fruit.*
> **Unas** canciones, **una** guitarra y   *A **few** songs, **a** guitar, and we have **a** party.*
> tenemos **una** fiesta.

◆ Masculine forms

un   *a, an*   **unos**   *a few, some*

> Tengo **un** abrigo nuevo.   *I have **a** new overcoat.*
> Compramos **unos** sobres.   *We bought **a few** envelopes.*

EJERCICIO
17·21

Los artículos indefinidos. Escribe el artículo indefinido. *Review the nouns in Spanish as you complete this exercise.*

1. _____ vez
2. _____ temblor
3. _____ verdad
4. _____ pasaje

5. _____ hospital
6. _____ crisis
7. _____ rubí
8. _____ sofá

9. _____ escalera
10. _____ manatí
11. _____ capitán
12. _____ pensión

EJERCICIO
17·22

Ahora, los plurales. Escribe los plurales de los artículos y los sustantivos del Ejercicio 17-21.

1. _____
2. _____
3. _____
4. _____
5. _____
6. _____

7. _____
8. _____
9. _____
10. _____
11. _____
12. _____

When are indefinite articles used in Spanish?

In some situations, the use of the indefinite articles in English and Spanish is equivalent. Use the indefinite articles

- to refer to one individual in a general group.

| Una sinfonía es **una obra de arte**. | *A symphony is **a work of art**.* |

That is, among many works of art, **una sinfonía** stands out as an example.

- to identify a person with a noun indicating his or her personal qualities.

| Eres **un ángel**. | *You are **an angel**.* |
| Ellos siempre han sido **unos cobardes**. | *They have always been **cowards**.* |

- to indicate an approximate amount with numbers and quantities.

| La bolsa cuesta **unos cincuenta euros**. | *The bag costs **about fifty euros**.* |
| En esta caja hay **unas tres docenas** de rosas. | *There are **about three dozen** roses in this box.* |

Note: Feminine nouns that begin with a stressed **a** or **ha** (**agua**, **águila**, **hacha**) take a masculine indefinite (or definite) article in the singular form. However, because they are feminine nouns, they take feminine adjectives.

| **Un arma** siempre es peligros**a**. | ***A weapon** is always dangerous.* |

EJERCICIO
17·23

¿Verdadero o falso?

_____ 1. Un ángel es una persona generosa.

_____ 2. El helado es un alimento bajo en calorías.

_____ 3. Un cobarde enfrenta a sus enemigos.

_____ 4. El gato es un animal doméstico.

_____ 5. Hay una frontera entre Estados Unidos y Canadá.

_____ 6. En una fábrica se usan maquinarias.

_____ 7. Un total es la suma de sus partes.

_____ 8. En unos desiertos hay camellos.

_____ 9. Una escultura es una obra musical.

_____ 10. Un coche alemán de lujo cuesta un ojo de la cara.

_____ 11. Romeo y Julieta son unos personajes de la novela *Don Quijote*.

When are indefinite articles *not* used in Spanish?

Remember *not* to use the indefinite articles

+ with nouns designating a nonspecific amount of material or materials.

¿Pones **tomate** en la paella?	*Do you put **any tomato** in the paella?*

+ with nouns of professions and occupations, nationality, or religion after **ser**.

Somos **electricistas**.	*We are **electricians**.*
Todos ellos son **venezolanos**.	*They are all **Venezuelans**.*
Son **judíos** de Grecia.	*They are **Jews** from Greece.*

If the noun is modified by an adjective or adjective phrase, the indefinite article is used.

Raúl es **un excelente carpintero**.	*Raúl is **an excellent carpenter**.*

Remember that nouns and adjectives of nationality and religion are *not* capitalized in Spanish.

+ when the noun is preceded by the following words: **cierto(a)**, **medio(a)**, **mil**, **otro(a)**, **qué**, or **tal(-es)**. Note the English equivalents in these examples.

Cierta persona te visita a menudo.	***A certain person** visits you often.*
Salimos en **media hora**.	*We will leave in **a half hour**.*
Perdieron **mil dólares** en la apuesta.	*They lost **one thousand dollars** on the bet.*
Compra **otro ramo** de flores.	*Buy **another bunch** of flowers.*
¡Qué mala suerte!	***What bad luck!***
No me cuentes **tal cosa**.	*Don't tell me **such a thing**.*

EJERCICIO
17·24

El artículo indefinido, ¿se usa o no? Escribe el artículo indefinido apropiado si es necesario. Si no es necesario, escribe una **X**.

1. _____ amigos de Mandy llegaron al aeropuerto.

2. Necesitamos _____ cita con el dentista.

3. Compré _____ revistas extranjeras.

4. Manuel, ¡_____ qué inteligente hombre eres!

5. Entrega estas cartas a _____ empleado de esa oficina.

6. Antonio Lázaro es _____ buen electricista.

7. Me lo dijo _____ cierta persona.

8. Yo no dije _____ tal cosa.

9. Marcos es _____ enfermero con mucha experiencia.

10. Lola, dame _____ otro helado.

¿Un chisme o un secreto a voces? Traduce. Usa el **Vocabulario útil**.

On Tuesday, Nidia was wearing a pair of dark glasses. Nidia went alone to a gallery. In front of a very modern French painting, she met Luis. They had a secret date. Later, Nidia and Luis went to a Japanese restaurant far away from the city. They sat in a secluded corner and they ordered some delicious dishes. At nine thirty in the evening, the Gonzálezes and the Suárezes arrived at the restaurant. What bad luck! A certain person started a rumor. Pablo Suárez is a gossipy man. The bad thing is that Nidia and Luis wanted to keep their secret. And now, the relationship between Nidia and Luis is an open secret.

Vocabulario útil

dark	**oscuro(a)**	secluded	**apartado(a)**
date	**la cita**	to keep	**guardar, proteger**
gossipy	**chismoso(a)**	to meet	**encontrarse (o > ue)**
open secret	**el secreto a voces**	to start a rumor	**correr un rumor**

Adjectives

Adjectives have different functions according to the role they play relative to the word they modify. One function is to limit or determine a noun. Adjectives in this category are demonstrative and possessive adjectives. For more detail, you may wish to refer to the unit on possessive adjectives and pronouns (Unit 21) in this book.

Mi reloj no funciona.	*My watch is not working.*
Esta rosa tiene un perfume fuerte.	*This rose has a strong fragrance.*

Another function associated with adjectives is complementing nouns, completing their meanings with various characteristics and qualities.

¿No quieres ese bolso **grande** y **barato**?	*Don't you want that **big**, **inexpensive** bag?*

Sometimes the role of adjectives is to specify the noun.

Quiero un auto **alemán**.	*I want a **German** car.*

The meaning of **auto** is made more precise by the adjective of nationality **alemán**. Note that, with some exceptions, descriptive adjectives in Spanish generally *follow* the nouns they modify. You will learn more about the placement of adjectives later in this unit.

Gender and number of adjectives in Spanish

Since the gender and number of adjectives in Spanish are closely associated with the nouns they modify, you may wish to review the unit on nouns and articles (Unit 17). Adjectives must agree in gender and number with the noun or pronoun they modify; therefore, adjectives are either feminine or masculine, singular or plural, according to the nouns they modify. Here are some gender and number rules for adjectives.

◆ Masculine adjectives that end in **-o** drop the **-o** and add **-a** for the feminine forms. To form the plural, both masculine and feminine, add **-s** to the singular ending.

SINGULAR	PLURAL
buen**o**, buen**a** (*good*)	buen**os**, buen**as**
perezos**o**, perezos**a** (*lazy*)	perezos**os**, perezos**as**
precios**o**, precios**a** (*precious*)	precios**os**, precios**as**

221

Esta camisa **negra** es importada de Italia.	*This **black** shirt is imported from Italy.*
Los zapatos **rojos** son de España.	*The **red** shoes are from Spain.*

◆ Numerous adjectives in Spanish have a single form for the masculine and feminine. If the adjective ends in -e, add -s for the plural. If it ends in a consonant, add -es.

SINGULAR	PLURAL
perseverant**e** (*persevering*)	perseverante**s**
débi**l** (*weak*)	débil**es**

una personalidad **agradable**	*a **pleasant** personality*
un cuento **interesante**	*an **interesting** story*
películas **populares**	***popular** movies*
un vino **francés** y pasteles **franceses**	***French** wine and **French** pastries*
un auto **veloz** y unos botes **veloces**	*a **fast** car and some **fast** boats*

A few spelling rules: Note that some adjectives may drop or add an accent mark when they are changed from singular to plural and vice versa. Adjectives of nationality are not capitalized. Remember to change **z** to **c** before adding the -es plural ending.

Here are some adjectives that have the same form in the masculine and feminine. Practice putting them in the plural.

agradable	pleasant	**feliz**	happy	**natural**	natural
azul	blue	**fuerte**	strong	**optimista**	optimistic
carmesí	red	**gris**	gray	**pesimista**	pessimistic
difícil	difficult, hard	**inferior**	inferior	**realista**	realistic
fácil	easy, simple	**interesante**	interesting	**triste**	unhappy
fatal	fatal	**mediocre**	mediocre	**verde**	green

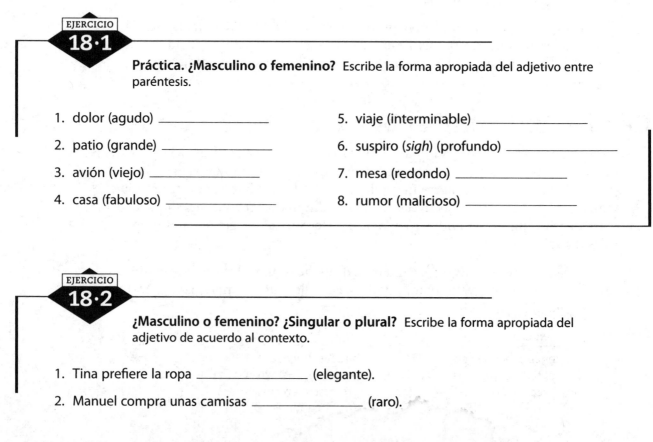

EJERCICIO 18·1

Práctica. ¿Masculino o femenino? Escribe la forma apropiada del adjetivo entre paréntesis.

1. dolor (agudo) _____

2. patio (grande) _____

3. avión (viejo) _____

4. casa (fabuloso) _____

5. viaje (interminable) _____

6. suspiro (*sigh*) (profundo) _____

7. mesa (redondo) _____

8. rumor (malicioso) _____

EJERCICIO 18·2

¿Masculino o femenino? ¿Singular o plural? Escribe la forma apropiada del adjetivo de acuerdo al contexto.

1. Tina prefiere la ropa _____ (elegante).

2. Manuel compra unas camisas _____ (raro).

3. Hay programas _____ (violento) en la tele.

4. Estos actores _____ (popular) no quieren firmar autógrafos.

5. Venden pendientes (*earrings*) _____ (azul).

6. ¿No has visto mi foto _____ (preferido)?

7. Prefiero el clima _____ (cálido).

8. Siempre me regalan corbatas _____ (feo) el día de mi cumpleaños.

EJERCICIO
18·3

En español. Escribe la frase en español. Coloca el adjetivo en el lugar apropiado.

1. *a beautiful day* _____

2. *a sad morning* _____

3. *a big hand* _____

4. *a pleasant aroma* _____

5. *a long song* _____

6. *a deep sleep* _____

7. *a sincere friend* [f.] _____

8. *a dedicated nurse* _____

9. *an interesting city* _____

10. *a difficult language* _____

11. *a terrible explosion* _____

12. *a brave soldier* _____

More about adjectives and their endings

◆ To form the feminine of adjectives ending in -**án**, -**dor**, and -**ón**, add -**a** to the masculine form.

   Note that the accent mark is not used in the feminine endings -**ana** and -**ona**. The plural of these adjectives is formed by adding -**es** to the masculine forms and -**s** to the feminine ending. Note that an accent mark is not used in the plural forms.

SINGULAR	PLURAL
charlat**án**/charlat**ana** (*talkative*)	charlatan**es**/charlatana**s**
pelead**or**/pelead**ora** (*feisty, aggressive*)	peleador**es**/peleador**as**
glot**ón**/glot**ona** (*gluttonous*)	gloton**es**/gloton**as**

Mi hermana es muy **habladora**.	*My sister is very **chatty**.*

- Adjectives of nationality (**gentilicios**) that end in **-o** drop the masculine ending and add **-a** to the feminine form. They are not capitalized in Spanish.

SINGULAR	PLURAL
mexican**o**/mexican**a** (*Mexican*)	mexican**os**/mexican**as**
peruan**o**/peruan**a** (*Peruvian*)	peruan**os**/peruan**as**

- Many adjectives of nationality have other endings, such as **-a, -án, -és, -ense**, and **-í**. These endings are both feminine and masculine.

Estos chocolates son **belgas**.	*These chocolates are **Belgian**.*
El idioma **catalán** se habla en Cataluña.	*The **Catalan** language is spoken in Catalonia.*
La nación **costarricense** es admirada por su tradición democrática.	*The **Costa Rican** nation is admired for its democratic tradition.*

- Use the masculine plural for an adjective that modifies a group of two or more nouns where at least one noun is masculine and one or more is feminine.

¿Adónde vas con el vestido y la chaqueta **viejos**?	*Where are you going with the **old** dress and jacket?*

- Compound adjectives add the plural to the last element.

Las sociedades **multiculturales** son más interesantes.	***Multicultural** societies are more interesting.*

EJERCICIO
18·4

Definiciones. Escribe la letra que indica el adjetivo que mejor completa la frase.

_____ 1. Juan trabaja mucho y bien. Es...	a. charlatán
_____ 2. Siempre dice lo que piensa. Es...	b. creativo
_____ 3. No dice la verdad. Es...	c. agresivo
_____ 4. Quiere trabajar menos. Es...	d. burlón (*mocking*)
_____ 5. Quiere ser rico. Es...	e. generoso
_____ 6. Prefiere pelear. Es...	f. mentiroso
_____ 7. Hace donaciones. Es...	g. ambicioso
_____ 8. Habla demasiado. Es...	h. trabajador
_____ 9. Se ríe de los demás. Es...	i. holgazán (*lazy*)
_____ 10. Tiene ideas diferentes. Es...	j. sincero

Where are adjectives placed in Spanish?

The position of adjectives in Spanish is related to the information they provide about the noun they modify. Adjectives that add information or describe qualities generally *follow* the noun. However, there are exceptions to this rule.

- ◆ Descriptive adjectives that emphasize intrinsic characteristics are placed before the noun.

  El **fiero** león pasea por la selva.   *The **ferocious** lion wanders in the jungle.*

  These adjectives stress certain inherent qualities. They appear more frequently in written Spanish and in literary style.

- ◆ Limiting adjectives, adjectives that indicate numbers and amounts, and possessive and demonstrative adjectives are placed before the noun.

Queremos **dos** helados.	*We want **two** ice creams.*
Hoy hay **menos** nieve.	*Today there is **less** snow.*
Mis problemas no son **tus** problemas.	*My problems are not **your** problems.*
Este edificio tiene **cuatro** ascensores.	***This** building has **four** elevators.*

  See Unit 21 for the study of possessive and demonstrative adjectives and Unit 26 for numbers.

  Adjectives that indicate numbers and amounts are called **indefinidos** when they do not designate specific numbers or amounts of things, people, or ideas.

  Here is a list of common adjectives of quantity, with their corresponding gender and number forms. Note that some have the same ending for both masculine and feminine.

algún/alguna/algunos/algunas	some
bastante/bastantes	enough
cuanto/cuanta/cuantos/cuantas	as much
mucho/mucha/muchos/muchas	many
ningún/ninguna/ningunos/ningunas	no, not any
poco/poca/pocos/pocas	few
suficiente/suficientes	sufficient
varios/varias	various, few

EJERCICIO
18·5

El adjetivo, ¿antes o después del sustantivo? Usa la forma apropiada del adjetivo entre paréntesis. Coloca tu respuesta en el lugar apropiado, antes o después del sustantivo.

1. El director traerá _____ informes _____ para sus empleados. (algún)

2. El director y el productor hablan de _____ temas _____. (filosófico)

3. No vamos a tomar _____ decisiones _____ antes de las cinco. (mucho)

4. En esta película, Cenicienta no consiguió _____ zapatillas _____ para ir a la fiesta. (ningún)

5. Esta película no va a ganar _____ premio _____ en el festival de cine. (ningún)

6. Esto va a ser un _____ proyecto _____ para nosotros. (difícil)

Some adjectives change meaning according to their position relative to the noun they modify. Placing these adjectives before the noun usually underscores an opinion, whether or not it is shared by others. Compare the change of meaning in the following examples.

Don Quijote es una **gran** novela.	Don Quixote *is a **great** novel.*
Viven en una casa **grande**.	*They live in a **large** house.*

Few would doubt calling *Don Quixote* a great novel. Placing the adjective before the noun emphasizes the significance of this work of art. In the second example, **grande**, following the noun, describes the size of the house. If we placed **grande** before **casa**, the meaning would change, and we would perceive a great house, adding the idea of "wonderful" or "famous" to the notion of size.

The following list includes other commonly used adjectives that change meaning according to their position with respect to the noun they modify.

	ENGLISH EQUIVALENT	
ADJECTIVE	BEFORE A NOUN	AFTER A NOUN
antiguo(a, os, as)	former	ancient
cierto(a, os, as)	(a) certain	sure
cualquier	any	any (old) . . .
grande	great	large
mismo(a, os, as)	same	himself, herself
nuevo(a, os, as)	different	new
puro(a, os, as)	nothing but	pure
simple	simple, easy	unsophisticated
único(a, os, as)	only	unique
viejo(a, os, as)	an old(-time) . . .	old

Use **gran** and **cualquier**, the shortened forms of **grande** and **cualquiera**, before singular feminine and masculine nouns.

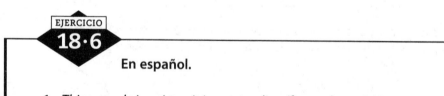

EJERCICIO
18·6

En español.

1. *This comedy is unique; it is outstanding (**fuera de serie**)!*

   _____

2. *My old friend Manolito wrote the script (**el guión**).*

   _____

3. *A former colleague came to the theater to watch the comedy.*

   _____

4. *The main character (**el protagonista**) is a simple man.*

_____

5. *Manolito always uses new ideas.*

_____

6. *Any person who comes to the theater will laugh.*

_____

Other adjective forms used before nouns: the shortened forms

When they precede the noun, certain adjectives have shortened forms (**apócopes**), that is, the masculine forms of several adjectives drop the **-o** ending when they are immediately followed by a masculine noun.

> Si me ayudas eres un **buen amigo**. }
> Eres un **amigo bueno** si me ayudas. } *If you help me, you are a **good friend**.*

The following list includes the basic adjectives and their shortened forms in context.

alguno (*some*)	**algún libro** (*some book*)
bueno (*good*)	**buen consejo** (*good advice*)
malo (*bad*)	**mal ejemplo** (*bad example*)
ninguno (*no, not any*)	**ningún soldado** (*no soldier*)
primero (*first*)	**el primer capítulo** (*the first chapter*)
tercero (*third*)	**el tercer año** (*the third year*)
uno (*a, an, one*)	**un poema** (*a poem*)

Note the accent mark on the shortened forms **algún** and **ningún**. Remember that **cien** and **ciento** are adjectives of quantity.

- **Cien** is used for the number *one hundred* before a plural noun (masculine or feminine).

  Tengo solamente **cien dólares** en el bolsillo. — *I only have **one hundred dollars** in my pocket.*

  La Casa de Representantes quiere **cien mil millones**. — *The House of Representatives wants **one hundred billion**.*

- **Ciento** appears in numbers 101 and higher.

  Hay **ciento noventa y nueve** sillas en este salón. — *There are **one hundred and ninety-nine** chairs in this room.*

San, the shortened form of the adjective **Santo**, is used with all masculine names of saints. Exceptions are **Santo Domingo** and **Santo Tomás**.

  San Francisco es una ciudad en California. — ***San Francisco** is a city in California.*

Y en tu caso... ¿Verdadero o falso?

_____ 1. Celebro el primer día del año, el Año Nuevo, en mi casa.

_____ 2. Ahora tengo ciento cincuenta dólares en mi billetera.

_____ 3. Hay algunos extraterrestres entre nosotros.

_____ 4. Si los padres fuman delante de los niños dan un mal ejemplo.

_____ 5. No termino de leer el primer capítulo si la novela es aburrida.

¿Dónde están los adjetivos? Identifica todos los adjetivos y subráyalos. _Remember that you may find some shortened forms and adjectives placed before the noun._

1. El viajero portugués trae un pasaporte vencido (_expired_).

2. El tercer año en la universidad es difícil y largo.

3. Han pasado tres meses.

4. Pablo Neruda, el gran poeta chileno, es un personaje curioso en una película italiana.

5. ¿Quién es el cantante famoso de San Juan?

Preguntas personales. _In your answers, place the adjectives in the appropriate place._

1. ¿Tienes algunos amigos en otros países?

_____

2. ¿Cuantas ciudades de los Estados Unidos conoces?

_____

3. ¿Qué programas cómicos te gustan?

_____

4. ¿Tienes un(-a) poeta favorito(a)? ¿Cómo se llama?

_____

5. ¿Has visitado el Viejo San Juan, en Puerto Rico?

_____

6. ¿Quieres un coche nuevo o un nuevo coche?

_____

Other considerations about the position of adjectives

More than one adjective can modify a noun. The rules for placement you have already learned still apply.

◆ Two or more adjectives may follow the noun and are usually linked by a conjunction or separated by a comma.

No es **impaciente o consentida**.   *She is not **impatient or spoiled**.*
Tiene un perro **simpático y pequeño**.   *He/She has a **pleasant, small** dog.*
El viaje fue **largo, tedioso**.   *The trip was **long, tedious**.*

◆ If, according to the rules, one of the adjectives precedes the noun, it remains in place. This applies to shortened forms or an adjective that conveys a different meaning when placed before the noun.

Vivían en un **gran** castillo **medieval**.   *They used to live in a **grand medieval** castle.*

EJERCICIO
18·10

En español. *Place the adjectives in their appropriate places.*

1. *He is courteous and generous.* _____

2. *We hear a loud and clear noise.* _____

3. *This chair costs three hundred dollars.* _____

4. *A glass of cold milk, please.* _____

5. *His office is on a long and narrow street.* _____

6. *There are some new stores on the first floor of this shopping center.*

_____

7. *Elly wants a brand new bicycle.* _____

Words that function as adjectives

Other parts of speech can function as adjectives.

- ◆ A noun + a preposition + another noun.

Rompí **la copa de cristal**.	*I broke the **crystal wineglass**.*
¿Te gusta mi **collar de perlas**?	*Do you like my **pearl necklace**?*

- ◆ Most past participles can complement a noun and function as adjectives. Remember that the regular past participles end in **-ado** and **-ido** and that many commonly used verbs have irregular participles. Consult Unit 10 and the Verb tables at the back of this book for past participles.

Las islas **situadas** al oeste de Ecuador son las Galápagos.	*The islands **situated** west of Ecuador are the Galápagos Islands.*
El plato **roto** está en la basura.	*The **broken** dish is in the garbage.*
La puerta está **cerrada**.	*The door is **closed**.*

EJERCICIO 18·11

En español.

1. *the diamond earrings* _____

2. *the open door* _____

3. *a summer dress* _____

4. *the broken records* _____

5. *some plastic bags* _____

6. *three paper baskets* _____

7. *a crystal dish* _____

8. *the written letter* _____

9. *my gold ring* _____

10. *the lost men* _____

EJERCICIO 18·12

En tu opinión... ¿Verdadero o falso?

_____ 1. Las pulseras de esmeraldas son valiosas.

_____ 2. El pollo asado es mi comida favorita.

_____ 3. Conviene tener una casa de verano.

_____ 4. En el invierno no uso ropa de algodón.

_____ 5. Una fina caja de chocolates es un regalo apropiado para una novia.

_____ 6. Patino en el lago congelado (*frozen*) en el invierno.

_____ 7. Siempre tengo un ramo de flores en mi sala.

_____ 8. Los zapatos de piel de cocodrilo son muy elegantes.

_____ 9. Hoy, he recibido tres cartas de amor.

_____ 10. Los cuentos de misterio me irritan.

Comparatives and superlatives

Comparatives

The qualities expressed by adjectives may be similar or equal to other qualities, more or less abundant than others, or superior to others. To express the degree of these qualities we use comparative and superlative forms.

Here are guidelines for the use of comparatives in Spanish.

◆ Express comparisons of *equality* with **tan** + adjective + **como**. The equivalent in English is *as* + adjective + *as*.

Soy **tan baja como** mi amiga María.	*I am **as short as** my friend María.*
Compré un abrigo **tan caro como** el tuyo.	*I bought a coat **as expensive as** yours.*

As usual, the adjective agrees with the noun that it modifies.

◆ Express comparisons of *inequality*, as follows.

Más + adjective + **que** is equivalent to English *more* + adjective + *than*.

Estos platos son **más ricos que** los platos italianos.	*These dishes are **more delicious than** Italian dishes.*

Menos + adjective + **que** is equivalent to English *less* + adjective + *than*.

Las novelas de amor son **menos interesantes que** las de misterio.	*Love stories are **less interesting than** mystery novels.*

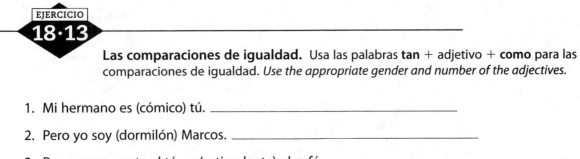

EJERCICIO
18·13

Las comparaciones de igualdad. Usa las palabras **tan** + adjetivo + **como** para las comparaciones de igualdad. *Use the appropriate gender and number of the adjectives.*

1. Mi hermano es (cómico) tú. _____

2. Pero yo soy (dormilón) Marcos. _____

3. Por eso me gusta el té: es (estimulante) el café. _____

4. No tengo noticias (interesante) los anuncios que acabo de leer.

   _____

5. Ah, esos pantalones son (caro) los que José compró ayer.

   _____

6. Mi casa es (viejo) la casa de mis abuelos. _____

7. ¿No crees que la salsa es (divertido) el regatón? _____

EJERCICIO
18·14

En español.

1. *Silk dresses are more expensive than cotton dresses.*

   _____

2. *These shoes are as comfortable as the red shoes.*

   _____

3. *To be in style (estar de moda) is less important than to save money.*

   _____

4. *You (tú) are as thrifty (ahorrativo) as my husband.*

   _____

5. *In my opinion, designing shoes is as creative as writing a poem.*

   _____

6. *Is peace of mind (tranquilidad) more necessary than wealth (riqueza)?*

   _____

7. *Isn't this translation less difficult than the previous exercise?*

   _____

Superlatives

Superlatives express the quality of the adjective to its maximum degree. Follow these rules for the use of superlatives.

◆ Use **más** + adjective + **de** or **menos** + adjective + **de** to express the maximum degree in comparison to others.

Estos son los días **más felices de** mi vida.	*These are the **happiest** days **of** my life.*
Raquel y Laura son las alumnas **menos apreciadas de** la clase.	*Raquel and Laura are the **least appreciated** students **of** the class.*

◆ Use the absolute superlative to express the maximum degree without comparing it to others. Use **muy** + adjective, or add one of the following endings: **-ísimo, -ísima, -ísimos, -ísimas**.

Las flores son **muy bellas**.
Las flores son **bellísimas**. } *The flowers are **very beautiful**.*

El joven es **muy inteligente**.
El joven es **inteligentísimo**. } *The young man is **very intelligent**.*

Spelling changes occur when certain adjective endings are dropped to add the superlative **-ísimo** endings. Adjectives that end in **-co, -go,** or **-z** change spelling to **qu, gu,** and **c**.

cómico	funny	**comiquísimo**
largo	long	**larguísimo**
feliz	happy	**felicísimo**

EJERCICIO
18·15

Los lugares de la ciudad. Práctica. Escribe la forma apropiada del superlativo absoluto que termina en **-ísimo, -ísimos, -ísima** e **-ísimas**.

1. un zoológico grande _____

2. un circo divertido _____

3. una avenida ancha (*wide*) _____

4. un teatro moderno _____

5. una universidad famosa _____

6. una playa bella _____

7. un restaurante caro _____

8. unas comidas variadas _____

9. una discoteca popular _____

10. un museo importante _____

Preguntas personales.

1. ¿Quién es la persona más importante de tu vida? _____

2. ¿Quién es, en tu opinión, un actor comiquísimo? _____

3. ¿Y una novela larguísima? _____

4. ¿Cuál es la fecha más importante del año para ti? _____

5. ¿Te gustaría ser famosísimo(a)? ¿Por qué? _____

6. ¿Quién es para ti una persona respetadísima? _____

Irregular comparative and superlative adjectives

Some adjectives have irregular comparative forms. Remember that irregular forms are usually the most common, both in English and Spanish.

	COMPARATIVE		SUPERLATIVE	
bueno(a, os, as)	**mejor(-es)**	better	**el/la mejor de** **los/las mejores de**	the best
malo(a, os, as)	**peor(-es)**	worse	**el/la peor de** **los/las peores de**	the worst
grande(s)	**mayor(-es)**	greater; older	**el/la mayor de** **los/las mayores de**	the greatest; the oldest
	más grande(-s)	larger	**el/la más grande de** **los/las más grandes de**	the largest
pequeño(a, os, as)	**menor(-es)**	lesser; younger	**el/la menor de** **los/las menores de**	the least; the youngest

¿Eres **el mayor de** todos los primos?
Ésta es **la peor de** todas las películas
  que he visto.

*Are you **the oldest of** all the cousins?*
*This is **the worst of** all the movies I have seen*
  (the worst movie I have [ever] seen).

En español.

1. *Pablo is the oldest brother.*

_____

2. *Rosa is the youngest of all.*

_____

3. *My uncle is older than your father.*

_____

4. *Felicia says she is twenty-five years old. She is younger than I thought.*

_____

5. *This game is more exciting than chess!*

_____

6. *Today, I received the worst grade in my French class.*

_____

7. *Well, tomorrow you (**tú**) will receive better news.*

_____

Other comparisons

Keep in mind the following details regarding comparisons in Spanish. Note that the English equivalent may not be a literal translation.

If the comparison is based on an adjective from a different clause, **de lo que** is used instead of **que** to translate *than*.

Esto es menos difícil **de lo que** pensábamos.

*This is less difficult **than** we thought.*

The comparison in **de lo que** is based on the adjective **difícil**.

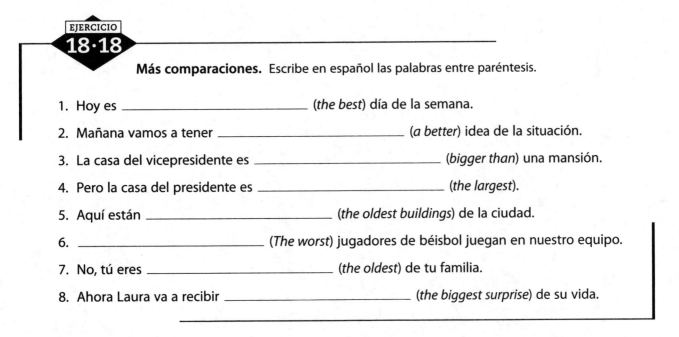

EJERCICIO
18·18

Más comparaciones. Escribe en español las palabras entre paréntesis.

1. Hoy es _____ (*the best*) día de la semana.

2. Mañana vamos a tener _____ (*a better*) idea de la situación.

3. La casa del vicepresidente es _____ (*bigger than*) una mansión.

4. Pero la casa del presidente es _____ (*the largest*).

5. Aquí están _____ (*the oldest buildings*) de la ciudad.

6. _____ (*The worst*) jugadores de béisbol juegan en nuestro equipo.

7. No, tú eres _____ (*the oldest*) de tu familia.

8. Ahora Laura va a recibir _____ (*the biggest surprise*) de su vida.

¡Ayúdeme, por favor! Traduce. Usa el **Vocabulario útil**.

Dear Dr. Blanco:

This is the first time I am writing to a women's magazine, but I need help. Amanda is a very good friend, but sometimes she is very annoying. She is the youngest of five sisters. My friend is very obstinate and competitive. If I buy a hat, she wants to have a more attractive hat. If I talk about my gold bracelet, she talks about her Colombian emerald ring. If I say I had a good day, Amanda's day is better. The worst is when we are with other friends. Some of her comments are pure fiction. She says she bought a brand new car, but it is really just a newer car. It is not bad to dream, but Amanda tells many lies and I do not know what to do. I need a big favor. What can I do to help my old friend?

Worried.

Vocabulario útil

annoying	**pesado(a)**	help	**la ayuda**
bracelet	**el brazalete, la pulsera**	lie, falsehood	**la mentira**
Colombian	**colombiano(a)**	obstinate	**obstinado(a)**
competitive	**competitivo(a)**	women's magazine	**una revista para mujeres**
friendship	**la amistad**	worried	**preocupado(a)**

Personal pronouns

A pronoun is used in place of one or more nouns or another word that refers to someone or something previously mentioned. If you have told your friends about your new boss's demanding personality and her love for coffee, they will understand your statement, "I will not make her any!" Your audience will understand that *her* refers to the new boss and *any* to coffee.

The use of pronouns prevents excessive repetition of nouns and reminds your audience who is doing what, how, to whom, etc. Remember that nouns can be part of either the subject or the predicate of the sentence. They function as subjects, direct objects, or indirect objects of a verb, or in prepositional phrases. Pronouns take the place of nouns and replace them in their functions as subjects or objects. According to the function or role they play, the forms of pronouns and their names change: subject pronouns, object pronouns, etc.

Subject pronouns

Because verb conjugation endings tell who the subject is, subject pronouns in Spanish are usually omitted.

¿A qué hora **comes**?	*At what time **do you eat**?*

The **-es** of the form **comes** reveals the subject **tú**. Pronouns may be used for clarification, as in the following example.

Ella sale ahora y **él no va**.	*She leaves now and he does not go.*

Subject pronoun forms

The following chart reviews **los pronombres personales de sujeto**.

SINGULAR SUBJECT PRONOUNS		PLURAL SUBJECT PRONOUNS	
yo	I	**nosotros/nosotras**	we
tú	you (fam.)	**vosotros/vosotras**	you (fam.)
usted (Ud.)	you (for.)	**ustedes (Uds.)**	you (for.)
él	he	**ellos**	they (masc., masc. & fem.)
ella	she	**ellas**	they (fem.)

Tú is the familiar form, used with friends, family, pets, and anyone you would treat with familiarity because of age, rank, etc. The **vosotros** form, the plural familiar subject pronoun, is used in Peninsular Spanish (Spain), but not in the Canary Islands. **Vosotros** is used in the same situations as **tú** but in the plural.

Usted and ustedes are used to show respect throughout the Hispanic world. Often, you will see the abbreviations Ud. and Uds. (or Vd. and Vds.). Most Spanish speakers, except in Peninsular Spain, use ustedes as the plural of the informal tú. The context of a message will clarify the intentions of the speaker.

Uses of the subject pronouns

In English, subject pronouns are necessary for identifying the subject of verbs. Spanish verb endings identify the subject in most situations, but it is sometimes necessary or preferable to include the subject pronoun. Use the Spanish subject pronouns when you wish to

- ◆ deliberately underscore the subject.

    Ellos saben mentir.   *They* (masc.) *know how to lie.*

- ◆ emphasize the speaker's message, especially with the verb **ser** or when the verb is understood.

    Ella sí estudia.   *She does study.*
    ¿Quién es? **Soy yo.**   *Who is it? It is I.*

    —¿Quién quiere un refresco?   *"Who wants a soft drink?"*
    —**Yo.** Y **ella**, una limonada.   *"I do. And for her, a lemonade."*

- ◆ clarify the subject in cases where the verb ending may indicate more than one grammatical person.

    ¡Elías miraba y **yo trabajaba!**   *Elías watched* while *I worked!*

- ◆ show respect by addressing a person or persons with the **Ud.** and **Uds.** formal forms. (**Usted** and **ustedes** are also known as the **pronombres de tratamientos, de cortesía o respeto.**)

    Entre Ud., por favor.   *Come in, please.*

As customs become more relaxed in many areas of the Spanish-speaking world, it is more usual to address a listener or an audience informally. However, it is still customary to use the **usted** and **ustedes** forms with persons

- ◆ to whom you owe respect because of a title, rank, or age.

    Sra. Perales, **dígame,** ¿dónde está   *Mrs. Perales, tell me, where is your passport?*
    su pasaporte?

- ◆ whom you have just met or whom you are unsure how to address.

    ¿Puede Ud. decirme su nombre?   *Can you tell me your name?*

Children and adolescents will often use the **tú** forms as soon as they meet each other.

Remember that in Spanish there is no equivalent of the English subject pronoun *it* in impersonal expressions.

    ¡Es importante!   *It is important!*
    Hace sol pero **llueve.**   *It's sunny, but it's raining.*

¿Cuál es el pronombre apropiado? Escribe el pronombre de sujeto que corresponde al sujeto de las oraciones siguientes.

1. Los astronautas estudian las condiciones atmosféricas. _____

2. ¿Estáis contentas en Barcelona? _____

3. ¿Viene Juan? _____

4. La artista donó tres de sus cuadros. _____

5. ¿Salimos? _____

6. Viven en esta casa. _____

7. ¡Pide la cena! _____

8. ¿Quieren una habitación con vista al mar? [formal] _____

¡Con énfasis! Escribe el pronombre para indicar énfasis. *The conjugated verb will tell you what person to choose.*

1. Susana es trabajadora pero _____ eres muy perezosa.

2. Carlos y yo somos realistas pero _____ [formal] creen que la vida es un cuento de hadas (*fairy tale*).

3. Nado muy bien, ¡_____ merezco (*deserve*) una medalla!

4. Nosotras no cocinamos bien pero _____ no saben preparar un té instantáneo.

5. Ahora ustedes van a dormir y _____ vamos a trabajar.

6. Ellos beben té pero _____ prefiero el té tailandés.

¿Tú o usted? Imagina que escribes una carta a estas personas. Marca una **X** detrás de la forma apropiada del pronombre de sujeto que debes usar.

1. tú _____ Ud. _____ el presidente de los Estados Unidos

2. Uds. _____ vosotras _____ tu amiga Ana y su hermana de Barcelona

3. tú _____ Ud. _____ Doña Ana, una señora de setenta y cinco años

4. tú _____ Ud. _____ tu prima

5. Uds. _____ vosotros _____ el Dr. Palermo y su esposa

6. tú _____ Ud. _____ el secretario general de las Naciones Unidas

7. tú _____ Ud. _____ el director de la escuela

8. Uds. _____ vosotros _____ unos desconocidos de cincuenta años de edad

9. Uds. _____ vosotros _____ los abuelos de tus amigos

10. tú _____ Ud. _____ un viejo amigo

En español. Usa los pronombres de sujeto solamente si son necesarios.

1. *You (**tú**) are what you eat.* _____

2. *They tell lies, I tell the truth.* _____

3. *It is raining.* _____

4. *Dr. Lagos, I need an appointment.* _____

5. *Mrs. Castro, can you hear me?* _____

6. *I work five days a week.* _____

7. *Who is it? It is she.* _____

8. *Where do you (**Uds.**) live?* _____

9. *Is it snowing now?* _____

10. *Do you (**tú**) read the newspaper every day?* _____

Pronouns as objects of prepositions

Almost identical to the subject pronoun forms, these pronouns always follow a preposition.

SINGULAR		PLURAL	
mí	me	**nosotros/nosotras**	us
ti	you (fam.)	**vosotros/vosotras**	you (fam. [Spain])
usted (Ud.)	you (for.)	**ustedes (Uds.)**	you (for. & fam.)
él	him, it (masc.)	**ellos**	them (masc., masc. & fem.)
ella	her, it (fem.)	**ellas**	them (fem.)
sí	yourself, himself, herself, itself		

Note that

◆ **mí**, **ti**, and **sí** are different from the subject pronouns.

◆ **mí** and **sí** have accent marks.

◆ **mí**, **ti**, and **sí**, combined with the preposition **con** (*with*), appear in the following forms.

conmigo   with me
contigo   with you (fam.)
consigo   with you (for.), with him(self), with her(self), with them(selves)

When are prepositional pronouns used in Spanish?

Prepositional pronouns appear as objects of prepositions.

Paco recibe una felicitación **de ella**.   *Paco receives a greeting card **from her**.*
Traen las maletas **consigo**.   *They bring the suitcases **with them**.*

Prepositional pronouns are also used

◆ with the preposition **a** to emphasize the direct object.

A ti no **te** aprecian.   *They do not appreciate **you**.*

◆ with the preposition **a** to make clear who is the indirect object or direct object.

Le toca **a ella**.   *It is **her** turn.*
Los veo **a ellos**.   *I see **them**.*

The forms of the prepositional pronouns have some exceptions. The subject pronoun forms **yo** and **tú** are used instead of **mí** and **ti** with the following prepositions.

entre   between
excepto   except
incluso   including
menos   except
salvo   except
según   according to

Entre tú y yo, están locos.   *Between you and me, they are crazy.*
Todos lo apoyan **excepto yo**.   *Everyone supports him **except me**.*

EJERCICIO
19·5

Práctica. Escribe la forma apropiada del pronombre.

1. para _____ (Marta)

2. de _____ (Lara y Raúl)

3. de acuerdo con _____ (yo)

4. en lugar de _____ (Uds.)

5. incluso _____ (tú)

6. menos _____ (vosotros)

7. por _____ (los chicos)

8. para _____ (las empleadas)

9. debajo de _____ (*it* [f.])

10. como _____ (nosotros)

11. delante de _____ (Ud.)

12. con _____ (tú)

13. con _____ (él)

14. según _____ (yo)

En español. Usa una de las preposiciones siguientes en cada frase.

acerca de	como	debajo de	excepto	para
cerca de	con	encima de	lejos de	sin

1. *We bring all the medicines with us* [m.]. _____

2. *She sent these flowers for you* (**tú**). _____

3. *Who put the pillow under it* [f.]? _____

4. *Lucy cannot live without them* [m.]. _____

5. *Who lives near me?* _____

6. *We all know the answer except him.* _____

7. *The house is far from you* (**Uds.**). _____

8. *The cat is on top of me.* _____

9. *She is like you* (**tú**). _____

10. *The press speaks about you* (**vosotras**). _____

Direct object pronouns

Object pronouns replace nouns. Direct object pronouns always answer the questions *What?* or *Whom?* If we hear the question "Who saw the movie?" and someone answers "She saw it," we understand that *it* refers to the implicit noun *the movie. It* clearly answers the question "What did she see?" Except for placement, direct object pronouns in Spanish function as they do in English.

Direct object pronoun forms

Direct object pronouns (**los objetos de complemento directo**) are as follows.

SINGULAR		PLURAL	
me	me	**nos**	us
te	you (fam.)	**os**	you (fam. [Spain])
lo	him, it (masc.), you (for. masc.)	**los**	them, you (for. & fam.)
la	her, it (fem.), you (for. fem.)	**las**	them, you (for. & fam.)

Note: In some parts of Spain, when referring to people, **le** is used instead of **lo**.

When are direct object pronouns used in Spanish?

As in English, direct object pronouns in Spanish, referring to a noun previously mentioned, are used to avoid repetition. In the simple affirmative, the direct object pronoun *precedes* both simple and compound conjugated verbs. In English, of course, the pronoun follows the verb.

Tina prepara **el postre**. Tina **lo** prepara.

*Tina prepares **dessert**. She prepares **it**.*

The direct object pronoun also precedes the verb in negative statements and questions.

—¿Has visto **mi reloj de oro**? ¿**Lo** has visto?
—No, no **lo** he visto.

*"Have you seen **my gold watch**? Have you seen **it**?"*
*"No, I haven't seen **it**."*

EJERCICIO
19·7

En el partido de béisbol. Contesta las preguntas. Sustituye los complementos directos con los pronombres correspondientes.

1. ¿Compraste las entradas? Sí, _____.

2. ¿Invitaste a Ana? No, _____.

3. ¿Llamaste a tus hermanos? No, _____.

4. ¿Tienes los binoculares? Sí, _____.

5. ¿Compraste los refrescos? No, _____.

6. ¿Lanzó Pepe la pelota? Sí, _____.

7. ¿Anotaron dos carreras? Sí, _____.

8. ¿Robaron dos bases? Sí, _____.

EJERCICIO
19·8

La astronomía. Usa el pronombre que necesitas para sustituir el sustantivo subrayado. Escribe la oración y coloca (*place*) el pronombre en el lugar apropiado.

1. Un astrónomo observa los planetas. _____

2. ¿Quiénes han visto un OVNI (*UFO*)? _____

3. Nosotros estudiamos las estrellas. _____

4. Ayer yo visité otro observatorio. _____

5. Tiene dos telescopios fabulosos en el segundo piso.

_____

6. Notamos <u>la Vía Láctea</u> (*Milky Way*) porque la noche está muy clara.

_____

7. Investigaremos <u>unos modelos espaciales</u>. _____

8. Ahora, saludamos <u>a la directora</u>. ¡Vamos! _____

EJERCICIO
19·9

En español. Coloca los pronombres en el lugar apropiado.

1. *I need her now.* _____

2. *She always helps me!* _____

3. *I wrote it [f.] for Gloria.* _____

4. *And I bought it [m.] with my money.* _____

5. *Did you (tú) visit them [m.]?* _____

6. *They respect me a lot.* _____

7. *Do you (tú) forgive me?* _____

8. *Oh, I know him very well.* _____

More about the position of direct object pronouns

Study the rules for the placement of direct object pronouns with the following verb constructions.

- ◆ With negative commands (**mandatos**), the pronoun precedes the command.

  No subas **las escaleras**. ¡No **las** subas!   *Don't climb **the steps**. Don't climb **them**!*

- ◆ With affirmative commands, attach the pronoun to the command.

  Llama **a Juanita**. ¡Lláma**la**!   *Call **Juanita**. Call **her**!*

Note the written accent mark on the command form + attached pronoun construction. If the stressed syllable on the command form is the next-to-last syllable (not counting the pronoun), add the accent mark.

En la cocina. Los pronombres y los mandatos. Sustituye el objeto directo con el pronombre correspondiente. *Remember to attach the direct object pronoun to the affirmative command.*

1. Compra los ingredientes. _____

2. No gastes dinero inútilmente. _____

3. Laven las papas. _____

4. Fríe la cebolla. _____

5. No quemes el arroz. _____

6. Guarden las botellas. _____

7. Baja la llama (*flame*). _____

El medio ambiente. En español.

1. *Protect the environment. Protect it now!* (tú)

   _____

2. *Write three posters. Write them!* (Uds.) _____

3. *Collect all plastic bottles. Collect them, please!* (tú)

   _____

4. *Recycle the newspapers. Recycle them!* (Uds.)

   _____

5. *Turn off the lights. Turn them off!* (Uds.) _____

6. *Save water. Save it, please!* (Uds.) _____

With infinitives and the **gerundio** (-**ando**, -**iendo**) forms, the pronoun may precede the first verb or conjugated form, *or* it may be attached to the infinitive or the **gerundio**.

No queremos comprar**lo**. / No **lo** queremos comprar.	*We do not want to buy **it**.*
Estoy leyéndo**lo**. / **Lo** estoy leyendo.	*I am reading **it**.*

Note the written accent mark on **leyéndolo**. When a pronoun is added to the -**ando**, -**iendo** form, the accent mark indicates the original stressed vowel.

Los infinitivos y los pronombres: las dos posibilidades. Sustituye los sustantivos con pronombres. Escribe las dos opciones: el pronombre antes del verbo y unido (*attached*) al infinitivo.

1. Voy a practicar deportes. _____/_____

2. ¿Quieres hacer este ejercicio? _____/_____

3. Vamos a hacer una apuesta (*bet*). _____/_____

4. No quiero perder mi dinero. _____/_____

5. Los chicos van a ganar el partido (*game*).

   _____/_____

6. Queremos gastar todo el dinero.

   _____/_____

7. Tú no sabes responder a esta pregunta.

   _____/_____

8. ¿Dónde quieres poner este pronombre?

   _____/_____

¿Qué están haciendo ahora? El complemento directo. Escribe la forma apropiada del pronombre del complemento directo subrayado. Únelo (*Attach it*) al gerundio -ando, -iendo.

1. Mirta está escondiendo <u>los chocolates</u>. _____

2. Álvaro está buscando <u>las zapatillas</u> (*slippers*).

   _____

3. Andy y Ann están viendo <u>la película</u>. _____

4. ¿Por qué Uds. están oyendo <u>esa música</u>? _____

5. ¿Quiénes están pagando <u>las cuentas</u>? _____

6. Los hermanos Díaz están leyendo <u>el periódico</u>.

   _____

7. Marco está bebiendo <u>una limonada fría</u>. _____

En español. Estamos disfrutando el concierto. *Write both possible constructions for* **gerundio** + *direct object pronouns.*

1. *We are watching it* [f.].

   _____/_____

2. *The musicians are playing it* [m.].

   _____/_____

3. *I am observing them* [m.].

   _____/_____

4. *Are you* (**Ud.**) *applauding it* (**la banda** [f.])?

   _____/_____

5. *The band is playing it* (**la marcha** [f.]).

   _____/_____

Indirect object pronouns

The indirect object usually tells *for whom* or *to whom* the action is done.

Carlos **me** dio un anillo.	*Carlos gave **me** a ring.*
Carlos **le** dio el anillo (**a ella**).	*Carlos gave the ring **to her**.*

Forms of the indirect object pronouns (**los objetos de complemento indirecto**) follow.

SINGULAR		PLURAL	
me	to me	**nos**	to us
te	to you (fam.)	**os**	to you (fam. [Spain])
le	to him, to her, to it, to you (for.)	**les**	to them (masc. & fem.), to you (for. & fam.)

The forms of the direct and indirect object pronouns are the same for the first and second persons, singular and plural. The third-person forms **le** and **les** are used for both feminine and masculine objects, as well as for the formal singular and plural forms **Ud.** and **Uds. Os** is the plural familiar indirect (and direct) object pronoun, used in Spain.

Le prometí que vendría.	*I promised (**whom?**) I would come.*

The above statement needs clarification. It is likely that the listener/reader does not know which individual was promised something (that is, that the speaker would come). Thus, the speaker needs to identify the antecedent of the indirect object (**le**).

Le prometí **a Carmen** que vendría.	*I promised **Carmen** I would come.*
Le prometí **a ella** que vendría.	*I promised **her** I would come.*

Where are indirect object pronouns placed?

The same rules for placement of the direct object pronouns apply to the indirect object pronouns. According to the general rule, indirect object pronouns are placed before both simple and compound forms of the conjugated verb. In English, the pronoun follows the verb.

Bettina **me** dio la maleta.	*Bettina gave **me** the suitcase.*
¿**Le** has dado tu palabra?	*Have you given **him**/**her** your word?*

The following is a select list of verbs that take a person as an indirect object in Spanish. Remember to use the indirect object pronoun with these verbs.

contar(le) algo (a alguien)	to tell something (to someone)
dar(le) algo (a alguien)	to give something (to someone)
decir(le) algo (a alguien)	to say something (to someone)
pedir(le) algo (a alguien)	to ask something (of someone)
regalar(le) algo (a alguien)	to give a present (to someone)
servir(le) algo (a alguien)	to serve something (to someone)
traer(le) algo (a alguien)	to bring something (to someone)

EJERCICIO
19·15

Los complementos indirectos. Escribe el pronombre para sustituir las palabras entre paréntesis.

1. _____ dio el dinero. (al empleado)

2. _____ envió una tarjeta postal. (a mí)

3. _____ devolví los libros. (a la bibliotecaria)

4. ¿_____ mostró sus intenciones? (a Ud.)

5. _____ repartimos los juguetes. (a los niños)

6. _____ reciclan las botellas. (a nosotros)

7. ¿_____ añadiste el coñac? (a la receta)

8. _____ pegaron un golpe (*hit*). (a ti)

EJERCICIO
19·16

Escribe en español. Después, subraya el pronombre de complemento indirecto.

1. *I sent you (**tú**) the letter.* _____

2. *You (**tú**) did not answer me.* _____

3. *Taly did not explain her problem to me.* _____

4. *Did she tell you (**Ud.**) about her engagement (**compromiso**)?*

_____

5. *She showed us her engagement ring (**anillo de compromiso**).*

_____

6. *Lynda prepares lunch for her.* _____

7. *They always ask me many questions.* _____

The placement of indirect object pronouns with commands, infinitives, and **gerundio** forms

The indirect object pronouns follow the same rules of placement as the direct object pronouns with commands (**mandatos**), infinitives, and **gerundio** forms.

- With negative commands, the pronoun precedes the command.

No me digas eso.   ***Don't tell me** that!*

- With affirmative commands, attach the pronoun to the command.

Tráele el desayuno a la cama.   ***Bring him/her** breakfast in bed.*

A written accent mark appears on the command form + attached pronoun construction. Remember to add the accent mark on the next-to-last syllable (not counting the pronoun) of the command form.

As with the direct object pronouns, with infinitives and the **gerundio**, either place the pronouns before the first verb or conjugated form, *or* attach them to the infinitive or **gerundio**.

Me dio el libro ayer.   *He/She **gave me** the book yesterday.*
Espero **darles** una buena noticia.   *I hope **to give you** good news.*
Estamos **comprándole** un sombrero.   *We are **buying him** a hat.*

Note the accent mark on **comprándole**. Remember to add it to the original stressed vowel of the **-ando**, **-iendo** forms when you attach object pronouns.

EJERCICIO
19·17

Los mandatos y los pronombres. Usa el pronombre de complemento indirecto que corresponde a las palabras entre paréntesis. Escribe la oración de nuevo y une el pronombre al mandato si es afirmativo.

1. Compren Uds. la revista (a Luisa). _____

2. Revisa la tarea (*homework*) (a los chicos). _____

3. Entreguen esta solicitud (*application*) (al director del programa).

_____

4. No digan una mentira (a sus jefes). _____

5. Devuelve los libros (a la bibliotecaria) (*librarian*).

   _____

6. Pida Ud. la visa (al cónsul). _____

7. No cuenten el final (a mí). _____

8. Regalen una torta (*cake*) de chocolate (al maestro).

   _____

9. Explique Ud. este problema (a su siquiatra). _____

10. Comenten este síntoma (a su doctor). _____

Los infinitivos y los pronombres. Sustituye las palabras entre paréntesis con el pronombre de objeto indirecto. *Write both options: the pronoun attached to the infinitive and the pronoun preceding the conjugated verb.*

1. Queremos llevar un regalo. (a tú tía)

   _____/_____

2. Debe pedir una excusa. (a su jefe)

   _____/_____

3. Voy a servir una paella. (a mis amigos)

   _____/_____

4. ¡No puedes decir mentiras! (a tus padres)

   _____/_____

5. Laura no quiere llevar las cajas. (a Ana y Luis)

   _____/_____

6. ¿Puedes prestar (*lend*) cien euros? (a nosotros)

   _____/_____

7. ¿Vais a servir un aperitivo? (a los clientes)

   _____/_____

8. Puedes hacer un favor. (a Miguel)

   _____/_____

¿Qué hacen? Sustituye el objeto indirecto entre paréntesis con el pronombre de complemento indirecto. Escribe la forma apropiada del pronombre y únelo al gerundio (-ando, -iendo).

1. Mirta está regalando los chocolates. (a los niños) _____

2. Álvaro está buscando las zapatillas. (para Uds.) _____

3. Los chicos están escribiendo una tarjeta. (a su tía) _____

4. ¿Por qué Uds. están tocando esa música? (para el público) _____

5. ¿Quiénes están pagando las cuentas? (a la tesorera) _____

6. Los hermanos Díaz están comentando el artículo. (a nosotros) _____

7. Marco está sirviendo una limonada fría. (a vosotros) _____

8. ¿Por qué tú no estás preparando la cena? (a mí) _____

9. Yo estoy lavando las sábanas (bedsheets). (para ti) _____

10. Nosotros estamos reciclando las botellas. (para la comunidad) _____

Los intercambios. En español. Place the pronouns before the conjugated verb.

1. We are sending them a postcard. _____

2. I am lending (prestar) you (tú) my bicycle.

_____

3. The bank is asking me for the money. _____

4. You (tú) are sending me a thousand dollars?

_____

5. I am writing you (Ud.) a note. _____

6. Are you (Uds.) making me an offer (oferta)?

_____

7. She is asking you (vosotros) a favor. _____

Double object pronouns

A direct object pronoun plus an indirect object pronoun can and frequently does appear with a verb in Spanish.

Prefiero escuchar sus comentarios.	*I prefer hearing his/her comments.*
Me los lee con frecuencia.	*He/She reads **them to me** frequently.*

Me is the indirect object indicating the person to whom he/she reads (**lee**). The second object **los** is the direct object pronoun replacing **sus comentarios**. The English equivalent is usually an object pronoun plus a prepositional phrase (*them to me*).

How are double object pronouns used in Spanish?

In daily communication, double object pronouns often simplify messages and avoid repetition. The placement of double pronouns is the same as single object pronouns. They appear before the conjugated form of the verb. The indirect object pronoun precedes the direct object pronoun.

¿Tu dinero? **Te lo** doy ahora mismo.	*Your money? I'm giving **it to you** now.*
Sheila **nos la** envió.	*Sheila sent **it to us**.*
Ella **se la** envió **a Marcos**. Y **se la** envió **a Lara y su hermana** también.	*She sent **it to Marcos**. And she sent **it to Lara and her sister**, too.*

Note that the indirect object pronoun form in the last example above is **se**. (You would expect **le** to appear in the construction **se la envió** of the first sentence and **les** in the construction **se la envió** of the second sentence.)

The indirect object pronouns **le** and **les** are changed to **se** when they are followed by **lo, los, la**, or **las**. For emphasis or clarification, a preposition plus noun or a preposition plus prepositional pronoun is usually added to this type of sentence.

Se la compré **a los niños**. No **se la** compré **a Uds**.	*I bought **it for the children**. I did not buy **it for you**.*

EJERCICIO
19·21

Están muy ocupados. Práctica. Sustituye los objetos de complemento directo e indirecto y escribe una frase con los pronombres en el orden correspondiente.

EJEMPLO   Rita prepara / un té tailandés / para mí. _Rita me lo prepara._

1. Tomás trae / los paquetes / a nosotros.

   _____

2. Él compra / los vegetales / a su tía.

   _____

3. El meteorólogo explica / el tiempo / a los televidentes (*TV viewers*).

   _____

4. Pero no dice / las malas noticias / a ellas.

   _____

5. Tomás entrega / la tarea / a su profesor.

_____

6. El agente de viajes hace / las reservaciones / para vosotros.

_____

7. El periodista presenta / muchas preguntas / a la senadora (*senator*).

_____

8. Mi peluquera (*hairdresser*) prepara / el tinte (*hair color*) / para mí.

_____

9. El policía da / una multa (*traffic ticket*) / al conductor.

_____

10. Ronnie lee / el periódico / a nosotros.

_____

The position of double object pronouns with commands, infinitives, and the gerundio

The position of double object pronouns with commands, the infinitive, and the **gerundio** is the same as the position of single object pronouns.

- ◆ With negative commands (**mandatos**), the pronouns precede the command.

    No **nos los** traigas.   *Do not bring **them to us**.*

- ◆ With affirmative commands, attach the pronouns to the command; the indirect object pronoun is followed by the direct object pronoun.

    Tráele el desayuno a la cama.   ***Bring him breakfast** in bed. **Bring it to him!***
    ¡Tráeselo!

- ◆ With infinitives and the **gerundio** (-**ando**, -**iendo**), either place the pronouns before the first verb or conjugated form *or* attach them to the infinitive or **gerundio**.

    Quieren **darles la noticia**. Sí, quieren   *They want to **give them the news**. Yes, they want*
    dárselas personalmente.   *to **give it to them** personally.*
    Estamos **comprándote** un traje.   *We are **buying you** a suit. Do you want to **try***
    ¿Quieres **probártelo?**   ***it on?***

Accent marks are added to the original stressed vowels: **tráeselo** and **probártelo**. Note that the reflexive pronoun (**te**) is also an indirect object pronoun in the last example above (**probártelo**).

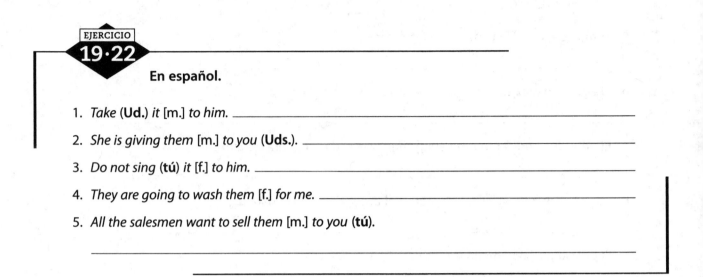

EJERCICIO
19·22

En español.

1. *Take (***Ud.***) it [m.] to him.* _____

2. *She is giving them [m.] to you (***Uds.***).* _____

3. *Do not sing (***tú***) it [f.] to him.* _____

4. *They are going to wash them [f.] for me.* _____

5. *All the salesmen want to sell them [m.] to you (***tú***).*

_____

The indirect object pronoun with **gustar** and other verbs

Certain verbs are always used in the third-person singular or plural with an indirect object pronoun. This is the case with **gustar**, which expresses likes and dislikes.

Me gusta el chocolate.	*I like chocolate.*
Me gustan las motocicletas también.	*I like motorcycles, too.*

This structure may take a bit of practice for English speakers learning Spanish. Note that the forms of **gustar** agree with the subject of each sentence. **El chocolate** is singular and the verb is in the third-person singular, **gusta**. In the second example, **gustan** in the plural agrees with the subject of the sentence, **las motocicletas**. Note the use of the definite article before each subject (**el chocolate, las motocicletas**), both of which follow the verbs, **me gusta(n)**.

The indirect object pronoun refers to the person who *likes* the subject: **el chocolate, las motocicletas**. The prepositional form of the pronoun is often used to clarify sentences with the third-person pronoun **le**: *A ella* **le gustan los objetos de cristal, pero** *a él* **le gustan los de cerámica.** (*She likes crystal objects, but he likes ceramic ones.*) The prepositional form may also be used for emphasis: *A mí* **me gustan las motocicletas.** (*I like motorcycles.*)

Of course, a noun or name can also be used to clarify which person likes or dislikes something or someone (and is the indirect object of **gustar**).

A Ana no **le gusta** bailar pero **a su hermano** sí **le gusta**.	*Ana does* ***not** **like** to dance, but ***her brother** **does like** it (**to dance**).*

Note: The subject of **gustar** may be an infinitive or more than one infinitive. The conjugation of **gustar** remains singular in either case: **Me gusta nadar y caminar.** (*I like to swim and to walk.*)

¿Te gusta viajar?	*Do you like traveling (to travel)?*
Y **me gusta nadar y caminar** por la playa también.	*And **I like swimming and walking** on the beach, too.*

EJERCICIO
19·23

¿**Qué les gusta?** Usa la forma del verbo **gustar** y el complemento indirecto apropiados. Escribe la oración completa.

1. A Patricia / gustar / ir de compras. _____

2. A los estudiantes no / gustar / los exámenes.

   _____

3. Y a los pacifistas no / gustar / las guerras.

   _____

4. A mí / gustar / viajar. _____

5. A los turistas / gustar / sacar fotos. _____

6. A tu amigo Javier / gustar / los refrescos.

   _____

7. ¿A ti / gustar / las flores? _____

8. ¿A quién no / gustar / la música mexicana?

   _____

EJERCICIO
19·24

En español.

1. *I know you (**Ud.**) like funny movies.* _____

2. *Children like to tease (**fastidiar**) my dog.*

   _____

3. *Do you (**tú**) like French food?* _____

4. *We do not like to get up early.* _____

5. *Sandra likes to learn new Spanish words.*

   _____

6. *Who does not like to travel?* _____

7. *Julia does not like this song.* _____

8. *Do you (**tú**) like orchids?* _____

Here are some other verbs conjugated like **gustar** in the third-person singular or plural with indirect object pronouns.

apasionar	to be mad about	**hacer falta**	to be in need of
encantar	to love (something)	**importar**	to care about
enloquecer	to be crazy about	**molestar**	to be bothered by
disgustar	to dislike; to hate	**parecer**	to seem; to appear to
faltar	to be missing	**sobrar**	to be left over
fascinar	to be fascinated	**tocarle a alguien**	to be one's turn

EJERCICIO
19·25

Preguntas personales.

1. ¿Qué te gusta más hacer en tu tiempo libre?

_____

2. ¿Y qué te apasiona? _____

3. ¿Qué te hace falta ahora? _____

4. ¿Cuándo te toca pagar la cuenta de la electricidad?

_____

5. ¿Te apasionan los deportes? _____

6. ¿Te molestan las críticas de tus enemigos?

_____

7. ¿Te enloquecen los anuncios (ads) por la radio?

_____

8. ¿Qué te disgusta más? _____

9. ¿Te sobra el dinero? _____

10. ¿Qué te encanta hacer en tus vacaciones?

_____

Sobre gustos hay mucho escrito. Traduce. Usa el **Vocabulario útil**.

"There is nothing written about good taste," says my friend Pablo. I have a different opinion, and I am going to express it. I do not like to sleep in a hammock. I love to go on vacation and swim in an Olympic pool. I like the good things in life, but in moderation. I love animals, and I hate horror movies. I love December because my family and I ski in the mountains. I go with my sister, and I love to compete with her.

Vocabulario útil

good taste	**el buen gusto**	Olympic pool	**la piscina olímpica**
hammock	**la hamaca**	to compete	**competir (e > i)**
horror film	**la película de horror**	to ski	**esquiar**

Relative pronouns

Reviewing a few points of grammar will help you understand the role played by relative pronouns (**los pronombres relativos**) in everyday communication. A relative pronoun always refers back to its *antecedent*, a noun or a pronoun previously mentioned in the sentence. In other words, relative pronouns serve as links or connectors between sentences or clauses. *That, those, which, who, whom,* and *whose* are used to introduce relative clauses in English.

Juan es el profesor **que enseña filosofía**.	*Juan is the professor **who teaches philosophy**.*

Antecedent means previous or prior. The antecedent in the above example, **el profesor**, is immediately followed by **que**, a relative pronoun that introduces a relative clause (**que enseña filosofía**). Relative clauses are always subordinate (dependent) clauses.

Velázquez es el autor de *Las Meninas*, **el cual** es mi cuadro favorito.	*Velázquez is the creator of* Las Meninas, ***which** is my favorite painting.*

The main (independent) clause in this case, **Velázquez es el autor de *Las Meninas***, makes complete sense; it stands on its own. The subordinate clause, **el cual es mi cuadro favorito**, embellishes the sentence; it adds meaning to the main sentence, but cannot stand on its own. This type of clause is called *nonrestrictive*, because it does not act upon or limit the content of the main clause.

However, in other sentences, the information in a dependent clause is necessary to understand the main clause. In this case, it is called a *restrictive* clause, because its presence limits the content of the main clause.

Las manzanas **que están podridas** no son saludables.	*The apples **that are rotten** are not healthful. (Rotten apples are not healthful.)*

Apples are considered a healthful fruit. If we take out the relative clause, **que están podridas**, the utterance would not make much sense.

Relative pronouns may refer to people, things, actions, events, or ideas. However, the correct pronoun must be used to convey the proper message. Observe the relative pronouns **que** and **quien** in the following sentences.

El libro **que está en la mesa** es mío.	*The book **that is on the table** is mine.*
El autor, **quien acaba de llegar de Francia**, firmó muchos libros.	*The author, **who has just arrived from France**, signed many books.*

258

The antecedent of the relative pronoun **quien** is always a person. Note that in English, relative pronouns (*that, which, who, whom*) are not necessarily included in a complex sentence. Note the English equivalent of the following example.

La playa **que nosotros visitamos** estaba desierta.

*The beach **we visited** was deserted.*

Que: When is the relative pronoun **que** used in Spanish?

The most common relative pronoun in Spanish, especially in conversational exchanges, is **que**, the equivalent of *that*. **Que** is never omitted in Spanish. Use **que** in a relative clause

◆ that refers to people, animals, things, ideas, or events in the singular or plural.

El hombre **que sale del banco ahora** lleva una maleta.

*The man **who is leaving the bank now** carries a suitcase.*

El pájaro **que canta** es mi regalo para ti.

*The bird **that is singing** is my gift to you.*

No queremos ir a la fiesta **que organizan los estudiantes**.

*We do not want to attend the party **(that) the students are organizing**.*

¿No vas a usar los zapatos **que compraste ayer**?

*Aren't you going to wear the shoes **that you bought yesterday**?*

◆ where it functions as the subject of a clause.

In the following example, **que**, referring back to **el guía**, functions as the subject of the verb (**llevó**) in the relative (dependent) clause.

Éste es el guía **que lo llevó al museo**.

*This is the guide **who took him to the museum**.*

◆ where it functions as the object of a clause.

In the example below, **que** refers back to the direct object (**al técnico**) of the verb (**recomiendo**) in the main clause. **Que** functions as the direct object of the verb (**llamamos**) in the relative (dependent) clause. (**Nosotros** [implied] is the subject of the relative clause.)

Te recomiendo al técnico **que llamamos ayer**.

*I recommend to you the technician **whom we called yesterday**.*

EJERCICIO
20·1

En mi ciudad. Práctica. Combina las dos frases en una oración. Usa el pronombre relativo **que**.

EJEMPLO   El libro dice "Romance nocturno". Es aburridísimo.

   El libro que dice "Romance nocturno" es aburridísimo.

1. La casa está cerca del puente. Es de María.

2. Vimos los tigres en el zoo. Son de la India.

_____

3. La escuela está cerrada. Es una institución privada.

_____

4. Los policías cuidan el banco. Están dormidos.

_____

5. Los árboles son más altos. Están en el parque.

_____

6. En la catedral hay unos turistas. Esperan ver unos cuadros de El Greco.

_____

EJERCICIO
20·2

Un poco de geografía. ¿Verdadero o falso?

_____ 1. La ciudad de Quito, que está en el hemisferio sur, es la capital de Perú.

_____ 2. Chile, un país que está en la costa del Pacífico, exporta muchas frutas.

_____ 3. En la ciudad de San Antonio, que está en Texas, hay poca herencia hispana.

_____ 4. La ciudad de Barcelona, que es famosa por las obras del arquitecto Antoni Gaudí, está en Cataluña, España.

_____ 5. La selva del Amazonas es parte de varios países hispanos que están en Suramérica.

_____ 6. La isla de Cuba, que atrae a muchos turistas, está a pocas millas de Cayo Hueso.

EJERCICIO
20·3

En español. Usa el pronombre relativo **que** en tus traducciones.

1. *While Jackie goes to the market, which is next to the movie theater, we watch a movie.*

_____

2. *The child who is with me is Jackie's son.*

_____

3. *The movie that we watch is not too interesting.*

_____

4. *Matt saw two women who did not pay for their tickets.*

_____

5. *Mark came to see a movie that is a foreign (**extranjero**) film.*

_____

6. *I bought the things that the children want, chocolates and refreshments.*

_____

Quien: When is the relative pronoun **quien** used in Spanish?

The English pronouns *who* and *whom* are the equivalents of **quien** and the plural form **quienes**. This relative pronoun, which refers only to people, is not used as frequently as **que**. It may appear in written language, to clarify the identity of the antecedent. Sometimes it is the equivalent of *whoever*.

Use **quien** (**quienes**) instead of **que** when the antecedent is a person, in a dependent clause where it functions as

- ◆ the subject of a verb.

    In the following example, **Fernando** is the subject of the verb **invita**. The relative pronoun **quien** in the dependent clause is the subject of **es**.

Fernando, **quien es un viejo amigo**, me invita a su boda.	*Fernando, **who is an old friend**, is inviting me to his wedding.*

- ◆ the object of a verb.

    In the following example, **quienes** is preceded by the preposition **a**: **a quienes**. This construction parallels the antecedent in the main clause, **al Dr. Salama** (which contains the contraction of the preposition **a** plus the definite article **el**). **A quienes** is the object of the verb **vimos**.

Saludamos al Dr. Salama y su esposa, **a quienes vimos ayer**.	*We said hello to Dr. Salama and his wife, **whom we saw yesterday**.*

The clause introduced with **quien** or **quienes** is separated from the main clause with commas. It is normally *nonrestrictive*.

En el baile de máscaras. Práctica. Combina las palabras en una oración. Usa el pronombre relativo **quien** o **quienes** de acuerdo al contexto. Escribe las comas.

EJEMPLO   Amelia / cumple años hoy / va a una fiesta de disfraces (*costume*)
_____ *Amelia, quien cumple años hoy, va a una fiesta de disfraces.* _____

1. El hombre / tiene un traje de Arlequín / es muy gordo.

   _____

2. El chico / trae un disfraz de Frankenstein / es muy bajo.

   _____

3. Los hombres / se visten como los siete enanitos (*dwarves*) / son muy viejos.

   _____

4. Una señora / parece la Bella Durmiente / está durmiendo en el sofá.

   _____

5. Un señor / viene con un traje de príncipe / no tiene aspecto aristocrático.

   _____

6. Las niñas / se ponen un disfraz de bruja (*witch*) / son muy simpáticas.

   _____

¿Quien o quienes? Usa la forma apropiada del pronombre de acuerdo al contexto.

1. Vimos a los camarógrafos (*cameramen*), _____ filmaron el documental.

2. Ésta es la narradora, _____ va a grabar la información del documental.

3. Los ayudantes, a _____ van a pagar un sueldo (*salary*), empiezan a trabajar mañana.

4. Un profesor de biología, _____ es el investigador del grupo, escribió el guión (*script*).

5. Saludamos al productor, a _____ conocen como el rey de los documentales.

6. Las actrices, _____ tienen un papel (*role*) muy corto, tienen miedo de los osos.

En español. Usa el pronombre relativo **quien, quienes** en tus traducciones.

1. *The man who is sitting to my right is from San Diego.*

   _____

2. *The people who bought the tickets today paid a high price.*

   _____

3. *The women whom you (**tú**) invited are dancing the rumba.*

   _____

4. *But I do not see their husbands, who were here.*

   _____

5. *Marlo, who is a good friend [f.], plays the piano.*

   _____

6. *Do you (**tú**) know the woman who is singing now?*

   _____

El que and el cual: When are the relative pronouns el que and el cual and their forms used in Spanish?

The relative pronoun forms of **que** with a definite article, **el que, los que, la que,** and **las que,** and the set of forms **el cual, los cuales, la cual,** and **las cuales** are interchangeable. Their English equivalents are *that, which, who,* and *whom.*

If you understand when to use **que** and **quien (quienes),** you are ready to use the alternate forms **el que, los que, la que,** and **las que** and **el cual, los cuales, la cual,** and **las cuales.** They add variety to a context that requires the use of many relative pronouns. Use these forms in dependent clauses where they

- ◆ function as the subject of a verb.

  El autor de *Don Quijote* es Cervantes,   *The author of* Don Quixote *is Cervantes,*
     el cual escribió otras novelas.   * who wrote other novels.*

- ◆ function as the object of a verb.

  In the following example, **el que** is preceded by the preposition **a (al que),** paralleling **a Eduardo** in the main clause.

  Saludamos a Eduardo, el hermano   *We said hello to Eduardo, Ali's brother,*
     de Ali, **al que vimos ayer.**   * whom we saw yesterday.*

◆ have two antecedents.

In this use, these forms refer to the person or thing physically farther away from the pronoun in the sentence.

Hay una foto de mis nietos, **la cual es muy simpática**.	*There is a photo of my grandchildren,* **which is very nice**.

Note that **quien** (**quienes**) and **el que**, **los que**, **la que**, or **las que** may be used as the indefinite subject of a verb. Their equivalents are *he who*, *those who*, etc.

Quien espera, desespera. }	*He who waits, loses hope.*
El que espera, desespera. }	

Práctica. Escribe la forma apropiada del pronombre, **el cual**, **los cuales**, **la cual**, **las cuales**.

1. Los hijos de Juan, _____ son mis colegas, viajarán al Oriente pronto.

2. Ellos viven en una casa muy bonita, _____ está al lado del río.

3. En la casa hay un salón, _____ está al lado de la escalera (*stairway*).

4. Juan también tiene dos hijas gemelas (*twins*), _____ hablan japonés.

5. Tienen libros en japonés, _____ solamente ellas pueden leer.

6. En esa casa hay dos colecciones de perlas orientales, _____ son muy valiosas.

Lo que and lo cual: When are the relative pronouns lo que and lo cual used in Spanish?

The antecedents of **lo que** and **lo cual** (interchangeable forms) are always ideas. They are neuter relative pronouns, more frequently used in writing than in speech. Their English equivalents are *that which*, *which*, *what*, or *whatever*. Follow these guidelines when using **lo que** and **lo cual**.

◆ Use **lo que** or **lo cual** to refer to a statement, concept, or idea previously mentioned.

Siempre llama después de las once de la noche, **lo que nos irrita**.	*He always calls after eleven at night,* **which irritates us**.

The idea of calling after a certain, inappropriate hour is understood or summed up in **lo que**. Remember that **lo cual** could also be used here.

◆ Use **lo que** to refer to a statement, concept, or idea that is understood because it has been discussed previously.

Lo que te avisó, no va a suceder.	**What** *he announced to you is not going to happen.*

¿Y en tu caso? Imagina que tú estás en cada una de estas situaciones. Escoge una frase para explicar tu reacción. *Note that more than one answer may be acceptable.*

me aburre	me enoja	me fascina	me gusta
me hace falta	me importa	me irrita	me interesa

1. No tengo dinero para comprar el auto que quiero, lo cual _____.

2. Voy a ir al gimnasio todos los días esta semana, lo cual _____.

3. Tengo que ir a casa de mi suegra (*mother-in-law*), lo que _____.

4. Hay una venta especial de zapatos esta semana, lo que _____.

5. Veo películas en mi computadora, lo cual _____.

6. Mis amigos me regalaron cien dólares para mi cumpleaños, lo que

    _____.

7. Este verano gané un viaje gratis a Cancún, lo cual _____.

8. Mañana es un día feriado (*holiday*), lo cual _____.

En español.

1. *The columnist reveals the actor's secrets, which is interesting.*

    _____

2. *What you (**tú**) want to know is in today's paper.*

    _____

3. *I always eat what I want.*

    _____

4. *The nutritionist recommends eating what is healthy.*

    _____

5. *My friends do not go to the gym often, which is not good.*

    _____

6. *Leonardo is not here, which worries me.*

    _____

7. *Do you (**Ud.**) see what I see now?*

    _____

8. *You (**Uds.**) are very generous, which is fabulous!*

    _____

Relative pronouns after prepositions

When relative pronouns are used after prepositions, they function as objects of a verb. In the example that follows, **al niño** is replaced in the relative clause by **a quien**, which is the direct object of **descubrieron**. Remember that a direct object answers the question *what*, *who*, or *whom*.

Castigaron al niño, **a quien descubrieron rompiendo la ventana.**	*They punished the boy, **whom they discovered breaking a window.***

◆ **El que, los que, la que, las que** and **el cual, los cuales, la cual,** and **las cuales** may be used after any preposition.

Abrimos la ventana **desde la cual vemos el valle.**	*We opened the window **from which we see the valley.***
La escuela **en la que ellos estudian** ganó el campeonato.	*The school **that they attend** won the championship.*
Daniela es una persona **en la cual se puede confiar.**	*Daniela is a person **whom you can trust.***

◆ **Que** may follow the prepositions **a, de, en,** and **con** if **que** does not refer to a person.

Éste es el auto **en que chocaron.**	*This is the car **in which they crashed.*** (*They crashed in this car.*)

◆ **Que** may follow the preposition **de** when the antecedent is a person.

Aquí entra el señor **de que hablamos.**	*Here comes the gentleman **about whom we talked.***

◆ **Quien** (**quienes**) and **el que** refer to people and may follow any preposition.

El hombre **con quien se casó Vera** es de Marruecos.	*The man **whom Vera married** is from Morocco.*

EJERCICIO
20·10

En la montaña. Práctica. Escribe la forma apropiada del pronombre **el cual, los cuales, la cual, las cuales, quien** o **quienes.**

1. Los jóvenes subieron una montaña desde _____ vieron un río.

2. Ellos vieron un puente muy viejo, por _____ pasaron.

3. Caminaron hasta una casa al lado de _____ había unos perritos.

4. La abuela preparó el almuerzo para _____ visitan su casa en el campo.

5. Los chicos buscan los cuchillos (*knives*), con _____ cortan la carne.

6. Comen todos excepto _____ no tienen hambre.

7. Después, llegó Pedro, con _____ todos quieren jugar al tenis.

8. También jugaron con las chicas, _____ no ganaron el partido de tenis.

Cuyo, cuya: When are the relative adjectives cuyo, cuya used in Spanish?

Cuyo (cuyos) and cuya (cuyas) mean *whose*. These are forms of a relative adjective referring to persons and things. They precede the noun they modify and must agree in gender and number with that noun.

Ésta es la señora **cuya tienda robaron anoche**.	*This is the lady **whose store was robbed** (**they robbed**) **last night**.*
Lazlo es un artista **cuyos cuadros se venden bien**.	*Lazlo is an artist **whose paintings are selling well**.*

Note that **cuyo** and its forms establish a relationship of possession. Each example sentence above could be divided into two parts. If you delete **cuya** and **cuyos** and replace them with a possessive adjective, the sentences become **Robaron *su* tienda anoche** and *Sus* **cuadros se venden bien**.

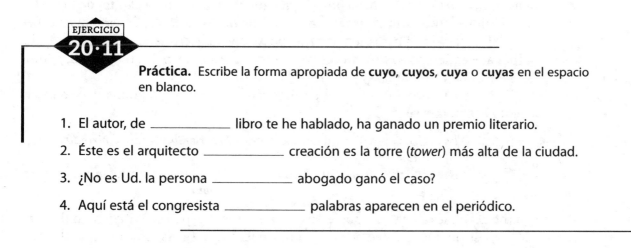

EJERCICIO 20·11

Práctica. Escribe la forma apropiada de **cuyo**, **cuyos**, **cuya** o **cuyas** en el espacio en blanco.

1. El autor, de _____ libro te he hablado, ha ganado un premio literario.

2. Éste es el arquitecto _____ creación es la torre (*tower*) más alta de la ciudad.

3. ¿No es Ud. la persona _____ abogado ganó el caso?

4. Aquí está el congresista _____ palabras aparecen en el periódico.

EJERCICIO 20·12

Las preparaciones para una reunión. Traduce. Usa el **Vocabulario útil** y la persona **usted**.

This is the ideal place for your business meeting. The three rooms (that) you need are on the ground floor, which is convenient. In the reception area, which is near the entrance, there are coffee, tea, and refreshments. Sheldon is the assistant whose name appears on your list. He is the person who can help you with the office equipment. On this list, you can see the names of our administrators, whom you can call at any time. Fred, the man with whom we talked, can open the balconies. There is a view of the lake, which is nice. If you need me, call the extension that is on my card.

Vocabulario útil

at any time	**en cualquier momento**	convenient	**cómodo(a)**
balcony	**el balcón**	ground floor	**el piso bajo**
business card	**la tarjeta**	office equipment	**el equipo de oficina**
business meeting	**la reunión de negocios**	reception area	**la recepción**

Possessive and demonstrative adjectives and pronouns

Possessive adjectives and pronouns

There are several ways of expressing possession both in Spanish and in English. The phrase *the capital of the United States* and its equivalent **la capital de los Estados Unidos** rely on similar prepositions, *of* and **de**, to indicate possession. Another way of expressing possession is with possessive adjectives and pronouns. Like other adjectives, possessive adjectives, which precede the noun they modify, limit the meaning of a noun: *my pen*, *your breakfast*.

Possessive pronouns have a similar relationship to the nouns they replace: "Not *my* pet, just *yours*."

Mis amigos preparan una fiesta de cumpleaños.	*My friends prepare a birthday party.*
Estas sandalias no son **mías**, son **tuyas**.	*These sandals are not **mine**; they are **yours**.*

In the examples above, the possessive forms reveal the person with whom the idea of possession is associated. **Mis** and **mías** refer to **yo**; **tuyas** indicates that the person **tú** owns the object **sandalias**. Possessive adjectives and possessive pronouns agree with their noun (= the object owned) in gender and in number.

Possessive adjective forms: the short forms and the long forms

There are two forms of the possessive adjectives (**los adjetivos posesivos**)—the short forms and the long forms. They all must agree in gender and in number with the items, ideas, etc., owned.

The short forms

The short forms consist of a single word. The subject pronouns of the persons who *own* the object, idea, relationship, etc., appear in the list below, for reference.

(yo) **mi, mis**	my
(tú) **tu, tus**	your (fam. sing.)
(él/ella, Ud.) **su, sus**	his/her, your (for. sing.), its
(nosotros/nosotras) **nuestro/nuestra, nuestros/nuestras**	our
(vosotros/vosotras) **vuestro/vuestra, vuestros/vuestras**	your (fam. pl. [Spain])
(ellos/ellas, Uds.) **su, sus**	their (masc., masc. & fem.), your (for. pl.)

tus zapatos y **tus** camisas	*your shoes and your shirts*
su libro y **su** libreta	*his/her/your/their book and his/her/your/their notebook*
nuestro abuelo y **nuestras** primas	*our grandfather and our (female) cousins*
sus amigos y **sus** maestras	*his/her/their friends and his/her/their (female) teachers*

Remember that

◆ the short forms of the possessive adjectives are placed *before* the nouns they modify.

◆ the singular short forms and the third-person plural do not have feminine and masculine forms.

◆ the masculine forms (**vuestro[s]** and **nuestro[s]**) end in -**o**, -**os**; the feminine forms (**vuestra[s]** and **nuestra[s]**) end in -**a**, -**as**.

◆ the forms **su** and **sus** may mean *his*, *her*, *your* (for.), *its*, or *their*. The context will help you determine the person the pronoun refers to.

Felipe trae a **su perro** al parque y Ana trae a **su gata**.	*Felipe brings **his (male) dog** to the park, and Ana brings **her (female) cat**.*
Alina y **sus hijas** bajan del autobús.	*Alina and **her daughters** step down from the bus.*
Los vendedores hablan con **sus clientes**.	*The salespeople talk to **their customers**.*

EJERCICIO
21·1

Práctica. Escribe la forma apropiada del adjetivo posesivo **mi, mis, tu, tus, su, sus, nuestro, nuestros, nuestra, nuestras, vuestro, vuestros, vuestra, vuestras** que corresponde a la persona entre paréntesis.

1. (Ana) _____ libros

2. (yo) _____ asunto (*matter, question*)

3. (Uds.) _____ maletas

4. (vosotros) _____ plan

5. (Pedro y Luisa) _____ pasaportes

6. (ellas) _____ viaje

7. (Ud.) _____ pluma

8. (nosotras) _____ relojes

9. (él) _____ palos de golf

10. (nosotros) _____ apartamento

11. (tú) _____ amistades

12. (mis hermanas) _____ casa

13. (mi esposo y yo) _____ jardín

14. (ellos) _____ vecinas

15. (mi gato) _____ cojín (*pillow*)

16. (Uds.) _____ banco

17. (yo) _____ tarjetas de crédito

18. (Felipe) _____ juguetes

19. (vosotros) _____ calcetines (*socks*)

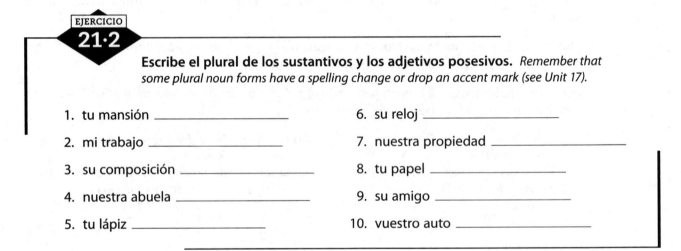

EJERCICIO

21·2

Escribe el plural de los sustantivos y los adjetivos posesivos. *Remember that some plural noun forms have a spelling change or drop an accent mark (see Unit 17).*

1. tu mansión _____

2. mi trabajo _____

3. su composición _____

4. nuestra abuela _____

5. tu lápiz _____

6. su reloj _____

7. nuestra propiedad _____

8. tu papel _____

9. su amigo _____

10. vuestro auto _____

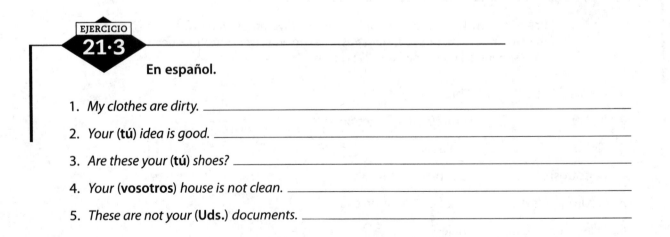

EJERCICIO

21·3

En español.

1. *My clothes are dirty.* _____

2. *Your (**tú**) idea is good.* _____

3. *Are these your (**tú**) shoes?* _____

4. *Your (**vosotros**) house is not clean.* _____

5. *These are not your (**Uds.**) documents.* _____

6. *Our apartment is not very large.* _____

7. *Do you (**tú**) want my notes?* _____

8. *Your (**Uds.**) plates are on the table.* _____

9. *Their chairs are here.* _____

10. *Where are my eyeglasses?* _____

The long forms

Spanish also has long forms of the possessive adjectives. They consist of one word and follow the noun.

LONG FORMS

(yo) **mío/mía, míos/mías**	mine
(tú) **tuyo/tuya, tuyos/tuyas**	yours (fam. sing.)
(él/ella, Ud.) **suyo/suya, suyos/suyas**	his, hers, yours (for. sing.)
(nosotros/nosotras) **nuestro/nuestra, nuestros/nuestras**	ours
(vosotros/vosotras) **vuestro/vuestra, vuestros/vuestras**	yours (fam. pl. [Spain])
(ellos/ellas, Uds.) **suyo/suya, suyos/suyas**	theirs, yours (for. pl.)

Compare the English equivalents in the following examples.

los zapatos y las camisas **tuyas**	*your shoes and your shirts*
el libro y la libreta **suyas**	*his/her/your/their book and his/her/your/ their notebook*
el abuelo **nuestro** y las primas **nuestras**	*our grandfather and our cousins*
los amigos **suyos** y las maestras **suyas**	*his/her/your/their friends and his/her/ your/their teachers*

Note that

- ◆ the long forms of the possessive adjectives *follow* the nouns they modify.

- ◆ all long forms have a masculine, a feminine, and their respective plural forms.

- ◆ **mío, mía, míos**, and **mías** have an accent mark.

- ◆ the third-person singular and plural forms have several translations in English. See the English equivalents of the examples above.

- ◆ *of mine, of yours, of ours*, etc. are other English equivalents of the long forms.

  ¿Encuentras unos amigos **míos**?   *Are you meeting some friends **of mine**?*

Práctica. *Use the long form of the possessive adjective that refers to the person(s) in each set of parentheses (**mío, mía, suyo,** etc.).*

1. (María y yo) el auto _____

2. (la secretaria) la computadora

   _____

3. (el médico) el consultorio _____

4. (yo) las medias _____

5. (ellos) la casa _____

6. (tú) las botas _____

7. (los maestros) las clases _____

8. (tú) los pantalones _____

9. (nosotros) la vida _____

10. (tú) la maleta _____

11. (Felipe y Ana) los hermanos _____

12. (yo) la amiga _____

En español. *Use the long forms of the possessive adjectives (**mío, tuyo, suyo,** etc.).*

1. *A friend of mine* [m.] *is a college professor.*

   _____

2. *I want to meet a cousin* [f.] *of his.* _____

3. *This obsession of yours* (**tú**) *with birds is very strange* (**raro**).

   _____

4. *This baseball team of ours is fabulous!*

   _____

5. *In this art exhibit* (**exposición**), *I see two pictures of his.*

   _____

When are the short and long forms of the possessive adjectives used in Spanish?

Although both the short and the long forms indicate who the possessor is and agree in number with the thing owned, they serve different purposes.

◆ The *long* forms emphasize who is the owner or contrast one possessor with another.

Este es **mi cepillo** de dientes y aquel es **el cepillo tuyo.**	*This is **my toothbrush,** and that one is **your toothbrush.***
Prefiero **el disco mío** y no **la canción tuya.**	*I prefer **my CD** and not **your song.***

♦ Because **su, sus, el suyo, la suya, los suyos,** and **las suyas** may not give you enough information to determine the owner, you may need to use a noun + **de** + the pronoun **él, ella, Ud., ellos, ellas,** or **Uds.** to clarify your message. See the following example.

—Aquí vienen Ana y Felipe. Pídele
  su donación.
—¿**La donación de ella** o **la donación
  de él?**

*"Here come Ana and Felipe. Ask **her** (**him**)
  for **her** (**his**) donation."*
*"**Her** donation or **his?**"*

EJERCICIO
21·6

¿De quién o quiénes son estas cosas? *Use the preposition* **de** + *the item* + *the
pronoun.*

EJEMPLO   ¿Es esta maleta tuya? (Ana)   ___Es la maleta de ella.___

1. Este pijama no es suyo. (Nina) _____

2. ¿Son éstas tus zapatillas? (Ana y Pepe) _____

3. Éste no es el peine (*comb*) mío. (Felipe) _____

4. ¿De quiénes son estas medicinas? (mis abuelos) _____

Possessive pronouns

Possessive pronouns (**pronombres posesivos**) are also used to indicate possession. They are the same as the long forms of the possessive adjectives. However, they are always expressed with the definite article.

POSSESSIVE PRONOUN FORMS

(yo) **el mío, la mía, los míos, las mías**	mine
(tú) **el tuyo, la tuya, los tuyos, las tuyas**	yours (fam. sing.)
(él/ella, Ud.) **el suyo, la suya, los suyos, las suyas**	his/hers, yours (for. sing.)
(nosotros/nosotras) **el nuestro, la nuestra, los nuestros, las nuestras**	ours
(vosotros/vosotras) **el vuestro, la vuestra, los vuestros, las vuestras**	yours (fam. pl. [Spain])
(ellos/ellas, Uds.) **el suyo, la suya, los suyos, las suyas**	theirs, yours (for. pl.)

mi libro y **el tuyo**	*my book and **yours***
Su auto es más moderno que **el mío.**	*Her car is more luxurious than **mine.***
Nuestra idea y **la suya** son buenas.	*Our idea and **yours** are good.*
Olvidé mi teléfono. ¿Puedo usar **el tuyo?**	*I forgot my phone. May I use **yours?***

Like other pronouns, possessive pronouns replace nouns previously mentioned. They take the place of nouns preceded by possessive adjectives. In the last example above (**mi teléfono**), the context refers to the owner, **yo,** and the thing owned, *my phone.* **El tuyo** avoids the repetitive **tu teléfono,** replacing the possessive adjective + noun with the possessive pronoun.

Remember these guidelines.

◆ Use the definite articles + the long form of the possessive adjectives to form the possessive pronouns. That is, the noun is dropped while the article + pronoun convey the message.

◆ All forms have a masculine form, a feminine form, and their respective plural forms.

◆ The third-person singular and plural forms have several translations in English (*yours, his, hers, theirs*).

You may need to use a definite article + **de** + the pronoun **él, ella, Ud., ellos, ellas,** or **Uds.** to clarify your message. To narrow down the meaning further, you may also use the name of the person.

—Aquí vienen Ana y Felipe. Es **su** cumpleaños.	*"Here come Ana and Felipe. It is **her** (**his**) birthday."*
—¿**El de ella** o **el de él**?	*"**Hers** or **his**?"*
—**El de Ana.**	*"**Hers** (**Ana's**)."*

Note that in English, the possessive form *hers* would suffice, and there would be no need for clarification. In Spanish, an attempt to answer this question with **el suyo** will likely be ambiguous.

Use the neuter possessive form **lo** + the masculine possessive pronoun to refer to a concept or idea.

Lo mío es mío.	*What is **mine** is mine.*
Lucía quiere **lo suyo**.	*Lucia wants what is **hers**.*

EJERCICIO
21·7

Cambia las palabras subrayadas. Usa la forma apropiada de los pronombres posesivos.

EJEMPLO   Tengo la silla de mi madre. ___*la suya*___

1. Me gusta la foto de Juan. _____

2. ¿Tienes tus fotos aquí? _____

3. Prefieren el postre (*dessert*) de Juliana. _____

4. No quieren probar mi receta. _____

5. ¿Por qué cierran las puertas del hotel? _____

6. Mi ventana está abierta. _____

7. Sus sábanas (*bedsheets*) son de seda (*silk*). _____

8. Pero tus toallas son de algodón (*cotton*). _____

9. ¡Acabo de encontrar el reloj de Armand en la basura! _____

10. Por suerte, nuestras cosas están todas aquí. _____

11. Tomo mis vitaminas por la mañana. _____

Vamos a hablar claramente. Escribe las palabras necesarias. *Use the definite article + the preposition* **de** *+ the pronoun* **él, ella, ellos, ellas, Ud.,** *or* **Uds.** *to replace the underlined words.*

1. las rosas de Ana y las suyas _____ (*his*)

2. mis promesas y las suyas _____ (*hers*)

3. el compromiso de Pedro y el suyo _____ (*theirs* [m.])

4. tu investigación y la suya _____ (*theirs* [f.])

5. mi problema y el suyo _____ (*yours* [formal pl.])

6. las palabras de Ana y las suyas _____ (*yours* [formal pl.])

7. mis sentimientos y los suyos _____ (*yours* [formal sing.])

8. el auto de Lucy y el suyo _____ (*yours* [formal sing.])

Preguntas personales. *Use the various possessive pronouns in your answers whenever possible:* **la mía, la de ellos,** *etc.*

1. ¿Prefieres tu casa o la de tus padres? _____

2. ¿Usas tu computadora en casa o la de tu oficina?

   _____

3. Si vas de viaje, ¿usas tus maletas o las de tus amigos?

   _____

4. ¿Escuchas tus discos o los de tus colegas? _____

5. ¿Gastas tu dinero o el de tus familiares (*relatives*)?

   _____

Lo mío es mío y lo tuyo es mío también. Traduce. Usa el **Vocabulario útil.**

*Some people are odd. They forget their pen at home and they want to use yours (**tú**). Then they put your pen in their pocket! They probably think what is mine is mine and what is yours is mine as well. That bothers me. My good friend Paul is an example. He reads my books all the time. If I cannot find a book of mine, I know it is at Paul's house or in his office. Where is our bilingual dictionary? It is not on my desk. It is on his desk, of course. And where is President Kennedy's biography? No, it is not at our municipal library. It is on that desk of his, in his den. Our nephew Allan always buys books for my birthday. If Paul is here, he reads my books first. Is Paul absentminded? Probably. But I am annoyed. I want my books. They are mine!*

Vocabulario útil

absentminded	**distraído(a), despistado(a)**	nephew	**el sobrino**
annoyed	**enojado(a)**	odd	**extraño(a), raro(a)**
bilingual	**bilingüe**	to bother	**molestar(le) a alguien**
biography	**la biografía**	to find	**encontrar (o > ue)**
den	**la sala de estar**	to forget	**olvidar**
library	**la biblioteca**		

Demonstrative adjectives

Demonstrative adjectives (**adjetivos demostrativos**) indicate the location of the noun they modify with respect to the speaker and the listener. An object, person, event, or concern may be close, not as close, or farther away from the speaker, or from the speaker and the person or persons being addressed.

Este autobús es muy cómodo.	*This bus is very comfortable.*
Ese año no viajamos.	*That year, we did not travel.*

Este autobús points to an object close to the speaker. **Ese año** indicates a time not as close as what is conveyed by **este**, yet not very far from the time the conversation takes place.

DEMONSTRATIVE ADJECTIVE FORMS

SINGULAR		PLURAL	
este, esta	this	**estos, estas**	these
ese, esa	that	**esos, esas**	those
aquel, aquella	that (over there)	**aquellos, aquellas**	those (over there)

Este dormitorio es mío.	*This bedroom is mine.*
Esa colcha es nueva.	*That bedspread is new.*
Aquellas ventanas están abiertas.	*Those windows over there are open.*

Remember that

♦ demonstrative adjectives precede the noun they modify and agree in gender and number with that noun.

♦ the singular masculine forms of demonstrative adjectives end in **-e** (**este, ese**) and **-el** (**aquel**), not **-o**.

Práctica. Usa la forma apropiada de los adjetivos demostrativos (**este, esta, estos, estas**).

1. _____ planeta
2. _____ zapatos
3. _____ jaguar
4. _____ sistema
5. _____ cuentas
6. _____ secretaria
7. _____ problemas
8. _____ parientes
9. _____ ciudad
10. _____ estaciones
11. _____ trabajador
12. _____ actitud

When are the different forms of the demonstrative adjectives used in Spanish?

Consider the location of the speaker and his or her interlocutor in the following situations.

♦ **Este, esta, estos,** and **estas** indicate a physical location, a matter, or a time close to the speaker and the person or person he or she addresses.

Conozco al dueño de **este restaurante**.	*I know the owner of **this restaurant**.*
Esta situación es muy delicada.	***This situation** is very delicate.*

♦ **Ese, esa, esos,** and **esas** refer to a place, a concern, or a time somewhat distant.

En **esa época**, no había teléfonos inalámbricos.	*At **that time**, there were no cordless phones.*

♦ When the forms of **ese, este,** and **aquel** follow the noun, they take on a condescending or affective connotation. The tone of the message underscores the meaning intended.

¿Por qué aceptas una invitación **del hombre ese**?	*Why do you accept an invitation **from a man like that**?*
Recuerdo mis vacaciones en Puerto Vallarta. **¡Qué días aquellos!**	*I remember my vacation in Puerto Vallarta. **Those beautiful days!***

♦ **Aquel, aquella, aquellos,** and **aquellas** refer to a place, a concern, or an era relatively far from the speaker and the interlocutor.

En **aquel momento** saltó con el paracaídas.	*At **that moment**, he jumped with the parachute (he parachuted out).*

There are three adverbs that help distinguish the respective locations or perspectives indicated by these pronouns. They are often used for emphasis.

Use Ud. **este** baño **aquí**.	*Use **this** bathroom **here**.*
Ponga Ud. **esa** toalla **allí**.	*Put **that** towel **there**.*
Cierre Ud. **aquella** puerta **allá**.	*Close **that** door **over there**.*

En el parque zoológico. Más práctica. Usa la forma apropiada del adjetivo demostrativo **ese, esa, esos, esas, aquel, aquella, aquellos, aquellas** entre paréntesis.

1. _____ monos (*monkeys*) (ese)

2. _____ jirafa (aquel)

3. _____ pájaro (ese)

4. _____ panteras (aquel)

5. _____ tigre (ese)

6. _____ leones (aquel)

7. _____ serpiente (ese)

8. _____ tiburón (*shark*) (aquel)

9. _____ osos panda (ese)

10. _____ elefante (aquel)

11. _____ hipopótamo (ese)

12. _____ rinoceronte (aquel)

En español. La comodidad en la casa. Escribe la forma apropiada (**este, ese, aquel,** etc.) de acuerdo al adverbio **aquí, allí** y **allá** entre paréntesis.

1. Ayer compré _____ sofá muy cómodo en la tienda nueva. (aquí)

2. Mira, necesito _____ lámparas modernas. (allí)

3. Quiero comprar también _____ colchón. (allá)

4. ¡_____ sábanas son de seda y muy suaves! (aquí)

5. Uf, _____ sillón es comodísimo pero cuesta demasiado. (allí)

6. ¿Qué te parecen _____ almohadas de plumas (*feather*)? (allá)

7. Me gustaría tener _____ mesa en la sala para poner los pies encima. (aquí)

8. ¿Sabes cuánto cuesta _____ cojín? (allí)

9. ¡_____ jarrones son horribles! (allá)

10. Necesito _____ mesita de noche. (aquí)

En español. En el parque.

1. *Many children come to this park with their parents.*

_____

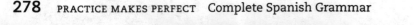

2. *Some women run in that area over there early in the morning.*

_____

3. *These swings (**los columpios**) are new and beautiful.*

_____

4. *My dog, Max, plays with those children over there.*

_____

5. *You (**tú**) can recycle plastic bottles in those bins (**los cubos**).*

_____

6. *I would like to roller-skate with you (**tú**) on that track (**la pista**).*

_____

7. *Look (**tú**), that man over there is sleeping under the tree.*

_____

8. *Do you (**tú**) want to participate in that baseball game?*

_____

Demonstrative pronouns

Demonstrative pronouns (**los pronombres demostrativos**) have the same forms as the demonstrative adjectives. Like other pronouns, they take the place of nouns.

DEMONSTRATIVE PRONOUN FORMS

SINGULAR		PLURAL	
éste, ésta	this one	**éstos, éstas**	these (ones)
ése, ésa	that one	**ésos, ésas**	those (ones)
aquél, aquélla	that one over there	**aquéllos, aquéllas**	those (ones over there)

Mi computadora es más rápida que **ésta**.	*My computer is faster than **this one**.*

Remember that demonstrative pronouns

◆ agree in gender and number with the nouns they replace.

◆ may have written accent marks (except the neuter forms **esto**, **eso**, and **aquello**). Note that contemporary writing often omits the accent mark.

Toma este globo y deja **ése** a ese niño.	*Take this balloon and leave **that one** for the other boy.*

The accent marks are only required for clarification if the context of the message is ambiguous. For the sake of practice, place the accent mark on the pronouns you write in the exercises that follow.

En el museo. Práctica. Cambia los sustantivos y usa solamente los pronombres. Use **ése, ésa, ésos, ésas** instead of the nouns.

1. la estatua _____
2. las fotos _____
3. la reproducción _____
4. el cuadro _____
5. las pinturas _____
6. la entrada _____
7. la tienda de regalos (*gift*) _____
8. el horario _____
9. los descuentos _____
10. el guía _____
11. el folleto (*flyer*) _____
12. las exposiciones _____

En español.

1. *This car is new, but that one is used (**usado**).*

_____

2. *Your (**tú**) camera is here, and these are Julia's and Mark's.*

_____

3. *Is this your (**tú**) backpack (**mochila**), or that one over there?*

_____

4. *This is my bag (**bolso**), and that one is mine, too.*

_____

5. *That one is my apartment building.*

_____

6. *Those over there are the tourists from Mexico.*

_____

7. *This bank and that one over there open at nine.*

_____

8. *That monument is more interesting than this one.*

_____

9. *What is that over there?* _____

The neuter forms of the demonstrative pronouns

The neuter demonstrative pronoun forms are used frequently in everyday communication and have specific functions.

esto	this
eso	that
aquello	that

Es difícil encontrar el trabajo ideal con el sueldo ideal. **Eso** es verdad.

It is difficult to find the ideal job with the ideal pay. That is true.

Observe that

- **esto**, **eso**, and **aquello** end in **-o**.

- these neuter forms do not have a written accent mark.

- neuter demonstrative pronouns refer to concepts or ideas. Usually they sum up or refer to an idea, a sentence, or a phrase that precedes the pronoun.

Pasamos la aspiradora y sacudimos los muebles. **Eso** es lo que hacemos.

We vacuum, and we dust the furniture. That is what we do.

- the neuter demonstratives also refer to something nonspecific or an object or idea not well known. They are often used in questions and exclamations.

—¿Qué es **eso**?
—¡**Eso** es una barbaridad!

"What is that?"
"That is horrible!"

Here are common expressions with the neuter form **eso**.

¿y eso?	why?
en eso	then
eso es	that is it
por eso	that is why

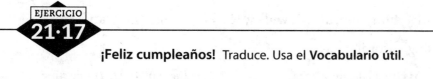

EJERCICIO
21·17

¡Feliz cumpleaños! Traduce. Usa el **Vocabulario útil**.

My birthday is tomorrow. That is good. But I have to clean my house, cook dinner, and clean the fish tank. And that is bad. Birthdays are days to celebrate. What is that? It is a flyer with information about a special cleaning service! That is fantastic! Why is that? Because I am going to dial this phone number right now! That's it! I am going to get my own birthday present. And I am going to ask for a discount with this coupon. This is fantastic!

Vocabulario útil

cleaning service	**el servicio de limpieza**	flyer	**el aviso**
coupon	**el cupón**	my own	**mi propio**
discount	**el descuento**	right now	**ahora mismo**
fish tank	**la pecera**	to dial	**marcar (un número de teléfono)**

Adverbs

An adverb is a modifier or a word that modifies other elements in a sentence: a verb, an adjective, or another adverb. Adverbs answer questions such as *how? how long? how much? when?* and *where?* They are easy to spot: Certain adverbs in English are made by adding *-ly* to an adjective. They emphasize the meaning of the verb: *I can **really** do it well. He spoke **softly**.*

In Spanish, there are several adjectives that may function as adverbs. When they are adverbs, they do not agree in number or gender. An example is **demasiado** (*too much*), an adverb of manner. In this example, it shows *how* the subject *works* (**trabaja**).

Ustedes trabajan **demasiado**.	*You work **too much**.*

However, in the following example, **demasiadas** agrees with the noun that follows it. In this sentence, as an adjective, it modifies **preguntas**.

Lola hace **demasiadas preguntas**.	*Lola asks **too many questions**.*

With all adverbs and adjectives in Spanish, it is important to understand the function of the words you choose and to select their appropriate forms.

Adverb forms in Spanish

Adverbs (**adverbios**) appear in a wide variety of forms. They can be

- a single word.

Los chicos llegan **ahora**.	*The boys are arriving **now**.*
¿Hablamos **luego**?	*Shall we talk **later**?*
Todavía no he terminado.	*I have not **yet** finished.*

- a compound word.

Salieron **anteayer**.	*They left **the day before yesterday**.*

Ahora, **luego**, and **todavía** are single words. **Anteayer** is a compound of two adverbs, **antes** and **ayer**. Note that, unlike in English, the adverb **todavía** does not come between the auxiliary verb and the participle in the compound tenses (**he terminado**). Compound tenses cannot be separated in Spanish.

282

The following list includes frequently used adverbs referring to place, time, quantity or measure, and manner.

PLACE		TIME	
abajo	down, downstairs	**ahora**	now
acá	over here	**anteanoche**	the night before last
afuera	out; outside	**anteayer**	the day before yesterday
allá	over there	**después**	later
allí	there	**ayer**	yesterday
aquí	here	**luego**	then, later
arriba	up, upstairs	**nunca**	never
cerca	near	**siempre**	always, all the time
debajo	under	**tarde**	late
delante	in front	**temprano**	early
detrás	behind	**todavía**	still
lejos	far	**ya**	already, right now

QUANTITY		MANNER	
bastante	enough	**bien**	well
demasiado	too much	**mal**	badly
mucho	much, a lot		
poco	little		
suficiente	enough		

EJERCICIO
22·1

El adverbio apropiado. Usa un adverbio para completar cada oración.

todavía	cerca	bien	nunca
lejos	poco	debajo	mal

1. No voy a la playa porque vivo _____ de la costa.

2. ¡Uds. _____ están listos para salir a tiempo!

3. Me siento _____, fantástico, y tengo ganas de nadar dos millas.

4. Vivo muy _____ de mi tía, a una milla, más o menos.

5. No puedo salir de casa _____ porque tengo que terminar mi trabajo.

6. Yo pongo el dinero _____ del colchón (*mattress*) para no perderlo.

7. ¿Te sientes _____? Siéntate en el sofá y descansa.

8. ¿El autor es _____ conocido? Necesita un nuevo publicista.

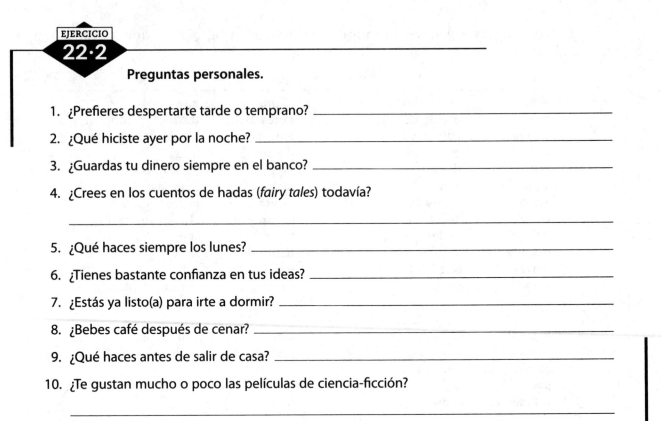

EJERCICIO

22·2

Preguntas personales.

1. ¿Prefieres despertarte tarde o temprano? _____

2. ¿Qué hiciste ayer por la noche? _____

3. ¿Guardas tu dinero siempre en el banco? _____

4. ¿Crees en los cuentos de hadas (*fairy tales*) todavía?

   _____

5. ¿Qué haces siempre los lunes? _____

6. ¿Tienes bastante confianza en tus ideas? _____

7. ¿Estás ya listo(a) para irte a dormir? _____

8. ¿Bebes café después de cenar? _____

9. ¿Qué haces antes de salir de casa? _____

10. ¿Te gustan mucho o poco las películas de ciencia-ficción?

   _____

EJERCICIO

22·3

Así soy yo. En español.

1. *There is always a reason to be happy.* _____

2. *I never have enough money.* _____

3. *I still have hopes to win the lottery.* _____

4. *Well, I dream a lot.* _____

5. *I expect too much from my friends.* _____

6. *Also, I have headaches frequently.* _____

7. *Besides, I don't complain (**quejarse**) often.* _____

8. *Later, I am going to take two aspirins.* _____

9. *But not yet, I want to wait.* _____

10. *Then, I will continue to talk about my personality.*

   _____

Compound adverbs

Compound adverbs in Spanish are formed with

- the feminine singular form of adjectives + the suffix -**mente**, equivalent to the English -*ly*.

    Los estudiantes trabajan **lentamente**.   *The students work **slowly**.*

- adjectives with a single form for the feminine and masculine + the suffix -**mente**. Such adjectives usually end in -**e** or a consonant (**fácil** [*easy*]). -**Mente** is added directly to the adjective.

    Eso se hace **fácilmente**.   *This is **easily** done.*
    La niña ríe **ruidosa y alegremente**.   *The girl laughs **loudly and happily**.*

Note: If the basic adjective has a written accent mark, the accent remains in place (**fácilmente**). If two or more adverbs ending in -**mente** are connected by conjunctions such as **y, ni**, or **pero**, only the final adverb in the series adds the suffix -**mente** (in the example above, **ruidosa y alegremente**).

Certain adverbs ending in -**mente** are more commonly seen in written language.

    Los niños cantaron **alegremente**.   *The children sang **happily**.*
    Finalmente, termina este programa.   *This program is **finally** ending.*

In everyday language, **alegremente** would likely be replaced by the adverbial expression **con alegría**, and **finalmente** by **por fin**. You will study such adverbial expressions later in this unit.

EJERCICIO
22·4

Práctica. Cambia los adjetivos a adverbios. Escribe la forma apropiada que termina en -**mente**.

1. ansioso _____

2. definitivo _____

3. lento _____

4. tímido _____

5. ágil _____

6. fácil _____

7. dulce _____

8. desgraciado _____

9. profundo _____

10. inmediato _____

11. total _____

12. obvio _____

13. claro _____

14. hábil _____

15. alegre _____

16. desafortunado _____

17. violento _____

18. completo _____

19. fuerte _____

20. rápido _____

Y en tu caso... ¿Verdadero o falso?

_____ 1. Probablemente recibiré una sorpresa agradable hoy.

_____ 2. Como lentamente.

_____ 3. Aprendo español rápidamente.

_____ 4. Trabajo tranquilamente en mi casa.

_____ 5. Hago mis ejercicios aeróbicos rápidamente.

_____ 6. Siempre duermo profundamente.

_____ 7. A menudo, me visto muy elegantemente.

_____ 8. Prefiero trabajar cómodamente en mi jardín.

_____ 9. Siempre saludo amablemente a todos mis vecinos.

_____ 10. Claramente sigo las instrucciones de mi médico.

En español.

1. *We do the exercises slowly.* _____

2. *Do you (**Uds.**) follow instructions carefully?*

_____

3. *Usually, we do not like to work on weekends.*

_____

4. *Obviously, this dog does not protect your (**Uds.**) house.*

_____

5. *Fortunately, you (**Uds.**) do not have too many jewels (**joyas**).*

_____

6. *You (**Uds.**) can easily protect your house with an alarm (**alarma**).*

_____

7. *Lisa speaks slowly and clearly.* _____

8. *She also speaks briefly.* _____

9. *Frankly, I do not like waiting.* _____

10. *Fortunately, I do not have much homework.*

_____

Other adverb forms: adverbial expressions

Groups of words may serve as adverbial expressions (**frases adverbiales**). Prepositions often tell where someone or something is; thus, many adverbial expressions consist of a preposition followed by other elements or parts of speech.

Here are the typical patterns.

◆ Preposition + an adjective

El auto salió **de repente**.	*The car left **suddenly**.*
Tengo que ir al dentista **de nuevo**.	*I have to go to the dentist **again**.*

◆ Preposition + a noun

Llegaron **de día**.	*They arrived **in the daytime**.*
Lo investigaron **a fondo**.	*They investigated it **thoroughly**.*

Here is a select list of commonly used fixed expressions.

a menudo	frequently, often	**de nuevo**	again
a veces	sometimes	**de pronto**	suddenly
al fin	finally	**de repente**	suddenly
al mismo tiempo	at the same time	**por desgracia**	unfortunately
con alegría	happily	**por fin**	finally
con facilidad	easily	**por suerte**	fortunately
con frecuencia	frequently	**por supuesto**	of course
con rapidez	quickly	**por último**	finally
con tristeza	sadly	**sin duda**	without a doubt
de día	in the daytime	**sin razón**	without (a) reason
de noche	at night		

EJERCICIO
22·7

La frase adverbial apropiada. Escribe en español la frase adverbial que aparece en inglés entre paréntesis. Recuerda: la expresión adverbial consiste de una preposición + adjetivo o sustantivo.

1. Barbara va al gimnasio _____ (*at night*).

2. No puede ir _____ (*in the daytime*) porque está muy ocupada.

3. Ella monta en bicicleta y habla por teléfono _____ (*at the same time*).

4. _____ (*Fortunately*) la bicicleta está cerca de la ventana y la recepción es buena.

5. Barbara va _____ (*frequently*) a la cafetería dentro del gimnasio.

6. _____ (*Sometimes*) ella pasa mucho tiempo charlando por teléfono.

7. _____ (*Without a doubt*) Barbara prefiere hablar, no hacer ejercicio.

8. Hoy, ella está _____ (*again*) practicando una rutina de aeróbicos.

Y en tu caso... ¿Verdadero o falso?

_____ 1. Por suerte, tengo muchos días feriados (*holidays*).

_____ 2. Por desgracia, no tengo suerte en la vida.

_____ 3. Siempre me despido con tristeza del Año Viejo.

_____ 4. Puedo viajar con rapidez en mi motocicleta.

_____ 5. Prefiero trabajar de día en mi computadora.

_____ 6. Me enseñaron que no debo hablar y comer al mismo tiempo.

_____ 7. A veces llego tarde a mis citas (*appointments*).

_____ 8. No puedo dormir bien de noche.

Regresa al ejercicio anterior. Escribe las frases adverbiales que aparecen en las preguntas 1–5.

1. _____

2. _____

3. _____

4. _____

5. _____

More adverbial expressions

In adverbial expressions, prepositions precede adjectives and nouns, and they may also precede verb forms or other adverbs.

Pedro regresó **al amanecer**.	*Pedro came back **at daybreak**.*
No puedo hacer dos cosas **al mismo tiempo**.	*I cannot do two things **at the same time**.*

Al amanecer is a combination of the contraction **al** + an infinitive. **Al mismo tiempo** consists of the contraction **al** + adjective + noun. Both are adverbial expressions of time. Consider the following lists as fixed expressions to be learned as lexical items.

The following adverbial expressions are formed with verb forms and other adverbs.

acá abajo	down here	**de ahora en adelante**	from now on
al anochecer	at nightfall	**de veras**	really, truly
al frente de	in front of	**de vez en cuando**	once in a while
al parecer	apparently	**desde aquí**	from here
al salir el sol	at sunrise	**desde entonces**	since then
allá arriba	up there	**hasta aquí**	up to here
cerca de	near (to)	**por lo visto**	apparently, evidently

EJERCICIO
22·10

En español. Usa una de las frases adverbiales de la lista anterior.

1. *Apparently, we want a better life.* _____

2. *Once in a while, we need to consider that life is short.*

_____

3. *Until now, we have worked a lot.* _____

4. *From now on, we are going to change our lifestyle* (**estilo de vida**)*.*

_____

5. *We are not going to get up at sunrise.* _____

6. *At nightfall, we can relax and forget about tomorrow.*

_____

7. *From here, we have a view of the river.* _____

8. *Up to now (here), this plan is boring.* _____

9. *Do we really have to change our lifestyle?*

_____

10. *From now (today) on, we cannot complain anymore.*

_____

Adjectives and nouns used as adverbs

Some adjectives and nouns are used as adverbs in idiomatic expressions. They are common in everyday Spanish. When used as adverbs, these forms are invariable; they do not change in gender or number.

La recepcionista habla **bajo**.	*The receptionist speaks **softly**.*
El hombre fue **directo** a la policía.	*The man went **directly** to the police.*
Hoy me siento **fatal**.	*Today I feel **bad(ly)**.*

Here are a few common adjectives or nouns used as adverbs.

alto	loudly	**fatal**	bad(ly)
bajo	softly	**fenómeno**	splendidly, wonderfully
claro	clearly	**fuerte**	loudly, strongly
directo	directly	**rápido**	quickly
duro	hard, intensely		

Comparisons with adverbs

Go back to the unit on adjectives (Unit 18) to review how to form comparisons of adjectives.
Adverbs also have comparative constructions. They may be equal to other adverbs, more or less abundant or intense than others, or superior to others. Use the following patterns to compare adverbs.

◆ For comparisons of *equality*, use **tan** + adverb + **como**.

Hablas **tan alto como** yo.	*You speak **as loudly as** I do.*

◆ For comparisons of *inequality*, use **menos** or **más** + adverb + **que**.

Estos días salimos **menos frecuentemente que** antes.	*These days, we go out **less frequently than** before.*
Trabajan **más lentamente que** los otros chicos.	*They work **more slowly than** the other boys.*

◆ If the comparison is based on an adjective or another adverb, **de lo que** is used instead of **que** as the equivalent of *than*.

Es más inteligente **de lo que** piensas.	*He is smarter **than** you think.*

◆ In comparisons that involve numerals, use **de** (not **que**).

Saben que tienen más **de** cuarenta días.	*They know they have more **than** forty days.*

EJERCICIO
22·11

Usa los adverbios. Escribe el adverbio en español. *Note that Nos. 2 and 7 require a comparative form.*

1. Por favor, habla _____ (*softly*).

2. Hoy salimos _____ (*faster*) ayer.

3. Nos vamos _____ (*immediately*) para la venta especial.

4. El delegado siempre habla _____ (*strongly*) delante de la asamblea.

5. Gritan _____ (*loudly*) y no se entiende lo que dicen.

6. Si te expresas _____ (*clearly*) vamos a tener una buena impresión.

7. Siempre hablas _____ (*louder*) nosotros.

When are adverbs used in Spanish?

Both in English and Spanish, adverbs are usually placed close to the word they modify. Adverbs and adverbial expressions add information in order to

- clarify the circumstances surrounding the action expressed by a verb: the time, the manner (for how long? how much?), or the place.

Ahora mismo compramos la moto.	*We are buying the motorcycle **right now**.*
Viajaremos **mucho**.	*We will travel **a lot**.*
Vamos a llegar **hasta allí**.	*We will get **over there**.*

- clarify the meaning of an adjective. Adverbs of manner are used in this way. The adverb usually precedes the adjective.

Paul está **obviamente listo** para salir.	*Paul is **obviously ready** to leave.*
Eres **demasiado bueno**.	*You are **too good**.*

Obviamente and **demasiado** modify and intensify **listo** and **bueno**.

- add precision to the meaning of another adverb.

¿Por qué van **tan despacio**?	*Why do they go **so slowly**?*
El proyecto va **muy rápido**.	*This project is moving **very fast**.*

In the examples above, **tan** adds emphasis to **despacio**, and **muy** does the same for **rápido**. Note that both **despacio** and **rápido** are adverbs; they are not adjectives. When used as an adjective, **rápido** agrees in number and gender with the noun it modifies: **los autos rápidos**. Adverbs and other words used as adverbs do not change.

- clarify the point of view of the communicator. See the following example, where the adverb is separated by commas.

Con mi ayuda, **claramente**, vas a pasar este examen.	***Clearly**, with my help, you will pass the exam.*

EJERCICIO
22·12

Ya voy a publicar mi libro. Traduce. Usa el **Vocabulario útil**.

Finally! The message is clearly on my answering machine. The editor of "Publicaciones Maravilla" accepted my novel. I am very happy. I want to call Lila right now. Obviously, she thinks I do not have enough talent to write a book. Naturally, she is jealous of my success. Lila always says she can do everything better than I. She frequently talks about a mysterious book she is going to publish soon. Without a doubt, Lila exaggerates frequently. Occasionally, she lies too. Can you keep a secret? She is definitely the inspiration for Chloe, the mean witch all my readers will hate.

Vocabulario útil

answering machine	**el contestador automático**	to exaggerate	**exagerar**
everything	**todo**	to hate	**odiar**
jealous	**celoso(a)**	to keep	**guardar**
mean (*adjective*)	**malo(a)**	to lie	**mentir (e > ie)**
reader	**el lector / la lectora**	to publish	**publicar**
right now	**ahora mismo**	witch	**la bruja**
success	**el éxito**		

Prepositions

Prepositions are used to indicate the relationship between words. The word itself ("pre-position") tells us it is placed before other words. Think of **preposiciones** as connectors, linking a noun, a pronoun, or a phrase to other words in a phrase or sentence.

Observe the relationship or connection established by the highlighted prepositions in the following examples.

Ellos trabajan **para mí**.	*They work **for me**.*
Mi casa está **cerca de la mansión**.	*My house is **close to the mansion**.*

Para and **de** introduce objects of prepositions. The words or phrases that follow the preposition are called the object of the preposition.

Spanish prepositions can present a challenge to English speakers. You will need to acquire them gradually. **Viajan *por* España** means *They are traveling **through** Spain*. If you change the preposition **por** to **para**, you alter the meaning of the sentence: **Viajan *para* España.** (*They are traveling **to** Spain.*)

Spanish speakers face similar challenges in learning English. *Get in*, *get in with*, and *get through* are only a few of the distinctions they must master. Note the Spanish equivalents: **entrar**, **quedar bien con**, **atravesar**. (A comedian, joking about the regional uses of words in the United States, objected to being told to *get on* the plane instead of to *get in* the plane. Getting *in* does sound more logical and safer than getting *on* a plane.) Significant changes in meaning can take place with a preposition.

As you study, it will be useful to group the common Spanish prepositions according to their form and meaning.

Frequently used prepositions in Spanish

Lists of prepositions, including verbs used with certain prepositions and idiomatic expressions with prepositions, appear in this unit. You may choose various study strategies. Memorizing may be helpful, as well as becoming aware of fixed expressions in context. The lists are provided as reference tools.

One-word (simple) prepositions

Prepositions appear in different forms. Here is a list of simple, or one-word, prepositions and their basic meanings.

a	to, at	hacia	toward
ante	before, in the presence of	hasta	until
bajo	under	para	for, in order to, to
con	with	por	for, by, through
contra	against	según	according to
de	of, from	sin	without
desde	from, since	sobre	over, above
en	in, on, into	tras	after
entre	between, among		

Práctica. Escribe la preposición apropiada.

| desde | por | hacia | sin | con |
| sobre | ante | según | entre | en |

1. Vamos a hacer este trabajo _____ tú y yo.

2. Si quiere, Ud. puede pagar la multa _____ una tarjeta de crédito.

3. La abogada defendió a su clienta _____ el juez.

4. El ladrón entró a la casa _____ la ventana.

5. Elena habla _____ un asunto muy interesante.

6. Viajamos _____ el norte, ¿verdad?

7. Pablo me saludó _____ la puerta de su casa.

8. Los niños no pueden ir a la fiesta _____ el permiso de los padres.

9. Mira, Carlos está _____ la sala de urgencia.

10. _____ Carmen, su hermano sale del hospital mañana por la mañana.

¿Verdadero o falso? Historia y geografía.

_____ 1. El Día de la Independencia de México es el cinco de mayo.

_____ 2. La Estrella Polar indica el Sur.

_____ 3. México es un país independiente desde hace dos siglos.

_____ 4. Según los historiadores, los indígenas de América Central construyeron pirámides.

_____ 5. Hasta el siglo XVI, los aztecas dominaron lo que hoy es México.

_____ 6. Hacia finales del siglo XVI, Cristóbal Colón llegó a las islas del Caribe.

_____ 7. Para llevar los tesoros de América a España, había que atravesar el mar Pacífico.

En español.

1. *Luisa cannot live without Jacob.* _____

2. *Jacob sent Luisa a card from Lima.* _____

3. *Jacob was traveling to Ecuador.* _____

4. *From the airport, he called Luisa.* _____

5. *He did not arrive in Quito until midnight.* _____

6. *Jacob found a coin under his pillow.* _____

7. *According to Luisa, he is superstitious.* _____

8. *With luck, Jacob will sell many of his products in Quito.*

_____

Compound prepositions

There are numerous compound prepositions (made up of two or more words). Many will already be familiar to you. Here are some **frases preposicionales**.

a cargo de	in charge of	**de vez en cuando**	from time to time
a causa de	because of	**debajo de**	beneath, under
a favor de	in favor of	**delante de**	in front of
a fines de	at the end of	**dentro de**	within, inside (of)
a mediados de	around	**desde luego**	of course
a partir de	from	**después de**	after
a pie	walking	**detrás de**	behind
a tiempo	on time	**en cambio**	on the other hand
a través de	through	**en (diez) días**	in (ten) days
además de	besides	**en efecto**	in fact
al norte de	to the north of	**en (una semana)**	in (one week)
al sur de	to the south of	**en vez de**	instead of
alrededor de	around	**encima de**	above, on top of
antes de	before	**enfrente de**	in front of
cerca de	near	**frente a**	in front of
de ahora en adelante	from now on	**fuera de**	outside of
de pie	standing	**lejos de**	far from

Práctica. Completa cada oración. Escoge la frase que indica la relación apropiada.

en una semana	a pie	además de	en cambio
de ahora en adelante	en vez de	a cargo de	a tiempo

1. Estoy en La Habana y voy a regresar _____ a mi casa en Miami.

2. Quiero disfrutar más con mi familia _____ regresar a casa y trabajar.

3. Yo estoy _____ mi oficina, y puedo tener más tiempo de vacaciones.

4. _____, mis empleados tienen que trabajar todos los días mientras yo disfruto mis vacaciones.

5. También, quiero visitar las playas, _____ pasar tiempo con mis primos.

6. Creo que yo, _____ voy a tener mucho más contacto con mis familiares.

7. Mis primos y yo vamos a ir _____ desde la casa a Centro Habana.

8. Nosotros debemos llegar _____ a una tienda para comprar regalos.

Preguntas personales.

1. ¿Terminas tu trabajo a tiempo?

_____

2. ¿Qué haces típicamente a mediados de la semana?

_____

3. ¿Estás a favor de una causa especial? ¿Qué causa?

_____

4. ¿Qué pones debajo de la cama?

_____

5. ¿Vas a pie a tu trabajo o a la escuela? ¿Por qué?

_____

6. ¿Qué hay cerca de tu casa?

_____

7. ¿Qué vas a hacer a fines de este verano?

_____

En español. Usa las expresiones que aparecen en la lista de frases preposicionales.

1. *The stores are far from our house.* _____

2. *My car is outside the garage.* _____

3. *Instead of sugar, the recipe (**receta**) says honey (**miel**).*

   _____

4. *From time to time, I run ten miles.* _____

5. *This meeting ends within an hour.* _____

6. *There are around fifteen birds in that tree.*

   _____

Relationships of commonly used prepositions and compound prepositions

Note that the same preposition may express a different relationship in different contexts.

Si vas **a** la fiesta, llámame. (movement)	*If you go **to** the party, call me.*
La fiesta es **a** las nueve. (time)	*The party is **at** nine o'clock.*

As part of adverbial phrases, prepositions can modify a verb. Simple and compound prepositions (**preposiciones simples** and **frases preposicionales**) can be classified and learned according to the relationships (of movement, place, time . . .) they establish. Remember that the same preposition can appear in a variety of adverbial phrases.

◆ Movement (**movimiento**). Prepositions of movement indicate a position or the direction where someone or something is going.

Van **a** la biblioteca.	*They go **to** the library.*
Ellos caminan **hacia** el edificio.	*They walk **toward** the building.*
No podemos correr **hasta** tu casa.	*We cannot run **to** your house.*
El avión sale **para** Londres.	*The plane leaves **for** London.*

◆ Location (**lugar**). These prepositions or prepositional phrases tell where someone or something is in relation to other people or things.

El gimnasio está **a la derecha** del auditorio.	*The gym is **to the right** of the auditorium.*
Los papeles están **en** mi oficina.	*The papers are **in** my office.*
Están **sobre** mi escritorio.	*They are **on top of** my desk.*
Mi oficina no está **lejos de** aquí.	*My office is not **far from** here.*
Voy a caminar **por** el barrio.	*I am going to walk **around** the neighborhood.*

- Time (**tiempo**). Most of these prepositions are used for other functions as well.

El concierto es **a** las ocho.	*The concert is **at** eight.*
No abren **antes de** las siete.	*They do not open **before** seven.*
¿**Hasta** cuando vas a esperar?	***Until** when will you wait?*
Llegan **para** fines de semana.	*They arrive **by** the weekend.*

- Other relationships. Most of these express relationships among people, things, or abstract ideas. They may establish a connection of means (**medio**), company (**compañía**), etc.

Siempre sale **con** sus hermanas.	*She always goes out **with** her sisters.*
¡Sales **sin** la maleta otra vez!	*You're leaving **without** your bag again!*
El paciente habló **acerca de** sus síntomas.	*The patient talked **about** his symptoms.*

EJERCICIO 23·7

¿Cuál? ¿Cuál es la frase preposicional o la preposición más lógica para completar la idea? Subraya la preposición o la frase preposicional de la respuesta.

1. Los turistas viajan (por | sin) la ciudad.

2. No quieren llegar (antes de | junto a) las diez al hotel.

3. Hay más de cuarenta personas (encima del | dentro del) autobús.

4. El grupo pasa (a favor de | a través de) una región de la costa.

5. Comen en un restaurante (debajo de | al lado de) la salida de la autopista.

6. Deciden explorar la costa (en vez de | enfrente de) regresar al hotel.

7. Por fin, van al hotel (dentro de | alrededor de) la medianoche.

8. Todos caminan (hacia | según) su cuarto.

9. Muchos duermen (contra | hasta) el mediodía.

10. Todos los turistas escriben (sobre | contra) la aventura cuando envían tarjetas a su familia.

EJERCICIO 23·8

En tu caso... ¿Es verdadero o falso? Indica con **V** o **F**.

_____ 1. No me levanto antes de las diez de la mañana los domingos.

_____ 2. Nunca voy al cine sin mis amigos.

_____ 3. Prefiero poner mis zapatos debajo de la cama.

_____ 4. Estoy a favor de la libertad de expresión para todos.

_____ 5. En mi casa, yo estoy a cargo de las compras en el supermercado.

_____ 6. De vez en cuando voy a un restaurante mexicano.

¿**Cuál?** ¿Qué clase de relación existe entre los elementos de la oración? Observa la preposición subrayada o frase preposicional subrayada. Indica la relación con la letra correspondiente: **M** (movimiento), **T** (tiempo), **L** (lugar) u **O** (otra).

_____ 1. Salen de la clase <u>antes de</u> las seis.

_____ 2. Podemos salir <u>hacia</u> el gimnasio.

_____ 3. ¿Pones tus cosas <u>en</u> la maleta?

_____ 4. Voy a cambiar <u>a partir de</u> hoy.

_____ 5. ¿Estás <u>a cargo de</u> lavar la ropa?

_____ 6. No caminan <u>alrededor de</u> la plaza.

_____ 7. Voy a votar <u>a favor de</u> esta candidata.

_____ 8. Estudio francés <u>en lugar de</u> español.

_____ 9. Van <u>a</u> la tienda.

_____ 10. Caminamos <u>a lo largo de</u> la playa.

The preposition a and the personal a

One of the basic functions of the preposition **a** is to indicate movement. Here are examples of some other functions of the preposition **a**.

Study the examples below and describe the different functions of **a**.

Prefiero ir **a pie**.	*I prefer to go **on foot**.*
Estamos **a cuatro millas** del aeropuerto.	*We are **four miles** from the airport.*
Los mejillones son **a dos dólares** la docena.	*Mussels are **two dollars** a dozen.*

In the examples above, the preposition **a** appears in adverbial expressions indicating ways or means to do something (**a pie**), distance (**a cuatro millas**), and price (**a dos dólares**). Later in this unit you will find a list of verbs that require **a** + an infinitive when they follow a conjugated verb. Here are some examples.

Vienen a ayudar.	*They come to help.*
¿Quieren **aprender a preparar** tacos?	*Do you want **to learn to prepare** tacos?*

A appears with other verbs in idiomatic expressions. Some examples are **sonar a** (*to sound like*) and **saber a** (*to taste like*).

¡Este postre **sabe a** ron!	*This dessert **tastes like** rum!*
Sus palabras **suenan a** amenaza.	*Her words **sound like** a threat.*

The "personal **a**" (different from the preposition **a**) is *required* in the following contexts.

◆ Before a noun if that direct object noun is a specific *person or persons*. Remember that **a** followed by the article **el** will result in the contraction **al**.

Llamo **a las chicas**.	*I am calling **the girls**.*
Veo **al cartero**.	*I see **the mail carrier**.*

Note: One exception to the use of the personal **a** before a direct object noun is the verb **tener**. *Do not* use the personal **a** after **tener** followed by a specific person or persons.

Tenemos parientes en San Francisco.	***We have relatives** in San Francisco.*

◆ With pronouns like **alguien, nadie**.

No veo **a nadie** en este restaurante.	*I do not see **anyone** in this restaurant.*

◆ With domestic animals, highlighting the bond of affection between human beings and pets.

La nena adora **a su gatito**.	*The little girl adores **her kitten**.*

EJERCICIO
23·10

En español. Usa la preposición **a**.

1. *This house smells like fish.* _____

2. *Are you calling Rosa or Manuel?* _____

3. *I love my canary!* _____

4. *They do not invite anyone to their anniversary (party).*

   _____

5. *My soup tastes like parsley (**perejil**).*

   _____

6. *Do you (**Uds.**) know anyone in this class?*

   _____

7. *The flowers are three dollars a dozen.*

   _____

8. *The train station is ten miles from my house.*

   _____

9. *Luisa takes care of (**cuidar**) my cat.*

   _____

Uses of prepositions and their English equivalents

A preposition may combine with other parts of speech, as follows.

- A noun + a preposition (often **de** or **para**) + another noun may modify a noun or a pronoun. The resulting phrase functions as an adjective. In English, a noun alone can serve as an adjective.

    Lee compra **la bandeja de cerámica**.   *Lee buys **the ceramic tray**.*
    Es **un tiesto para flores**.   *It is **a flowerpot**.*

- A preposition + a noun modifies a verb. The result is an adverbial expression.

    Pelea **sin cuidado**.   *He fights **carelessly** (without care).*
    Trabajo **con paciencia**.   *I work **patiently** (with patience).*

- Certain prepositions followed by an infinitive are equivalent to the present participle (*-ing* form) in English. Remember to use the Spanish infinitive form after these prepositions.

    Al regresar a Italia, fueron a Nápoles.   ***Upon returning** to Italy, they went to Naples.*
    ¿Cómo entras al cine **sin pagar**?   *How do you go into the movie theater **without paying**?*

The following prepositions are used in front of infinitives in this way.

al	upon	**en lugar de**	instead of
antes de	before	**en vez de**	instead of
con	with	**hasta**	until
de	of	**sin**	without
después de	after		

EJERCICIO
23·11

En español. Escribe en español la frase entre paréntesis.

1. Preferimos descansar _____ (*instead of walking*).

2. _____ (*After entering*) a la sala, puedes sentarte en el sofá.

3. _____ (*Upon finishing*) la merienda (*snack*), vamos a ver el programa de noticias.

4. Voy a cerrar la ventana _____ (*without making*) ruido (*noise*).

5. Marta hace sus tareas _____ (*with speed*).

6. En cambio, Ruth no sabe hacer nada _____ (*in peace*).

7. Tomamos café _____ (*upon arriving*) a la cafetería.

8. _____ (*Instead of washing*) la ropa, prefiero escuchar la radio.

The uses of para and por

For is the basic English equivalent of both **para** and **por**. However, these two prepositions change meaning in context. If you choose **para** or **por** incorrectly, you may cause confusion.

If you say **trabajo *por* Marco**, the listener will understand that you are taking over Marco's responsibilities and you are working *instead of* him. If you say **trabajo *para* Marco**, you mean that you do some work for Marco or he is your boss. The distinction between **para** and **por** is sometimes rather subtle in Spanish.

Use **para** to indicate the following relationships.

◆ Purpose. **Para** indicates the *purpose* of an action or goal, equivalent to the English phrase *in order to*. It may indicate the purpose or the use of an action, an event, or an object.

Comemos **para** vivir.	*We eat (**in order**) **to** live.*
Bill estudia **para** enfermero.	*Bill studies **to be** a nurse.*
La reunión es **para** comentar el libro.	*The meeting is **to** discuss the book.*
Necesito una caja **para** mis cosas.	*I need a box **for** my things.*

◆ Comparison. **Para** indicates the *contrast* of an idea, person, object, or situation in order to distinguish it from others in the same group or category.

Para una revista de modas, es muy cara.	***For** a fashion magazine, it is very expensive.*
Es precoz **para ser** un niño de siete años.	*He is precocious **for** a seven-year-old boy.*

◆ Deadlines. **Para** indicates date, time, and deadlines in the future. Some English equivalents are *for*, *by*, and *on*.

La cita es **para** el martes por la mañana.	*The appointment is **for** Tuesday morning.*
Termina el informe **para** las diez.	*Finish the report **by** ten o'clock.*

◆ Destination. The intended destination preceded by **para** may be a place or a person.

¿Éste es el libro **para** el profesor?	*Is this the book **for** the professor?*
¿Sale ella **para** África?	*Is she leaving **for** Africa?*

EJERCICIO
23·12

Un poco de lógica. Escribe la letra que corresponde a la respuesta.

_____ 1. Hay que gastar mucho

_____ 2. Tienen que estudiar más

_____ 3. Deben salir ahora

_____ 4. Habla muy bien el alemán

_____ 5. El taxi es

_____ 6. Necesitas una casa grande

_____ 7. Este trabajo es

_____ 8. Estás muy alta

a. para la señora.

b. para tener solamente diez años.

c. para tener más espacio.

d. para el lunes a las cuatro en punto.

e. para comprar este auto nuevo.

f. para llegar a tiempo.

g. para ser español.

h. para pasar el examen.

En español. Usa la preposición **para**. *As you do the exercise, notice the different English equivalents for* **para**.

1. *For a liberal, he has traditional ideas.* _____

2. *Are you (tú) training for the Olympic games?*

   _____

3. *I need a lamp for my bedroom.* _____

4. *They must be here by four o'clock.* _____

5. *This coffee is for us.* _____

6. *Lucille reads the newspaper in order to find an apartment.*

   _____

7. *Is this letter for Susan?* _____

8. *We are leaving for San Francisco.* _____

9. *What do you (tú) need this money for?* _____

10. *I need the money for a new computer.* _____

Use **por** to indicate the following relationships.

◆ Exchange. **Por** expresses the idea "in exchange for."

¡Compra los zapatos **por** $20!	*Buy the shoes for $20!*
Quiero cambiar mi auto **por** tu moto.	*I want to exchange my car for your motorcycle.*

◆ Moving through. **Por** indicates the action of moving through a space.

Corrieron **por** el parque.	*They ran through the park.*

◆ Duration of time. **Por** expresses how long something took.

Estudiaron **por** tres horas.	*They studied for three hours.*

◆ Expressions of time. **Por** is found in the fixed expressions of time: **por la tarde, por la mañana, por la noche**, etc.

Nos vamos **por la mañana**.	*We leave in the morning.*

◆ Movement. **Por** is used to talk about transportation, as the equivalent of *by means of*.

El turista viene **por** tren.	*The tourist comes by train.*

◆ Reason. **Por** points out a reason or rationale, as the equivalent of *because of*.

Por no jugar bien no vas a ganar el partido.	*Because you do not play well, you are not going to win the game.*

Por is also used

* to introduce the agent of the passive voice.

El caso fue estudiado **por** los especialistas.	*The case was studied **by** the specialists.*

* to express the equivalent of *per.*

¿Escribes sólo veinte palabras **por minuto**?	*You can type only twenty words **per minute**?*

* to express the equivalent of *for* when it follows these verbs: **enviar** (*to send*), **ir** (*to go*), **preguntar** (*to ask*), **venir** (*to come*), **regresar** (*to come back*), and **volver** (*to come back*).

Ella me **envió por** pan.	*She sent me **out for** bread.*
Regresamos por los paquetes.	*We came back for the packages.*
Pregunten por Manuel.	*Ask for Manuel.*

* to indicate *to be about to do something* or *to be in favor of something or someone* with **estar** + **por** + infinitive.

Estamos por terminar.	*We are about to finish.*
Ellos están por un aumento de sueldo.	*They support a pay raise.*

EJERCICIO
23·14

Preguntas para un amigo. Usa la preposición **por** y la forma **tú** para los verbos.

1. *Do you go to work by train or by car?* _____

2. *Are you about to finish your work now?* _____

3. *Do you send your greetings by e-mail?* _____

4. *Do you run through the park often?* _____

5. *Good heavens (**Caramba**)! Did you buy those shoes for three hundred dollars?*

   _____

6. *Do you drive on the highway at sixty-five miles per hour?*

   _____

7. *Do you return home in the afternoon or in the evening?*

   _____

8. *And finally, are you for the liberals or for the conservatives?*

   _____

Por in common idiomatic expressions

Por appears in commonly used idiomatic expressions. This list is provided as a reference.

por ahí, allí	around there	**por lo general**	generally
por ahora	for now	**por lo menos**	at least
por aquí	this way	**por lo visto**	apparently
por cierto	by the way	**por poco**	almost
por Dios	for God's sake	**por separado**	separately
por ejemplo	for example	**por si acaso**	just in case
por eso	that is why	**por supuesto**	of course
por favor	please	**por último**	finally
por fin	finally		

EJERCICIO 23·15

Una conversación entre dos amigos. ¿Cuál es la expresión más apropiada para completar la idea? Subraya la respuesta.

1. Oye, Pedro, (por ejemplo | por ahí) viene Antonio.

2. (Por lo visto | Por favor), ¿puedes prestarme tus lentes de sol?

3. ¡(Por separado | Por supuesto)! Pero, ¿por qué necesitas mis lentes?

4. (Por lo visto | Por separado) no sabes que le debo dinero a Antonio.

5. ¿De verdad? (Por lo general | Por cierto), tú me debes a mí veinticinco dólares.

6. ¡(Por ejemplo | Por Dios)! Yo no recuerdo eso.

7. (Por lo general | Por lo menos) no digas mentiras. Sabes la verdad.

8. ¡Ay! (Por favor | Por si acaso), ten un poco de paciencia.

9. (Por ahí | Por fin) dices la verdad.

10. Sí, pero (por eso | por poco) ayúdame. No quiero que Antonio me vea aquí.

EJERCICIO 23·16

¿Por o para? Escribe la preposición apropiada.

1. El avión sale _____ México en dos horas.

2. Los estudiantes van a estar en Acapulco _____ diez días.

3. Allí, no van a poder encontrar un hotel _____ poco dinero.

4. _____ ser jóvenes, son muy responsables.

5. _____ la mañana, quieren tomar el sol.

6. _____ el viernes, ya podemos llamarlos a Tijuana.

7. Van a pasar _____ la casa de unas amigas de Carmen.

8. Espero que ellos nos llamen _____ teléfono.

En español. Usa **por** o **para**, de acuerdo al contexto.

1. *We work instead of Lidia.* _____

2. *They pass through the tunnel.* _____

3. *He has at least two cars.* _____

4. *Because of her illness (**enfermedad**), she is not here.*

_____

5. *My friend comes by my office.* _____

6. *He comes by train.* _____

7. *He will be here by four o'clock.* _____

Y en tu caso... ¿Verdadero o falso?

_____ 1. Debes tener 21 años para votar en los Estados Unidos.

_____ 2. Puedes recibir una multa (*ticket*) si conduces a ochenta millas por hora.

_____ 3. Trabajas mejor por la mañana y no por la tarde.

_____ 4. Tienes que terminar un proyecto especial para el sábado.

_____ 5. Entras a tu casa por la puerta del garaje.

_____ 6. Sales para México la semana que viene.

_____ 7. Siempre llevas un cepillo para el pelo.

Explica por qué. *Explain why either* **por** *or* **para** *is used in each of the following sentences. Indicate destination, movement, exchange, etc. in your answers.*

1. Salen para Moscú esta tarde. _____

2. Viajan por avión. _____

3. Van a llegar para las cuatro. _____

4. Pagaron trescientos euros por los billetes. _____

5. Para un viaje tan largo, el billete es barato. _____

6. Viajan para asistir a un congreso. _____

7. Viajan por el oeste de Europa. _____

8. Viajan por necesidad. _____

9. Van a estar en Moscú por una semana. _____

10. Por último, van a visitar a unos amigos. _____

Verbs that require the preposition a or de + an infinitive in Spanish

In Spanish, some conjugated verbs always require **a**, **de**, or another preposition when followed by an infinitive (**Me decido a salir.** *I decide to go out.*). Other conjugated verbs are followed directly by the infinitive (**Querríamos comer** ahora. *We would like to eat now.*).

Whether or not they are followed by infinitives, prepositions often determine the meaning of Spanish verbs: **regresar** means *to return*. **Regresar a** means *to return to* with the intention of doing something, while **regresar de** implies *to return from*.

Regresaron a terminar el trabajo.	*They returned to do the work.*
Elisa **regresó de San Pedro** anoche.	*Elisa returned from San Pedro last night.*

The following lists of commonly used verbs are provided for vocabulary study and as a reference tool. Entries in a good all-Spanish or bilingual dictionary will show prepositions used with verbs, often in examples. Consult your dictionary for verbs not found here.

Some verbs may be categorized according to the preposition they require. The following list includes verbs followed by the preposition **a**, before an infinitive and/or before a predicate noun. Context will tell you if an infinitive or a noun is appropriate. (Stem-changing verbs are indicated in parentheses.)

acercarse a	to approach, come close to	**montar a**	to ride
		oler a (o > ue)	to smell of
aprender a	to learn to	**oponerse a**	to oppose, be opposed to
asistir a	to attend	**ponerse a**	to start to
atreverse a	to dare to	**quedarse a**	to stay, remain (back) to
comenzar a (e > ie)	to start to	**regresar a**	to go back to
convidar a	to invite to	**resistirse a**	to resist
correr a	to run to	**saber a**	to taste like
decidirse a	to decide to	**salir a**	to go out to
empezar a (e > ie)	to begin to	**sonar a (o > ue)**	to sound like
enseñar a	to teach to	**venir a**	to come to
inspirar a	to inspire to	**volver a (o > ue)**	to return (something) to; to do (something) again
invitar a	to invite to		
ir a	to go to		
llegar a	to arrive to/at; to succeed in		

EJERCICIO
23·20

¿Cuál es la respuesta? Escribe la equivalencia en español de las palabras en inglés. *You may want to review the previous list of infinitives followed by the preposition a.*

1. Mi habitación _____ (*smells like*) rosas.

2. Esas palabras _____ (*sound like*) mentiras (*lies*).

3. Gandhi me _____ (*inspires to*) buscar soluciones pacíficas.

4. Muchas personas no _____ (*dare to*) aprender una lengua extranjera.

5. No quiero aprender a _____ (*to ride*) caballo con un pony.

6. Sus padres _____ (*are opposed to*) su matrimonio con Carla.

Verbs with other prepositions

The prepositions **de, con,** and **por** also connect conjugated verbs with an infinitive or with a predicate noun. Learn the following verbs along with their prepositions.

acabar de	to have just
acordarse de (o > ue)	to remember (*someone or something*)
alegrarse de	to be glad about
alegrarse por	to be happy for
amenazar con	to threaten with
casarse con	to marry
consentir en (e > ie)	to consent to
consistir en	to consist of
dejar de	to stop (*doing something*)
insistir en	to insist on
olvidarse de	to forget about (*someone or something*)
soñar con (o > ue)	to dream of/about
terminar de	to finish (*doing something*)

¿Cuál es la preposición apropiada? Subraya tu respuesta.

1. Carla está enamorada (con | de) Juan.

2. Laura se casa (con | a) Martín.

3. Yo sueño (de | con) ver a mis amigos en Colorado.

4. La profesora insiste (con | en) estos datos acerca de la comunidad hispana.

5. Paula, deja (con | de) hablar y empieza a trabajar ya.

6. Nos alegramos (de | para) verlos aquí.

7. ¿Vienen Uds. (en | a) el mes de mayo?

8. El meteorólogo se olvidó (de | por) dar el pronóstico del tiempo para mañana por la tarde.

Verbs that require a preposition in English but not in Spanish

Note that some Spanish verbs that *don't* require a preposition have English equivalents that do. Anglophones will be tempted to try to translate these verbs literally, adding a preposition where it doesn't exist. Learn this list of Spanish verbs without prepositions by picturing them in context (**bajar las escaleras**, *to go down the steps*).

In context, the verbs in this list are all followed by a direct object noun (or preceded by a direct object pronoun). Don't forget to include the personal **a** when the direct object noun is a specific person (**Busco a Carlos**. *I am searching for Carlos.*).

apagar	to turn off (*a light*)
bajar	to go down
borrar	to cross out
botar	to throw away
buscar	to look for
caerse	to fall down
colgar (o > ue)	to hang up
encender (e > ie)	to light up
escuchar	to listen to
esperar	to wait for
mirar	to look at
pagar	to pay for
poder	to be able to
poner	to turn on (*an appliance*)
quitar(se)	to take off
sacar	to take out
salir	to go out
subir	to go up

Las noticias. Traduce. Usa el **Vocabulario útil**.

I go down the steps, I go into the living room, I turn on the TV, and I listen to the news. I dream of a day full of good news. For example, foreign leaders do not threaten with a new international conflict, the financial experts do not report dreadful details about the economy, and I stop thinking of the world's problems. I am not selfish, for God's sake. I only want one day of peace and happy thoughts. What news do I want to hear? For example, that we are all for peace and against war, that we are glad to have the simple things in life. Today, I am going to turn off the television, and I am going to look for my shovel to work in the garden.

Vocabulario útil

detail	**el detalle**	news	**las noticias**
dreadful	**horrible**	peace	**la paz**
financial	**financiero(a)**	selfish	**egoísta**
foreign	**extranjero(a)**	shovel	**la pala**
full	**lleno(a)**	thought	**el pensamiento**
leader	**el líder**	to report	**reportar**

Indefinite and negative words and expressions

You are probably already familiar with most of the words and expressions in this unit. Indefinite and negative words can be adjectives (**alguno**[a], *some*), pronouns (**nadie**, *no one, nobody*), or adverbs (**nunca**, *never*).

Algunas personas no viajan por avión.	*Some people do not travel by plane.*
Nadie está aquí.	*No one is here.*
No sale **nunca**.	*He never goes out.*

Algo and **nada** may be *pronouns* that describe something imprecise and, therefore, indefinite.

Algo puede cambiar.	*Something may change.*

Yet these two words serve as *adverbs* in situations such as the following.

Marta se siente **algo** mejor ahora.	*Marta feels somewhat better now.*
No me gusta esta situación **nada**.	*I do not like this situation at all.*

Conjunctions may also be used as indefinite and negative words. *Note*: **O... o...** and **ni... ni...** are always used in pairs.

O salimos **o** nos quedamos.	*Either we go or we stay.*
Ni fumo **ni** bebo.	*I neither smoke nor drink.*

By grouping these expressions together as indefinite and negative words, we can focus on their uses and contrast them with their English equivalents.

Indefinite and negative words in Spanish

Indefinite and negative words may refer to people or things. You will learn them more easily as contrasting pairs, as they are presented in the following list.

INDEFINITE		NEGATIVE	
algo	something, somewhat	**nada**	nothing
alguien	someone, somebody, anyone, anybody	**nadie**	no one, nobody, not anyone
algún, -a, -o, -as, -os	some, somebody	**ningún**, -a, -o, -as, -os	no, none
o... o...	either . . . or . . .	**ni... ni...**	neither . . . nor . . .
sí	yes	**no**	no
siempre	always	**nunca, jamás**	never
también	also	**tampoco**	neither

310

Y en tu caso... ¿Verdadero o falso?

_____ 1. Nunca digo mentiras.

_____ 2. Siempre digo lo que siento.

_____ 3. No sé nada de la situación económica de mis amigos.

_____ 4. Tampoco sé cuáles son los problemas de mis vecinos.

_____ 5. Tengo algunos problemas en mi trabajo.

_____ 6. Nadie vive conmigo en mi casa.

_____ 7. Jamás he visitado México.

_____ 8. Conozco a alguien que habla árabe.

En español.

1. *No one works in this office.* _____

2. *Some people (**personas**) are nicer than others.*

   _____

3. *I never ask questions.* _____

4. *I do not talk much, either.* _____

5. *Sometimes, I need help.* _____

6. *Do you (**Ud.**) speak German, too?* _____

7. *She eats either potatoes or rice only.* _____

8. *Neither you (**tú**) nor I.* _____

When are indefinite and negative words used in Spanish?

Here is a summary of the uses of indefinite and negative words in Spanish.

- ◆ **Alguien** and **nadie** refer only to *people*.

Alguien me manda flores a la oficina todos los viernes.	*Someone sends me flowers at my office every Friday.*
No veo **a nadie** en el salón de fiestas.	*I **don't** see **anyone** in the ballroom.*

  Note the personal **a** in the second example above; **nadie** is the direct object of the verb **veo.**

- **Algo** and **nada** refer only to *things or ideas*.

¿Vas a hacer **algo**?	*Are you going to do **anything (something)**?*
Nada va a cambiar.	***Nothing** is going to change.*

- The forms **algún/alguna/alguno/algunas/algunos** and **ningún/ninguna/ninguno/ningunas/ningunos** may refer to both *people* and *things*. A spelling rule requires a written accent mark on **algún** and **ningún** when the **-o** ending of the adjectives **alguno** and **ninguno** is dropped, and these words (masculine, singular) precede the noun.

Algunos estudiantes no quieren estudiar pero **ningún profesor** está de acuerdo.	***Some students** do not want to study, but **none of the professors** agrees.*

  Note: The form **alguno(a)**, when used as an adjective, follows the noun and may replace the negative **ninguno(a)**. **Algún** always precedes the noun.

Las leyes no son respetadas por **criminal alguno**.	***No criminal** respects the laws.*
Algún día vamos a viajar al espacio.	***One day**, we are going to travel into space.*

- Use the negative adverb **no** before the conjugated verb or before the pronoun if an object pronoun precedes the verb.

No beben vino.	*They **do not (don't)** drink wine.*
No los quieren aquí.	*They **don't** want **them** here.*

- Two or even three negative words may be used in Spanish in the same sentence. Remember that if a negative follows a verb, the verb must also be preceded by a negative.

Nunca viene **nadie** a las fiestas de Mary. **Nadie** viene **nunca** a las fiestas de Mary. }	***No one** ever comes to Mary's parties.*
¿**No** traes **ni** dinero **ni** tu documento de identidad al trabajo?	*You bring **neither** your money **nor** your ID to work?*

- Use **jamás**, **nada**, **nadie**, **ninguno**, and **nunca** in questions when you expect a negative answer. These words add emphasis to the message.

¿Conoces a **nadie** más cómico que Ramón?	*Do you know **anyone** funnier than Ramón?*

EJERCICIO
24·3

En el partido de fútbol. Escoge la palabra más apropiada para completar la oración.

algo	alguien	nadie	siempre
algunos	nunca	ni	o

1. Ayer, sucedió _____ muy inusual en el estadio.

2. _____ he visto un equipo de fútbol tan desilusionado.

3. No ganamos el partido porque _____ pudo anotar un gol.

4. _____ los jugadores estaban cansados, _____ estaban confundidos.

5. ¡_____ de los fans estaban llorando!

6. _____ sacó un pañuelo para secarse las lágrimas.

7. _____ celebramos en Casa Manolo cuando ganamos el partido.

8. _____ yo _____ mis amigos fuimos a Casa Manolo.

EJERCICIO
24·4

¡No! Contesta las preguntas en forma negativa. *You may need more than one negative word in your answers.*

1. ¿Hay refrescos en la nevera? _____

2. ¿Quiere Ud. dormir o jugar al fútbol? _____

3. ¿Van ellos a algún lugar interesante este fin de semana?

   _____

4. ¿Tienen alguna esperanza (*hope*) Uds. de encontrar el anillo perdido?

   _____

5. ¿Sabes donde están las preguntas y las respuestas para la tarea?

   _____

6. ¿Tienen tiempo para ayudarme? _____

7. ¿Vas a visitar a tus suegros siempre? _____

8. ¿Vas a saludar a tus tíos también? _____

9. ¿Celebran Uds. algún día especial esta semana?

   _____

10. ¿Conocen ellos a alguien de nuestra familia?

    _____

11. ¿Tienes algo que añadir (*add*)? _____

EJERCICIO
24·5

Preguntas personales. Contesta en forma negativa.

1. ¿Conoces a alguien en Australia? _____

2. ¿Tienes algún amigo especial? _____

3. ¿Has visitado alguna vez algún país interesante?

   _____

4. ¿Estudias siempre al amanecer (*at daybreak*)?

   _____

5. ¿Vas siempre al cine los sábados por la tarde?

   _____

6. ¿Te ayuda alguien a hacer los ejercicios de este libro?

   _____

7. ¿Haces algo para evitar el cansancio (*fatigue*)?

   _____

8. ¿Tienes algunas ideas para ganar más dinero?

   _____

9. ¿Has respondido jamás tantas preguntas personales?

   _____

10. ¿Tienes algo importante que hacer después de terminar este ejercicio?

   _____

EJERCICIO 24·6

En español. *Remember that it may be necessary to use more than one negative word in Spanish. Use* **algo, nada, nunca,** *etc.*

1. *I am somewhat preoccupied.* _____

2. *Is there someone in this room?* _____

3. *No one wants to do anything.* _____

4. *Manny neither took the photos nor filmed* (**filmar**) *the meeting.*

   _____

5. *Do we need to find Peter or Sandra?* _____

6. *Someday, we are going to finish this work.*

   _____

7. *They do not like this work at all.* _____

8. *They will never do this.* _____

Other negative expressions

Some of the words you have studied in this unit are also used in multiword negative expressions. These expressions serve as adverbs, prepositions, or conjunctions and are common in everyday conversation. They can be memorized as lexical items.

NEGATIVE EXPRESSIONS

ahora no	not now	**no importa**	it does not matter
de ninguna manera	no way, certainly not	**no... más que**	no more than
ni hablar	certainly not	**todavía no**	not yet
ni siquiera	(not) even	**ya no**	no more, no longer
ni... tampoco	neither . . .		

EJERCICIO
24·7

Un poco de sentido común. Para responder a cada comentario, escribe la letra que indica la respuesta más apropiada.

_____ 1. Yo no sé dónde está tu auto.

_____ 2. ¿Ha empezado la película?

_____ 3. ¿Puedes comprar dos refrescos?

_____ 4. Pero, ¿no tienes dinero?

_____ 5. ¿Quieres salir al baño ahora?

_____ 6. ¿Estás cómodo en tu asiento?

a. No puedo, no tengo dinero.

b. No, la butaca es dura.

c. Todavía no. En unos diez minutos.

d. Ni siquiera diez centavos.

e. Ni yo tampoco.

f. Ahora, no.

The conjunctions **pero** and **sino** and negative expressions

Sino is a conjunction, a word that is used to link words, phrases, and sentences that have the same grammatical function.

No veo a tu hermano **sino** a tu primo.	*I do not see your brother **but (rather)** your cousin.*
Ellos no hablaron **sino** gritaron en la charla.	*They did not speak **but (rather)** screamed at the get-together.*

In the sentence **No veo *a tu hermano* sino a tu primo**, the direct object of **veo** is **a tu hermano** and **sino a tu primo** completes the direct object. The repeated personal **a** indicates the role of the direct object. In the second half of the sentence, **veo** is understood after **sino**: (**veo**) **a tu primo**. In Spanish, **sino** is referred to as a **conjunción adversativa**, always used after negative statements to state a counter position or contrast. **Sino** communicates the idea *on the contrary* or *rather*.

Sino may also indicate a restriction, equivalent to *only* in English in situations such as the following.

No espera **sino que** tú defiendas tus ideas.	*He wants **only that** you defend your ideas.*
Las hijas de Marsha no compran **sino** camisas de seda.	*Marsha's daughters buy **only** (do not buy **anything but**) silk shirts.*

Pero is another conjunction equivalent to *but* in English. The contrast expressed by **pero** is not as absolute. The meaning of **pero** is closer to *however* or *instead*.

Quieren papas fritas **pero** sin sal.	*They want french fries, **but** without salt.*
Vamos, **pero** no podemos gastar mucho dinero.	*Let's go, **but** we cannot spend much money.*

When are **pero** and **sino** used in Spanish?

Both **pero** and **sino** are used to state contrasts. When in doubt, think of the message you want to communicate to your audience.

◆ **Pero** communicates the idea of *however, instead*.

Venden buenos productos **pero** son muy caros.	*They sell good products, **but** (**however**) they are expensive.*

◆ **Sino** is used only after a negative statement, and its meaning is closer to *on the contrary* or *but rather*.

No les gustan las películas de horror **sino** las películas cómicas.	*They do not like horror movies, **but** (**on the contrary**) funny movies.*
No entraron **sino que** salieron.	*They did not come in, **but** (**instead**) went out.*

Note, in the example above, that if you contrast two conjugated verbs, you should use **sino que**.

EJERCICIO
24·8

Las cosas claras. Completa las oraciones con una corrección. Escribe la corrección con la palabra entre paréntesis y la conjunción **sino**.

EJEMPLO   La plata no es un vegetal. (un mineral)
   La plata no es un vegetal sino un mineral.

1. El sol no es un planeta. (una estrella)

   _____

2. Blanca Nieves no es un personaje (*character*) real. (ficticio)

   _____

3. La astronomía no es un deporte. (una ciencia)

   _____

4. El inglés no es la lengua oficial de Portugal. (Inglaterra)

   _____

5. La paella no es un plato típico mexicano. (español)

   _____

6. El ballet no es un juego. (un arte)

   _____

7. Un crucigrama no es un problema. (un pasatiempo)

_____

8. Un perro no es una persona. (un animal)

_____

9. La luna no es una estrella. (un satélite)

_____

_____

EJERCICIO
24·9

¿Pero, sino o sino que? Decide si debes usar **pero**, **sino** o **sino que**. Escribe la palabra apropiada en cada oración.

1. Tienen muchos problemas _____ son felices.

2. No pueden caminar _____ correr para llegar a tiempo.

3. Tampoco saben esquiar _____ quieren aprender.

4. No escalaron la montaña _____ descansaron en el río.

5. Pescaron varias truchas (*trout*) _____ no las llevaron a casa.

6. Montaron en bicicleta _____ también nadaron toda la tarde en la playa.

7. Les gusta bucear (*dive*) _____ no tienen el equipo.

8. No ganaron el partido _____ quedaron en segundo lugar.

9. Tú sabes patinar muy bien _____ casi nunca practicas en el parque.

10. No queremos que se vayan _____ nos acompañen al lago.

EJERCICIO
24·10

Secretos y rumores. Traduce. Usa el **Vocabulario útil**.

*I am going to tell you (**tú**) something, but do not reveal this to anybody, to no one! Carmen has a boyfriend! Neither you nor your friends know him. She says that no one understands her. Carmen never tells her secrets. Ah, but I know some of her secrets. Carmen says she is twenty-nine years old. But she is a few years older. She never celebrates her birthday. Either she is afraid of old age or she is very silly. No, she is not silly, she is obsessive. And do you know what? Carmen went to a plastic surgeon to get rid of some of her wrinkles.*

Vocabulario útil

besides	**además**	silly	**ridículo(a); tonto(a)**
old age	**la vejez**	to get rid of	**eliminar**
reveal	**revelar**	wrinkle	**la arruga**

Interrogative and exclamatory words

Interrogative words and expressions

Asking questions is one of the most useful linguistic functions we can learn in a new language. The responses we get let us gauge how well we are communicating. The five *W* English question words gather information on any topic: *who? what? when? where?* and *why?* In Spanish, the first three of these basic questions start with a /k/ sound: **¿quién?**, **¿qué?**, and **¿cuándo?** Note that interrogative words require a written accent mark. Each is preceded by an inverted question mark; a standard question mark ends each written question.

Interrogative words in Spanish

Interrogative words (**palabras interrogativas**) can be adjectives followed by a noun (**¿Cuántos** alumnos? ***How many** students?*), while some are adverbs (**¿Dónde** vives? ***Where** do you live?*). Others are pronouns (**¿Cuál** necesitas? ***Which one** do you need?*).

Here are the most commonly used interrogative words.

¿Cuál? ¿Cuáles?	Which one(s)?
¿Cuándo?	When?
¿Cuánto? ¿Cuánta?	How much?
¿Cuántos? ¿Cuántas?	How many?
¿Cómo?	How?
¿Dónde?	Where?
¿Adónde?	Where (to)?
¿De dónde?	Where from?
¿Qué?	What?
¿Para qué?	What for?
¿Por qué?	Why?
¿Quién? ¿Quiénes?	Who?
¿A quién? ¿A quiénes?	Whom?
¿De quién? ¿De quiénes?	Whose?

¿Cuál es la palabra interrogativa apropiada? Escoge la palabra interrogativa para cada pregunta. Usa cada palabra solamente una vez.

cómo	cuál	dónde	cuánto	cuántos
qué	cuáles	cuándo	cuánta	cuántas

1. ¿_____ está Pablo?

2. ¿_____ son tus colores preferidos?

3. ¿_____ hora es?

4. ¿_____ es la fiesta? ¿El lunes?

5. ¿_____ horas trabajas cada día?

6. ¿_____ dinero ganas?

7. ¿_____ días trabajas a la semana?

8. ¿_____ es tu actividad favorita?

9. ¿_____ es tu casa, grande o pequeña?

10. ¿_____ agua bebes cada día?

Other uses of interrogative words and expressions

In addition to the equivalents given above, some Spanish interrogative words have other uses.

◆ Use **¿Cómo?** to ask someone to repeat information you missed or did not understand. The English equivalent in this case is *What?*

—Necesito diez dólares.   *"I need ten dollars."*
—**¿Cómo?**   *"What?"*

◆ **¿Qué?** is also used to clarify information.

—**¿Qué** dijiste?   *"What did you say?"*

◆ **¿Cuál?** and its plural form **¿cuáles?** are pronouns used to indicate *which one* and the plural *which ones* in most areas of the Spanish-speaking world. Use this word to ask about a choice. If the interrogative word is followed by a noun, use the adjective **¿qué?** instead.

El traje rojo y el azul son bonitos.   *The red suit and the blue one are beautiful.*
    ¿Cuál prefieres?   ***Which (one)** do you prefer?*
¿Qué blusa vas a usar?   ***Which** blouse are you going to wear?*

Here are two ways of requesting the same information about today's date, with **¿cuál?** and **¿qué?**

    ¿Qué fecha es hoy?   ***What's the date today?***
    ¿Cuál es la fecha?   ***What's the date?***

The noun **fecha** follows the interrogative adjective **¿qué?**, and **¿cuál?** is followed by a verb. However, **¿cuál?** and **¿cuáles?** followed by a noun are used instead of **¿qué?** in some areas of the Hispanic world.

◆ **¿Cuántos?** and the feminine form **¿cuántas?** are adjectives if followed by a noun, and they are pronouns if they refer to a noun previously mentioned and understood from the context. They agree in gender and number with the noun. The English equivalent is *how many?*

¿Cuántos chicos y **cuántas** chicas hay en este salón?	*How many boys and how many girls are there in this room?*

◆ **¿Cuánto?** (*how much?*) seeks information about amounts.

¿Cuánto cuesta esta nevera?	*How much does this refrigerator cost?*

◆ **¿Adónde?** and **¿dónde?** both refer to places. **¿Adónde?** is directional; it appears with verbs indicating motion. **¿Dónde?** asks for locations.

¿Adónde vas con tanta prisa?	*Where are you going in such a hurry?*
¿Dónde está mi reloj?	*Where is my watch?*

◆ Prepositions may precede a question word in Spanish, changing the meaning of the basic interrogative word. Don't try to translate the English equivalents word for word.

—**¿Con quién** hablas?	*"Who(m) are you talking to?"*
—Con mi novio.	*"My boyfriend."*
—**¿A quién** esperas?	*"Who(m) are you waiting for?"*
—A mi hermana.	*"My sister."*

EJERCICIO
25·2

Una entrevista. Escribe una pregunta apropiada para cada respuesta. Usa la forma **Ud.** de los verbos.

1. _____ Mi nombre es Julián del Portal.

2. _____ Soy de Carabobo, Venezuela.

3. _____ No, no soy dentista. Soy pediatra.

4. _____ Pues, soy muy dedicado a mi profesión, y muy modesto.

5. _____ Claro que sí, soy muy puntual.

6. _____ ¡Caramba! Es tarde. Son las cinco y media. ¡Hasta pronto!

EJERCICIO
25·3

¿Sabes la respuesta? Contesta en español.

1. ¿En qué mes celebramos el Mes de la Hispanidad en los Estados Unidos? _____

2. ¿De dónde es el origen del chocolate? _____

3. ¿Quién es el compañero de Don Quijote? _____

4. ¿Cuál es la capital de Uruguay? _____

5. ¿Qué dos idiomas se hablan en Paraguay? _____

6. ¿Cuáles son las capitales de Chile y Puerto Rico? _____

EJERCICIO
25·4

En el banco. En español. Usa la persona **Ud.**

1. *Who is next?* _____

2. *What is your name, sir?* _____

3. *How (**En qué**) can I help you?* _____

4. *What (day) is your birthday (**fecha de nacimiento**)?* _____

5. *Where do you work?* _____

6. *How long can you stay?* _____

¿Para qué? ¿Por qué?: When are they used in Spanish?

Both **¿para qué?** and **¿por qué?** are the equivalent of *why?* in English. In Spanish, these expressions have slightly different functions.

◆ Use **¿para qué?** to ask about a *purpose*, literally, *what for?* Note that the answer to this question does not start with **porque** (*because*) but with **para**.

    —¿**Para qué** necesitas tanto dinero?   *"Why do you need so much money?"*
    —**Para comprar** los palos de golf.   *"(In order) to buy golf clubs."*

◆ Use **¿por qué?** when you want to find out a *reason*. Expect **porque** (*because*)—one word and no accent mark—in the reply to your question.

    —¿**Por qué** necesitas tanto dinero?   *"Why do you need so much money?"*
    —**Porque voy a comprar** los palos   *"Because I am buying golf clubs."*
    de golf.

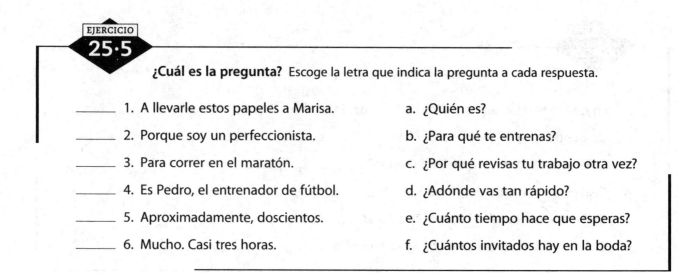

¿Cuál es la pregunta? Escoge la letra que indica la pregunta a cada respuesta.

_____ 1. A llevarle estos papeles a Marisa.

_____ 2. Porque soy un perfeccionista.

_____ 3. Para correr en el maratón.

_____ 4. Es Pedro, el entrenador de fútbol.

_____ 5. Aproximadamente, doscientos.

_____ 6. Mucho. Casi tres horas.

a. ¿Quién es?

b. ¿Para qué te entrenas?

c. ¿Por qué revisas tu trabajo otra vez?

d. ¿Adónde vas tan rápido?

e. ¿Cuánto tiempo hace que esperas?

f. ¿Cuántos invitados hay en la boda?

Interrogative words and expressions in indirect questions

Interrogative words may also be incorporated into sentences as indirect questions. Indirect questions restate a direct question that has been posed by a third person.

Tu papá pregunta **qué** necesitas.
Él quiere saber **adónde** vas.

Your dad asks (is asking) **what** *you need.*
He wants to know **where** *you are going.*

Remember that the interrogative words incorporated into indirect questions require accent marks. Indirect questions may be in different tenses. The example below is in the past + future tense.

El pasajero **preguntó a qué hora saldrá** el tren para Bilbao.

The passenger **asked at what time** *the train* **will leave** *for Bilbao.*

Y en tu caso... Verdadero o falso?

_____ 1. Tus amigos siempre te preguntan cuánto gastas en tus compras.

_____ 2. Siempre sabes qué programa hay en la tele.

_____ 3. Tus parientes siempre quieren saber con quiénes vas a pasar las fiestas.

_____ 4. Te preguntan cuántos años tienes en una entrevista para un trabajo.

_____ 5. Tú sabes quiénes son tus vecinos.

_____ 6. Quieres saber cómo se llama el presidente de México.

_____ 7. Tu maestro(a) de español pregunta cuántos años has estudiado español.

_____ 8. El agente de viajes te pregunta adónde irás de vacaciones este año.

El interrogatorio. En español.

1. *Ask your friend [m.] who is sitting over there.*

   _____

2. *The police ask where you were [preterit] last night.*

   _____

3. *The detective asks at what time you arrived at the disco.*

   _____

4. *Your mother is asking where you went after midnight.*

   _____

5. *They ask when this interrogation will end.*

   _____

Exclamations

Written language has devices that express what voice modulation, facial expressions, etc., do in spoken communication. Exclamations (**palabras y expresiones exclamativas**), for example, usually convey strong feelings. Some interrogative words and expressions are used in exclamations accompanied by exclamation marks. Note the inverted exclamation mark that precedes each expression; a standard exclamation mark ends the sentence.

¡Cuánto...! ¡Cuánta...!	How much . . . !
¡Cuántos...! ¡Cuántas...!	How many . . . !
¡Cuán...!	How . . . ! (*in literary style*)
¡Cómo...!	How . . . !
¡Qué...!	What . . . !
¡Porque...!	Because . . . !
¡Quién...! ¡Quiénes...!	Who . . . !

¡Cuántas flores! Pero hoy no es nuestro aniversario.	*So many flowers! But today isn't our anniversary.*
¡Qué sorpresa!	*What a surprise!*
¡Cuánto trabajas!	*How much you work! (You work so much!)*
¡Qué casa (tan) horrible!	*What an ugly house!*

Note that the optional adverb **tan** preceding the adjective **horrible** adds emphasis to the exclamation. The adverb **más** is also used this way for emphasis.

EJERCICIO
25·8

En la peluquería. Subraya la exclamación apropiada.

1. ¡(Qué | Cuánto) color de pelo tan horrible!

2. ¡(Qué | Cuánto) dinero por un corte de pelo!

3. ¡(Cuánto | Cuántos) clientes salen contentos con el servicio!

4. ¡(Quién | Quiénes) tuviera ese pelo tan bonito!

5. ¡(Cuánto | Cuántos) colores de pelo diferentes!

6. ¡(Cómo | Qué) rápido trabaja ese peluquero!

7. ¡(Cuánto | Cuántos) tiempo tengo que esperar!

8. ¡(Cómo | Qué) mala suerte! Mi peluquero no puede darme una cita para el viernes.

EJERCICIO
25·9

¿Cómo respondes? Usa la exclamación apropiada.

_____ 1. Este examen es muy difícil.	a. ¡Qué sabrosa!
_____ 2. Me gané la lotería.	b. ¡Qué fáciles!
_____ 3. Está ganando mi equipo.	c. ¡Qué barato!
_____ 4. Me gusta la comida del restaurante.	d. ¡Qué mala suerte!
_____ 5. Solamente cuestan tres dólares.	e. ¡Qué partido tan bueno!
_____ 6. No son difíciles los exámenes.	f. ¡Cuánto dinero!
_____ 7. Hay más de ochenta mil personas.	g. ¡Cuánto sabes!
_____ 8. Recibí el premio al mejor alumno.	h. ¡Cuánta gente!

¡Qué día! Traduce. Usa el **Vocabulario útil.**

Mario cannot take me to my doctor today. Why didn't he call me last night? What bad luck! Now I have to take a taxi. Why are so many cars on the expressway? How much traffic! Dr. Domínguez' office is far, and the fare is around twenty-five dollars. Too much money for this service! Oh! And now it is raining, too. What a horrible day! Finally, I am now at my doctor's office. There are a lot of patients in the waiting room. I probably will spend two or three hours here. How annoying! Now I can approach the window. What? The receptionist gave me bad news. My appointment is tomorrow? What a day!

Vocabulario útil

annoying	**desagradable**	how annoying!	**¡qué pesado!; ¡qué rabia!**
around	**alrededor de, más o menos**	to approach	**acercar(se)**
doctor's office	**la consulta**	to spend	**pasar**
expressway	**la autopista**	waiting room	**la sala de espera**
fare	**la tarifa**	window	**la ventanilla**

Numbers

Cardinal numbers

Here is a list of Spanish cardinal numbers (**los números cardinales**). Note alternative spellings for some numbers under 30.

0	**cero**	23	**veintitrés, veinte y tres**
1	**uno**	24	**veinticuatro, veinte y cuatro**
2	**dos**	25	**veinticinco, veinte y cinco**
3	**tres**	26	**veintiséis, veinte y seis**
4	**cuatro**	27	**veintisiete, veinte y siete**
5	**cinco**	28	**veintiocho, veinte y ocho**
6	**seis**	29	**veintinueve, veinte y nueve**
7	**siete**	30	**treinta**
8	**ocho**	31	**treinta y uno**
9	**nueve**	32	**treinta y dos**
10	**diez**	33	**treinta y tres**
11	**once**	34	**treinta y cuatro**
12	**doce**	35	**treinta y cinco**
13	**trece**	36	**treinta y seis**
14	**catorce**	37	**treinta y siete**
15	**quince**	38	**treinta y ocho**
16	**dieciséis, diez y seis**	39	**treinta y nueve**
17	**diecisiete, diez y siete**	40	**cuarenta**
18	**dieciocho, diez y ocho**	50	**cincuenta**
19	**diecinueve, diez y nueve**	60	**sesenta**
20	**veinte**	70	**setenta**
21	**veintiuno, veinte y uno**	80	**ochenta**
22	**veintidós, veinte y dos**	90	**noventa**

100	**ciento (cien)**	800	**ochocientos/ochocientas**
101	**ciento uno/una**	900	**novecientos/novecientas**
200	**doscientos/doscientas**	1.000	**mil**
300	**trescientos/trescientas**	2.000	**dos mil**
400	**cuatrocientos/cuatrocientas**	100.000	**cien mil**
500	**quinientos/quinientas**	1.000.000	**un millón**
600	**seiscientos/seiscientas**	1.000.000.000	**mil millones**
700	**setecientos/setecientas**		

Cardinal numbers may be used as adjectives or pronouns. If they precede a noun, they function as an adjective. Note the following rules for the use of cardinal numbers in Spanish.

- Instead of commas, Spanish uses periods to indicate the value of units, and commas instead of periods to indicate decimals.

Recibimos **12.532** votos.	*We got **12,532** votes.*
Este libro cuesta **$22,30**.	*This book costs **$22.30**.*

- If a number ending in **uno** (*one*) precedes a noun, it agrees with that noun in gender. The masculine form drops the **-o** and the feminine changes to **una**. All other numbers are invariable.

No tengo **veintiún** dólares.	*I do not have **twenty-one** dollars.*
Hay **treinta y una** señoras esperando.	*There are **thirty-one** women waiting.*

Note the accent mark on **veintiún** in the first example above.

- The numbers 16 to 19 and 21 to 29 may be spelled in two ways: in one word or with three words, as in **dieciséis** or **diez y seis**. The one-word spelling requires an accent mark and reflects contemporary spelling preference.

El **dieciocho** es mi número favorito.	***Eighteen** is my favorite number.*

- Use **y** to separate tens and units only. Note the different construction in the English equivalent.

Tienes **treinta y siete** años solamente.	*You are only **thirty-seven** years old.*
Pagaron **cuatrocientos cuarenta y cinco** dólares.	*They paid **four hundred forty-five** dollars.*

- If a noun does not follow the number, a number ending in **uno** does not change to **un**. The noun omitted is understood from previous information.

—¿Cuántos chicos hay en esta clase?	*"How many boys are there in this class?"*
—**Treinta y uno.**	*"Thirty-one."*

- Compounds that end in **-ciento** also agree with the noun that follows them.

Trajeron **doscientas esmeraldas** colombianas.	*They brought **two hundred** Colombian **emeralds**.*

- **Cien** indicates the number, quantity, or amount before **mil** and **millones**.

Hay **cien mil dólares** para tu proyecto.	*There is **one hundred thousand dollars** for your project.*
Dicen que el dictador tiene **cien millones de dólares** en el banco.	*They say the dictator has **a hundred million dollars** in the bank.*

Note that the preposition **de** follows **millón** or **millones** in Spanish, preceding a noun.

En español. Escribe los números que aparecen entre paréntesis.

1. _____ personas (35)

2. _____ habitantes (2.341)

3. _____ castillos (322)

4. _____ lápices (16)

5. _____ billetes (67)

6. _____ caballeros (71)

7. _____ maletas (100)

8. _____ copias (502)

9. _____ alumnas (26)

10. _____ soldados (100.000)

11. _____ días (31)

12. _____ millas (*miles*) (700)

13. _____ de dólares (1.000.000)

14. _____ tarjetas (51)

When do we use cardinal numbers?

Cardinal numbers are used

◆ to count.

Veinticuatro, veinticinco...	*Twenty-four, twenty-five . . .*

◆ to express arithmetic problems.

dividido por, entre   divided by (÷)

Sesenta **entre** tres son veinte.	*Sixty divided by three is twenty.*
Ochenta **dividido por** diez son ocho.	*Eighty divided by ten is eight.*

más, y   plus (+)

Dos **y** once son trece.	*Two plus eleven is thirteen.*
Cinco **más** cuatro son nueve.	*Five plus four is nine.*

menos   minus (−)

Cien **menos** veinticinco son setenta y cinco.	*One hundred minus twenty-five is seventy-five.*

por   multiplied by (×)

Nueve **por** tres son veintisiete.	*Nine multiplied by three is twenty-seven.*

- to tell time (**la hora**). The third-person singular form of **ser** (**es, era**) is used for *one o'clock* and any time that includes **la una: la una y diez minutos**. The third-person plural of **ser** (**son, eran**) is used for all other times.

Es **la una** en punto.	*It's exactly **one o'clock**.*
Son **las cuatro y diez**.	*It is **four ten**.*
Eran **las cinco y veinte** cuando salieron de clase.	*It was **five twenty** when they left the classroom.*

The arithmetic expressions **menos** (*minus*) and **y** (*and, plus*) are also used to tell time. The fraction **media** (*half*) is used to indicate the half hour. For telling time in English, **menos** = *to* and **y** = *past*.

Son las dos **y** cuarto. Salimos a las tres **menos** cuarto.	*It is a quarter **past** two. We leave at a quarter **to** three.*
¿Podemos irnos a las dos **y media**?	*May we leave at **half past** two?*

As in English, cardinal numbers are also used to tell time in Spanish: **las dos y quince** (*two fifteen*), **dos y cuarenta y cinco** (*two forty-five*), and **dos y treinta** (*two thirty*).

Note that the preposition **a** + **la** or **a** + **las** + the time is equivalent to *at* + time in English. Use the expressions of time **de la mañana** (*in the morning*), **de la tarde** (*in the afternoon*), and **de la noche** (*at night*) to indicate a more precise time. They translate A.M. and P.M. in English.

- to express dates. Note the use of **ser**.

¿Qué día **es** hoy? Hoy **es** el 3 de noviembre.	*What day **is** today? Today **is** November 3.*
Mi cumpleaños no **es** el primero de mayo.	*My birthday **is** not on May first.*

All days of the month are indicated with cardinal numbers except **el primero** (*the first*). In English, the preposition *on* is used where Spanish uses the definite article **el** to indicate when an event takes place. To tell the date, the order of the words in Spanish is different from English. **Hoy es el cinco de mayo** is the equivalent of *Today is May 5*. However, it is also possible to use an expression with **estar a** + the day of the month.

Estamos a quince de marzo.	*It is March 15.*

Here are the months of the year in Spanish.

enero	January	**julio**	July
febrero	February	**agosto**	August
marzo	March	**septiembre**	September
abril	April	**octubre**	October
mayo	May	**noviembre**	November
junio	June	**diciembre**	December

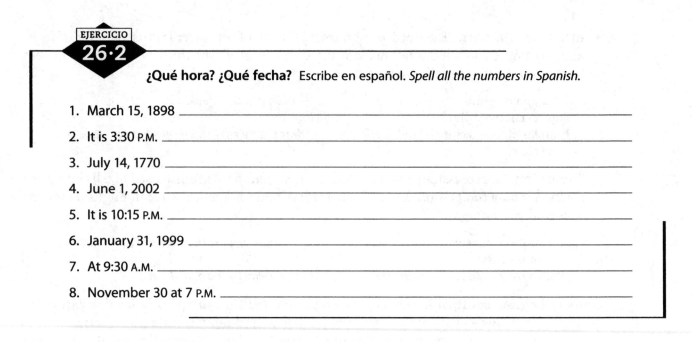

EJERCICIO
26·2

¿Qué hora? ¿Qué fecha? Escribe en español. *Spell all the numbers in Spanish.*

1. March 15, 1898 _____

2. It is 3:30 P.M. _____

3. July 14, 1770 _____

4. June 1, 2002 _____

5. It is 10:15 P.M. _____

6. January 31, 1999 _____

7. At 9:30 A.M. _____

8. November 30 at 7 P.M. _____

EJERCICIO
26·3

Preguntas personales.

1. ¿Cuántos años tienes? _____

2. ¿Qué día celebras tu cumpleaños? _____

3. ¿Cuál es tu número de la suerte (*lucky*)? _____

4. Escribe el número de tu distrito postal (*zip code*). _____

5. ¿Qué hora tienes? _____

6. ¿Cuánto dinero quieres ganar a la semana? _____

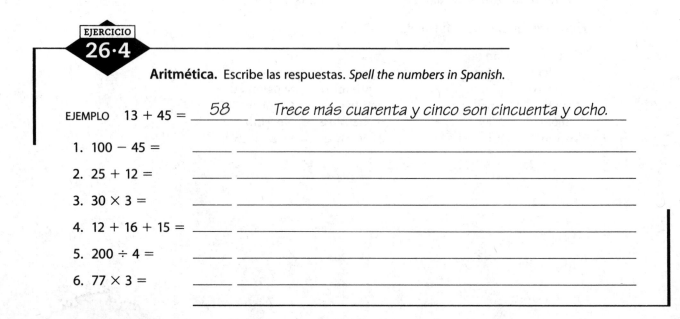

EJERCICIO
26·4

Aritmética. Escribe las respuestas. *Spell the numbers in Spanish.*

EJEMPLO   13 + 45 = ___*58*___   *Trece más cuarenta y cinco son cincuenta y ocho.*

1. 100 − 45 = _____

2. 25 + 12 = _____

3. 30 × 3 = _____

4. 12 + 16 + 15 = _____

5. 200 ÷ 4 = _____

6. 77 × 3 = _____

¿Verdadero o falso?

_____ 1. El primero de enero es la celebración de Año Nuevo.

_____ 2. El mes de abril tiene treinta y un días.

_____ 3. Veinticinco más treinta son setenta.

_____ 4. Hay más de treinta millones de hispanos en los Estados Unidos.

_____ 5. En un año bisiesto (*leap*) febrero tiene veintisiete días.

_____ 6. Cincuenta es el número de estados de los Estados Unidos.

_____ 7. Celebramos el Día de las madres el catorce de febrero.

_____ 8. Vivimos en el siglo (*century*) veintiuno.

_____ 9. Hay 102 senadores en el senado de los Estados Unidos.

_____ 10. Hay doce rosas en una docena.

En español.

1. *There are more than one hundred television channels.*

_____

2. *Many American families have only one child (**hijo**).*

_____

3. *Many American households (**hogares** [m.]) have three television sets.*

_____

4. *One cannot buy much with twenty-five dollars.*

_____

5. *There are thirty-two pieces (**pieza**) in a chess set (**juego de ajedrez**).*

_____

6. *We work fifty weeks every year.*

_____

7. *Lincoln's birthday is February 12.*

_____

Ordinal numbers

Ordinal numbers (**números ordinales**) are used to assign a place in a series. They may function as adjectives or as pronouns. The following are the ordinal numbers used in Spanish.

primero(a)	first	**sexto(a)**	sixth
segundo(a)	second	**séptimo(a)**	seventh
tercero(a)	third	**octavo(a)**	eighth
cuarto(a)	fourth	**noveno(a)**	ninth
quinto(a)	fifth	**décimo(a)**	tenth

Ordinal numbers in Spanish are used in the following ways.

◆ After the ordinal number **décimo** (*tenth*), cardinal numbers are used to indicate the order in a series, and they usually follow the noun.

Éste es el congreso **15** de esta organización.   *This is the **15th** convention of this organization.*

◆ Ordinals can function as adjectives and nouns.

El segundo día, fueron a la playa.   *The second day, they went to the beach.*
Es **la segunda** vez que llamo.   *This is **the second time** I'm calling.*
Marcos es **el tercero**.   *Marcos is **the third** (one).*

◆ When **primero** and **tercero** are used as adjectives and precede a masculine noun, they drop the **-o**.

En primer lugar, tú debes hacer tu trabajo.   *In the first place, you should do your work.*
Ellos viven en **el tercer piso**.   *They live on **the third floor**.*

Ordinal numbers in English are often printed with *-th* following the number, as in *5th*. Spanish printed equivalents are: **1º**, **2ª**, **3er**, **5ta**, etc. Note that the suffixes of the abbreviations reflect the final letter or letters of the ordinal number written out.

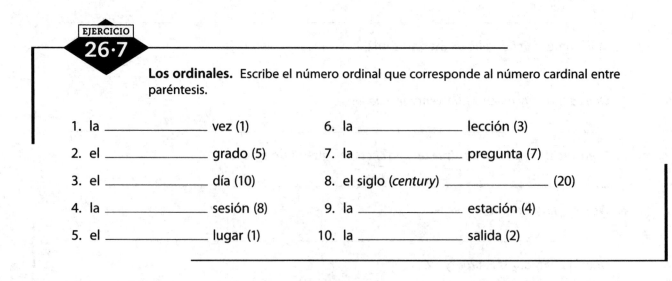

EJERCICIO
26·7

Los ordinales. Escribe el número ordinal que corresponde al número cardinal entre paréntesis.

1. la _____ vez (1)

2. el _____ grado (5)

3. el _____ día (10)

4. la _____ sesión (8)

5. el _____ lugar (1)

6. la _____ lección (3)

7. la _____ pregunta (7)

8. el siglo (*century*) _____ (20)

9. la _____ estación (4)

10. la _____ salida (2)

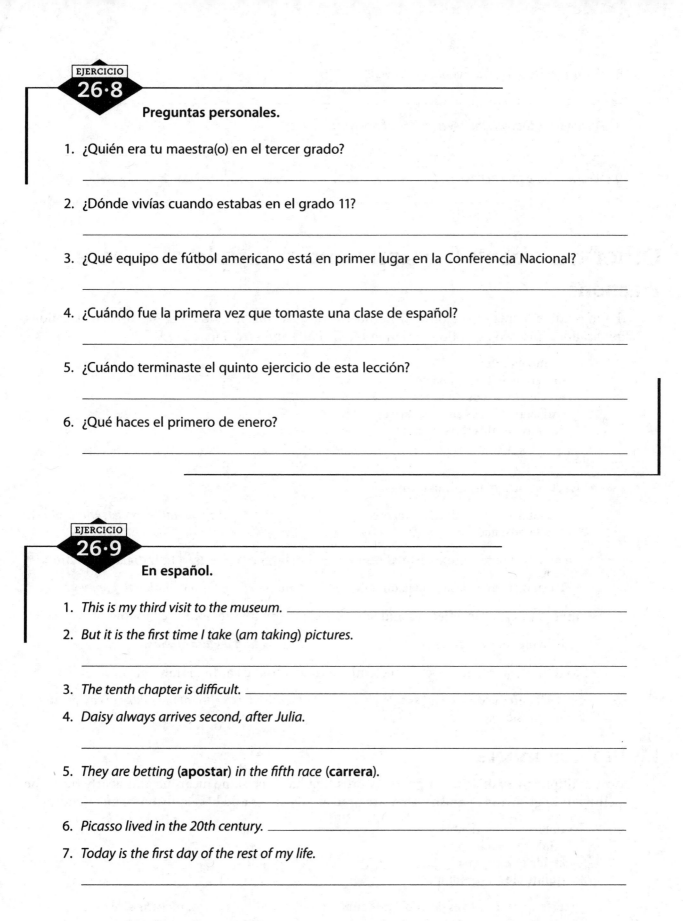

EJERCICIO
26·8

Preguntas personales.

1. ¿Quién era tu maestra(o) en el tercer grado?

   _____

2. ¿Dónde vivías cuando estabas en el grado 11?

   _____

3. ¿Qué equipo de fútbol americano está en primer lugar en la Conferencia Nacional?

   _____

4. ¿Cuándo fue la primera vez que tomaste una clase de español?

   _____

5. ¿Cuándo terminaste el quinto ejercicio de esta lección?

   _____

6. ¿Qué haces el primero de enero?

   _____

EJERCICIO
26·9

En español.

1. *This is my third visit to the museum.* _____

2. *But it is the first time I take (am taking) pictures.*

   _____

3. *The tenth chapter is difficult.* _____

4. *Daisy always arrives second, after Julia.*

   _____

5. *They are betting (**apostar**) in the fifth race (**carrera**).*

   _____

6. *Picasso lived in the 20th century.* _____

7. *Today is the first day of the rest of my life.*

   _____

8. *December is the twelfth month of the year.*

_____

9. *Fortunately, today is the seventh day of the week.*

_____

10. *We live on the fourth floor.* _____

Other numbers: fractions and multiple numbers
Fractions

The masculine forms of the ordinal numbers you just finished studying are used in fractions (**quebrados**). The two exceptions are **medio** (*one half*) and **tercio** (*one third*).

medio, la mitad	½
un tercio, la tercera parte	⅓
un cuarto, la cuarta parte	¼
tres cuartos, tres cuartas partes	¾
dos tercios, dos terceras partes	⅔

Note that

◆ fractions are masculine nouns.

Un tercio de la población prefiere   ***One-third*** *of the population prefers this product.*
este producto.

◆ an article + a feminine ordinal number + **parte(s)** may be used to indicate a fraction.

La cuarta parte de la población no votó.   ***One-fourth*** *of the population did not vote.*

◆ **medio** (*half*) is an adjective and agrees in gender with the noun that follows it.

Bebí **medio vaso** de agua.   *I drank **half a glass** of water.*

◆ to indicate a fraction above one tenth, add **-avo** to the cardinal number.

Recibí **un doceavo** de mi sueldo en   *I received **a twelfth** of my salary in commissions.*
comisiones.

Multiple numbers

Most multiples in Spanish are cognates (words that have the same meaning and nearly the same spelling in English and Spanish). They are used as adjectives and have only one gender ending.

doble	double
triple	triple
cuádruple	quadruple
quíntuple	quintuple

Este apartamento es **de doble tamaño**.   *This apartment is **double the size**.*
Quieren **triples ganancias** de sus   *They want **triple earnings** from their*
inversiones.   *investments.*

Note that the equivalent in English includes *the*, a definite article, in *double the size*.

Escribe en español.

1. ⅓ of the population _____

2. a double ration _____

3. ½ orange _____

4. half a day _____

5. ⅔ of my salary _____

6. the 6th column _____

7. ⅛ of a yard _____

8. quadruple profits (**ganancias**) _____

¿Sumar, restar, dividir o multiplicar? Traduce. Usa el **Vocabulario útil**.

*Every day we see numbers: We add, multiply, subtract, and divide. We see a sign on the turnpike and we read: "Sixty-five miles per hour." We go to a store and we want to buy towels and another signs says: "Second floor." We want to multiply our fortune with a lottery ticket or with the stock market. We sit in front of the computer and search the database. The price of gold can go up twenty percent by the second month of next year. We can double our money. Yet, if we gain five percent, we are lucky! Probably, we spend twenty-five percent of our time shopping, looking for bargains, and spending money. And we need to remember birthday dates. Mine is February 11. In this twenty-first century, we have computers and cell phones with calculators. We can do our arithmetic tasks easily. Be careful (**tú**): spend less and save more!*

Vocabulario útil

arithmetic	**aritmético(a)**	task	**la tarea**
bargain	**la ganga; la oferta**	to add	**sumar**
database	**la base de datos**	to be lucky	**tener suerte**
earn	**ganar**	to divide	**dividir**
fortune	**la suerte; la riqueza**	to double	**doblar**
next year	**el año que viene;**	to go up	**subir**
	el próximo año	to multiply	**multiplicar**
percent	**el por ciento**	to subtract	**restar**
stock	**la acción (en la bolsa**	turnpike	**la pista de peaje**
	de valores)		

Verb tables

Regular verbs

Simple tenses

Indicative mood

PRESENT

hablar	hablo	hablas	habla	hablamos	habláis	hablan
comer	como	comes	come	comemos	coméis	comen
vivir	vivo	vives	vive	vivimos	vivís	viven

PRETERIT

hablar	hablé	hablaste	habló	hablamos	hablasteis	hablaron
comer	comí	comiste	comió	comimos	comisteis	comieron
vivir	viví	viviste	vivió	vivimos	vivisteis	vivieron

IMPERFECT

hablar	hablaba	hablabas	hablaba	hablábamos	hablabais	hablaban
comer	comía	comías	comía	comíamos	comíais	comían
vivir	vivía	vivías	vivía	vivíamos	vivíais	vivían

FUTURE

hablar	hablaré	hablarás	hablará	hablaremos	hablaréis	hablarán
comer	comeré	comerás	comerá	comeremos	comeréis	comerán
vivir	viviré	vivirás	vivirá	viviremos	viviréis	vivirán

CONDITIONAL

hablar	hablaría	hablarías	hablaría	hablaríamos	hablaríais	hablarían
comer	comería	comerías	comería	comeríamos	comeríais	comerían
vivir	viviría	vivirías	viviría	viviríamos	viviríais	vivirían

AFFIRMATIVE AND NEGATIVE COMMANDS

hablar (tú)	habla	no hables	**vivir (tú)**	vive	no vivas
hablar (Ud.)	hable	no hable	**vivir (Ud.)**	viva	no viva
hablar (vosotros)	hablad	no habléis	**vivir (vosotros)**	vivid	no viváis
hablar (Uds.)	hablen	no hablen	**vivir (Uds.)**	vivan	no vivan

comer (tú)	come	no comas
comer (Ud.)	coma	no coma
comer (vosotros)	comed	no comáis
comer (Uds.)	coman	no coman

Subjunctive mood

hablar	hable	hables	hable	hablemos	habléis	hablen
comer	coma	comas	coma	comamos	comáis	coman
vivir	viva	vivas	viva	vivamos	viváis	vivan

IMPERFECT **-ra** FORMS

hablar	hablara	hablaras	hablara	habláramos	hablarais	hablaran
comer	comiera	comieras	comiera	comiéramos	comierais	comieran
vivir	viviera	vivieras	viviera	viviéramos	vivierais	vivieran

IMPERFECT **-se** FORMS

hablar	hablase	hablases	hablase	hablásemos	hablaseis	hablasen
comer	comiese	comieses	comiese	comiésemos	comieseis	comiesen
vivir	viviese	vivieses	viviese	viviésemos	vivieseis	viviesen

Compound tenses

Use a form of auxiliary **haber** plus the past participle of a verb (**hablado, comido, vivido**).

Indicative Mood

PRESENT PERFECT

hablar	he	has	ha	hemos	habéis	han	**hablado**
comer	he	has	ha	hemos	habéis	han	**comido**
vivir	he	has	ha	hemos	habéis	han	**vivido**

PLUPERFECT

hablar	había	habías	había	habíamos	habíais	habían	**hablado**
comer	había	habías	había	habíamos	habíais	habían	**comido**
vivir	había	habías	había	habíamos	habíais	habían	**vivido**

PRETERIT PERFECT

hablar	hube	hubiste	hubo	hubimos	hubisteis	hubieron	**hablado**
comer	hube	hubiste	hubo	hubimos	hubisteis	hubieron	**comido**
vivir	hube	hubiste	hubo	hubimos	hubisteis	hubieron	**vivido**

FUTURE PERFECT

hablar	habré	habrás	habrá	habremos	habréis	habrán	**hablado**
comer	habré	habrás	habrá	habremos	habréis	habrán	**comido**
vivir	habré	habrás	habrá	habremos	habréis	habrán	**vivido**

CONDITIONAL PERFECT

hablar	habría	habrías	habría	habríamos	habríais	habrían	**hablado**
comer	habría	habrías	habría	habríamos	habríais	habrían	**comido**
vivir	habría	habrías	habría	habríamos	habríais	habrían	**vivido**

Subjunctive Mood

hablar	haya	hayas	haya	hayamos	hayáis	hayan	**hablado**
comer	haya	hayas	haya	hayamos	hayáis	hayan	**comido**
vivir	haya	hayas	haya	hayamos	hayáis	hayan	**vivido**

PLUPERFECT **-ra** FORMS

hablar	hubiera	hubieras	hubiera	hubiéramos	hubierais	hubieran	**hablado**
comer	hubiera	hubieras	hubiera	hubiéramos	hubierais	hubieran	**comido**
vivir	hubiera	hubieras	hubiera	hubiéramos	hubierais	hubieran	**vivido**

PLUPERFECT **-se** FORMS

hablar	hubiese	hubieses	hubiese	hubiésemos	hubieseis	hubiesen	**hablado**
comer	hubiese	hubieses	hubiese	hubiésemos	hubieseis	hubiesen	**comido**
vivir	hubiese	hubieses	hubiese	hubiésemos	hubieseis	hubiesen	**vivido**

Verbs with spelling changes

-**Ger** or -**gir** infinitives change **g** to **j** before -**o** and -**a**.

PRESENT INDICATIVE

| **escoger** | escojo | escoges | escoge | escogemos | escogéis | escogen |

PRESENT SUBJUNCTIVE

| **escoger** | escoja | escojas | escoja | escojamos | escojáis | escojan |

-**Guir** infinitives change **gu** to **g** before -**o** and -**a**.

PRESENT INDICATIVE

| **extinguir** | extingo | extingues | extingue | extinguimos | extinguís | extinguen |

PRESENT SUBJUNCTIVE

| **extinguir** | extinga | extingas | extinga | extingamos | extingáis | extingan |

-**Cer** and -**cir** infinitives change **c** to **z** before -**o** and -**a**.

PRESENT INDICATIVE

| **vencer** | venzo | vences | vence | vencemos | vencéis | vencen |

PRESENT SUBJUNCTIVE

| **vencer** | venza | venzas | venza | venzamos | venzáis | venzan |

-**Car** infinitives change **c** to **qu** before -**e**.

| **explicar** | expliqué | explicaste | explicó | explicamos | explicasteis | explicaron |

| **explicar** | explique | expliques | explique | expliquemos | expliquéis | expliquen |

-**Gar** infinitives change **g** to **gu** before -**e**.

| **llegar** | llegué | llegaste | llegó | llegamos | llegasteis | llegaron |

| **llegar** | llegue | llegues | llegue | lleguemos | lleguéis | lleguen |

-**Zar** infinitives change **z** to **c** before -**e**.

| **cruzar** | crucé | cruzaste | cruzó | cruzamos | cruzasteis | cruzaron |

| **cruzar** | cruce | cruces | cruce | crucemos | crucéis | crucen |

Verbs with stem changes

Infinitives in -**ar** change stem **e** to **ie**, **o** to **ue**, and **u** to **ue**.

cerrar

| PRESENT INDICATIVE | cierro | cierras | cierra | cerramos | cerráis | cierran |
| PRESENT SUBJUNCTIVE | cierre | cierres | cierre | cerremos | cerréis | cierren |

contar

| PRESENT INDICATIVE | cuento | cuentas | cuenta | contamos | contáis | cuentan |
| PRESENT SUBJUNCTIVE | cuente | cuentes | cuente | contemos | contéis | cuenten |

jugar

| PRESENT INDICATIVE | juego | juegas | juega | jugamos | jugáis | juegan |
| PRESENT SUBJUNCTIVE | juegue | juegues | juegue | juguemos | juguéis | jueguen |

Infinitives in -**er** change stem **e** to **ie** and **o** to **ue**.

perder

| PRESENT INDICATIVE | pierdo | pierdes | pierde | perdemos | perdéis | pierden |
| PRESENT SUBJUNCTIVE | pierda | pierdas | pierda | perdamos | perdáis | pierdan |

mover

| PRESENT INDICATIVE | muevo | mueves | mueve | movemos | movéis | mueven |
| PRESENT SUBJUNCTIVE | mueva | muevas | mueva | movamos | mováis | muevan |

Infinitives in -**ir** change stem **e** to **i**, **e** to **ie** and **i**, and **o** to **ue** and **u**.

pedir

PRESENT INDICATIVE	pido	pides	pide	pedimos	pedís	piden
PRETERIT INDICATIVE	pedí	pediste	pidió	pedimos	pedisteis	pidieron
PRESENT SUBJUNCTIVE	pida	pidas	pida	pidamos	pidáis	pidan
IMPERFECT SUBJUNCTIVE	pidiera	pidieras	pidiera	pidiéramos	pidierais	pidieran

mentir

PRESENT INDICATIVE	**miento**	**mientes**	**miente**	mentimos	mentís	**mienten**
PRETERIT INDICATIVE	mentí	mentiste	mintió	mentimos	mentisteis	mintieron
PRESENT SUBJUNCTIVE	**mienta**	**mientas**	**mienta**	mintamos	mintáis	**mientan**
IMPERFECT SUBJUNCTIVE	mintiera	mintieras	mintiera	mintiéramos	mintierais	mintieran

morir

PRESENT INDICATIVE	**muero**	**mueres**	**muere**	morimos	morís	**mueren**
PRETERIT INDICATIVE	morí	moriste	murió	morimos	moristeis	murieron
PRESENT SUBJUNCTIVE	**muera**	**mueras**	**muera**	muramos	muráis	**mueran**
IMPERFECT SUBJUNCTIVE	muriera	murieras	muriera	muriéramos	murierais	murieran

Infinitives in -**uir** add **y** to the stem before the endings.

huir

PRESENT INDICATIVE	huyo	huyes	huye	huimos	huís	huyen
PRETERIT INDICATIVE	huí	huiste	huyó	huimos	huisteis	huyeron
PRESENT SUBJUNCTIVE	huya	huyas	huya	huyamos	huyáis	huyan
IMPERFECT SUBJUNCTIVE	huyera	huyeras	huyera	huyéramos	huyerais	huyeran

Irregular verbs

Indicative mood

PRESENT

caber	**quepo**	cabes	cabe	cabemos	cabéis	caben
caer	**caigo**	caes	cae	caemos	caéis	caen
dar	**doy**	das	da	damos	**dais**	dan
decir	**digo**	dices	dice	decimos	decís	dicen
estar	**estoy**	estás	está	estamos	estáis	están
haber	**he**	**has**	**ha**	**hemos**	habéis	**han**
hacer	**hago**	haces	hace	hacemos	hacéis	hacen
ir	**voy**	**vas**	**va**	**vamos**	**vais**	**van**
oír	**oigo**	**oyes**	**oye**	**oímos**	oís	**oyen**
poner	**pongo**	pones	pone	ponemos	ponéis	ponen
saber	**sé**	sabes	sabe	sabemos	sabéis	saben
salir	**salgo**	sales	sale	salimos	salís	salen
ser	**soy**	**eres**	**es**	**somos**	**sois**	**son**
tener	**tengo**	**tienes**	**tiene**	tenemos	tenéis	**tienen**
traer	**traigo**	traes	trae	traemos	traéis	traen
valer	**valgo**	vales	vale	valemos	valéis	valen
venir	**vengo**	**vienes**	**viene**	venimos	venís	**vienen**
ver	**veo**	ves	ve	vemos	**veis**	ven

PRETERIT

andar	anduve	anduviste	anduvo	anduvimos	anduvisteis	anduvieron
caber	cupe	cupiste	cupo	cupimos	cupisteis	cupieron
dar	di	diste	dio	dimos	disteis	dieron
decir	dije	dijiste	dijo	dijimos	dijisteis	dijeron
estar	estuve	estuviste	estuvo	estuvimos	estuvisteis	estuvieron
haber	hube	hubiste	hubo	hubimos	hubisteis	hubieron
hacer	hice	hiciste	hizo	hicimos	hicisteis	hicieron
ir	fui	fuiste	fue	fuimos	fuisteis	fueron
poder	pude	pudiste	pudo	pudimos	pudisteis	pudieron
poner	puse	pusiste	puso	pusimos	pusisteis	pusieron
querer	quise	quisiste	quiso	quisimos	quisisteis	quisieron
saber	supe	supiste	supo	supimos	supisteis	supieron
ser	fui	fuiste	fue	fuimos	fuisteis	fueron
tener	tuve	tuviste	tuvo	tuvimos	tuvisteis	tuvieron
traducir	traduje	tradujiste	tradujo	tradujimos	tradujisteis	tradujeron
traer	traje	trajiste	trajo	trajimos	trajisteis	trajeron
venir	vine	viniste	vino	vinimos	vinisteis	vinieron
ver	vi	viste	vio	vimos	visteis	vieron

IMPERFECT

ir	iba	ibas	iba	íbamos	ibais	iban
ser	era	eras	era	éramos	erais	eran
ver	veía	veías	veía	veíamos	veíais	veían

FUTURE

caber	cabré	cabrás	cabrá	cabremos	cabréis	cabrán
decir	diré	dirás	dirá	diremos	diréis	dirán
haber	habré	habrás	habrá	habremos	habréis	habrán
hacer	haré	harás	hará	haremos	haréis	harán
poder	podré	podrás	podrá	podremos	podréis	podrán
poner	pondré	pondrás	pondrá	pondremos	pondréis	pondrán
querer	querré	querrás	querrá	querremos	querréis	querrán
saber	sabré	sabrás	sabrá	sabremos	sabréis	sabrán
salir	saldré	saldrás	saldrá	saldremos	saldréis	saldrán
tener	tendré	tendrás	tendrá	tendremos	tendréis	tendrán
valer	valdré	valdrás	valdrá	valdremos	valdréis	valdrán
venir	vendré	vendrás	vendrá	vendremos	vendréis	vendrán

CONDITIONAL

caber	cabría	cabrías	cabría	cabríamos	cabríais	cabrían
decir	diría	dirías	diría	diríamos	diríais	dirían
haber	habría	habrías	habría	habríamos	habríais	habrían
hacer	haría	harías	haría	haríamos	haríais	harían
poder	podría	podrías	podría	podríamos	podríais	podrían
poner	pondría	pondrías	pondría	pondríamos	pondríais	pondrían
querer	querría	querrías	querría	querríamos	querríais	querrían
saber	sabría	sabrías	sabría	sabríamos	sabríais	sabrían
salir	saldría	saldrías	saldría	saldríamos	saldríais	saldrían
tener	tendría	tendrías	tendría	tendríamos	tendríais	tendrían
valer	valdría	valdrías	valdría	valdríamos	valdríais	valdrían
venir	vendría	vendrías	vendría	vendríamos	vendríais	vendrían

Subjunctive mood

PRESENT SUBJUNCTIVE

caber	quepa	quepas	quepa	quepamos	quepáis	quepan
caer	caiga	caigas	caiga	caigamos	caigáis	caigan
dar	dé	des	dé	demos	deis	den
estar	esté	estés	esté	estemos	estéis	estén
haber	haya	hayas	haya	hayamos	hayáis	hayan
hacer	haga	hagas	haga	hagamos	hagáis	hagan
ir	vaya	vayas	vaya	vayamos	vayáis	vayan
poner	ponga	pongas	ponga	pongamos	pongáis	pongan
saber	sepa	sepas	sepa	sepamos	sepáis	sepan
salir	salga	salgas	salga	salgamos	salgáis	salgan
ser	sea	seas	sea	seamos	seáis	sean
traer	traiga	traigas	traiga	traigamos	traigáis	traigan
valer	valga	valgas	valga	valgamos	valgáis	valgan
ver	vea	veas	vea	veamos	veáis	vean

IMPERFECT -ra SUBJUNCTIVE

andar	anduviera	anduvieras	anduviera	anduviéramos	anduvierais	anduvieran
caber	cupiera	cupieras	cupiera	cupiéramos	cupierais	cupieran
dar	diera	dieras	diera	diéramos	dierais	dieran
decir	dijera	dijeras	dijera	dijéramos	dijerais	dijeran
estar	estuviera	estuvieras	estuviera	estuviéramos	estuvierais	estuvieran
haber	hubiera	hubieras	hubiera	hubiéramos	hubierais	hubieran
hacer	hiciera	hicieras	hiciera	hiciéramos	hicierais	hicieran
ir	fuera	fueras	fuera	fuéramos	fuerais	fueran
poder	pudiera	pudieras	pudiera	pudiéramos	pudierais	pudieran
poner	pusiera	pusieras	pusiera	pusiéramos	pusierais	pusieran
querer	quisiera	quisieras	quisiera	quisiéramos	quisierais	quisieran
saber	supiera	supieras	supiera	supiéramos	supierais	supieran
ser	fuera	fueras	fuera	fuéramos	fuerais	fueran
tener	tuviera	tuvieras	tuviera	tuviéramos	tuvierais	tuvieran
traducir	tradujera	tradujeras	tradujera	tradujéramos	tradujerais	tradujeran
traer	trajera	trajeras	trajera	trajéramos	trajerais	trajeran
venir	viniera	vinieras	viniera	viniéramos	vinierais	vinieran
ver	viera	vieras	viera	viéramos	vierais	vieran

Spanish-English glossary

A

abismo (*m.*) abyss
abogado/a (*m./f.*) lawyer
abrazar to embrace, hug
abril (*m.*) April
abrir to open
abuelo/a (*m./f.*) grandfather/ grandmother
aburrido/a bored; boring
aburrir to bore; **aburrirse** to get bored
accidente (*m.*) accident
aceite (*m.*) oil (*cooking; motor*)
aceituna (*f.*) olive
aceptar to accept
acerca de about
aconsejar to advise
acordarse (**o > ue**) (**de**) to remember
acostar (**o > ue**) to put to bed; **acostarse** to go to bed
acostumbrarse (**a**) to get used (to)
actitud (*f.*) attitude
actuar to act; to behave
acuerdo (*m.*) agreement; **estar de acuerdo** to agree
adelgazar to lose weight
adentro inside
adivinar to guess
adolescente (*m./f.*) teenager; adolescent
¿adónde? where to?
aduana (*f.*) customs
advertir (**e > ie**) to advise, warn
aerolínea (*f.*) airline
aeropuerto (*m.*) airport
afeitarse to shave
aficionado/a (*m./f.*) fan
afuera outside; **afueras** (*f.pl.*) suburbs
agente de viajes (*m./f.*) travel agent
agosto (*m.*) August
agradable pleasant
agregar to add (up)
aguacero (*m.*) downpour, shower
aguinaldo (*m.*) bonus; Christmas gift
ahora now
ahorrar to save (up)
aire (*m.*) air; **al aire libre** outdoors
ajedrez (*m.*) chess

ajo (*m.*) garlic
alcalde (*m.*) mayor
alcanzar to reach
alegría (*f.*) happiness
alejarse to walk away
alemán (*m.*) German (*language*); **alemán** (**alemana**) German (*person*)
alfombra (*f.*) rug; carpet
algo something; anything
algodón (*m.*) cotton
alguien someone, somebody; anybody
allí there
almohada (*f.*) pillow
almorzar (**o > ue**) to eat lunch
almuerzo (*m.*) lunch
alquilar to rent
alquiler (*m.*) rent
alrededor (**de**) around
amable nice, kind
amar to love
amarillo/a yellow; (*m.*) yellow (*color*)
ambiente (*m.*) environment; **medio ambiente** (*m.*) environment
ambos/as both
amistad (*f.*) friendship
amistoso/a friendly
amor (*m.*) love
ancho/a wide
andar to walk
anfitrión (**anfitriona**)(*m./f.*) host/ hostess
anillo (*m.*) ring
anoche last night
anónimo/a anonymous
anteojos (*m.pl.*) eyeglasses
antes (**de**) before; beforehand
antipático/a unpleasant
anuncio (*m.*) commercial; advertisement
añadir to add
año (*m.*) year
apagar to turn off
aparcamiento (*m.*) parking lot, parking space
aparcar to park
aparecer to appear
apenas hardly

aprender to learn
aprobar (**o > ue**) to approve
aquí here
arañar to scratch
árbol (*m.*) tree
archivo (*m.*) file
arena (*f.*) sand
arete (*m.*) earring
armario (*m.*) closet; cabinet
arquitecto/a (*m./f.*) architect
arreglar to fix; to repair
arreglo (*m.*) repair
arroz (*m.*) rice
arruga (*f.*) wrinkle
artículo (*m.*) item; article
ascensor (*m.*) elevator
así in this way
asistente (*m./f.*) assistant; **asistente de vuelo** flight attendant
asistir (**a**) to attend
aspiradora (*f.*) vacuum cleaner; **pasar la aspiradora** to vacuum
astronauta (*m./f.*) astronaut
asunto (*m.*) matter
asustar to scare; **asustarse** to get scared
atacar to attack
aterrizar to land
atleta (*m./f.*) athlete
atraer to attract
aumento (*m.*) raise; increase
aunque although
autobús (*m.*) bus
autopista (*f.*) expresssway; **autopista de peaje** (*f.*) turnpike
ave (*f.*) bird
avergonzado/a embarrassed
averiguar to find out
avión (*m.*) airplane
avisar to let know
ayer yesterday
ayuda (*f.*) help
ayudar to help
azúcar (*m.*) sugar

B

bailar to dance
baile (*m.*) dance

bajo/a short; low

ballena (*f.*) whale; **observar ballenas** (*f.*) whale watching

baloncesto (*m.*) basketball

banco (*m.*) bank

bandera (*f.*) flag

bañar to bathe; **bañarse** to take a bath

baño (*m.*) bath; bathroom

baraja (*f.*) deck of cards

barato/a inexpensive

barco (*m.*) boat; ship

barrer to sweep

barrio (*m.*) neighborhood

bastante enough

bastar to suffice

basura (*f.*) garbage; trash

baúl (*m.*) trunk

bebé (*m.*) baby

beber to drink

béisbol (*m.*) baseball

belleza (*f.*) beauty

bendecir (**e > i**) to bless

beso (*m.*) kiss

biblioteca (*f.*) library

bicicleta (*f.*) bicycle

bien well

bienestar (*m.*) well-being

bilingüe bilingual

billete (*m.*) ticket

billetera (*f.*) wallet

boca (*f.*) mouth

boda (*f.*) wedding

boleto (*m.*) ticket

bolígrafo (*m.*) pen

bolsa (*f.*) purse; pocketbook; bag

bolsillo (*m.*) pocket

bombero/a (*m./f.*) firefighter

bombilla (*f.*) lightbulb

bosque (*m.*) woods; forest

botón (*m.*) button

breve brief

brillar to shine

broma (*f.*) joke

bronceador (*m.*) suntan oil

bruja (*f.*) witch

bueno/a good

burbuja (*f.*) bubble

buscar to look for, search for

butaca (*f.*) armchair

buzón (*m.*) mailbox

C

caballo (*m.*) horse

cabello (*m.*) hair

caber to fit

cabeza (*f.*) head

cada every; each

caer to fall; **caerse** to fall down

café (*m.*) coffee; brown

cafetería (*f.*) cafeteria; coffee shop

caja (*f.*) box

cajero/a (*m./f.*) cashier

calcetines (*m.*) socks

cálido/a warm

callarse to be quiet

calle (*f.*) street

calor (*m.*) heat; warmth

calvo/a bald

cama (*f.*) bed

cámara (*f.*) camera

cambiar to change

cambio (*m.*) change; exchange rate; **en cambio** on the other hand

camino (*m.*) road

camisa (*f.*) shirt

camiseta (*f.*) T-shirt

campaña (*f.*) campaign

campeón (campeona) (*m./f.*) champion

campeonato (*m.*) championship

canción (*f.*) song

candidato/a (*m./f.*) candidate

cansado/a tired

cansar to tire; **cansarse** to get tired

cantante (*m./f.*) singer

cantar to sing

cantidad (*f.*) amount

capital (*f.*) capital city; **capital** (*m.*) capital wealth

capítulo (*m.*) chapter

carácter (*m.*) character; temper

cárcel (*f.*) jail; prison

carne (*f.*) meat

caro/a expensive

carrera (*f.*) career

carretera (*f.*) highway

carta (*f.*) letter; card

casado/a married

casarse (con) to marry, get married (to)

casi almost

caso (*m.*) case

castillo (*m.*) castle

catálogo (*m.*) catalogue

cazar to hunt

cebolla (*f.*) onion

celebrar to celebrate

celoso/a jealous

cena (*f.*) dinner

cenar to eat dinner

centro (*m.*) center; downtown

centro comercial (*m.*) shopping mall/center

cepillar(se) to brush (oneself) (*hair, teeth*)

cepillo (*m.*) brush

cerebro (*m.*) brain

ceremonia (*f.*) ceremony

cerrado/a closed

cerrar (**e > ie**) to close

cerveza (*f.*) beer

césped (*m.*) lawn

chaqueta (*f.*) jacket

charlar to chat

cheque (*m.*) check

chico/a (*m./f.*) boy/girl; small

chimenea (*f.*) fireplace

chisme (*m.*) gossip

chiste (*m.*) joke

chocar to crash

cielo (*m.*) sky

ciencia (*f.*) science

cierto/a certain; true

cigarro (*m.*) cigar

cine (*m.*) movie theater; movies

cinta (*f.*) tape

cinturón (*m.*) belt

cita (*f.*) date; appointment

clase (*f.*) class

clasificar to classify

cliente/clienta (*m./f.*) client; customer

clima (*m.*) climate

cocinar to cook

cocinero/a (*m./f.*) cook; chef

coger to catch, grab

cohete (*m.*) rocket

cola (*f.*) line; tail

colchón (*m.*) mattress

colgar (**o > ue**) to hang (up)

collar (*m.*) necklace

comedor (*m.*) dining room

comenzar (**e > ie**) to begin, start

comer to eat

cometa (*m.*) comet; (*f.*) kite

cómico/a funny

comida (*f.*) food; meal

comisión (*f.*) commission

como as

¿cómo? how?

cómodo/a comfortable

compañero/a (*m./f.*) classmate; colleague; **compañero/a de cuarto** roommate

compañía (*f.*) company

competir (**e > i**) to compete

componer to compose

comportarse to act, behave

compra (*f.*) purchase; **ir de compras** to go shopping

comprar to buy, purchase

comprender to understand, comprehend

compromiso (*m.*) commitment; engagement

con with

con tal (de) que provided that

conceder to grant

concierto (*m.*) concert

concluir to conclude

concurso (*m.*) contest

conducir to drive; to conduct, lead

confesar (**e > ie**) to confess

confianza (*f.*) trust

congelar to freeze

congreso (*m.*) convention; congress

conjugar to conjugate
conocer to know, be acquainted with
conquistar to conquer
conseguir (e > i) to get; to succeed in
consejo (*m.*) advice
consentir (e > ie) to consent, allow
constituir to constitute, make up
construir to construct, build
consultorio (*m.*) doctor's office
contado (al contado) (for) cash
contaminación (*f.*) contamination; pollution
contar (o > ue) to count
contener to contain
contestar to answer
contra against
contraseña (*f.*) password
contribuir to contribute
convencer to convince
convenir (en) to agree (to)
convertir (e > ie) to turn into
convidar to invite
copa (*f.*) wineglass
corazón (*m.*) heart
corbata (*f.*) necktie
corregir (e > i) to correct
correo (*m.*) mail; **echar al correo** to mail (*a letter*)
correr to run
cortar to cut
corte (*m.*) cut; **corte de pelo** (*m.*) haircut
cortés polite
cortina (*f.*) curtain
cosa (*f.*) thing
cosecha (*f.*) harvest
costar (o > ue) to cost
costumbre (*f.*) custom, habit
crecer to grow
creer to believe
criar to raise
crimen (*m.*) crime
cristal (*m.*) crystal
cruzar to cross
cuadra (*f.*) city block
cuadro (*m.*) painting
cualquier(a) any
cuando when; **cuando quiera** whenever
cuanto/a whatever; **¿cuánto?** how much?; **¡cuánto!** how!
cuarto (*m.*) room
cubrir to cover
cuchara (*f.*) spoon
cuchillo (*m.*) knife
cuenta (*f.*) bill
cuento (*m.*) story; **cuento de hadas** fairy tale
cuestión (*f.*) issue; matter
cuidado (*m.*) care
cuidadosamente carefully

cuidadoso/a careful
cuidar to care for; **cuidarse** to take care of oneself
culpa (*f.*) blame; **tener la culpa** to be to blame
culpar to blame
cultivar to grow plants
cumpleaños (*m.*) birthday
cuñado (*m.*) brother-in-law
curso (*m.*) class, course
cuyo/a whose

D

dama (*f.*) lady, woman; **damas** checkers
dañar to break; to damage
daño (*m.*) injury; damage; **hacer daño** to hurt, do damage
dar to give; **dar un paseo** to take a walk; **darse cuenta de** to realize
debajo de under
deber ought to; must
decidir to decide
decir (e > i) to say, tell
defender (e > ie) to defend
dejar to leave (out); to allow
delgado/a thin; slim
demasiado too much
demostrar (o > ue) to demonstrate
dentro de inside
dependiente (*m./f.*) clerk
depositar to deposit
deprimido/a depressed
derecha (*f.*) right; **a la derecha** to the right
derecho (*m.*) right (*privilege*)
desaparecer to disappear
desastre (*m.*) disaster
desayunar to have breakfast
desayuno (*m.*) breakfast
descansar to rest
descortés impolite
describir to describe
descubrir to discover
desde from
deseo (*m.*) wish; desire
desfile (*m.*) parade
deshacer to undo
desierto (*m.*) desert
desmayarse to faint
despedirse (e > i) to say good-bye
despertar(se) (e > ie) to wake up
después later; **después de** afterwards
destacar(se) to stand out
destruir to destroy
desvestirse (e > ie) to undress (oneself)
detener to stop; to arrest
devolver (o > ue) to return
día (*m.*) day; **día feriado** (*m.*) holiday
diamante (*m.*) diamond

diario (*m.*) diary; newspaper
dibujo (*m.*) drawing
diciembre (*m.*) December
diente (*m.*) tooth
dieta (*f.*) diet; **estar a dieta** to be on a diet
difícil hard, difficult
dificultad (*f.*) difficulty
dinero (*m.*) money
Dios; dios (*m.*) God; god
diploma (*m.*) diploma
dirección (*f.*) address
dirigir to direct
disculparse to excuse oneself
discutir to discuss; to argue
diseñador(a) (*m./f.*) designer
diseño (*m.*) design
disfraz (*m.*) disguise, costume
distancia (*f.*) distance
distinto/a different
diversión (*f.*) amusement, fun; **parque de diversiones** (*m.*) amusement park
divertirse (e > ie) to have fun
doblar to turn
docena (*f.*) dozen
documento (*m.*) document
dólar (*m.*) dollar
doler (o > ue) to hurt
dolor (*m.*) ache; pain
domingo (*m.*) Sunday
donde where; **¿dónde?** where?
dondequiera wherever
dormir (o > ue) to sleep; **dormirse** to fall asleep
dormitorio (*m.*) bedroom
drama (*m.*) play
ducha (*f.*) shower
ducharse to take a shower
dudar to doubt
dulce sweet
durante during
durar to last
duro/a hard

E

echar to pour; **echarse** to rest; **echar de menos** to miss someone, something
edad (*f.*) age
edificio (*m.*) building
educar to educate
egoísta selfish
ejército (*m.*) army
elección (*f.*) election
elegir (e > i) to elect
embajador(a) (*m./f.*) ambassador
emboscada (*f.*) ambush
emisora (*f.*) radio station
emocionante exciting
empacar to pack
empezar (e > ie) to begin

empleado/a (*m./f.*) employee
empleo (*m.*) job; work
empresa (*f.*) enterprise
enamorado/a (*m./f.*) lover;
  estar enamorado/a to be in love
encantador(a) charming
encender (e > ie) to light; to kindle
encima de on top of
encontrar (o > ue) to find;
  encontrarse con to meet with
enemigo/a (*m./f.*) enemy
energía (*f.*) energy
enero (*m.*) January
enfermarse to get sick
enfermedad (*f.*) illness
enfermero/a (*m./f.*) nurse
enfermo/a sick
enfrente (de) in front (of)
engañar to deceive
enigma (*m.*) enigma; puzzle
enojado/a angry
enojarse to get angry
ensalada (*f.*) salad
ensayar to rehearse
ensayo (*m.*) rehearsal
enseñar to teach
entender (e > ie) to understand
entero/a entire
entonces then
entrada (*f.*) entrance; admission
entrar to enter
entre between
entregar to deliver
entrenar to train
entrevista (*f.*) interview
enviar to send
envolver (o > ue) to wrap
equipaje (*m.*) equipment; luggage
equipo (*m.*) team; gear
equivocarse to make a mistake
error (*m.*) error; mistake
escalera (*f.*) staircase; stairs; ladder
escena (*f.*) scene
escenario (*m.*) stage
escoger to select
esconder to hide
escrito/a written; **por escrito**
  in writing
escritorio (*m.*) desk
escuchar to listen
escuela (*f.*) school; **escuela**
  secundaria high school
esmeralda (*f.*) emerald
espacio (*m.*) space; room
espalda (*f.*) back
espejo (*m.*) mirror
esperar to hope; to wait (for)
espía (*m./f.*) spy
esposo/a (*m./f.*) husband/wife
esquiar to ski
esquina (*f.*) corner
establecer to establish

estación (*f.*) season; station
estacionar to park
estado (*m.*) state
Estados Unidos (*m.*) United States
estampilla (*f.*) stamp
estante (*m.*) shelf
estar to be; **estar a dieta** to be on a
  diet
estómago (*m.*) stomach
estornudar to sneeze
estrella (*f.*) star; **estrella de cine**
  movie star
estudiante (*m./f.*) student
estudios (*m.*) studies
estupendo/a great
examen (*m.*) exam
excursión (*f.*) day trip
exigir to demand
éxito (*m.*) success; **tener éxito** to be
  successful
exitoso/a successful
exposición (*f.*) exhibit
extinguir to extinguish
extranjero/a foreign
extraño/a strange; odd

F

fábrica (*f.*) factory
falda (*f.*) skirt
faltar to be lacking, be absent
fama (*f.*) fame
fantasía (*f.*) fantasy
fantasma (*m.*) ghost
farmacia (*f.*) pharmacy
fascinar to fascinate
fastidiar to bother
favor (*m.*) favor
febrero (*m.*) February
felicidad (*f.*) happiness
feliz happy
ferrocarril (*m.*) railroad
fiebre (*f.*) fever
fiesta (*f.*) party
fin (*m.*) end; **fin de semana** weekend
financiero/a financial
fingir to pretend
firma (*f.*) signature
firmar to sign
flan (*m.*) custard
flor (*f.*) flower
florero (*m.*) vase
flotar to float
fondo (*m.*) bottom
forma (*f.*) shape; **en buena forma**
  in good shape
foto (*f.*) photo
francés (*m.*) French (*language*);
  francés (francesa) French (*person*)
frase (*f.*) sentence; phrase
frecuencia (*f.*) frequency;
  con frecuencia frequently, often
fregar (e > ie) to wash (*dishes*)

freír (e > i) to fry
fresa (*f.*) strawberry
fresco/a cool
frío/a cold
frontera (*f.*) border
fuego (*m.*) fire
fuera outside
fumar to smoke
funcionar to work, run (*machinery*)
fútbol (*m.*) soccer
fútbol americano (*m.*) football

G

gafas de sol (*f.pl.*) sunglasses
gana (*f.*) desire; **tener ganas de**
  to feel like
ganador(a) (*m./f.*) winner
ganar to win; to earn
ganga (*f.*) bargain
gasolina (*f.*) gasoline
gastar to spend
gato (*m.*) cat
gente (*f.*) people
gigante (*m.*) giant
gimnasio (*m.*) gym; gymnasium
girar to turn
gobernador(a) (*m./f.*) governor
goma (*f.*) glue; **goma de borrar** eraser
gota (*f.*) drop
gozar to enjoy
grabadora (*f.*) recorder
grabar to record
graduarse to graduate
gran great; grand
grande big; large
grave serious
gravedad (*f.*) gravity
griego (*m.*) Greek (*language*);
  griego/a Greek (*person*)
guante (*m.*) glove
guapo/a handsome; good-looking
guardar to keep; **guardar cama**
  to stay in bed
guerra (*f.*) war
guía (*m./f.*) guide; **guía de turismo**
  (*f.*) travel guide
guitarra (*f.*) guitar
gustar to like; to be pleasing
gusto (*m.*) taste

H

habitación (*f.*) room
hablar to speak, talk
hacer to make; to do; **hacer ejercicio**
  to exercise; **hacer una pregunta**
  to ask a question
hamaca (*f.*) hammock
hambre (*f.*) hunger
hamburguesa (*f.*) hamburger
hasta until
hecho (*m.*) fact
helado (*m.*) ice cream

herido/a wounded
hermano/a (*m./f.*) brother/sister
hervir (e > ie) to boil
hidrante de incendios (*m.*) fire hydrant
hielo (*m.*) ice
hierba (*f.*) grass
hipoteca (*f.*) mortgage
hogar (*m.*) home
hoja (*f.*) leaf
hombre (*m.*) man
hombro (*m.*) shoulder
honrado/a honest
horario (*m.*) schedule
horno (*m.*) oven
hotel (*m.*) hotel
hoy today
huelga (*f.*) strike
hueso (*m.*) bone
huésped (*m./f.*) guest
huevo (*m.*) egg
huir to flee
humano/a human
humilde humble
humor (*m.*) humor
huracán (*m.*) hurricane

I

idioma (*m.*) language
iglesia (*f.*) church
igual equal; same
imaginarse to imagine
impedir (e > i) to prevent
impermeable (*m.*) raincoat
imponer to enforce
importante important; **importarle a alguien** to be important
importar to import
impuesto (*m.*) tax
incendio (*m.*) fire
incluir to include
incluso including
incómodo/a uncomfortable
influir to influence
información (*f.*) information
ingeniero/a (*m./f.*) engineer
Inglaterra (*f.*) England
inglés (*m.*) English (*language*); **inglés (inglesa)** English (*person*)
insistir to insist
intentar to try
interés (*m.*) interest
interesar to interest
introducir to present
inundación (*f.*) flood
inundar to flood
invertir (e > ie) to invest
investigar to investigate
invierno (*m.*) winter
invitación (*f.*) invitation
invitado/a (*m./f.*) guest
invitar to invite

ir to go; **irse** to go away; **ir de compras** to go shopping
izquierda left; **a la izquierda** to the left

J

jamás never; not ever
jardín (*m.*) garden
jaula (*f.*) cage
jefe/a (*m./f.*) boss; employer
jirafa (*f.*) giraffe
joven young
joya (*f.*) jewel
joyas (*f.*) jewelry
joyería (*f.*) jewelry store
juego (*m.*) game
jueves (*m.*) Thursday
juez(a) (*m./f.*) judge
jugar (o > ue) (a) to play (*a game or sport*)
juguetería (*f.*) toy store
juicio (*m.*) trial
julio (*m.*) July
junio (*m.*) June
juntos/as together
justificar to justify
justo/a fair; just
juventud (*f.*) youth

L

lado (*m.*) side; **al lado de** next to
ladrar to bark
ladrón (ladrona) (*m./f.*) thief
lago (*m.*) lake
lágrima (*f.*) tear
lámpara (*f.*) lamp
lana (*f.*) wool
langosta (*f.*) lobster
lanzador(a) (*m./f.*) pitcher (*baseball*)
lanzar to throw
largo/a long
lástima (*f.*) pity; shame
lavaplatos (*m.*) dishwasher
lavar to wash; **lavarse** to wash oneself
leche (*f.*) milk
lechuga (*f.*) lettuce
lectura (*f.*) reading
leer to read
legumbre (*f.*) vegetable
lejos far; **lejos de** away from
lenguaje (*m.*) language
lentes (*m.pl.*) eyeglasses
lento/a slow
león (*m.*) lion
letra (*f.*) letter (*of the alphabet*); **letra mayúscula** capital letter; **letra minúscula** lowercase letter
levantarse to stand up; to get up
ley (*f.*) law
leyenda (*f.*) legend
libertad (*f.*) freedom; liberty

libra (*f.*) pound
libre free
librería (*f.*) bookstore
libro (*m.*) book
líder (*m./f.*) leader
limonada (*f.*) lemonade
limpiar to clean
limpio/a clean
línea (*f.*) line; **línea aérea** (*f.*) airline; **en línea** online
listo/a ready; smart
llamada (*f.*) call; **llamada telefónica** phone call
llamar to call
llave (*f.*) key
llegar to arrive; **llegar a ser** to become
llenar to fill
lleno/a full
llevar to carry; to wear
llorar to cry
llover (o > ue) to rain
lluvia (*f.*) rain
lluvioso/a rainy
loco/a crazy
lograr to achieve, succeed
lotería (*f.*) lottery
lucha (*f.*) fight; struggle
luego later; then
lugar (*m.*) place
luna (*f.*) moon
luna de miel (*f.*) honeymoon
lunes (*m.*) Monday
luz (*f.*) light

M

madera (*f.*) wood
maduro/a ripe
maestro/a (*m./f.*) teacher
mago/a (*m./f.*) magician
maldecir (e > i) to curse
maleta (*f.*) suitcase
maletero (*m.*) trunk
malo/a bad; evil
mancha (*f.*) spot
manejar to drive; to manage
manga (*f.*) sleeve
mano (*f.*) hand; **dar una mano** to give a hand
manta (*f.*) blanket
mantel (*m.*) tablecloth
mantener to maintain
mantequilla (*f.*) butter
manzana (*f.*) apple
mañana (*f.*) morning; (*adv.*) tomorrow
maratón (*m.*) marathon
maravilloso/a wonderful
marcharse to leave
marido (*m.*) husband
mariposa (*f.*) butterfly
marrón (*m.*) brown
martes (*m.*) Tuesday

martillar to hammer
martillo (*m.*) hammer
marzo (*m.*) March
más more
máscara (*f.*) mask
materia (*f.*) matter; (school) subject
mayo (*m.*) May
mayor older; larger
mecánico/a (*m./f.*) mechanic
media (*f.*) stocking
medianoche (*f.*) midnight
medio/a half; (*m.*) middle
mediodía (*m.*) noon
medir (e > i) to measure
mejor better
menor younger
menos less
mensaje (*m.*) message; **mensaje de texto** (*m.*) text message
mentir (e > ie) to lie, tell a lie
mentira (*f.*) lie
mentiroso/a (*m./f.*) liar
merecer to deserve
mes (*m.*) month
mesero/a (*m./f.*) waiter, waitress
meta (*f.*) goal
meter to put
metro (*m.*) meter; subway
mezclar to blend
mientras while
miércoles (*m.*) Wednesday
mil (*m.*) thousand
milla (*f.*) mile
mirar to watch, look at
mismo/a same; **lo mismo** the same thing
misterio (*m.*) mystery
mitad (*f.*) half
modales (*m.pl.*) manners
modelo (*m./f.*) model
mojado/a wet
molestar to bother
moneda (*f.*) coin; change
mono (*m.*) monkey
monstruo (*m.*) monster
montar to ride (*horseback*); **montar en bicicleta** to ride a bike
monumento (*m.*) monument
morder (o > ue) to bite
mordida (*f.*) bite
morir (o > ue) to die
mosca (*f.*) (house)fly
mosquito (*m.*) mosquito
mostrar (o > ue) to show
mover (o > ue) to move
mucho/a much; many; a lot
mudarse to move, change residence
mueble (*m.*) piece of furniture; **muebles** furniture
muela (*f.*) tooth; molar; **muela del juicio** wisdom tooth
muerte (*f.*) death

muerto/a dead
mujer (*f.*) woman
multa (*f.*) fine; traffic ticket
mundo (*m.*) world; **todo el mundo** everybody
muñeca (*f.*) doll; wrist
museo (*m.*) museum
música (*f.*) music

N

nacer to be born
nada nothing; **de nada** you are welcome
nadar to swim
nadie nobody; no one
naranja (*f.*) orange
nariz (*f.*) nose
naturaleza (*f.*) nature
navaja (*f.*) razor
Navidad (*f.*) Christmas
necesitar to need
negar (e > ie) to deny
negociante (*m./f.*) businessman/ businesswoman
negocio (*m.*) business; **empresa de negocios** (*f.*) company
nervioso/a nervous
nevada (*f.*) snowfall
nevar (e > ie) to snow
niebla (*f.*) fog
nieto/a (*m./f.*) grandson/ granddaughter
nieve (*f.*) snow
ninguno/a (ningún) none; not any
noche (*f.*) night; **por la noche** at night
nombre (*m.*) name
nota (*f.*) note
notas (*f.pl.*) grades
noticias (*f.pl.*) news
novia (*f.*) girlfriend; fiancée; bride
noviembre (*m.*) November
novio (*m.*) boyfriend; fiancé; groom
nube (*f.*) cloud
nublado/a cloudy
nuevo/a new; **de nuevo** again
número (*m.*) number
nunca never

O

o... o... either ... or ...
obedecer to obey
octubre (*m.*) October
ocupado/a busy
odiar to hate
odio (*m.*) hatred
odontología (*f.*) dentistry
ofrecer to offer
oír to hear
ojalá God willing
ojo (*m.*) eye

oler (o > ue) to smell; to (have a) smell
olimpiadas (*f.*) Olympic Games
oliva (*f.*) olive
olvidar to forget
oponer to oppose
ordenado/a neat
organizar to organize
orgulloso/a proud
oro (*m.*) gold
oscuridad (*f.*) darkness
oscuro/a dark
oso (*m.*) bear
otoño (*m.*) autumn
otro/a another
OVNI (*m.*) UFO

P

pagar to pay
página (*f.*) page
pájaro (*m.*) bird
palabra (*f.*) word
palacio (*m.*) palace
pálido/a pale
pan (*m.*) bread
panadería (*f.*) bakery
panadero/a (*m./f.*) baker
pantalla (*f.*) screen
pantalones (*m.pl.*) pants
papa (*f.*) potato
papá (*m.*) father; dad
papel (*m.*) paper; role
papelería (*f.*) stationery store
paquete (*m.*) package
par (*m.*) pair
parada (*f.*) (bus) stop
paraguas (*m.*) umbrella
parecer to seem; **parecerse a** to look like
pared (*f.*) wall
pariente (*m./f.*) relative
parrilla (*f.*) grill; **a la parrilla** grilled
partido (*m.*) game
pasajero/a (*m./f.*) passenger
pasar to pass
pasatiempo (*m.*) hobby
pasillo (*m.*) hallway
pastel (*m.*) cake
patata (*f.*) potato
patinar to skate
pato (*m.*) duck
pavo (*m.*) turkey
payama (*f.*) pajamas
payaso/a (*m./f.*) clown
paz (*f.*) peace
pedazo (*m.*) piece
pedir (e > i) to ask for
pegar to glue; to hit
peinar(se) to comb (one's hair)
peine (*m.*) comb
película (*f.*) movie
peligro (*m.*) danger

peligroso/a dangerous

pelo (*m.*) hair

peluquería (*f.*) hairdresser's shop; barber shop

pensar (**e** > **ie**) to think; **pensar en** to think about; **pensar de** to have an opinion

peor worse

pequeño/a small, little

percha (*f.*) hanger

perder (**e** > **ie**) to lose; **perder el tiempo** to waste time

perezoso/a lazy

periódico (*m.*) newspaper

periodista (*m./f.*) journalist

perla (*f.*) pearl

permiso (*m.*) permission; **con permiso** excuse me

permitir to permit, allow

perseguir (**e** > **i**) to pursue

personaje (*m.*) character

pertenecer to belong

pesadilla (*f.*) nightmare

pesado/a annoying

pesar to weigh

pescado (*m.*) fish (*for eating*)

peso (*m.*) weight

pez (*m.*) fish (*in water*)

pie (*m.*) foot; **estar de pie** to be standing

piel (*f.*) skin

pierna (*f.*) leg

pijama (*m.*) pajamas

píldora (*f.*) pill

pintor(a) (*m./f.*) painter

pintura (*f.*) paint

pirámide (*f.*) pyramid

piscina (*f.*) swimming pool

piso (*m.*) floor; apartment

pista (*f.*) clue; track; **pista de hielo** (*f.*) ice-skating rink

plancha (*f.*) (clothes) iron

planchar to iron

planeta (*m.*) planet

plata (*f.*) silver

plátano (*m.*) banana

playa (*f.*) beach

población (*f.*) population

poco/a little; **hace poco** a short time ago

poder (**o** > **ue**) to be able to

policía (*m./f.*) police officer; (*f.*) police force

política (*f.sing.*) politics

político/a (*m./f.*) politician

poner to put; **ponerse** to become; to put on clothing; **ponerse a dieta** to go on a diet

porque because

portero/a (*m./f.*) goalkeeper; goalie

poseer to possess, own

postre (*m.*) dessert

precio (*m.*) price

preferir (**e** > **ie**) to prefer

premio (*m.*) prize

preocupado/a worried

preocuparse to worry

preparar to prepare

presentación (*f.*) presentation; introduction

préstamo (*m.*) loan

prestar to loan, lend

primavera (*f.*) spring

primero/a first

primo/a (*m./f.*) cousin

prisa (*f.*) hurry; **de prisa** quickly

probar (**o** > **ue**) to prove; to taste

probarse (**o** > **ue**) to try on

problema (*m.*) problem

producir to produce

profesión (*f.*) profession

profesional (*m./f.*) professional

programa (*m.*) program

progreso (*m.*) progress

prohibido/a prohibited

promesa (*f.*) promise

prometer to promise

pronóstico (*m.*) forecast

pronto soon

pronunciación (*f.*) pronunciation

propina (*f.*) tip

proponer to propose

proteger to protect

próximo/a next

prueba (*f.*) quiz

publicar to publish

publicidad (*f.*) publicity; advertisement

público (*m.*) public; audience

pueblo (*m.*) town

puente (*m.*) bridge

puesto (*m.*) place; job

pulgada (*f.*) inch

pulsera (*f.*) bracelet

punto (*m.*) point; **punto de vista** point of view; **en punto** on the dot

puro/a pure

Q

que that; than; **¿qué?** what?

quedar(se) to stay, remain

quehacer (*m.*) chore, task

queja (*f.*) complaint

quejarse (**de**) to complain (about)

quemar to burn

querer (**e** > **ie**) to want; **querer decir** to mean

querido/a dear

queso (*m.*) cheese

quien who; **¿quién?** who?

quienquiera whoever

química (*f.*) chemistry

quitar(se) to take off, remove

quizás perhaps

R

rabia (*f.*) rage

radio (*m./f.*) radio

rama (*f.*) branch (*tree*)

ramo (*m.*) bouquet (*of flowers*)

rana (*f.*) frog

rápidamente quickly

rápido/a fast

raqueta (*f.*) (tennis) racket

raro/a odd

rato (*m.*) while; **pasar un buen rato** to have a good time

razón (*f.*) reason; **tener razón** to be right

realizar to achieve; to fulfill

rebaja (*f.*) special sale

rebajar de peso to lose weight

recepción (*f.*) reception

receta (*f.*) recipe; prescription

recetar to prescribe

rechazar to reject

recibir to receive

reciclar to recycle

recoger to pick up, gather

reconocer to recognize

recordar (**o** > **ue**) to remember

recuerdo (*m.*) memory; souvenir; **recuerdos** regards

recurso (*m.*) resource

reducir to reduce, cut down

referir (**e** > **ie**) to refer

refresco (*m.*) refreshment; soft drink

refrigerador (*m.*) refrigerator

regalar to give a present

regalo (*m.*) gift

regar (**e** > **ie**) to water

regla (*f.*) rule; ruler

rehacer to redo, remake

reina (*f.*) queen

reír(se) (**e** > **i**) to laugh

relajarse to relax

relámpago (*m.*) lightning

reloj (*m.*) watch; clock

renunciar to quit (*a job, etc.*)

reñir(se) (**e** > **i**) to quarrel

repetir (**e** > **i**) to repeat

reportaje (*m.*) report

resfriado (*m.*) (head) cold; **tener un resfriado** to have a cold

resolver (**o** > **ue**) to solve, resolve

respirar to breathe

respuesta (*f.*) answer

restaurante (*m.*) restaurant

reunión (*f.*) meeting

reunir(se) to gather, meet

revista (*f.*) magazine

rey (*m.*) king

rezar to beg; to pray

rico/a rich; tasty

ridículo/a ridiculous

riqueza (*f.*) wealth

risa (*f.*) laughter

robar to rob, steal
robo (*m.*) robbery
robótica (*f.*) robotics
rodilla (*f.*) knee; **de rodillas** kneeling
rogar (**o > ue**) to pray; to beg
rompecabezas (*m.*) puzzle
romper to break
ropa (*f.*) clothing
ropero (*m.*) closet
roto/a broken
rubí (*m.*) ruby
rubio/a blond(e)
rueda (*f.*) wheel
ruido (*m.*) noise
ruso (*m.*) Russian (*language*);
　ruso/a (*m./f.*) Russian (*person*)

S

sábado (*m.*) Saturday
saber to know; **saber de** to know
　about
sabio/a wise
sabor (*m.*) flavor
sabroso/a delicious
sacar to take out; **sacar una foto**
　to take a picture
sacudir to shake; **sacudir el polvo**
　to dust (*furniture*)
sal (*f.*) salt
sala (*f.*) living room; **sala de juntas**
　boardroom
salchicha (*f.*) sausage
salida (*f.*) exit
salir to come out; to leave
saltar to jump
salud (*f.*) health
saludable healthy
saludar to greet
saludo (*m.*) greeting
sangre (*f.*) blood
sano/a healthy
secadora (*f.*) (clothes) dryer
secar(se) to dry (oneself)
seco/a dry
secreto (*m.*) secret
secundaria (*f.*) high school
sed (*f.*) thirst
seda (*f.*) silk
seguir (**e > i**) to follow, continue
seguro/a safe
sello (*m.*) stamp
selva (*f.*) jungle; **selva tropical** rain
　forest
semáforo (*m.*) traffic light
semana (*f.*) week
semilla (*f.*) seed
sentado/a sitting; seated
sentarse (**e > ie**) to sit down, be
　seated
sentir (**e > ie**) to regret; **sentirse**
　to feel
septiembre (*m.*) September

Serie Mundial (*f.*) World Series
servilleta (*f.*) napkin
servir (**e > i**) to serve
siempre always
siglo (*m.*) century
siguiente next; following
silla (*f.*) chair
sillón (*m.*) armchair
sin without
sobrar to be left over
sobre (*m.*) envelope
sociedad (*f.*) society; company
sofá (*m.*) sofa, couch
sol (*m.*) sun
solamente only
soldado (*m./f.*) soldier
solicitud (*f.*) application
solo/a alone; (*adv.*) **solo** only; just
sombra (*f.*) shade; shadow
sombrero (*m.*) hat
sonar (**o > ue**) to ring; **sonar a**
　to sound like
sonreír (**e > i**) to smile
sonrisa (*f.*) smile
soñar (**o > ue**) (**con**) to dream (of)
sopa (*f.*) soup
sostener to sustain; to support
sótano (*m.*) basement
subir to climb, go up
subrayar to underline
sucio/a dirty
suegro/a (*m./f.*) father-in-law/
　mother-in-law
sueldo (*m.*) salary
suelo (*m.*) floor
sueño (*m.*) dream
suéter (*m.*) sweater
suficiente enough
sufrir to suffer
sugerir (**e > ie**) to suggest
supersticioso/a superstitious
suponer to suppose
sur (*m.*) south
sustituir to substitute

T

tabaco (*m.*) tobacco; cigar
taladrar to drill
talla (*f.*) size (*for clothing*)
tamaño (*m.*) size
también also, too
tampoco neither, not either
tanto/a so much
taquilla (*f.*) box office
tardar to take time
tarde late
tarjeta (*f.*) card; **tarjeta de crédito**
　credit card
taza (*f.*) cup; mug
té (*m.*) tea
teatro (*m.*) theater
tela (*f.*) cloth; fabric

teléfono (*m.*) telephone
televisión (*f.*) television; television
　(set)
tema (*m.*) theme; topic
temblar (**e > ie**) to tremble; to shake
temer to fear
temor (*m.*) fear
temprano early
tenedor (*m.*) fork
tener to have; **tener que** to have to
terminar to finish
terremoto (*m.*) earthquake
tesoro (*m.*) treasure
tiempo (*m.*) time; weather; **a tiempo**
　on time
tienda (*f.*) store
tierra (*f.*) land; earth
tijeras (*f.pl.*) scissors
toalla (*f.*) towel
tocar to touch; to play (*an instrument*)
todavía still; yet
todo (*m.*) all; everything
tolerar to tolerate
tomar to take; to drink; **tomar una**
　decisión to make a decision
tomate (*m.*) tomato
tonto/a silly; ridiculous
tormenta (*f.*) storm
torta (*f.*) cake
tostada (*f.*) toast
tostar (**o > ue**) to toast
trabajar to work
trabajo (*m.*) work; job
traducir to translate
traer to bring; to carry
tráfico (*m.*) traffic
trágico/a tragic
traje (*m.*) suit; **traje de baño** bathing
　suit
tranquilo/a peaceful, calm
tratar to treat; **tratar de** to try to (*do*
　something)
tren (*m.*) train
triste sad
tristeza (*f.*) sadness
tropezar (**e > ie**) to stumble;
　tropezar con to bump into
trueno (*m.*) thunder

U

último/a last
único/a only; unique
unir to unite
uva (*f.*) grape

V

vaca (*f.*) cow
vacaciones (*f.pl.*) vacation
vacío/a empty
valer to be worth; **valer la pena**
　to be worthwhile
valor (*m.*) value

variedad (*f.*) variety
varios/as several
vaso (*m.*) glass
vecindario (*m.*) neighborhood
vecino/a (*m./f.*) neighbor
vehículo (*m.*) vehicle
vela (*f.*) candle
vencer to conquer
vendedor(a) (*m./f.*) salesperson
vender to sell
venir to come
venta (*f.*) sale
ventana (*f.*) window
ventanilla (*f.*) box office; car window
ver to see
verano (*m.*) summer
verdad (*f.*) truth

vestido (*m.*) dress
vestir(se) (**e > i**) to dress
vez (*f.*) (*pl.* **veces**) time; **de vez en cuando** from time to time
viajar to travel
viaje (*m.*) trip
vida (*f.*) life
vidrio (*m.*) glass
viejo/a old
viento (*m.*) wind
viernes (*m.*) Friday
vigilar to watch over; to guard
vino (*m.*) wine; **vino tinto** red wine
vista (*f.*) view
vitamina (*f.*) vitamin
vivir to live
vivo/a alive

volar (**o > ue**) to fly
voleibol (*m.*) volleyball
volver (**o > ue**) to return
voz (*f.*) voice
vuelo (*m.*) flight

W

web (*f.*) Web; **página web** (*f.*) Web page

Y

ya already

Z

zapatería (*f.*) shoe store
zapatilla (*f.*) slipper
zapato (*m.*) shoe

English-Spanish glossary

A

a un, una
a lot mucho/a
about acerca de
accept aceptar
accident accidente (*m.*) **by accident**
  por casualidad
ache dolor (*m.*)
achieve lograr; realizar
acquire adquirir (e > ie)
across a través (de); por
act actuar; comportarse
action movie una película de acción
actor actor (*m.*)
actress actriz (*f.*)
add agregar; añadir
address dirección (*f.*)
admire admirar
advice consejo (*m.*)
advise advertir (e > ie); aconsejar
afraid asustado/a; **to be afraid of**
  tener miedo de
after; afterwards después (de)
afternoon tarde (*f.*)
again otra vez; de nuevo
against contra
agent agente (*m./f.*)
agree (*to do something*) convenir (en);
  to agree with estar de acuerdo con
air aire (*m.*)
airline aerolínea (*f.*)
alive vivo/a
all todo (*m.*); **all day long** todo el día
allow consentir (e > ie); dejar;
  permitir
already ya
also también
although aunque
always siempre
ambassador embajador(a) (*m./f.*)
ambush emboscada (*f.*)
among entre
amount cantidad (*f.*)
amusement diversión (*f.*); **amusement
  park** parque de atracciones, parque
  de diversiones (*m.*)
and y; e (*preceding a word starting
  with* **i** *or* **hi**)

anecdote anécdota (*f.*)
angry enfadado/a, enojado/a
anniversary aniversario (*m.*)
annoy molestar
annoying pesado/a
anonymous anónimo/a
another otro/a
answer respuesta (*f.*); contestar;
  responder
any; anything algo; cualquiera;
  cualquier cosa
anyway de cualquier forma
anywhere; not anywhere en cualquier
  parte; en ninguna parte
apparently al parecer; por lo visto
appear aparecer
apple manzana (*f.*)
application solicitud (*f.*);
  formulario (*m.*)
appointment cita (*f.*)
approve aprobar (o > ue)
April abril (*m.*)
architect arquitecto/a (*m./f.*)
armchair butaca (*f.*); sillón (*m.*)
army ejército (*m.*)
around alrededor (de)
arrange arreglar
arrest detener
arrive llegar
article artículo (*m.*)
as como; **as much as** tanto como;
  as soon as tan pronto como
ask preguntar
ask (**for**) pedir (e > i)
asleep dormido/a
assignment tarea (*f.*)
astronaut astronauta (*m./f.*)
athlete atleta (*m./f.*)
attack atacar
attend asistir a
attitude actitud (*f.*)
attract atraer
audience público (*m.*)
August agosto (*m.*)
aunt tía (*f.*)
autumn otoño (*m.*)
away from lejos de; **to go away** irse
  (*irr.*)

B

baby bebé (*m.*)
back (*adv.*) atrás
backyard jardín; patio (*m.*)
bad malo/a
bad mood mal humor (*m.*)
bag bolsa (*f.*)
baker panadero/a (*m./f.*)
bakery panadería (*f.*)
bald calvo/a
ball pelota (*f.*)
banana plátano (*m.*)
bank banco (*m.*)
bargain ganga (*f.*)
bark ladrar
baseball béisbol (*m.*)
baseball field campo de pelota (*m.*)
basement sótano (*m.*)
basketball baloncesto (*m.*)
bath; bathroom baño (*m.*)
bathe bañar(se)
bathing suit traje de baño (*m.*)
be ser; estar
beach playa (*f.*)
bear oso (*m.*)
because porque
become ponerse; hacerse
bed cama (*f.*)
bedroom dormitorio (*m.*)
beer cerveza (*f.*)
before antes (de)
beg rogar (o > ue); rezar
begin comenzar; empezar (e > ie)
beginning principio (*m.*)
behave comportarse
believe creer
belong pertenecer
belt cinturón (*m.*)
best mejor
better mejor
between entre
bicycle bicicleta (*f.*)
big grande; gran
bilingual bilingüe
bill cuenta (*f.*)
bird pájaro (*m.*); (el) ave (*f.*)
birthday cumpleaños (*m.*)
bite mordida (*f.*); morder (o > ue)

blame culpa (*f.*); culpar; **to be blamed** tener la culpa
blanket manta (*f.*)
blend mezclar
block (*city*) manzana; cuadra (*f.*)
blond(e) rubio/a
blood sangre (*f.*)
boardroom sala de juntas (*f.*)
boat barco (*m.*)
boil hervir (e > ie)
bomb bomba (*f.*)
bone hueso (*m.*)
book libro (*m.*)
bookstore librería (*f.*)
border frontera (*f.*)
bored; boring aburrido/a
born (to be) nacer
boss jefe/a (*m./f.*)
bother fastidiar; molestar
bottom fondo (*m.*)
bouquet ramo de flores (*m.*)
box caja (*f.*)
box office taquilla (*f.*); ventanilla (*f.*)
boy chico (*m.*)
boyfriend novio (*m.*)
bracelet pulsera (*f.*); brazalete (*m.*)
brain cerebro (*m.*)
branch (*tree*) rama (*f.*)
brave valiente
bread pan (*m.*)
break romper; quebrar
breakfast desayuno (*m.*); **to have breakfast** desayunar
breathe respirar
brick ladrillo (*m.*)
bride novia (*f.*)
bridge puente (*m.*)
bring traer
bring back devolver (o > ue)
broken roto/a; dañado/a
brother hermano (*m.*)
brother-in-law cuñado (*m.*)
brown marrón (*m.*), *adj.*
brush cepillo (*m.*)
brush (oneself) cepillar(se)
build construir
building edificio (*m.*)
bump into tropezar(se) con (e > ie)
burn quemar
bury enterrar (e > ie)
bus autobús (*m.*)
business negocio (*m.*); **businessman/ businesswoman** negociante (*m./f.*)
busy ocupado/a
butter mantequilla (*f.*)
butterfly mariposa (*f.*)
button botón (*m.*)
buy comprar
by por; **by accident** por casualidad

C

cabinet armario (*m.*)
café café (*m.*)
cafeteria cafetería (*f.*)
cage jaula (*f.*)
cake torta (*f.*); pastel (*m.*)
call llamada (*f.*)
call (oneself) llamar(se)
calorie caloría (*f.*)
camera cámara (*f.*)
candidate candidato/a (*m./f.*)
candle vela (*f.*)
candy caramelos (*m.pl.*)
capital (*city*) capital (*f.*)
capital (*wealth*) capital (*m.*)
card tarjeta (*f.*); carta (*f.*)
cards (*deck of*) baraja (*f.*)
care cuidado (*m.*); cuidar; **to care for** (*a person*) cuidar a; **to care for oneself** cuidarse
career carrera (*f.*)
careful cuidadoso/a
carefully con cuidado, cuidadosamente
carpet alfombra (*f.*)
case caso (*m.*)
castle castillo (*m.*)
cat gato (*m.*)
catalogue catálogo (*m.*)
catch agarrar; coger
celebrate celebrar
center centro (*m.*)
century siglo (*m.*)
ceremony ceremonia (*f.*)
chair silla (*f.*)
champion campeón (campeona) (*m./f.*)
championship campeonato (*m.*)
change cambio (*m.*); cambiar
chapter capítulo (*m.*)
character personaje (*m.*); carácter (*m.*)
charming encantador(a)
check cheque (*m.*)
checkers damas (*f.pl.*)
cheese queso (*m.*)
chemistry química (*f.*)
chess ajedrez (*m.*)
choose elegir (e > i); escoger
chore tarea (*f.*)
Christmas Navidad (*f.*)
cigar puro (*m.*); cigarro (*m.*)
class clase (*f.*)
classify clasificar
classmate compañero/a de clase (*m./f.*)
clean limpio/a; limpiar
clerk dependiente (*m./f.*)
client cliente (*m.*); clienta (*f.*)
climate clima (*m.*)
climb subir
clock reloj (*m.*)
close cerca

close cerrar (e > ie)
closed cerrado/a
closet armario (*m.*)
clothes, clothing ropa (*f.*)
cloudy nublado/a
clown payaso/a (*m./f.*)
clue pista (*f.*)
coffee café (*m.*)
coffee-colored marrón
coffee shop cafetería (*f.*)
coin moneda (*f.*)
cold resfriado (*m.*) (*illness*); frío (*m.*) (*temperature*); **to have a cold** tener un resfriado
colleague compañero/a (*m./f.*)
comb peine (*m.*)
comb (one's) hair peinar(se)
come venir
comet cometa (*m.*)
comfortable cómodo/a
commercial anuncio (*m.*); aviso (*m.*)
company compañía (*f.*); sociedad (*f.*); empresa de negocios (*f.*)
compete competir (e > i)
complain quejar(se) de
complaint queja (*f.*)
complete acabar; terminar
compose componer
concert concierto (*m.*)
confess confesar (e > ie)
conjugate conjugar
constitute constituir
construct construir
contain contener
contamination contaminación (*f.*)
contest concurso (*m.*)
continue continuar; seguir (e > ie)
contract contrato (*m.*)
convince convencer
cook cocinero/a (*m./f.*); cocinar
corner esquina (*f.*); rincón (*m.*)
cost costar (o > ue)
cotton algodón (*m.*)
count contar (o > ue)
counter mostrador (*m.*)
couple par (*m.*); **a couple of** un par de
coupon cupón (*m.*)
course curso (*m.*), clase (*f.*); **of course** por supuesto
courteous cortés
cover cubrir
cow vaca (*f.*)
crazy loco/a
credit card tarjeta de crédito (*f.*)
crime crimen (*m.*)
cross cruz (*f.*); **cross** (*the street*) cruzar; pasar
cry llorar
crystal cristal (*m.*)
cup taza (*f.*)
curtain cortina (*f.*)
custom costumbre (*f.*)

customer cliente (*m./f.*)
customs aduana (*f.*)
cut cortar

D

dance baile (*m.*); bailar
danger peligro (*m.*)
dangerous peligroso/a
dark oscuro/a
darkness oscuridad (*f.*)
date fecha (*f.*); cita (*f.*)
day día (*m.*)
daybreak al amanecer
dead muerto/a
dear querido/a
death muerte (*f.*)
deceive engañar
December diciembre (*m.*)
decide decidir
defend defender (e > ie)
delicious delicioso/a, sabroso/a, rico/a
deliver entregar
demand exigir
demonstrate demostrar (o > ue)
dentistry odontología (*f.*)
deny negar(se) (e > ie)
depend depender (de)
deposit depositar
depressed deprimido/a
describe describir
desert desierto (*m.*)
deserve merecer
desire deseo (*m.*)
desk escritorio (*m.*)
dessert postre (*m.*)
destroy destruir
diamond diamante (*m.*)
diary diario (*m.*)
die morir (o > ue)
diet dieta (*f.*); ponerse a dieta
different diferente; distinto/a
difficult difícil
difficulty dificultad (*f.*)
dine cenar
dining room comedor (*m.*)
dinner cena (*f.*); **to have dinner** cenar
dirty sucio/a
disappear desaparecer
disaster desastre (*m.*)
discover descubrir
discuss discutir
dish plato (*m.*)
dishwasher lavaplatos (*m.sing.*)
dissolve disolver (o > ue)
do hacer; **to have nothing to do with** no tener nada que ver con
document documento (*m.*)
dollar dólar (*m.*)
doubt duda (*f.*); dudar
down abajo
downtown centro (*m.*)
dozen docena (*f.*)

draw dibujar
dream sueño (*m.*); soñar (o > ue); **to dream of** soñar con
dress vestido (*m.*); vestir(se) (e > i)
drill taladro (*m.*); taladrar
drink bebida (*f.*); beber; tomar
drive conducir; manejar
drop gota (*f.*)
drugstore farmacia (*f.*)
drunk borracho/a
dry seco/a; secar(se)
dryer secadora (*f.*)
duck pato (*m.*)
during durante
dust polvo (*m.*); sacudir (*clean*)

E

each cada
early temprano
earn ganar
earring pendiente (*m.*), arete (*m.*)
earth tierra (*f.*)
earthquake terremoto (*m.*)
eat comer; **to eat lunch** almorzar (o > ue)
education educación (*f.*)
effort esfuerzo (*m.*)
egg huevo (*m.*)
either (neither) tampoco
either . . . or . . . o... o...
elect elegir (e > i)
election elección (*f.*)
elevator ascensor (*m.*)
embarrassed avergonzado/a
employee empleado/a (*m./f.*)
employer jefe/a (*m./f.*)
empty vacío/a; vaciar
end fin (*m.*); acabar; terminar
enemy enemigo/a (*m./f.*)
energy energía (*f.*)
engagement compromiso (*m.*)
England Inglaterra (*f.*)
English inglés (*m.*) (*language*)
enigma enigma (*m.*)
enjoy gozar de; disfrutar de
enough bastante; suficiente
enter entrar
enterprise empresa (*f.*)
entire entero/a
entrance entrada (*f.*)
envelope sobre (*m.*)
environment medio ambiente (*m.*)
equal igual
equipment equipaje (*m.*)
error error (*m.*)
establish establecer
evening noche (*f.*); **in the evening** por la noche
every cada
everybody, everyone todos; todo el mundo
everything todo (*m.*)

everywhere en (por) todas partes
exam examen (*m.*)
exciting emocionante
exercise hacer ejercicio
exhibit exposición (*f.*)
exit salida (*f.*)
expensive caro/a
explain explicar
express expresar(se)
extinguish extinguir
eye ojo (*m.*)
eyeglasses anteojos (*m.pl.*); lentes (*m.pl.*)

F

face cara (*f.*)
fact hecho (*m.*)
fair justo/a
fairy tale cuento de hadas (*m.*)
fall (*season*) otoño (*m.*)
fall (down) caer(se)
familiar familiar; **to be familiar with** conocer
fan aficionado/a (*m./f.*)
fantasy fantasía (*f.*)
far lejos
fast rápido/a
father padre (*m.*); papá (*m.*)
father-in-law suegro (*m.*)
favorite favorito/a
fear temor (*m.*); tener miedo de
February febrero (*m.*)
feel sentir(se) (e > ie); **to feel like** tener ganas de
fever fiebre (*f.*)
few pocos; **a few** unos cuantos
fiancé/fiancée prometido/a (*m./f.*); novio/a (*m./f.*)
fight lucha (*f.*); pelear; reñir
file archivo (*m.*)
fill (up, out) llenar
film película (*f.*)
finally al fin; por fin
finance finanzas (*f.pl.*)
financial financiero/a
find encontrar (o > ue); **to find out** averiguar
fine bien
fine (*traffic ticket*) multa (*f.*)
fingernail uña (*f.*)
finish terminar
fire fuego (*m.*); incendio (*m.*)
fire (*dismiss*) despedir (e > i)
fire hydrant hidrante de incendios (*m.*)
firefighter bombero/a (*m./f.*)
fireplace chimenea (*f.*)
first primero/a
fish pescado (*m.*) (*for eating*); pez (*m.*)
fit caber
fix arreglar

flag bandera (*f.*)
flan (*custard*) flan (*m.*)
flavor sabor (*m.*)
flee huir
float flotar
flood inundación (*f.*); inundar
floor suelo (*m.*); piso (*m.*) (*level*)
flower flor (*f.*)
fly mosca (*f.*); volar (o > ue)
fog niebla (*f.*)
foggy nublado/a
follow seguir (e > i)
following siguiente
food comida (*f.*)
fool tonto/a (*m./f.*); engañar
foot pie (*m.*); **on foot** a pie
football fútbol americano (*m.*)
for para; por
forecast pronóstico (*m.*)
foreign extranjero/a
forest bosque (*m.*); selva (*f.*)
forever para siempre
forget olvidar
fork tenedor (*m.*)
fortunately por suerte
free libre
freedom libertad (*f.*)
freeway autopista (*f.*)
freeze congelar
French francés (*m.*) (*language*)
frequently con frecuencia; frecuentemente
Friday viernes (*m.*)
friendly amistoso/a
friendship amistad (*f.*)
frighten asustar
frog rana (*f.*)
from de; **from time to time** de vez en cuando
fry freír (e > i)
fulfill realizar
full lleno/a
fun diversión (*f.*); **to have fun** divertirse (e > ie)
funny cómico/a; chistoso/a
furious furioso/a
furniture mueble (*m.*) (*one piece*); muebles (*m.pl.*)

G

gain weight engordar
game juego (*m.*); partido (*m.*)
garbage basura (*f.*)
garden jardín (*m.*)
garlic ajo (*m.*)
gasoline gasolina (*f.*)
generally por lo común, por lo general, generalmente
genuine auténtico/a
German alemán (*m.*) (*language*)
get obtener; conseguir (e > i)
ghost fantasma (*m.*)

giant gigante (*m.*)
gift regalo (*m.*)
giraffe jirafa (*f.*)
girl chica (*f.*); niña (*f.*)
girlfriend novia (*f.*)
give dar
glass vaso (*m.*); vidrio (*m.*)
glove guante (*m.*)
glue goma de pegar (*f.*); pegar
go ir; **to go away** ir(se); **to go to bed** acostarse (o > ue)
goal gol (*m.*); meta (*f.*)
goalkeeper portero/a (*m./f.*)
God; god Dios (*m.*); dios (*m.*)
God willing ojalá
gold oro (*m.*)
good bueno/a
gossip chisme (*m.*); chismorrear
governor gobernador(a) (*m./f.*)
grab agarrar; coger
grades notas (*f.pl.*)
grand gran; grande
granddaughter nieta (*f.*)
grandfather abuelo (*m.*)
grandmother abuela (*f.*)
grandson nieto (*m.*)
grape uva (*f.*)
grass hierba (*f.*)
great gran, grande; estupendo/a
Greek griego (*m.*) (*language*)
greet saludar
greeting saludo (*m.*)
grill parrilla (*f.*); asar a la parrilla
groom novio (*m.*)
grow crecer; cultivar (*plants*)
guest invitado/a (*m./f.*)
guide guía (*m./f.*); **travel guide** guía de turismo (*m./f.*)
guitar guitarra (*f.*)
guy chico (*m.*)
gym gimnasio (*m.*)

H

hair cabello (*m.*); pelo (*m.*)
haircut corte de pelo (*m.*)
hallway pasillo (*m.*)
hamburger hamburguesa (*f.*)
hammer martillo (*m.*); martillar
hammock hamaca (*f.*)
hand mano (*f.*); **to give a hand** dar una mano
handsome guapo/a
hang (up) colgar (o > ue)
hanger percha (*f.*); perchero (*m.*)
happen pasar; suceder
happiness felicidad (*f.*)
happy feliz
hard duro/a; difícil
hardly apenas
harvest cosecha (*f.*)
hat sombrero (*m.*)
hate odiar

have tener; **to have fun** divertirse; **to have something to do with** tener que ver con
head cabeza (*f.*)
health salud (*f.*)
healthy saludable; sano/a
hear oír
heart corazón (*m.*)
help ayuda (*f.*); ayudar
here aquí
hide esconder
highway autopista (*f.*); carretera (*f.*)
hold sostener
holiday fiesta (*f.*), día feriado (*m.*)
home hogar (*m.*)
honest honrado/a
honeymoon luna de miel (*f.*)
hope esperanza (*f.*); esperar
horse caballo (*m.*)
host anfitrión (*m.*)
hostess anfitriona (*f.*)
hotel hotel (*m.*)
how? ¿cómo?; **how much?** ¿cuánto?; **how!** ¡cuánto!
hug abrazo (*m.*); abrazar
human humano/a
humble humilde
humor humor (*m.*)
hunger (el) hambre (*f.*); **to be hungry** tener hambre
hunt cazar
hurricane huracán (*m.*)
hurry prisa (*f.*); **to be in a hurry** tener prisa
hurt doler (o > ue); hacer daño
husband esposo (*m.*)

I

ice hielo (*m.*)
ice cream helado (*m.*)
ice skating patinar
ice-skating rink pista de hielo (*f.*)
ill enfermo/a
illness enfermedad (*f.*)
imagine imaginar(se)
immediately en seguida, inmediatamente
impede impedir (e > i); dificultar
import importar
important importante; **to be important** importarle a alguien
inch pulgada (*f.*)
include incluir
increase aumentar
influence influencia (*f.*); influir (en)
information información (*f.*)
innocent inocente
insane loco/a
inside adentro; dentro (de)
insist (on) insistir (en)
instead of en vez de
interest interés (*m.*); interesar

interpreter intérprete (*m./f.*)
introduce presentar
introduction presentación (*f.*)
invest invertir (e > ie)
investigate investigar
invitation invitación (*f.*)
invite invitar
iron plancha (*f.*); planchar
item artículo (*m.*)
itinerary itinerario (*m.*)

J

jaguar jaguar (*m.*)
jail cárcel (*f.*)
jam mermelada (*f.*)
January enero (*m.*)
jealous celoso/a
jewel joya (*f.*)
jewelry joyas (*f.*); **jewelry store** joyería (*f.*)
job empleo (*m.*); trabajo (*m.*)
joke broma (*f.*); chiste (*m.*)
joy alegría (*f.*); felicidad (*f.*)
judge juez(a) (*m./f.*)
July julio (*m.*)
jump brincar; saltar
June junio (*m.*)
jungle selva (*f.*)
just justo/a; (*adv.*) sólo; solamente
justice justicia (*f.*)
justify justificar

K

keep guardar
key llave (*f.*)
king rey (*m.*)
kiss beso (*m.*)
kitchen cocina (*f.*)
knee rodilla (*f.*)
kneel arrodillarse, estar de rodillas
knife cuchillo (*m.*)
know saber; conocer; **to know about** saber de; **to know how** saber; **to let know** avisar

L

lack carecer; **to be lacking** hacer falta
ladder escalera (*f.*)
lake lago (*m.*)
lamp lámpara (*f.*)
land tierra (*f.*); aterrizar
language idioma (*m.*); lenguaje (*m.*)
large grande
last último/a; **last night** anoche; **to last** durar
late tarde
later más tarde; luego
laugh reír(se) (e > i)
law ley (*f.*)
lawn césped (*m.*)
lawyer abogado/a (*m./f.*)
lazy perezoso/a

leader líder (*m./f.*)
leaf hoja (*f.*)
learn aprender
leave salir; irse; **to leave behind** dejar
left izquierda (*f.*); **to the left** a la izquierda
leftovers sobras (*f.pl.*)
leg pierna (*f.*)
legend leyenda (*f.*)
lemonade limonada (*f.*)
lend prestar
less menos
lesson lección (*f.*)
let dejar; permitir
letter carta (*f.*); letra (*of alphabet*) (*f.*)
lettuce lechuga (*f.*)
liar mentiroso/a (*m./f.*)
liberty libertad (*f.*)
library biblioteca (*f.*)
lie mentira (*f.*); **to tell a lie** mentir (e > ie)
lie down acostarse (o > ue)
life vida (*f.*)
light luz (*f.*); encender (e > ie)
lightbulb bombilla (*f.*)
lightning relámpago (*m.*)
like gustarle a uno; **to feel like** tener ganas de
line cola (*f.*); línea (*f.*); **online** en línea
lion león (*m.*)
listen (to) escuchar
little pequeño/a; un poco
live vivir
lively animado/a
living room sala (*f.*); sala de estar (*f.*)
loan préstamo (*m.*); prestar; **home loan** hipoteca (*f.*)
lobster langosta (*f.*)
lock cerradura (*f.*); candado (*m.*); encerrar (e > ie)
long largo/a; **a long time** mucho tiempo; **how long?** ¿cuánto tiempo?
look (at) mirar; **to look for** buscar; **to look like someone** parecerse a alguien
lose perder (e > ie); **to lose weight** adelgazar; bajar de peso
lot mucho/a
lottery lotería (*f.*)
love amor (*m.*); amar, querer; **to be in love with** estar enamorado de; **to fall in love with** enamorarse de
lucky afortunado/a; **to be lucky** tener suerte
luggage equipaje (*m.*)
lunch almuerzo (*m.*); almorzar (o > ue)

M

mad (*angry*) enojado/a
magazine revista (*f.*)
magician mago/a (*m./f.*)

mail correo (*m.*); echar al correo
mailbox buzón (*m.*)
maintain mantener
make hacer; **to make a decision** tomar una decisión
male varón (*m.*)
mall centro comercial (*m.*)
man hombre (*m.*)
manager gerente (*m./f.*)
manners los modales (*m.pl.*)
many muchos/as
marathon maratón (*m.*)
March marzo (*m.*)
married casado/a
marry casarse (con); **to get married** casarse (con)
mask máscara (*f.*)
matter asunto (*m.*); **to matter** importar
mattress colchón (*m.*)
May mayo (*m.*)
mayor alcalde (*m.*)
meal comida (*f.*)
meanwhile mientras tanto
measure medida (*f.*); medir (e > i)
meat carne (*f.*)
mechanic mecánico/a (*m./f.*)
medicine medicina (*f.*)
meet conocer; **to meet with** encontrarse con (o > ue)
meeting reunión (*f.*)
merit merecer
message mensaje (*m.*)
messy desordenado/a
meter metro (*m.*)
midday mediodía (*m.*)
middle medio (*m.*); **in the middle** en medio de
midnight medianoche (*f.*)
mile milla (*f.*)
milk leche (*f.*)
minute minuto (*m.*)
mirror espejo (*m.*)
miss echar de menos
mistake error (*m.*); **to make a mistake** equivocarse
model modelo (*m./f.*)
Monday lunes (*m.*)
money dinero (*m.*)
monkey mono (*m.*)
monster monstruo (*m.*)
month mes (*m.*)
moon luna (*f.*)
more más
morning mañana (*f.*)
mortgage hipoteca (*f.*)
mosquito mosquito (*m.*)
mother mamá (*f.*); madre (*f.*)
mother-in-law suegra (*f.*)
mouth boca (*f.*)
move mover(se) (o > ue); **to change residence** mudarse

movie película (*f.*)

movies cine (*m.sing.*)

much mucho/a; **too much** demasiado

multiply multiplicar

museum museo (*m.*)

music música (*f.*)

must deber de; tener que; **one must** hay que

mystery misterio (*m.*)

N

name nombre (*m.*); llamar(se)

nap siesta (*f.*)

napkin servilleta (*f.*)

nature naturaleza (*f.*)

near cerca

neat ordenado/a

necklace collar (*m.*)

need necesidad (*f.*); necesitar

neighbor vecino/a (*m./f.*)

neighborhood barrio (*m.*); vecindario (*m.*)

neither tampoco

nephew sobrino (*m.*)

nervous nervioso/a

never nunca; jamás; **never ever** nunca más

new nuevo/a

news noticias (*f.pl.*)

newspaper diario (*m.*); periódico (*m.*)

next al lado de; próximo/a; siguiente

nice amable; simpático/a

niece sobrina (*f.*)

night noche (*f.*); **at night** por la noche

nightmare pesadilla (*f.*)

nobody; no one nadie

noise ruido (*m.*)

none ningún; ninguno/a

noon mediodía (*m.*)

nose nariz (*f.*)

not any; not a single one ningún; ninguno/a

not anything nada

not ever jamás

note nota (*f.*)

nothing nada

novel novela (*f.*)

November noviembre (*m.*)

now ahora

nowhere en ninguna parte

number número (*m.*)

numerous muchos/as; numerosos/as

O

obey obedecer

occur ocurrir; pasar

October octubre (*m.*)

odd extraño/a; raro/a

of de; **of course** por supuesto

offer oferta (*f.*); ofrecer

often a menudo; frecuentemente; muchas veces

oil aceite (*m.*); **suntan oil** bronceador (*m.*)

old viejo/a

older mayor

olive oliva (*f.*); aceituna (*f.*)

Olympic Games olimpiadas (*f.*)

once una vez; **once in a while** de vez en cuando

onion cebolla (*f.*)

only sólo, solamente; único/a

open abrir

orange naranja (*f.*)

organize organizar

otherwise de lo contrario; de otro modo

outside fuera

oven horno (*m.*)

owe deber

own tener

owner dueño/a (*m./f.*)

P

pack empacar

package paquete (*m.*)

page página (*f.*)

pain dolor (*m.*)

painful doloroso/a; **to be painful** doler (o > ue)

paint pintura (*f.*); pintar

painter pintor(a) (*m./f.*)

painting cuadro (*m.*)

pajamas pijama (*m.*); payama (*f.*)

palace palacio (*m.*)

pale pálido/a

pants pantalones (*m.pl.*)

paper papel (*m.*); informe (*m.*)

parade desfile (*m.*)

park parque (*m.*); aparcar; estacionar

parking space aparcamiento (*m.*)

partner socio/a (*m./f.*)

party fiesta (*f.*)

passenger pasajero/a (*m./f.*)

passport pasaporte (*m.*)

password contraseña (*f.*)

pay pagar

peace paz (*f.*)

pearl perla (*f.*)

pen bolígrafo (*m.*); pluma (*f.*)

people gente (*f.*); personas (*f.pl.*)

perhaps quizás

permit permitir; dejar

pet animal doméstico (*m.*)

pharmacy farmacia (*f.*)

phone call llamada telefónica (*f.*)

photo foto (*f.*); fotografía (*f.*)

pick escoger; **to pick up** recoger

picture pintura (*f.*); cuadro (*m.*)

piece pedazo (*m.*)

pillow almohada (*f.*)

pitcher (*baseball*) lanzador(a) (*m./f.*)

pity lástima (*f.*)

place lugar (*m.*); poner

planet planeta (*m.*)

play drama (*m.*); jugar (u > ue); **to play an instrument** tocar un instrumento; **to play a game** jugar un juego; **to play a joke** gastar una broma

please por favor; agradar

pleasant agradable

pleasing agradable

pocket bolsillo (*m.*)

point punto (*m.*); **point of view** punto de vista

police force policía (*f.*); cuerpo de policía (*m.*)

policeman policía (*m.*)

policewoman policía (*f.*)

polite cortés; educado/a

politician político/a (*m./f.*)

politics política (*f. sing.*)

pollution contaminación (*f.*)

pool piscina (*f.*); alberca (*f.*)

population población (*f.*)

possess poseer; tener

poster cartel (*m.*); poster (*m.*)

potato patata (*f.*); papa (*f.*)

pound libra (*f.*)

pray rezar; rogar (o > ue)

prefer preferir (e > ie)

prepare preparar

prescription receta médica (*f.*)

present regalo (*m.*); presentar

pretend fingir

price precio (*m.*)

prince príncipe (*m.*)

princess princesa (*f.*)

principal (*school*) director(a) (*m./f.*)

prison prisión (*f.*); cárcel (*f.*)

prize premio (*m.*)

problem problema (*m.*)

produce producir

profession profesión (*f.*); carrera (*f.*)

professional profesional (*m./f.*)

program programa (*m.*)

progress progreso (*m.*)

prohibited prohibido/a

promise promesa (*f.*); prometer

pronunciation pronunciación (*f.*)

propose proponer

protect proteger

proud orgulloso/a

prove probar (o > ue)

provided that con tal que

public público (*m.*); audiencia (*f.*)

publicity publicidad (*f.*)

publish publicar

purchase compra (*f.*); comprar

pure puro/a

purse bolsa (*f.*)

pursue perseguir (e > i)

put poner; **to put on oneself** ponerse; **to put into** meter en

puzzle enigma (*m.*); rompecabezas (*m.sing.*); **crossword puzzle** crucigrama (*m.*)

pyramid pirámide (*f.*)

Q

quality calidad (*f.*)

quarrel pelea (*f.*), riña (*f.*); reñir, pelear

queen reina (*f.*)

question pregunta (*f.*); (*issue*) cuestión (*f.*)

quick rápido/a

quickly rápidamente

quiet tranquilo/a; callar(se)

quit renunciar a

quite bastante

quiz prueba (*f.*)

R

racket (*tennis*) raqueta (*f.*)

radio radio (*m./f.*); **radio station** emisora (*f.*)

railroad ferrocarril (*m.*); tren (*m.*)

rain lluvia (*f.*)

raincoat impermeable (*m.*)

rain forest selva tropical (*f.*)

rainy lluvioso/a

raise aumento (*m.*); (*a child*) criar; levantar

rate velocidad (*f.*); **exchange rate** cambio (*m.*)

razor navaja de afeitar (*f.*)

reach llegar a; alcanzar (*un objetivo*)

read leer

ready listo/a

real verdadero/a

realize darse cuenta de

really de veras

receive recibir

reception recepción (*f.*)

recipe receta (*f.*)

recognize reconocer

recommend recomendar (e > i)

record grabar

recorder grabadora (*f.*)

recycle reciclar

redo rehacer

reduce reducir

refrigerator refrigerador (*m.*)

regret sentir (e > i)

rehearsal ensayo (*m.*)

rehearse ensayar

reject rechazar

relax relajarse

remain quedarse

remake rehacer

remember acordarse (o > ue) de; recordar

remove quitar(se)

rent alquiler (*m.*); alquilar

repair arreglo (*m.*), reparación (*f.*); arreglar, reparar

repeat repetir (e > i)

report informe (*m.*); reportaje (*m.*)

request pedir (e > i)

resolve resolver (o > ue)

resource recurso (*m.*)

respect respetar

rest descansar

restaurant restaurante (*m.*)

retire jubilar(se)

return regresar; (*something*) devolver (o > ue)

rice arroz (*m.*)

rich rico/a

riddle enigma (*m.*)

ride (*horseback*) montar; **to ride a bike** montar en bicicleta

ridiculous ridículo/a; tonto/a

right derecha (*f.*); (*privilege*) derecho (*m.*); **to the right** a la derecha; **to be right** tener razón

right now ahora mismo

ring anillo (*m.*); sortija (*f.*); sonar (o > ue)

ripe maduro/a

river río (*m.*)

road camino (*m.*)

rob robar

robotics robótica (*f.*)

rocket cohete (*m.*)

role papel (*m.*); **to play the role of** hacer el papel de

room cuarto (*m.*); habitación (*f.*)

roommate compañero/a (*m./f.*)

routine rutina (*f.*)

ruby rubí (*m.*)

rug alfombra (*f.*)

rule regla (*f.*)

ruler regla (*f.*)

run correr; (*machine*) funcionar

run away huir

Russian ruso (*m.*) (*language*)

S

sad triste

sadness tristeza (*f.*)

safe seguro/a

salad ensalada (*f.*)

salary sueldo (*m.*)

sale venta (*f.*); **special sale** rebaja (*f.*)

salesperson vendedor(a) (*m./f.*)

salt sal (*f.*)

same mismo/a; **the same** lo mismo; igual

sand arena (*f.*)

Saturday sábado (*m.*)

save ahorrar; **to save a life** salvar una vida

say decir (e > i); **to say good-bye** despedirse (e > i)

scare asustar; **to get scared** asustarse

scene escena (*f.*)

schedule horario (*m.*)

school escuela (*f.*); **high school** secundaria (*f.*)

science ciencia (*f.*)

scissors tijeras (*f.pl.*)

scratch arañar

scream gritar

screen pantalla (*f.*)

scrub fregar (e > ie)

search busca (*f.*); búsqueda (*f.*); buscar

season estación (*f.*)

seat asiento (*m.*); sentar(se) (e > ie)

seated sentado/a

secret secreto (*m.*)

see ver

seem parecer

seldom rara vez

select escoger

selfish egoísta

sell vender

send mandar; enviar

sentence frase (*f.*); oración (*f.*)

separately por separado

September septiembre (*m.*)

serious grave

serve servir (e > i)

server camarero/a (*m./f.*); mesero/a (*m./f.*)

set juego (*m.*)

several varios/as

shade sombra (*f.*)

shadow sombra (*f.*)

shame lástima (*f.*); pena (*f.*)

shape forma (*f.*); **in good shape** en buena forma

shave afeitar(se)

shelf estante (*m.*)

shine brillar

ship barco (*m.*)

shoe zapato (*m.*)

shop ir de compras

shopping mall/center centro comercial (*m.*)

short corto/a

shoulder hombro (*m.*)

shovel pala (*f.*)

show mostrar (o > ue)

shower aguacero (*rain*) (*m.*); ducha (*f.*); ducharse

shut cerrar (e > ie)

shy tímido/a

sick enfermo/a; **to get sick** enfermarse

sign anuncio (*m.*); letrero (*m.*); firmar

signature firma (*f.*)

silly ridículo/a, tonto/a

silver plata (*f.*)

sing cantar

sister hermana (*f.*)
sit down sentarse (e > ie)
size talla (*f.*); tamaño (*m.*)
skate patín (*m.*); patinar
ski esquiar
sky cielo (*m.*)
sleep dormir (o > ue)
sleepy soñoliento/a; **to be sleepy** tener sueño
sleeve manga (*f.*)
slim delgado/a
slipper zapatilla (*f.*)
slow lento/a
small pequeño/a
smart listo/a
smell oler (o > ue)
smile sonrisa (*f.*); sonreír (e > i)
smoke humo (*m.*); fumar
snake culebra (*f.*); serpiente (*f.*)
sneeze estornudar
snow nieve (*f.*); nevar
snowfall nevada (*f.*)
snowstorm nevada (*f.*)
Snow White Blanca Nieves
so tan
so many tantos/as
so much tanto/a
so that para que
soap jabón (*m.*)
soccer fútbol (*m.*)
society sociedad (*f.*)
socks calcetines (*m.pl.*)
sofa sofá (*m.*)
soldier soldado (*m./f.*)
some algunos/as
somebody; someone alguien
something algo
sometimes a veces
song canción (*f.*)
soon pronto
sorry (I'm) lo siento
sound sonar (o > ue)
soup sopa (*f.*)
south sur (*m.*)
souvenir recuerdo (*m.*)
space espacio (*m.*)
speak hablar
spend gastar
spoon cuchara (*f.*)
spring primavera (*f.*)
spy espía (*m./f.*)
stage escenario (*m.*)
stain mancha (*f.*)
stairway escalera (*f.*)
stamp sello (*m.*); estampilla (*f.*)
stand up levantar(se)
star estrella (*f.*); **movie star** estrella de cine (*f.*)
start empezar (e > ie)
state estado (*m.*)
stay quedarse
steal robar

still todavía
stomach estómago (*m.*)
stop parada (*f.*); dejar de; impedir (e > i)
store tienda (*f.*)
storm tormenta (*f.*)
story cuento (*m.*)
stove cocina (*f.*)
strange extraño/a, raro/a
strawberry fresa (*f.*)
street calle (*f.*)
strict estricto/a
strike huelga (*f.*)
strong fuerte
student estudiante (*m./f.*)
studies estudios (*m.pl.*)
study estudiar
stumble tropezar (e > ie)
subtract restar
suburbs afueras (*f.pl.*)
subway metro (*m.*)
success éxito (*m.*)
successful exitoso/a; **to be successful** tener éxito
such tal; **such a thing** tal cosa
suddenly de repente
suffer sufrir
suffering sufrimiento (*m.*)
sugar azúcar (*m./f.*)
suggest sugerir (e > ie)
suit traje (*m.*); **bathing suit** traje de baño (*m.*)
suitcase maleta (*f.*)
summer verano (*m.*)
sun sol (*m.*)
Sunday domingo (*m.*)
sunglasses gafas de sol (*f.pl.*)
superstitious supersticioso/a
support mantener
suppose suponer
sweater suéter (*m.*)
sweep barrer
sweet dulce
swim nadar
swimming pool piscina (*f.*)
swing columpio (*m.*); columpiarse

T

table mesa (*f.*)
tablecloth mantel (*m.*)
take tomar; **to take off** despegar; **to take off clothing** quitar(se) ropa
tale cuento (*m.*)
talk hablar
tape cinta (*f.*)
task tarea (*f.*)
taste gusto (*m.*); probar (o > ue)
tax impuesto (*m.*)
tea té (*m.*)
teach enseñar
teacher maestro/a (*m./f.*)
tear lágrima (*f.*)

teenager adolescente (*m./f.*)
telephone teléfono (*m.*); **on the telephone** por teléfono
television televisión (*f.*); televisor (*m.*)
tell decir (e > i)
tennis tenis (*m.*)
test examen (*m.*); probar (o > ue)
text message mensaje de texto (*m.*)
theater teatro (*m.*)
theme tema (*m.*)
then entonces
theory teoría (*f.*)
therefore por lo tanto
thief ladrón (ladrona) (*m./f.*)
thin delgado/a; flaco/a
thing cosa (*f.*)
think pensar (e > ie); **to think of** pensar en
thirst sed (*f.*); **to be thirsty** tener sed
thousand mil (*m.*)
through por; a través de
throw lanzar; tirar
thunder trueno (*m.*)
Thursday jueves (*m.*)
ticket boleto (*m.*); **round-trip ticket** billete de ida y vuelta; multa (*f.*)
time tiempo (*m.*); vez (*f.*); **on time** a tiempo; **from time to time** de vez en cuando
tip propina (*f.*)
tired cansado/a; **to be tired** estar cansado/a
toast tostada (*f.*); tostar (o > ue)
together juntos/as
tolerate tolerar
tomato tomate (*m.*)
tomorrow mañana
ton tonelada (*f.*)
tonight esta noche
too también
tooth diente (*m.*); muela (*f.*); **wisdom tooth** muela del juicio (*m.*)
toothpaste pasta de dientes (*f.*)
top (of) encima de
touch tocar
tour excursión (*f.*)
towel toalla (*f.*)
town pueblo (*m.*); población (*f.*)
toy juguete (*m.*)
traffic tráfico (*m.*); **traffic light** semáforo (*m.*)
tragic trágico/a
train tren (*m.*); entrenar(se)
translate traducir
trash basura (*f.*)
travel viajar
travel agent agente de viajes (*m./f.*)
tray bandeja (*f.*)
treasure tesoro (*m.*)
tree árbol (*m.*)
trial juicio (*m.*); proceso (*m.*)
trip viaje (*m.*); **day trip** excursión (*f.*)

truck camión (*m.*)
true cierto/a; verdadero/a
trunk baúl (*m.*); maletero (*m.*)
truth verdad (*f.*)
try intentar; tratar de; **to try on clothing** probar(se) (o > ue)
T-shirt camiseta (*f.*)
Tuesday martes (*m.*)
tunnel túnel (*m.*)
turkey pavo (*m.*)
turn doblar; **to turn off** apagar; girar
turnpike autopista de peaje (*f.*)

U

UFO OVNI (*m.*)
umbrella paraguas (*m.sing.*)
uncle tío (*m.*)
uncomfortable incómodo/a
under debajo de
underline subrayar
understand comprender; entender (e > ie)
undo deshacer
undress desvestir(se) (e > i)
unfortunately por desgracia, desgraciadamente
unite unir
United States Estados Unidos (*m.pl.*)
university universidad (*f.*)
unless a menos que
unpleasant antipático/a
until hasta
up arriba
use usar
usually por lo general; generalmente

V

vacation vacaciones (*f.pl.*)
variety variedad (*f.*)
vase florero (*m.*); jarrón (*m.*)
vegetable vegetal (*m.*)
vehicle vehículo (*m.*)
videotape grabar, filmar
view vista (*f.*)
visit visita (*f.*)
vitamin vitamina (*f.*)
voice voz (*f.*)

volleyball voleibol (*m.*)
vote votar

W

wait esperar
waiter camarero (*m.*); mesero (*m.*)
waitress camarera (*f.*); mesera (*f.*)
wake despertar(se) (e > ie)
wake up despertarse (e > ie)
walk andar; caminar; **to walk away** alejarse
wall pared (*f.*)
wallet billetera (*f.*)
want querer (e > ie)
war guerra (*f.*)
warm cálido/a, tibio/a; **to be warm** tener calor; **warm-up exercise** ejercicio de calentamiento (*m.*)
warn advertir (e > ie)
wash lavar(se); **to wash dishes** fregar (e > ie)
waste malgastar; **to waste time** perder (e > ie) el tiempo
watch (*time*) reloj (*m.*)
watch mirar
water (el) agua (*f.*); regar (e > ie)
wealth riqueza (*f.*)
wealthy rico/a
wear llevar; usar
Web web (*f.*); red informática (*f.*)
wedding boda (*f.*)
Wednesday miércoles (*m.*)
week semana (*f.*)
weekend fin de semana (*m.*)
weigh pesar
weight peso (*m.*)
welcome bienvenido/a; **you're welcome** de nada
well bien
well-being bienestar (*m.*)
wet mojado/a; **to get wet** mojarse
whale ballena (*f.*); **whale watching** observar las ballenas
what? ¿qué?, ¿cómo?
whatever cuanto/a
whenever cuando quiera
where donde; **where?** ¿dónde?
wherever dondequiera

while mientras; rato (*m.*)
who quien; **who?** ¿quién?
whoever quienquiera
wide ancho/a
wife esposa (*f.*)
win ganar
wind viento (*m.*)
window ventana (*f.*); **car window** ventanilla (*f.*)
wine vino (*m.*); **red wine** vino tinto
winner ganador(a) (*m./f.*)
winter invierno (*m.*)
wise sabio/a
wish deseo (*m.*); desear; querer (e > ie)
witch bruja (*f.*)
with con; **with me** conmigo; **with you** contigo
within dentro de
without sin
woman mujer (*f.*)
wonderful maravilloso/a
wood madera (*f.*)
woods bosque (*m.*)
word palabra (*f.*)
work trabajo (*m.*); empleo (*m.*); trabajar; (*machine*) funcionar
world mundo (*m.*)
World Series Serie Mundial (*f.*)
worry preocupación (*f.*); preocuparse
worse peor
worth valor (*m.*); **to be worth** valer
wounded herido/a
wrap envolver (o > ue)
wrinkle arruga (*f.*)
wrist muñeca (*f.*)
write escribir
written escrito/a
wrong equivocado/a; **to be wrong** no tener razón

Y

year año (*m.*)
yellow amarillo/a
yesterday ayer
yet todavía
young joven
younger menor

Answer key

1 The present tense of regular verbs, irregular verbs, and verbs with spelling changes

1·1
1. vive
2. trabaja
3. estudia
4. planean
5. sube
6. saca
7. conversas
8. necesita

1·2
1. Yo preparo la cena.
2. Los niños suben la escalera.
3. Mis gatos beben leche.
4. El cliente suma la cuenta.
5. La mamá de Carli habla al reportero / a la reportera.
6. La actriz teme a los críticos.
7. Tus amigos comen fajitas.

1·4
1. Hoy Martha y Linus celebran su aniversario.
2. Sus parientes llegan a tiempo.
3. Varios amigos conversan en la sala.
4. En el patio, los chicos escuchan música latina.
5. El olor a enchiladas circula por toda la casa.
6. Los niños beben limonada.

1·6
1. V
2. V
3. F
4. F
5. V

1·7
1. Hace... que estudio español.
2. Uso la computadora desde hace...
3. Hace... años que los Estados Unidos son una nación independiente.
4. Usamos la Internet desde hace... años.
5. Escucho música clásica desde hace... / No escucho música clásica.

1·9
1. V
2. F
3. F
4. F
5. V

1·10
1. doy
2. ponen
3. ven
4. cabemos
5. traigo
6. caigo
7. haces
8. salgo

1·11
1. Compongo canciones para mis amigos.
2. Propongo un brindis.
3. Reponen el dinero en mi cuenta.
4. Ud. distrae al público.
5. Las niñas deshacen el rompecabezas.

1·12
1. b
2. a
3. h
4. c
5. f
6. g
7. e
8. d

1·13
1. conduzco
2. salen
3. conozco
4. ofrece
5. merezco
6. obedecen
7. perteneces
8. conoce

1·14
1. Merezco un aumento de sueldo.
2. ¿Salgo ahora?
3. Agradezco tu amistad.
4. No pertenezco a este grupo.
5. Traduzco las instrucciones.
6. ¡Rara vez impongo mis ideas!
7. Permanezco callado(a).

1·15
1. Hay una persona.
2. Hay diez programas.
3. Voy ahora.
4. No oigo música.
5. ¿Ve Ud. el autobús?
6. Digo la verdad.
7. Tienen tiempo.
8. Detienen el coche.

1·16
1. está
2. hay
3. llegan
4. es; digo
5. vienen
6. tiene
7. oyes
8. van

1·17
1. exijo
2. escojo
3. extingo
4. recojo
5. venzo
6. protejo
7. convenzo
8. finjo

1·18
1. No hay neblina esta mañana.
2. El reloj da las diez y media.
3. Hace sol ahora. / Hay sol ahora.
4. El público da gritos en el estadio.
5. El capitán le da un abrazo al portero.

1·21
1. ¿Tienes hambre?
2. Tenemos sed.
3. Lori hace una visita a su primo.
4. Mario le da un abrazo a su amigo.
5. Tienen prisa.
6. Tienes razón esta vez.
7. No tengo miedo.
8. ¿Tiene Ud. frío?

1·22
1. e
2. b
3. h
4. a
5. d
6. f
7. c
8. g

1·23 Detesto los lunes. Empezamos otra semana con la misma rutina. Hablo con mis vecinos acerca del fin de semana, nuestra familia y nuestras costumbres en casa. A veces mi esposo me ayuda con los quehaceres de la casa. Pasa la aspiradora y barra la terraza. Juan, el esposo de Lidia, lava la ropa. ¡Tienen una lavadora y una secadora nueva! Y a Juan le gusta planchar las camisas. El esposo de Marta, Mauricio, prepara la cena casi todas las noches. Tiene una parrilla nueva en el patio, un regalo de Marta para su cumpleaños. ¡Ahora, Marta no cocina! Mi otra vecina, Susana, vive con su suegra y ella ayuda también. Necesito más ayuda de mi esposo, mi madre o los aparatos electrodomésticos. ¡Trabajo demasiado!

2 The present tense of verbs with stem changes

2·1
1. prefiero
2. recomienda
3. enciende
4. entienden
5. gobierna
6. piensa
7. cierra

2·2
1. gobierna
2. defiende
3. comienza
4. hiela
5. entiende
6. nos sentamos

2·3

1. podemos
2. cuesta
3. encuentra
4. suelo
5. almuerzo
6. juego
7. llueve
8. recordamos

2·4

1. Truena.
2. Recuerdo.
3. Cuesta diez dólares.
4. Ella envuelve el regalo.
5. Silvia cuenta los billetes.
6. Jugamos ahora.
7. Muestras las fotos.
8. Huelen las flores.

2·5

1. prefiere
2. miente
3. presienten
4. advierten
5. mientes
6. siento
7. convierten
8. refiere

2·6

1. El agua hierve.
2. Martha no miente.
3. Se siente bien.
4. Se divierten.
5. Usted miente.
6. Preferimos jugar ajedrez.

2·7

1. ¿Sonríes cuando ves a tus colegas?
2. ¿Sigues las reglas en el trabajo?
3. ¿Mides tus palabras cuando hablas con tu supervisor(-a)?
4. ¿Te ríes / Te burlas de tus amigos?
5. ¿Te vistes de manera apropiada?
6. ¿Te despides cuando sales al final del día?

2·8

1. c
2. b
3. d
4. a
5. f
6. e

2·9

1. F
2. V
3. V
4. V
5. F
6. F

2·11

1. V
2. F
3. V
4. V
5. V
6. V

2·12

1. entiende
2. quieres
3. nos resfriamos
4. continúa
5. Enviamos
6. concluye

2·13 Tengo una manía: leo y escribo novelas de detectives. Cuando sueño, puedo escribir más novelas. Los miércoles tengo una sesión con mi nueva siquiatra, la Dra. Salazar. Ella sugiere la terapia de hipnosis para mi bienestar. Yo prefiero no hablar acerca del tratamiento. Confieso que es difícil escribir novelas. Yo le muestro un capítulo de mi novela. Ella escucha. Yo sugiero leer el texto en voz alta. La Dra. Salazar no responde. Me siento nervioso. Me muerdo las uñas mientras describo a mi héroe. Quiero defender las ideas en mi novela. La Dra. Salazar no responde. Yo sigo leyendo mi novela. El detective, mi héroe, mide seis pies. En este capítulo él sigue a la esposa de su cliente, una mujer bella, pero ella desaparece. ¡De repente, suena el teléfono y la Dra. Salazar se despierta! Me despido. Fuera de la oficina me río. El poder de mis palabras puede hipnotizar a mi público. ¡La Dra. Salazar duerme mientras yo hablo!

3 Ser and estar

3·1

1. F
2. F
3. V
4. V
5. F
6. V

3·2

1. Este es Manuel Ortiz.
2. Es de Puerto Rico.
3. Esta es su asistente, Leticia.
4. Ella es ecuatoriana.
5. Ellos son nuestros amigos.
6. Manuel es un atleta excelente.

3·3	1. e	4. b
	2. a	5. c
	3. f	6. d

3·4	1. Son, está	4. es
	2. está	5. son
	3. está	6. es

3·5	1. telling time; present progressive form	4. characteristic
	2. temporary condition	5. time an event takes place
	3. temporary physical condition	6. occupation

3·6	1. está	4. Están
	2. está	5. están
	3. estar	6. Es

3·7	1. Estoy deprimido(a) pero no estoy loco(a).	5. Bueno, tengo hambre y estoy cansado(a).
	2. Estos no son mis zapatos.	6. ¿Estamos listos para salir?
	3. ¿Por qué están Uds. aquí?	7. El partido es en el estadio de la universidad.
	4. ¡Uds. no están seguros!	

3·8	1. c	4. d
	2. b	5. a
	3. f	6. e

3·9	1. Estamos a 25 de abril.	4. ¿Estás de acuerdo conmigo?
	2. Está a punto de terminar.	5. Están de vacaciones.
	3. Estamos por la paz.	6. El jefe está de vuelta.

3·10 Arturo Pérez, su esposa y sus hijos son de Texas. Los antepasados de Arturo son de las Islas Canarias, España. Él tiene cincuenta y cinco años, es bilingüe y es abogado. Es agradable, tenaz y muy honesto. Ahora está a punto de empezar una campaña para ser juez. Él piensa que es el candidato ideal para este cargo. Melina, su esposa, está de acuerdo con él y está lista para ayudar a Arturo en su campaña. Ella es muy compasiva y está orgullosa del éxito profesional de su esposo. La familia de Arturo espera celebrar su victoria. Ángel, el nieto de Arturo, cree que su abuelo puede ser la estrella de un nuevo programa de TV en un canal hispano en San Antonio: "El juez Arturo". Ángel dice que el español está de moda.

4 The preterit tense

4·1	1. robaron	5. sospechamos
	2. perdió	6. Escuchaste
	3. corrí	7. salió
	4. dispararon	8. Compraron

4·2	1. Anteanoche Ana regresó a casa.	5. El detective Rojas y su asistente resolvieron el caso la semana pasada.
	2. Esta mañana, Pilar envió tres mensajes electrónicos al banco.	6. Esta mañana a las ocho, el doctor visitó a su nuevo paciente.
	3. Roberto viajó a San Antonio el mes pasado.	
	4. Hace diez años me mudé a este edificio.	

4·4	1. 2	4. 1
	2. 4	5. 3
	3. 5	

4·5	1. compramos un televisor para ver películas.	4. llegamos a las tres y charlamos con mi tía.
	2. comimos comida mexicana, tomamos un refresco y lavamos los platos.	5. nos dimos cuenta de que el perro de Matilde es feísimo.
	3. visitamos a mi tía Matilde.	

4·7
1. Busqué
2. Llegué
3. lancé
4. Jugué
5. almorcé
6. saqué
7. Organicé
8. Toqué
9. Gocé

4·8
1. Pagué
2. Empecé
3. Busqué
4. Toqué
5. Jugué
6. Coloqué
7. Almorcé
8. Practiqué
9. Expliqué
10. Abracé

4·9
1. Alfonso leyó una novela gótica de Ruiz Zafón.
2. Su hermano se cayó de la silla.
3. ¡Oímos sus gritos!
4. Sus perros ladraron y contribuyeron al ruido.
5. El gato huyó de la casa.
6. Alfonso construyó esa casa hace muchos años.
7. Yo intuí que esta familia está loca.

4·10
1. leyó
2. incluyó
3. intuyó
4. distribuyeron
5. contribuyó
6. concluyeron

4·11
1. consiguieron
2. prefirió
3. durmieron
4. sonrió
5. pidieron
6. sirvió
7. se rió
8. se vistió
9. pidieron
10. se divirtieron, disfrutaron

4·12
1. En el gimnasio, Marisa consiguió terminar sus ejercicios temprano.
2. Se vistió y llegó al cine a las seis de la tarde.
3. Compró su entrada y pidió un refresco.
4. Una chica joven le sirvió la bebida y sonrió.
5. En el teatro, Marisa se sentó y miró los comerciales.
6. ¡Cuántos comerciales! ¡Pagó para ver una película, no anuncios comerciales aburridos!
7. Marisa durmió por una hora.
8. Se despertó veinte minutos antes del final de la película.

4·13
1. Alberto no pudo.
2. Anoche Rita puso las llaves sobre la mesa.
3. La maleta no cupo en el maletero.
4. Ayer hubo una reunión.
5. Estuvieron aquí.
6. Puse el tenedor en la gaveta.
7. Tuvimos que ir a la tienda.
8. ¿Estuvieron Uds. en la fiesta?
9. Mis amigos tuvieron un accidente.

4·14
1. No dije una mentira.
2. Trajo un pastel.
3. Tradujeron los ejercicios.
4. Hicimos el trabajo.
5. Tú viniste tarde.
6. Tim hizo la tarea.
7. ¿Vinieron ellos?

4·15
1. hizo
2. trajo
3. dio
4. fuimos
5. puse
6. vino
7. produjeron
8. propusimos
9. pude
10. supuso

4·16
1. Ayer conocí a Lily, la nueva secretaria.
2. Supe que habla tres idiomas.
3. Pero ella no pudo terminar su primera tarea a tiempo.
4. Ella no quiso trabajar después de las cinco.
5. Lily tradujo tres documentos.
6. Hizo un trabajo estupendo.
7. Yo leí los documentos.
8. Supimos la noticia al día siguiente.
9. Lily se fue antes de las cinco y no regresó al día siguiente.
10. No quise creerlo. ¡Necesitamos una nueva secretaria!

4·17
1. F
2. F
3. V
4. F
5. V
6. V
7. F
8. F

4·18   Una librería no es solamente un lugar para comprar libros impresos. Ayer pasé horas en mi librería favorita. Me senté en el piso y leí un par de revistas. Con la copia de una novela nueva, me mudé a una silla muy cómoda cerca del café. Decidí tomar una taza de té verde. Entonces escuché mis canciones favoritas en mi computadora portátil. Después fui a la sección de libros en español y supe que *Matemáticas, ¿dónde estás?* ¡es un libro de verdad! Nunca entendí las matemáticas pero elegí la edición de bolsillo. Fui a la caja registradora y no quise comprarlo en la tienda. Encontré una promoción en línea con un quince por ciento de descuento y con envío gratis. Por supuesto, ¡tuve que hacer cuentas para saber el precio verdadero!

5   The imperfect tense

5·1
1. caminaba
2. se ponía
3. nadaba, dormía
4. jugábamos
5. corría
6. volvía
7. comía
8. Quería
9. prefería
10. soñábamos

5·2
1. Jugaba
2. Aprendía
3. Arreglaba
4. Tocaba
5. Recibía
6. Leía
7. Vivía
8. Miraba
9. Tenía
10. Cantaba

5·3
1. íbamos
2. eran
3. eran
4. éramos
5. veían
6. era
7. veían
8. iban

5·4
1. salía
2. montaban
3. bailábamos
4. tenían
5. sabían
6. conocíamos
7. tocaban
8. podía
9. quería

5·5
1. Ana compraba chocolates.
2. (Yo) escribía postales.
3. (Ella) nadaba.
4. Ud. llamaba a menudo.
5. Ustedes y yo trabajábamos.
6. Ellos iban a la biblioteca.
7. Tú ayudabas siempre.
8. Louise y tú ahorraban dinero.

5·6
1. Todos los días (ella) descansaba después de almorzar.
2. Casi siempre ponían azúcar en el café.
3. A veces, usted se levantaba temprano.
4. De vez en cuando Sheila se quedaba en casa.
5. Generalmente el tren llegaba tarde por la mañana.
6. Muchas veces perdía el autobús.
7. Mi madre casi nunca dormía.

5·7
1. Cuando tenía veinte años, yo vivía en Ponce, Puerto Rico.
2. Todas las mañanas iba a mi clase de español.
3. Usualmente, mi clase terminaba al mediodía.
4. Mis amigos y yo queríamos quedarnos en una ciudad agradable.
5. A menudo iba al mercado para hablar con las personas del lugar.
6. De vez en cuando echaba de menos a mi familia.
7. Pero casi nunca quería regresar a casa.
8. Los domingos, Carla y Jorge me llevaban a su casa a cenar.
9. Jorge hacía chistes pero no eran cómicos.

5·8
1. X
2. Todas las mañanas
3. Usualmente
4. X
5. A menudo
6. De vez en cuando
7. casi nunca
8. Los domingos
9. X

5·9
1. pensaba
2. decía
3. sentían
4. comprabas
5. estaba
6. salías

5·10
1. dormía
2. Había
3. quería
4. era
5. tenían
6. prefería
7. ayudaban

5·11
1. Dormía
2. Se bañaba
3. Leía
4. eran
5. Entraba
6. Miraba
7. hablaba
8. Regresaba

5·13 Charlotte viaja frecuentemente / con frecuencia. Cuando era niña, visitaba a su tía en Alaska. Hacían excursiones con guía para observar las ballenas. Cuando era estudiante en una universidad, quería ser bióloga marina. En aquellos días, prefería viajar al Caribe. En la primavera hacía una reserva de un viaje de ida y vuelta. Siempre viajaba en un vuelo directo a Punta Cana, en la República Dominicana. Como de costumbre, facturaba su equipaje y entraba a la puerta de embarque. Al aterrizar, recogía su maleta y pasaba por la aduana. La maleta era pesada porque llevaba el equipo para bucear. Del aeropuerto, iba en un autobús a un hotel en la Bahía de Samaná. Al día siguiente estaba lista para una experiencia emocionante: observar las ballenas en un clima cálido. ¡Charlotte podía observar y estudiar más ballenas en el Caribe que en Alaska!

6 More about the preterit and the imperfect

6·1
1. Eran
2. salió
3. oyó
4. tenía
5. decidió
6. escuchó
7. regresó
8. fue
9. Era
10. se sintió

6·2
1. El domingo era mi día favorito. Me levantaba tarde y leía el periódico en la cama.
2. Ese domingo fue diferente.
3. Me levanté temprano, me vestí rápidamente y salí a montar en bicicleta por el barrio.
4. Era una mañana bonita. Hacía fresco también.
5. Mientras yo montaba en bicicleta, había mucha gente activa en el parque.
6. Dos mujeres jóvenes hacían jogging mientras un perro las seguía.
7. Un señor mayor hacía ejercicio en el parque y dos niños jugaban.
8. De repente, tanta actividad me hizo sentir cansado(a).
9. Entonces, volví a casa, guardé la bicicleta y preparé una taza de chocolate caliente.

6·3
2. a specific, particular Sunday
3. a series of specific actions that took place in the past
8. observe the nature of the verb, **hacer**, and the expression of time, **de repente**
9. sequence of actions completed in the past

6·4
1. Mientras yo hacía mi trabajo, un(-a) paciente me llamó por teléfono.
2. Ella hablaba y de repente, colgó el teléfono.
3. Yo buscaba un documento cuando alguien tocó a la puerta.
4. Mi asistente abrió la ventanilla mientras yo rellenaba el formulario.

6·5
1. leía novelas de ciencia-ficción a menudo.
2. salía con mis amigos todos los fines de semana.
3. ponía la mesa para la cena todas las noches.
4. no me preocupaba mucho nunca.
5. era muy impaciente siempre.

6·6
1. El lunes
2. El fin de semana pasado
3. Anoche
4. Hace dos meses
5. Ayer
6. Esta mañana

6·7
1. salió
2. Hacía
3. Vimos
4. ganaron
5. creían/creyeron
6. eran
7. tocaba

6·8
1. **a las ocho en punto**; specific time
2. background description
3. **el mes pasado**; specific time
4. **ese día**; specific time
5. **creían/creyeron**; both express a mental or emotional action
6. **eran**; **ser** describes people's inherent qualities, an action of indefinite duration
7. two simultaneous actions in the past

6·10
1. se hizo
2. se puso
3. me puse
4. nos hicimos
5. te pusiste
6. se volvió

6·11 Hace cinco años María Luisa se casó con Jacobo. Él estudió cinco años en Miami y se hizo ingeniero. La ceremonia fue por la tarde en una bella capilla en Santo Domingo. Después de la boda, la recepción empezó a las nueve en punto de la noche en una vieja mansión. Mientras los invitados esperaban a la novia y al novio, charlaron y tomaron bebidas. De pronto escucharon música y se dieron cuenta de que los recién casados estaban allí. Los invitados esperaban para ver a María Luisa y su padre bailar. De repente, escucharon un "merengue", un baile típico de la República Dominicana. Esta es una tradición dominicana y los invitados disfrutaron el baile. Entonces, Jacobo bailó con María Luisa. Todos los acompañaron y bailaron toda la noche. Nadie quería dejar de bailar. Jacobo y María Luisa se escaparon a eso de la una y media de la mañana. Al día siguiente salieron en un crucero desde la Florida a las Islas Británicas para su luna de miel.

7 The future and the conditional

7·1
1. bajaré
2. viajarán
3. cocinaremos
4. pedirán
5. leeremos
6. decidirán
7. recibirán
8. bailarán
9. cooperarán
10. venderás
11. temerá
12. elegirán

7·2
1. estará
2. llevará
3. recogeré
4. iremos
5. pasarán
6. se mudarán

7·3
1. Prepararás la cena.
2. Los niños no jugarán los videojuegos.
3. El/La vendedor(-a) sumará la cuenta.
4. La mamá de Carly no hablará a su vecino(a).
5. Mis amigos comerán en La Valentina.
6. Mi hermana y yo esperaremos.

7·4
1. saldremos
2. habrá
3. encontrarás
4. querrás
5. podrá/tendremos
6. vendrán

7·5
1. recibirá
2. podrás
3. saldrán
4. irán
5. invitará
6. sabrás

7·7
1. será
2. irá
3. habrá
4. llegará
5. vendrán

7·9
1. Esta noche no lloverá en Las Vegas.
2. La probabilidad de aguaceros aumentará el lunes en el Sur de California.
3. Un frente frío llegará a Santa Fe este fin de semana.
4. Habrá chubascos aislados en San Marcos.
5. En Albuquerque, la temperatura bajará a cuarenta y cinco grados.
6. Tres pulgadas de nieve se acumularán en Chicago.

7·10
1. voy a exigir
2. va a venir
3. van a hacer
4. van a pagar
5. vamos a recibir
6. voy a levantar
7. va a llover

7·11 El mes que viene, mi amiga Rosa irá a una competencia en un canal local de televisión. Hasta entonces, Rosa practicará su canción favorita todos los días. Ella tiene la fuerza de voluntad para ganar. Rosa se levantará temprano por la mañana, tocará el piano y cantará su canción favorita delante de un espejo. Su vecino, Manuel, dice que necesita tapones para los oídos. ¿Por qué? ¡Manuel escuchará la misma canción una y otra vez todos los días! Rosa intentará cambiar su apariencia. Correrá cinco millas todas las noches y comerá menos. Cambiará el color de su pelo o usará una peluca y comprará un vestido rojo. Rosa cree que ella será la mejor concursante y ganará el primer premio. Tendrá un minuto de fama. Rosa cree que va a obtener una audición para un espectáculo de variedades. ¿Ganará? ¿Habrá un final totalmente inesperado y sorprendente? ¡Quién sabe!

7·12
1. subiría
2. compraría
3. plancharían
4. investigaría
5. leerían
6. comeríais

7·13
1. llamarían
2. esperaría
3. ofreceríamos
4. llevarían
5. tomaría
6. ayudaría

7·14
1. ¿Comerían Uds. las tortillas?
2. Los niños no jugarían con este juguete.
3. ¿Quién traería la cerveza?
4. Pedro no se reiría.
5. Yo no leería esta novela.
6. El cartero traería las revistas.

7·15
1. salgo, saldría
2. hay, habría
3. Puedo, Podría
4. quiero, querría

7·16
1. Habría demasiado ruido.
2. ¿Irían ellos también?
3. Carlos sonreiría.
4. ¿Quién vendría?

7·17
1. Fregaría...
2. Iría...
3. Saldría...
4. Cenaría...

7·18
1. haría
2. tendríamos
3. encontraría
4. dormiría
5. valdría
6. llegaría
7. vendría
8. saldría

7·19
1. e
2. a
3. d
4. c
5. f
6. b

7·20
1. Ocurriría después de la medianoche.
2. ¿Qué hora sería cuando Cynthia salió?
3. Un ladrón entraría en la casa.
4. Vería el cuadro en la sala.
5. Un cómplice lo ayudaría.
6. Pondría el cuadro en un camión.

7·22 A Josefina le gustaría visitar Ecuador en diciembre. Ella haría ejercicio, perdería peso y así podrá escalar uno de los volcanes cerca de Quito. Ella no gastará dinero en comida chatarra y preparará su almuerzo todos los días. Creo que ella sería más saludable, también. Josefina abrirá una cuenta de ahorros en el banco. Ella ahorraría cien dólares todas las semanas. Pero, quién sabe, Josefina no es ahorrativa. Ella necesitará la disciplina y un plan para alcanzar su meta. ¡Yo viajaría con ella a Ecuador! Me encantaría ver la Avenida de los Volcanes y disfrutar unas vacaciones. Exploraríamos muchos lugares interesantes y descubriríamos/disfrutaríamos de los platos ecuatorianos.

8 Reflexive verbs and reflexive constructions

8·1
1. me desayuno
2. me miro
3. me afeito
4. Me quito
5. me ducho
6. me seco
7. me cepillo

8·2
1. Me corto las uñas.
2. Lana se peina.
3. Nos lavamos las manos.
4. Los payasos se maquillan.
5. Me tapo con una manta.
6. La recepcionista se lima las uñas.

8·3
1. se viste
2. se prueban
3. se desviste
4. se despiden
5. me acuesto
6. se duerme

8·4
1. Me enojo.
2. Se enferma fácilmente.
3. Nos aburrimos en esta clase.
4. Ud. se olvida de las reglas.
5. Inés se alegra.
6. ¡Se vuelve un animal!
7. ¿Cómo se acuerdan Uds.?
8. Se disgustan.
9. Me divierto con las películas.
10. Marcos se enloquece.

8·6
1. prepara
2. se prepara
3. te enfermas
4. enferma
5. prueba
6. se prueba
7. se quita
8. quita
9. me llevo
10. llevamos
11. acuesta
12. se acuesta

8·7
1. te levantes
2. Súbase
3. te asustes
4. Acostaos
5. Quítense
6. te duermas
7. quítense
8. prepárate

8·8
1. ¡Pruébenselos!
2. Carlos, póntelo.
3. No se afeiten aquí.
4. Córtalo, Laura.
5. ¡Séquela!
6. Acérquense.
7. Prepárenlos.
8. Por favor, llévatelos.

8·10
1. d
2. i
3. h
4. a
5. j
6. g
7. f
8. c
9. b
10. e

8·11 Carlos y Alexandra van de compras a menudo. Alex se prueba los vestidos caros de la tienda pero Carlos no se enoja. Generalmente, ella no gasta mucho dinero pero se demora mucho tiempo comprando. Alex va al probador, se desviste, se prueba varios vestidos de diseñadores famosos, se mira en el espejo y se olvida de Carlos. Él se cansa de esperar, se sienta en un sofá y se duerme. Mientras Carlos duerme, Alex se va a la zapatería y se pone varios pares de zapatos. Después, se va a la sección de perfumería y maquillaje y se compra algunos productos de belleza. Sabe que Carlos no se enoja porque ella no gasta mucho dinero. Luego, Alex se despide de la vendedora y se reúne con Carlos. Él se despierta. Se sorprende porque Alex lleva muchos paquetes y se preocupa un poco. Alex dice que ella no gasta mucho dinero y Carlos se tranquiliza. Se van a la cafetería y meriendan. Como de costumbre, ya es tarde y ellos deciden que no vale la pena visitar el departamento de caballeros.

8·12
1. Amanda y yo nos abrazamos.
2. ¡Ustedes se ven en el espejo!
3. Los dos equipos se admiran mutuamente.
4. Los niños siempre se pelean entre ellos.
5. ¿Uds. se conocen?
6. Nos ayudamos mutuamente.
7. Mi esposo y yo nos respetamos.
8. Carlos y su hermano se hablan todos los días.
9. ¿Os veis a menudo?
10. Mis amigos se saludan.
11. Nos entendemos.
12. Julia y Jena se cepillan el cabello.

8·14
1. se pone
2. te haces
3. nos ponemos
4. se vuelve
5. te pones
6. se ponen
7. se hace
8. nos ponemos

8·15
1. Lina se pone brava cuando trabaja mucho.
2. ¡Me pongo muy nervioso(a) cuando gritas!
3. La gente se vuelve loca cuando hay fiesta.
4. ¡No te pongas bravo(a)!
5. ¿Quién se hace experto sin la experiencia?

8·16 Un día, Ariela se levantó temprano. Se miró en el espejo. Se lavó la cara. Se pintó los labios con la nueva barra de labios y se peinó (el pelo). Tenía un peinado nuevo, una cola de caballo. Estaba feliz/contenta con su nuevo look/aspecto. Entonces, se vistió. Se puso un conjunto nuevo. Salió de la casa y vio a su nueva vecina, Zoe. Ariela y Zoe se miraron. Se saludaron y después se rieron. ¡Tenían el mismo peinado y el mismo conjunto! Ariela sacó su cámara, ellas sonrieron y ahora tienen la foto. Desde entonces, Ariela y Zoe se hablan todos los días. Se sienten almas gemelas.

9 The progressive tenses

9·1
1. está patinando
2. están bebiendo
3. estamos esquiando
4. está aplaudiendo
5. estás jugando
6. estoy sacando
7. están discutiendo
8. están compartiendo

9·2
1. oyendo
2. huyendo
3. destruyendo
4. construyendo
5. atrayendo
6. contribuyendo

9·3
1. sirviendo
2. hirviendo
3. siguiendo
4. riñendo
5. compitiendo
6. diciendo

9·4
1. Ahora, Marcos se está levantando / está levantándose.
2. Lola se está bañando / está bañándose; se está dando / está dándose un baño.
3. Pedro se está afeitando / está afeitándose en el baño.
4. No me estoy cepillando / estoy cepillándome los dientes.
5. ¿Estás vendiéndolos? / ¿Los estás vendiendo?
6. ¿Quién lo está esperando / está esperándolo a Ud. en el lobby?

9·5
1. está escondiendo
2. está dando
3. están gritando
4. están esperando
5. Está durmiendo
6. está viviendo

9·6
1. Los fanáticos están viendo un buen juego.
2. Ahora no está lloviendo.
3. El equipo está jugando bien.
4. El entrenador está animando a sus jugadores.
5. Un vendedor de cerveza está subiendo las escaleras.
6. Él está gritando: "¡Cacahuates, cerveza!"
7. Ahora, la banda está tocando música.
8. Los fanáticos están divirtiéndose.
9. El otro equipo está perdiendo el juego.

9·7
1. estaba buscando
2. estaban rellenando
3. estaba escribiendo
4. estaban respondiendo
5. estaba recibiendo
6. estaban haciendo
7. estaba cambiando
8. estaba tomando
9. estaba leyendo

9·9
1. Miriam sigue cantando la misma canción.
2. Mi hijo anda buscando trabajo.
3. ¿Quién continúa haciendo ruido?
4. Iremos buscando una respuesta.
5. No seguirán mintiendo.
6. (Ella) Está perdiendo la esperanza.
7. Continuará apoyando a sus amigos.
8. ¿Estabas tú trabajando en esta oficina ayer?

9·10
1. buscando
2. ir
3. Nadar
4. encontrar
5. disfrutando
6. bronceándose
7. flotando
8. durmiendo

9·11 ¿Qué estoy haciendo? Ahora mismo estoy escribiendo un reporte para mi clase de robótica. A la vez, estoy mirando un video de una universidad en Japón. Un hombre joven que está estudiando odontología está taladrando la muela de una paciente. Ahora están saliendo lágrimas de sus ojos. También está agitando las manos. La paciente no está sonriendo, está dando gritos porque siente mucho dolor. ¡Pobrecita! Tal vez necesita anestesia para este procedimiento. Al escuchar sus gritos, el estudiante está nervioso. ¡Ja, un asistente le está trayendo un vaso de agua al estudiante! Creo que te vas a reír. La paciente no es real. El estudiante está practicando con un robot. Por lo menos, el estudiante no está torturando a una paciente.

10 Compound tenses: the present perfect and the past perfect

10·1
1. hemos caminado
2. has acabado
3. han salido
4. he comido
5. ha llegado

10·3
1. El Dr. Taylor ha llegado.
2. No he hablado con él.
3. ¿Has llamado?
4. Lola ha encendido la tele en la sala de espera.
5. La enfermera / El enfermero no ha salido.
6. ¿Quién se ha llevado mi revista?
7. El examen ha terminado.

10·4
1. he leído
2. ha traído
3. Ha oído
4. ha reído
5. han sonreído
6. ha caído
7. han creído

10·5
1. ha disuelto
2. ha puesto
3. ha escrito/impreso
4. ha abierto
5. Has resuelto
6. he hecho
7. han vuelto

10·6
1. He descubierto que hay un ratón en mi habitación.
2. Yo no me he repuesto de la experiencia.
3. Yo le he descrito la escena a mi vecina Rosa.
4. Ella ha propuesto llamar a un exterminador.
5. Ella ha predicho el fin de mi problema.

10·8
1. c
2. d
3. a
4. j
5. i
6. h
7. g
8. f
9. e
10. b

10·9
1. F
2. F
3. V
4. F
5. V
6. V
7. V

10·10 Siempre he querido una casa nueva. Finalmente, nos hemos mudado a nuestra nueva casa. Hemos descubierto algunas sorpresas. He escrito una lista de las reparaciones. Hemos arreglado una gotera en el techo. Hemos comprado nuevas herramientas y yo he aprendido a usar el martillo. ¡Yo he reparado una pared y he cambiado muchas bombillas! Afortunadamente, no me he roto las uñas ni me he fracturado un dedo. Y nos hemos reído también. Hemos invitado a muchos amigos. Ellos han venido a ayudarnos y han traído comida y regalos. He oído muchas veces que los amigos son como familia. He descubierto que eso es verdad.

10·11
1. habían salido
2. había empezado
3. habían entrado
4. había devuelto
5. habían vivido
6. habíamos sacado

10·12
1. Habíamos terminado tres ejercicios de este capítulo.
2. Habíamos llamado a mi hermana antes de ir al mercado.
3. Habíamos preparado el desayuno.
4. Habíamos abierto las ventanas en tu habitación.
5. No habíamos terminado el trabajo hasta las once de la mañana.
6. Habíamos hecho una cita para un corte de pelo.

10·13
1. F
2. V
3. V
4. V
5. F

10·14
1. visto
2. predicho
3. disuelto
4. repuesto
5. impuesto
6. caído

10·15 *Possible answers:* había aprendido, había bajado, me había casado, había comprado, había conseguido, había dejado, había empezado, había liquidado, había pagado, había publicado

10·16
1. Después de haber ganado el primer premio, Marcela está muy orgullosa.
2. Al haber tenido una conversación con nosotros, Mirta decidió aceptar nuestra invitación.
3. Después de haber conocido a Carmela, Marcos supo la verdad.
4. Por haber salido tan tarde, perdimos el vuelo.
5. Después de haber trabajado toda la semana, nosotros nos merecemos unas vacaciones.
6. Por no haber revisado el precio, pagamos demasiado.
7. Al haber terminado tu trabajo antes de la fecha de entrega, tú mereces un descanso.
8. Por haber hecho todos los ejercicios en este capítulo, ahora escribo mejor en español.

10·17 Hace varias semanas, Beni y Celia habían organizado una excursión a San Diego. Ellos habían vivido allí varios años. A Beni siempre le encanta hacer bromas. Había decidido sorprender a su amigo Pablo. Beni y Celia estacionaron su auto frente a la casa de Pablo. Celia había llevado la videocámara para grabar una película de la visita. Tocaron a la puerta pero nadie respondió. Regresaron a su auto y vieron una patrulla. El agente de policía les había dado una multa por estacionar muy cerca del hidrante. ¿Quién había llamado a la policía? ¡Pablo! Él siempre ha sospechado de las intenciones de otras personas. Él había visto el auto estacionado frente a su casa. Pensó que eran unos intrusos. Celia filmó la escena cuando Pablo y Beni por fin se abrazaron.

11 Compound tenses: the future perfect and the conditional perfect

11·1
1. habrán salido
2. habrá comido
3. habrá cerrado
4. habrás dormido
5. habrá recibido
6. se habrán sacado
7. se habrá recuperado
8. habré olvidado

11·3
1. habrá creído
2. se habrá cubierto
3. habrán oído
4. habremos hecho
5. habré resuelto
6. habrán visto

11·4
1. El tiempo habrá mejorado mañana.
2. El mecánico habrá arreglado el auto.
3. Yo habré llenado el tanque de gasolina.
4. ¿Habrás recogido la ropa en la lavandería?
5. Habré comprado las frutas en el mercado.
6. Habremos pagado las cuentas del mes.

11·6
1. habrá estudiado
2. habré dicho
3. habrá salido
4. habrán pagado
5. habrán visto
6. habrás sido
7. habrá recibido
8. habrá empezado

11·7 Hoy habré recibido quince mensajes de desconocidos: tres ofertas de tarjetas de crédito, dos anuncios de una píldora milagrosa que cura todos los padecimientos, seis proposiciones deshonestas, dos chistes y dos cartas que debo reenviar a otros usuarios. ¿Quién habrá mandado tantos mensajes electrónicos? ¿Cuántas personas habrán recibido esta información? ¿Quién habrá averiguado las direcciones de tanta gente? El espacio cibernético habrá creado posibilidades infinitas de comunicación a gran velocidad, pero no ha previsto el gran número de mensajes ridículos y sospechosos que recibimos todos los días. Este mensaje dice que si envío esta carta a diez personas, en tres días habré recibido una sorpresa muy agradable. ¡Y estas personas habrán devuelto el mismo mensaje diez veces más! Pero si no envío la carta, en una semana habré visto un cambio desfavorable en mi vida. ¿Qué habré descubierto en tres días? Voy a conducir con cuidado... por si acaso.

11·8
1. habría tomado
2. Habrías llevado
3. se habrían puesto
4. habríamos sacado
5. habrían caminado
6. habrían comprado

11·9
1. habría roto
2. habría cubierto
3. habrían vuelto
4. habríamos oído
5. habría puesto
6. se habrían caído

11·11
1. Nosotros habríamos leído todo el periódico.
2. Yo habría buscado el crucigrama.
3. Lisa habría pedido la sección de deportes.
4. Los chicos habrían peleado por las comiquitas.
5. Fernando habría revisado los anuncios clasificados.
6. Mi madre habría cortado los cupones.

11·12
1. habríamos terminado
2. habría salido
3. se habría casado
4. habría ido
5. habría cancelado
6. habría visto

11·13
1. Te habría dado el dinero.
2. Ella habría descansado todo el día.
3. ¿Habrían ido al partido de béisbol?
4. Habrían comido los chocolates pero yo no los dejé.
5. Yo habría dormido bien pero me llamaste a las dos de la mañana.
6. Habría lavado la ropa pero la lavadora se rompió.

11·15 El miércoles pasado yo estaba esperando a Rafael a la entrada de un parque de diversiones. Rafael es siempre muy puntual. Eran las cinco y media y no había llegado. ¿Rafael habría olvidado la cita? ¡Imposible! ¿Habría tenido un accidente? Yo lo habría llamado pero no tenía mi teléfono celular. ¿No habría ido Rafael al cine en vez de al parque? ¡Qué va! Me habría llamado. Por fin vi a Rafael. Me dijo que habría llegado a tiempo pero había sido imposible. No sabía que tenía que llenar el tanque de gasolina. Rafael se quedó varado sin gasolina en medio de la autopista de peaje. ¡Qué tontería!

12 The passive voice and passive constructions

12·1
1. El auto fue arreglado por Carlos.
2. Los exámenes fueron cancelados por la profesora.
3. La cena fue preparada por los cocineros.
4. Las pólizas de seguro fueron vendidas por el agente.
5. Los empleados fueron despedidos por el jefe.

12·2
1. El proyecto será aprobado por una comisión.
2. El equipo será instalado por una compañía local.
3. Todos los voluntarios serán entrenados por nuestro gerente.
4. Muchos premios de la rifa serán donados por varias familias.
5. El lazo de la inauguración será cortado por la reina de la feria.
6. Las entradas serán vendidas en la taquilla.
7. Todos los niños serán recibidos por un payaso.
8. El último día será celebrado con fuegos artificiales.

12·3

1. V	4. V	7. F
2. V	5. F	8. V
3. F	6. V	9. V

12·4 Una noticia de última hora. Un coche con un viajero peculiar fue descubierto en la Avenida Simón Bolívar. Un león fue visto en el asiento trasero del auto. Las autoridades fueron avisadas inmediatamente. El conductor fue detenido por la policía. El auto era conducido por una dama misteriosa cuya identidad aun es desconocida. La dama y el león fueron finalmente identificados como miembros del Circo Moderno. Cuando fue interrogada, la extravagante dama presentó a su león, Bebé. La misteriosa dama ofreció mucha información a la prensa. Fue revelado que Bebé lleva una correa con diamantes. El incidente ha sido considerado como un truco publicitario.

12·5

1. f	4. e
2. b	5. d
3. a	6. c

12·7

1. se visten	4. se abre
2. se colocan	5. se envuelven
3. se limpian	6. se cierran

12·8

1. V	4. V
2. F	5. F
3. V	6. V

12·9
1. Se venden carros usados aquí.
2. Se dice que el crimen no paga.
3. No se aceptarán tarjetas de crédito.
4. Aquí se hablan inglés y español.
5. El museo se inaugurará mañana.

12·10 "Uno se informa, se prepara y busca tesoros perdidos en el fondo del mar. Se sabe que en las aguas del Mar Caribe se descubren muchos tesoros enterrados. El buque español *Santa Margarita* fue descubierto por unos buzos que buscaban tesoros. ¡Más de dos millones de dólares en oro y joyas se recuperaron de ese barco! ¡Y del buque *Atocha* casi cincuenta toneladas de plata y miles de esmeraldas del tamaño de una nuez! Pero te tienes que preparar. Te compras el mejor equipo de buceo, te buscas un lugar ideal para tu aventura y te vas a buscar tu tesoro". Esas palabras fueron dichas por un experto cazador de tesoros. Te crees esas palabras, te compras tu equipo con tu tarjeta de crédito, te vas a buscar tesoros, te olvidas de la realidad, te pasas la vida debajo del océano y te arruinas antes de encontrar tu tesoro hundido en el fondo del mar.

13 The subjunctive mood: the present and the present perfect subjunctive tenses in noun clauses

13·1
1. lees
2. compre
3. cantemos
4. comes
5. escribe
6. se casan

13·2
1. esté
2. ayude
3. preparen
4. bebas
5. recibamos
6. comprenda

13·3
1. Quiero que practiques el tango y la salsa.
2. Marcos desea que almorcemos en este restaurante.
3. Prefieren que expliquemos nuestro plan.
4. Queremos que usted busque la respuesta.
5. La cajera duda que ustedes paguen en efectivo.
6. El público prefiere que Lamas toque la guitarra.
7. Marta y yo dudamos que él saque el dinero.

13·4
1. El/La entrenador(-a) quiere que el partido empiece a tiempo mañana.
2. Ella prefiere que todos los jugadores se despierten más temprano.
4. Dudo que todos Uds. comprendan/entiendan las reglas para jugar tenis.
5. Nuestros rivales quieren que nosotros perdamos el partido mañana.
6. Prefiero que Ud. se siente en la segunda fila, cerca del césped.
7. El/La asistente del entrenador / de la entrenadora duda que Bernardo defienda su título con dignidad.

13·6
1. siga
2. advierta
3. pida
4. sugiera
5. consienta

13·7
1. continúe
2. influyan
3. sustituya
4. concluya
5. destruyan
6. envíes

13·8
1. Pedro quiere que ellos traigan los nuevos CDs.
2. Mi madre prefiere que tú hagas la lista.
3. Quieren que usted vea los resultados.
4. Ella prefiere que ustedes salgan inmediatamente.
5. Dudo que la película valga la pena.
6. Sheila espera que su maleta quepa en el auto.

13·9
1. el secretario / la secretaria traiga los papeles.
2. el/la asistente salga.
3. el/la contador(-a) vea los documentos.
4. el presidente / la presidenta sepa sus deseos de ganar más dinero.
5. sus empleados sean corteses.

13·10
1. d
2. e
3. c
4. a
5. f
6. b

13·11
1. busque
2. lleguen
3. mida
4. acabemos
5. firme

13·13   1. Dudamos que los chicos lleguen antes de las ocho.
2. Me dice que abra la ventana ahora.
3. ¿Quién desea contar un cuento?
4. Quiero que ustedes comprendan mi punto de vista.
5. El inspector ve que la carretera necesita arreglos.
6. Ella sugiere que trabajemos en su proyecto.

13·14   3. no dependent clause introduced by **que**
5. **ve**, the verb in the main clause, does not communicate doubt or uncertainty

13·15   Creo que mi nueva compañera de cuarto no es muy amable. Quiero que sepa que estoy enojada. Prefiero que discutamos este asunto pronto. Ella no quiere que me sienta cómoda en nuestro apartamento. Nuestro contrato prohíbe que tengamos mascotas en el apartamento pero ella quiere quedarse con su loro, Tonto. Bueno, la verdad es que Tonto se despierta a las 5:30 todas las mañanas y yo prefiero dormir tarde los fines de semana. Voy a pedirle que busque otro apartamento.

13·17
1. estés	4. recomiendes	7. lleguen
2. sepas	5. conoces	8. recojan
3. vengan	6. puedan	9. subas

13·18   La empresa Telemast anuncia hoy la llegada de su nuevo gerente general. Bob espera que el nuevo gerente sea un hombre simpático y flexible. Más vale que el nuevo jefe entienda que Bob llega tarde a la oficina de vez en cuando. Bob desea crear una buena primera impresión y hoy llega a tiempo. Ojalá el nuevo gerente entienda que los empleados necesitan más tiempo para almorzar. Es importante que permita que sus empleados hagan llamadas personales desde la oficina. Ojalá que el nuevo jefe sea muy paciente y no sea muy exigente. Sin embargo, es muy probable que Bob reciba una gran sorpresa. La persona que ahora ocupa el cargo de gerente general acaba de llegar a Telemast. Es la señora Almagro. Es muy conocida entre sus amigos como la "Dama de hierro".

13·19
1. haya seguido	4. hayan perdido	7. hayan permitido
2. haya tenido	5. haya aceptado	8. hayan terminado
3. haya despegado	6. haya roto	9. hayas entregado

13·20   1. Sentimos que Ana haya llegado.
2. Espero que hayan entregado el paquete.
3. Será necesario que tú hayas leído los libros antes de la reunión.
4. Su esposo espera que ella haya devuelto el sombrero nuevo a la tienda.
5. Los viajeros se alegran de que el avión haya salido a tiempo.
6. El agente exigirá que el director haya pagado a los actores antes del fin de semana.

13·21
1. haya subido	4. hayan vendido
2. haya reducido	5. haya rebajado
3. hayan disminuido	6. haya sido

13·22   Me alegro de que Pamela haya aprendido técnicas nuevas en el trabajo. Es increíble que haya tomado tantos cursos de informática. ¡Ojalá que sus padres hayan ayudado a pagar los costos de las clases virtuales! Parece mentira que Pam haya terminado todas las clases a distancia. Es probable que haya compartido sus respuestas con su profesor a través de la pantalla electrónica de su computadora, en casa, ¡en sus cómodos pijamas! Es sorprendente que en las últimas décadas muchas carreras hayan cambiado tanto.

14 More uses of the subjunctive: adverb and relative clauses

14·1
1. acabe	5. vean
2. ayude	6. termine
3. tengas	7. necesite
4. cierre	

14·2
1. para que
2. antes (de) que
3. sin que
4. en caso de que
5. a menos que
6. para que
7. en caso de que

14·3
1. Diego invita a sus colegas a un restaurante en Miami para que prueben platos típicos de Argentina.
2. Diego no va a un restaurante a menos que tenga un buen menú.
3. Él sugiere un plato de pasta en caso de que sus amigos no quieran comer churrasco, un plato de carne a la parrilla.
4. Los camareros siempre sirven un plato con aperitivos antes de que los clientes decidan el plato fuerte.
5. Hay una pantalla grande en la terraza para que / de modo que los clientes vean programas de televisión y videos de Argentina.
6. Un video muestra una competencia reciente de tango para que / de modo que los clientes sepan que los ganadores son de Japón y Colombia.

14·4
1. g
2. i
3. h
4. d
5. a
6. e
7. c
8. f
9. b

14·5
1. dure
2. entre
3. pida
4. entregue
5. gastes
6. salgan

14·6
1. Leeré el mensaje tan pronto como pueda.
2. Trae la revista para que leas el artículo.
3. Acabaremos el informe de modo que / para que Uds. encuentren la información.
4. Cada vez que el teléfono suene, Marsha contestará.
5. Uds. trabajarán aunque estén cansados.
6. La recepcionista llamará a los clientes después de que termine la reunión.

14·8
1. tenemos
2. llegue
3. tengan
4. gasta
5. tiene
6. duermo
7. pueda
8. es
9. sale
10. es

14·9
1. habitual action
3. uncertainty; the action may occur in the future
5. habitual action
7. the action will occur after the action in the main clause
8. habitual action

14·10 Quiero jubilarme pronto, tan pronto como sea posible. Yo quiero dejar de trabajar cuando cumpla 55 años. Tengo veinticinco años para ganar dinero. Por eso escucho los consejos de mis amigos. Mi amigo Pete es extremadamente conservador y sugiere que ponga mi dinero en el banco. Dice que tan pronto como reciba mi cheque este mes, debo ahorrar el veinticinco por ciento de mi salario. Marcia es la gerente de un banco y ella cree que debo comprar una propiedad para que el precio suba y, ¡yo gane mucho dinero! Mark es más agresivo. Él dice que si yo no invierto mi dinero en la bolsa de valores, no voy a dejar de trabajar hasta que tenga setenta años. ¿Y si la bolsa baja y pierdo todo mi dinero? Por si acaso, compro billetes de lotería de vez en cuando.

14·11
1. La pareja busca un auto que no sea caro.
2. ¿Hay un gato que no sea limpio?
3. Queremos encontrar a alguien que pueda ayudarnos.
4. La gente necesita un amigo que sea confiable.
5. No hay ningún niño que no necesite mucha atención.

14·12
1. pague
2. resuelva
3. ofrezca
4. coma
5. suba
6. hagan
7. haya

14·13
1. venda
2. está
3. sepa
4. sea
5. empieza
6. vive
7. pueda

14·15
1. Marcos busca un jugador de tenis que pueda ganar el partido.
2. ¿Conocen Uds. una tienda que venda productos mexicanos?
3. Necesitamos una oficina que sea grande y barata.
4. No hay nada que tú puedas hacer para resolver este problema.
5. Prefiero un amigo que sea honesto.
6. ¡No hay nadie que comprenda este mensaje!

14·16
1. cualquier
2. quienquiera
3. dondequiera
4. adondequiera
5. cualquiera

14·17
1. busque
2. coma
3. sepa
4. llegue
5. piensa
6. diga
7. aceptemos
8. recuerde

14·18
1. Tania es muy lista diga lo que diga la gente.
2. Tal vez tengamos suerte hoy si vendemos tantos productos como ella vendió ayer.
3. Es probable que Tania llegue antes de las ocho para decorar la vitrina.
4. Tal vez Tania reciba un aumento de sueldo pronto.
5. Aunque tú no lo creas, ella quiere tener su propio negocio.
6. Trabaje donde trabaje / Dondequiera que ella trabaje, tendrá éxito.

14·19
1. Tal vez
2. Por muy barato que sea
3. Por mucho que llames
4. Cuesten lo que cuesten
5. Sea como sea
6. Cuando quiera que vayan

14·20 No voy a ver a Daniela hasta después del 15 de abril. Ella no contesta mis llamadas aunque yo deje diez mensajes en su contestadora. Ella es muy perezosa y no toma decisiones hasta el último minuto. Aunque no quiera, tiene que llenar los formularios de la declaración de impuestos y buscar todos los recibos para declarar sus gastos. Ella se enferma y no descansará hasta que complete su declaración de impuestos. Va a sufrir un ataque de histeria a menos que alguien resuelva su problema. Necesita un contable que quiera ayudarla en tan poco tiempo. ¡Quizás ella encuentre esto emocionante! Daniela debe cambiar. Dice un refrán español: "No dejes para mañana lo que puedas hacer hoy".

15 The subjunctive mood past tenses: the imperfect and the pluperfect subjunctive

15·1
1. caminaran
2. vivieran
3. saliera
4. durmiera
5. cantara
6. fueras
7. se cayeran
8. costara
9. sirviera
10. trajeran

15·2
1. viniera, viniese
2. tocaras, tocases
3. encontrara, encontrase
4. terminara, terminase
5. pagaran, pagasen
6. cerraran, cerrasen
7. supiera, supiese
8. hablaran, hablasen

15·3
1. Era/Fue necesario que ellos esperaran veinte minutos para comprar las entradas.
2. Joe le pidió a Mary que comprara chocolates.
3. Mary compró refrescos en caso de que tuvieran sed.
4. Ann y Mary querían asientos que estuvieran cerca de la pantalla.
5. Ellos no querían ver los comerciales antes de que empezara la película.
6. Jack se fue del cine antes de que terminara la película.

15·4
1. nos divirtiéramos / nos divirtiésemos...
2. leyéramos/leyésemos...
3. probáramos/probásemos...
4. fuera/fuese...
5. trajera/trajese...

15·5
1. trabajara
2. pudiera
3. conocieran
4. diera
5. recogieran
6. mantuviera
7. visitaran
8. tuvieran

15·6
Sabrina tenía el pelo castaño, largo y lacio. Fue a la peluquería y le dijo a su peluquero que le cortara el pelo. Pete, el peluquero, le sugirió que cambiara el color de su cabello. Sabrina siempre había querido que su pelo fuera diferente. Decidió que quería ser rubia. Pete buscó un color que le gustara a Sabrina. Ella prefería un color que fuera claro. Tres horas y media después de que él cambiara el color del pelo, Pete comenzó a usar las tijeras. Cuando Pete terminó, Sabrina se miró al espejo. ¡Y vio a una mujer muy diferente! Cuando Sabrina volvió a casa, entró y su esposo no habló mucho. Él parecía confundido. Antes de que Sabrina le pidiera su opinión, su esposo dijo: "¿Y por qué no un permanente también?"

15·7
1. ¿Pudiera Ud. abrir la puerta, por favor?
2. Quisiera entrar.
3. Ud. debiera terminar ahora.
4. Ud. debiera cerrar la puerta ahora.
5. Yo no quisiera comprar esta corbata.
6. Debiera pedir perdón por mis errores.

15·8
1. e
2. d
3. g
4. b
5. f
6. c
7. a

15·9
1. hubieran/hubiesen salido
2. hubiera/hubiese permitido
3. hubiéramos/hubiésemos querido
4. hubiera/hubiese podido
5. hubieras/hubieses escrito

15·10
1. hubieran pasado
2. hubiera creído
3. hubiera mentido
4. se hubieran sentado
5. hubiera cometido
6. hubiera afirmado

15·11
1. ellos hubieran salido de su oficina.
2. Elías hubiera creado una nueva campaña.
3. todos hubieran escuchado sus sugerencias.
4. hubiera visto el nombre "Burbujas" en una botella de champú.
5. hubieran visto a un extraterrestre.

15·13
1. tuviéramos
2. dejara
3. quisiera
4. fuera
5. tuvieran
6. fuera

15·14
1. pudiera
2. compite
3. tuviera
4. hubiese perdido
5. pudiera
6. compramos

15·15
1. hubiera jugado
2. hubieras entendido
3. hubiera tenido
4. hubiéramos escuchado
5. hubiera leído
6. hubiera ahorrado
7. hubieran hecho
8. hubieras salido

15·17 Es necesario mantener el equilibrio de la naturaleza para preservar la vida de los hombres y los animales. Si no hubiéramos destruido muchos recursos naturales habríamos podido mantener una mejor situación económica y social en nuestro mundo. Si no hubiéramos ignorado las consecuencias, habríamos salvado muchas selvas tropicales. Consumimos mucha energía y eso es un problema. Pero todos queremos conducir/manejar un auto, tener electrodomésticos en casa y vivir una vida cómoda. Si usáramos más energía solar, energía eólica y otras energías renovables, protegeríamos el medio ambiente. Y si protegiéramos especies en peligro de extinción en un parque, fomentaríamos el ecoturismo. Ayudaríamos a nuestro planeta si tomáramos medidas para proteger el medio ambiente.

16 The commands

16·1
1. Abra
2. Pase
3. Escriba
4. Lea
5. Deposite
6. Compre

16·2
1. sigan
2. Escojan
3. Obtengan
4. Muestren
5. Recojan
6. lleguen

16·3
1. No lleguen tarde al trabajo.
2. Saluden al huésped.
3. Lleven el equipaje a la habitación.
4. Enciendan las luces en la habitación.
5. No hagan preguntas indiscretas.
6. Cierren la puerta y regresen a la recepción.

16·4
1. c
2. e
3. a
4. d
5. b

16·5
1. Esté Ud. aquí a las dos.
2. ¡Sean Uds. generosos!
3. No vayan Uds.
4. Sepa Ud. la verdad.
5. No den Uds. dinero.

16·6
1. hable
2. repita
3. explique
4. escuche
5. cuelgue
6. Llame

16·7
1. Pique 3 dientes de ajo y una cebolla.
2. Corte 8 tomates, 1 pepino y 1 pimiento verde.
3. Mezcle los vegetales con el ajo y la cebolla.
4. Añada 4 cucharadas de aceite de oliva, 2 cucharadas de vinagre y 1 cucharadita de sal.
5. Añada 2 tazas de agua fría.
6. Mezcle la pimienta.
7. Ponga el gazpacho frío en el refrigerador por 1 ó 2 horas.
8. Sirva la sopa fría con pan frito y perejil picado.

16·8
1. Llegue hasta la primera señal de stop.
2. Doble a la izquierda en la esquina.
3. Maneje/Conduzca cinco cuadras y doble a la derecha.
4. Pague el peaje en la caseta.
5. Estacione/Aparque el auto en nuestro garaje.
6. Deje las llaves en el auto.

16·9
1. Trabaja
2. Prepara
3. Huye
4. Bebe
5. Sube
6. Comienza
7. Baja
8. Revisa
9. Piensa
10. Escucha
11. Ayuda
12. Empieza
13. Duerme
14. Cuelga

16·10
1. Di
2. Haz
3. Ve
4. Pon
5. Ven

16·11
1. Pon tus libros aquí.
2. Haz la tarea.
3. Di la verdad.
4. Ten cuidado.
5. Ve a la escuela ahora.
6. Sé buena.

16·12
1. uses
2. pidas
3. hagas
4. repitas
5. des

16·13
1. Ven, vayas
2. Escribe, olvides
3. Saca, pierdas
4. Devuelve, compres
5. Lee, traigas
6. Sal, demores

16·14
1. comas, consume
2. Haz, corre
3. Duerme, bebas
4. Juega, ve
5. Respira, piensa

16·15
1. Comprad
2. Leed
3. Escuchad
4. Despertad
5. Aplaudid

16·16
1. ¡No juguéis a la pelota! Tocad el piano.
2. ¡No cerréis los sobres! Escribid las direcciones primero.
3. ¡No vayáis ahora! Esperad diez minutos más.
4. ¡No paguéis la cuenta todavía! Añadid la propina.
5. ¡No cortéis los tomates! Pelad los pepinos.

16·17
1. Cámbialo.
2. Lávalo.
3. Llénalo.
4. Límpialas.
5. Revísalas.

16·18
1. Dile la verdad. ¡Dísela!
2. Cómprenle la muñeca. ¡Cómprensela!
3. ¡Háblele Ud. al / a la gerente!
4. Quejaos al / a la asistente de vuelo.

16·19
1. Cambiemos
2. Recitemos
3. Hablemos
4. Repasemos
5. Tomemos
6. enojemos
7. Compremos
8. olvidemos

16·20
1. Naveguemos
2. Investiguemos
3. Empecemos
4. Busquemos
5. hagamos

16·21
1. Alquilémoslo.
2. Dibujémoslos.
3. Compongámoslas.
4. Incluyámosla.
5. Vendámoslas.

16·22 ¡No quiero oír el anuncio otra vez! "¡Visítenos! ¡Maneje/Conduzca uno de nuestros nuevos modelos! ¡Déjenos su auto viejo y salga en su auto nuevo! ¡Compre hoy y pague luego! ¡Compare nuestros precios! ¡No se deje engañar por otras agencias! ¡Aproveche la oferta de fin de año! ¡No olvide que tenemos préstamos con intereses bajos!" Y después las voces de una pareja que dicen: "¡Vamos ahora mismo y compremos el auto de nuestros sueños!" Y yo les diría: "¡No se engañen! ¡No paguen un ojo de la cara! ¡No firmen un contrato por cinco años! ¡Escuchen a este tonto y ahorren dinero y dolores de cabeza!"

17 Nouns and articles

17·1
1. M
2. M
3. M
4. M
5. X
6. M
7. M
8. X
9. M
10. X
11. M
12. X

17·2
1. la
2. la
3. la
4. la
5. el
6. la
7. la
8. la
9. el
10. el
11. la
12. la

17·3
1. La dermatitis
2. la dosis
3. El tenor
4. el equipaje
5. la estación
6. La fealdad

17·4
1. El arpa
2. El hacha
3. La campeona
4. La gerente
5. El águila
6. La estrella
7. El marqués
8. El mes

17·5
1. el limonero
2. el portugués
3. El rojo, el blanco, el azul
4. El peral
5. El lunes
6. el lavaplatos
7. el sacacorchos
8. el paraguas
9. El alemán
10. Las Islas

17·6
1. la profesora
2. la maestra
3. la periodista
4. la reina
5. la pintora
6. la actriz
7. la madre
8. la gerente
9. la yegua
10. la comandante
11. la artista
12. la bailarina

17·7
1. V
2. V
3. F
4. V
5. V
6. F

17·8
1. la estudiante
2. el león
3. la abogada
4. el manzano
5. la pera
6. la emperatriz
7. el marido, el esposo
8. el yerno
9. la heroína
10. la turista
11. la víctima
12. la papa

17·9
1. los señores
2. las reinas
3. las almas
4. los aviones
5. las leonas
6. las flores
7. las cárceles
8. los restaurantes
9. las carnes
10. las aguas
11. las guías
12. los padres
13. los temores
14. los domingos

17·10
1. las sopas
2. las residencias
3. los pasajes
4. las mujeres
5. los relojes
6. las españolas
7. los bebés
8. los manteles
9. los rubís, los rubíes
10. las canciones
11. las luces
12. las regiones

17·11
1. Mis vacaciones terminan el domingo.
2. Voy a ver las panteras en el zoológico mañana.
3. Ahora Lina y yo nos ponemos las gafas de sol.
4. Este hotel está en las afueras de Madrid.
5. Viajamos de noche y descansamos en un coche cama.
6. Lina nunca trae el paraguas.

17·12
1. los gemelos
2. los domingos
3. los binoculares
4. las tesis
5. las tijeras
6. las gafas

17·13
1. Los, la
2. Los, los
3. Los, los
4. El, la
5. Los, las
6. Las, los
7. Los, el

17·14
1. La
2. los
3. los
4. X
5. los
6. X
7. la
8. las
9. la
10. las
11. el

17·15
1. Hoy tengo una cita a las nueve y media de la mañana.
2. Me pongo el abrigo y los guantes antes de salir.
3. El/La asistente del / de la dentista habla portugués y español.
4. Me duele la muela del juicio.
5. Las caries pueden causar dolor/dolores.
6. Los viernes siempre llego a casa tarde.
7. Sin embargo, hoy iré a casa a eso de las once y media.
8. ¡Necesito descansar! La cabeza me va a doler también.

17·16
1. diez centavos la docena
2. los Goya de hoy
3. los López
4. los Estados Unidos
5. doce dólares la yarda
6. (el) trabajar duro
7. las (islas) Galápagos
8. el presidente Roosevelt
9. (el) comer y (el) beber

17·17
1. la
2. la
3. la
4. Los
5. la
6. X
7. X
8. la

17·20
1. Lee la frase "lo bueno, lo malo y lo feo".
2. Lo importante es estudiar.
3. Nadar es el mejor ejercicio.
4. Carlos I (Primero) es también Carlos V (Quinto).
5. Busca el águila en el cuadro.
6. Éste es el libro del Sr. Gómez.
7. No vamos a La Mancha.
8. ¿Quién no quiere ir al museo?
9. Lo mejor es dormir después del viaje.
10. ¡Mira lo fácil que está esto!

17·21
1. una
2. un
3. una
4. un
5. un
6. una
7. un
8. un
9. una
10. un
11. un
12. una

17·22
1. unas veces
2. unos temblores
3. unas verdades
4. unos pasajes
5. unos hospitales
6. unas crisis
7. unos rubís, unos rubíes
8. unos sofás
9. unas escaleras
10. unos manatís, unos manatíes
11. unos capitanes
12. unas pensiones

17·23
1. V
2. F
3. F
4. V
5. V
6. V
7. V
8. V
9. F
10. V
11. F

17·24
1. Unos
2. una
3. unas
4. X
5. un
6. un
7. X
8. X
9. un
10. X

17·25 El martes, Nidia llevaba unas gafas oscuras. Nidia fue sola a una galería. Delante de un cuadro francés muy moderno, ella se encontró con Luis. Tenían una cita secreta. Después, Nidia y Luis fueron a un restaurante japonés lejos de la ciudad. Se sentaron en una esquina apartada y pidieron unos platos deliciosos. A las nueve y media de la noche los González y los Suárez llegaron al restaurante. ¡Qué mala suerte! Cierta persona empezó a correr un rumor. Pablo Suárez es un hombre chismoso. Lo malo es que Nidia y Luis querían guardar su secreto. Y ahora, la relación entre Nidia y Luis es un secreto a voces.

18 Adjectives

18·1
1. agudo
2. grande
3. viejo
4. fabulosa
5. interminable
6. profundo
7. redonda
8. malicioso

18·2
1. elegante
2. raras
3. violentos
4. populares
5. azules
6. preferida
7. cálido
8. feas

18·3
1. un día bonito
2. una mañana triste
3. una mano grande
4. un aroma (un perfume) agradable
5. una canción larga
6. un sueño profundo
7. una amiga sincera
8. una enfermera dedicada / un enfermero dedicado
9. una ciudad interesante
10. un idioma/lenguaje, una lengua difícil
11. una explosión terrible
12. un soldado valiente

18·4
1. h
2. j
3. f
4. i
5. g
6. c
7. e
8. a
9. d
10. b

18·5
1. algunos informes
2. temas filosóficos
3. muchas decisiones
4. ningunas zapatillas
5. ningún premio
6. proyecto difícil

18·6
1. ¡Esta comedia es única, fuera de serie!
2. Mi viejo amigo, Manolito, escribió el guión.
3. Un antiguo colega vino al teatro para ver la comedia.
4. El protagonista es un hombre simple.
5. Manolito siempre usa ideas nuevas.
6. Cualquier persona que venga al teatro se va a reír.

18·8
1. El viajero <u>portugués</u> trae un pasaporte <u>vencido</u>.
2. El <u>tercer</u> año en la universidad es <u>difícil</u> y <u>largo</u>.
3. Han pasado <u>tres</u> meses.
4. Pablo Neruda, el <u>gran</u> poeta <u>chileno</u>, es un personaje <u>curioso</u> en una película <u>italiana</u>.
5. ¿Quién es el cantante <u>famoso</u> de San Juan?

18·10
1. Es cortés y generoso.
2. Escuchamos un ruido alto y claro.
3. Esta silla cuesta trescientos dólares.
4. Un vaso de leche fría, por favor.
5. Su oficina está en una calle larga y estrecha.
6. Hay algunas tiendas nuevas en el primer piso de este centro comercial.
7. Elly quiere una bicicleta nueva.

18·11
1. los pendientes/zarcillos de diamantes
2. la puerta abierta
3. un vestido de verano
4. los discos rotos
5. algunas bolsas de plástico
6. tres cestas (cestos) de papel
7. un plato de cristal
8. la carta escrita
9. mi anillo de oro
10. los hombres perdidos

18·13
1. tan cómico como
2. tan dormilón como
3. tan estimulante como
4. tan interesantes como
5. tan caros como
6. tan vieja como
7. tan divertida como

18·14
1. Los vestidos de seda son más caros que los vestidos de algodón.
2. Estos zapatos son tan cómodos como los zapatos rojos.
3. Estar de moda es menos importante que ahorrar dinero.
4. Eres tan ahorrativo(a) como mi esposo.
5. En mi opinión, diseñar zapatos es tan creativo como escribir un poema.
6. ¿Es la tranquilidad más necesaria que la riqueza?
7. ¿No es esta traducción menos difícil que el ejercicio anterior?

18·15
1. grandísimo
2. divertidísimo
3. anchísima
4. modernísimo
5. famosísima
6. bellísima
7. carísimo
8. variadísimas
9. popularísima
10. importantísimo

18·17
1. Pablo es el hermano mayor.
2. Rosa es la menor de todas.
3. Mi tío es mayor que tu padre.
4. Felicia dice que tiene veinticinco años. Ella es menor de lo que pensaba.
5. ¡Este juego es más emocionante que el ajedrez!
6. Hoy recibí la peor nota de mi clase de francés.
7. Bueno, mañana recibirás mejores noticias.

18·18
1. el mejor
2. una mejor
3. más grande/mayor que
4. la más grande / la mayor
5. los edificios más viejos
6. Los peores
7. el/la mayor
8. la sorpresa más grande

18·19 Querida Dra. Blanco:

Es la primera vez que escribo a una revista para mujeres pero necesito ayuda. Amanda es muy buena amiga pero a veces ella es muy pesada. Ella es la menor de cinco hermanas. Mi amiga es muy obstinada y competitiva. Si compro un sombrero, Amanda quiere tener un sombrero más atractivo. Si hablo de mi pulsera de oro, ella habla de su anillo de esmeraldas colombianas. Cuando comento que he tenido un día bueno, el día de Amanda es mejor. Lo peor es cuando estamos con otros amigos. Algunos de sus comentarios son puras ficciones. Dice que compró un auto nuevo pero es realmente un nuevo auto. No es malo soñar pero Amanda dice muchas mentiras y no sé qué hacer. Necesito un gran favor. ¿Qué puedo hacer para ayudar a mi vieja amiga?

Preocupada.

19 Personal pronouns

19·1
1. ellos
2. vosotras
3. él
4. ella
5. nosotros/nosotras
6. ellos/ellas/ustedes
7. tú
8. Uds./ellos/ellas

19·2
1. tú
2. Uds.
3. yo
4. ellos/ellas/ustedes
5. nosotros/nosotras
6. yo

19·3
1. Ud.
2. vosotras
3. Ud.
4. tú
5. Uds.
6. Ud.
7. Ud.
8. Uds.
9. Uds.
10. tú

19·4

1. Eres lo que comes.
2. Ellos dicen mentiras, yo digo la verdad.
3. Llueve / Está lloviendo.
4. Dr. Lagos, necesito una cita.
5. Sra. Castro, ¿me escucha Ud.?
6. Trabajo cinco días a la semana.
7. ¿Quién es? Es ella.
8. ¿Dónde viven Uds.?
9. ¿Está nevando?
10. ¿Lees el periódico todos los días?

19·5

1. ella
2. ellos
3. conmigo
4. Uds.
5. tú
6. vosotros
7. ellos
8. ellas
9. ella
10. nosotros
11. Ud.
12. contigo
13. con él
14. según yo

19·6

1. Traemos todas las medicinas con nosotros.
2. Ella envió/mandó estas flores para ti.
3. ¿Quién puso la almohada debajo de ella?
4. Lucy no puede vivir sin ellos.
5. ¿Quién vive cerca de mí?
6. Todos sabemos la respuesta excepto él.
7. La casa está lejos de ustedes.
8. El gato está encima de mí.
9. Ella es como tú.
10. La prensa habla acerca de vosotras.

19·7

1. las compré
2. no la invité
3. no los llamé
4. los tengo
5. no los compré
6. la lanzó
7. las anotaron
8. las robaron

19·8

1. Un astrónomo los observa.
2. ¿Quiénes lo han visto?
3. Nosotros las estudiamos.
4. Ayer yo lo visité.
5. Los tienen en el segundo piso.
6. La notamos porque la noche está muy clara.
7. Los investigaremos.
8. Ahora, la saludamos. ¡Vamos!

19·9

1. La necesito ahora.
2. ¡Ella me ayuda siempre!
3. La escribí para Gloria.
4. Y lo compré con mi dinero.
5. ¿Los visitaste?
6. Ellos/Ellas me respetan mucho.
7. ¿Me perdonas?
8. Ah, lo conozco muy bien.

19·10

1. Cómpralos.
2. No lo gastes inútilmente.
3. Lávenlas.
4. Fríela.
5. No lo quemes.
6. Guárdenlas.
7. Bájala.

19·11

1. Protege el medio ambiente. ¡Protégelo ahora!
2. Escriban tres pósters. ¡Escríbanlos!
3. Recoge todas las botellas de plástico. ¡Recógelas, por favor!
4. Recicle los periódicos. ¡Recíclelos!
5. Apaguen las luces. ¡Apáguenlas!
6. Ahorre agua. ¡Ahórrela, por favor!

19·12

1. Los voy a practicar. / Voy a practicarlos.
2. ¿Lo quieres hacer? / ¿Quieres hacerlo?
3. La vamos a hacer. / Vamos a hacerla.
4. No lo quiero perder. / No quiero perderlo.
5. Los chicos lo van a ganar. / Los chicos van a ganarlo.
6. Lo queremos gastar todo. / Queremos gastarlo todo.
7. Tú no la sabes responder. / Tú no sabes responderla.
8. ¿Dónde lo quieres poner? / ¿Dónde quieres ponerlo?

19·13

1. Mirta está escondiéndolos.
2. Álvaro está buscándolas.
3. Andy y Ann están viéndola.
4. ¿Por qué Uds. están oyéndola?
5. ¿Quiénes están pagándolas?
6. Los hermanos Díaz están leyéndolo.
7. Marco está bebiéndola.

19·14
1. La estamos mirando. / Estamos mirándola.
2. Los músicos lo están tocando. / Los músicos están tocándolo.
3. Los estoy observando. / Estoy observándolos.
4. ¿La está Ud. aplaudiendo? / ¿Está Ud. aplaudiéndola?
5. La banda la está tocando. / La banda está tocándola.

19·15
1. Le
2. Me
3. Le
4. Le
5. Les
6. Nos
7. Le
8. Te

19·16
1. Te envié la carta.
2. No me contestaste.
3. Taly no me explicó su problema.
4. ¿Le contó acerca de su compromiso?
5. Nos enseñó/mostró su anillo de compromiso.
6. Lynda le prepara el almuerzo.
7. Siempre me hacen muchas preguntas.

19·17
1. Cómprenle la revista.
2. Revísales la tarea.
3. Entréguenle esta solicitud.
4. No les digan una mentira.
5. Devuélvele los libros.
6. Pídale la visa.
7. No me cuenten el final.
8. Regálenle una torta de chocolate.
9. Explíquele este problema.
10. Coméntenle este síntoma.

19·18
1. Queremos llevarle un regalo. / Le queremos llevar un regalo.
2. Debe pedirle una excusa. / Le debe pedir una excusa.
3. Voy a servirles una paella. / Les voy a servir una paella.
4. ¡No puedes decirles mentiras! / ¡No les puedes decir mentiras!
5. Laura no quiere llevarles las cajas. / Laura no les quiere llevar las cajas.
6. ¿Puedes prestarnos cien euros? / ¿Nos puedes prestar cien euros?
7. ¿Vais a servirles un aperitivo? / ¿Les vais a servir un aperitivo?
8. Puedes hacerle un favor. / Le puedes hacer un favor.

19·19
1. regalándoles
2. buscándoles
3. escribiéndole
4. tocándole
5. pagándole
6. comentándonos
7. sirviéndoos
8. preparándome
9. lavándote
10. reciclándole

19·20
1. Les estamos enviando una tarjeta.
2. Te estoy prestando mi bicicleta.
3. El banco me está pidiendo el dinero.
4. ¿Me estás enviando mil dólares?
5. Le estoy escribiendo a Ud. una nota.
6. ¿Me están haciendo Uds. una oferta?
7. Os está pidiendo un favor.

19·21
1. Tomás nos los trae.
2. Él se los compra.
3. El meteorólogo se lo explica.
4. Pero no se las dice.
5. Tomás se la entrega.
6. El agente de viajes os las hace.
7. El periodista se las presenta.
8. Mi peluquera me lo prepara.
9. El policía se la da.
10. Ronnie nos lo lee.

19·22
1. Lléveselo.
2. Se los está dando.
3. No se la cantes.
4. Van a lavármelas.
5. Todos los vendedores quieren vendértelos.

19·23
1. A Patricia le gusta ir de compras.
2. A los estudiantes no les gustan los exámenes.
3. Y a los pacifistas no les gustan las guerras.
4. A mí me gusta viajar.
5. A los turistas les gusta sacar fotos.
6. A tu amigo Javier le gustan los refrescos.
7. ¿A ti te gustan las flores?
8. ¿A quién no le gusta la música mexicana?

19·24
1. Sé que le gustan las películas cómicas.
2. A los niños les gusta fastidiar a mi perro.
3. ¿Te gusta la comida francesa?
4. No nos gusta levantarnos temprano.
5. A Sandra le gusta aprender palabras nuevas en español.
6. ¿A quién no le gusta viajar?
7. A Julia no le gusta esta canción.
8. ¿Te gustan las orquídeas?

19·26 "Sobre gustos no hay nada escrito", dice mi amigo Pablo. Yo tengo una opinión diferente y la voy a expresa~~r~~
No me gusta dormir en una hamaca. Me encanta ir de vacaciones y nadar en una piscina olímpica. Me gu~~stan~~
las cosas buenas de la vida, pero con moderación. Me encantan los animales y me disgustan las películas ~~de~~
horror. Me encanta diciembre porque mi familia y yo esquiamos en las montañas. Voy con mi hermana ~~y me~~
encanta competir con ella.

20 Relative pronouns

20·1
1. La casa que está cerca del puente es de María.
2. Los tigres que vimos en el zoo son de la India.
3. La escuela que está cerrada es una institución privada.
4. Los policías que cuidan el banco están dormidos.
5. Los árboles que son más altos están en el parque.
6. En la catedral hay unos turistas que esperan ver unos cuadros de El Greco.

20·2
1. F		4. V	
2. V		5. V	
3. F		6. V	

20·3
1. Mientras Jackie va al mercado que está al lado del cine, nosotros vemos una película.
2. El niño que está conmigo es el hijo de Jackie.
3. La película que vemos no es muy interesante.
4. Matt vio a dos mujeres que no pagaron sus entradas.
5. Mark vino a ver una película que es extranjera.
6. Compré las cosas que los niños quieren: chocolates y refrescos.

20·4
1. El hombre, quien tiene un traje de Arlequín, es muy gordo.
2. El chico, quien trae un disfraz de Frankenstein, es muy bajo.
3. Los hombres, quienes se visten como los siete enanitos, son muy viejos.
4. Una señora, quien parece la Bella Durmiente, está durmiendo en el sofá.
5. Un señor, quien viene con un traje de príncipe, no tiene aspecto aristocrático.
6. Las niñas, quienes se ponen un disfraz de bruja, son muy simpáticas.

20·5
1. quienes		4. quien	
2. quien		5. quien	
3. quienes		6. quienes	

20·6
1. El hombre quien está sentado a mi derecha es de San Diego.
2. La gente quien compró los boletos hoy pagó un precio alto. / Las pers~~on~~as quienes compraron los boletos hoy pagaron un precio alto.
3. Las mujeres a quienes invitaste están bailando la rumba.
4. Pero no veo a sus esposos, quienes estaban aquí.
5. Marlo, quien es una buena amiga, toca el piano.
6. ¿Conoces a la mujer quien está cantando ahora?

20·7
1. los cuales		4. las cuales	
2. la cual		5. los cuales	
3. el cual		6. las cuales	

20·9
1. El/La columnista revela los secretos del actor, lo cual es interesante.
2. Lo que tú quieres saber está en el periódico de hoy.
3. Siempre como lo que quiero.
4. El/La nutricionista recomienda comer lo que es saludable.
5. Mis amigos no van al gimnasio con frecuencia, lo cual no es bueno.
6. Leonardo no está aquí, lo cual me preocupa.
7. ¿Ve Ud. lo que yo veo ahora?
8. ¡Ustedes son muy generosos, lo cual es fabuloso!

20·10
1. la cual	5. los cuales
2. el cual	6. quienes
3. la cual	7. el cual / quien
4. quienes	8. las cuales / quienes

20·11
1. cuyo
2. cuya
3. cuyo
4. cuyas

20·12 Este es el lugar ideal para su reunión de negocios. Las tres salas que Ud. necesita están en el piso bajo, lo cual es muy cómodo. En la recepción, la cual está cerca de la entrada, hay café, té y refrescos. Sheldon es el asistente cuyo nombre aparece en su lista. Él es la persona quien le puede ayudar con el equipo de oficina. En esta lista Ud. puede ver los nombres de nuestros administradores, a quienes Ud. puede llamar en cualquier momento. Fred, el hombre con quien hablamos, puede abrir los balcones. Hay una vista al lago, la cual es agradable. Si me necesita, llame a la extensión que está en mi tarjeta.

21 Possessive and demonstrative adjectives and pronouns

21·1
1. sus	6. su	11. tus	16. su
2. mi	7. su	12. su	17. mis
3. sus	8. nuestros	13. nuestro	18. sus
4. vuestro	9. sus	14. sus	19. vuestros
5. sus	10. nuestro	15. su	

21·2
1. tus mansiones	5. tus lápices	8. tus papeles
2. mis trabajos	6. sus relojes	9. sus amigos
3. sus composiciones	7. nuestras	10. vuestros autos
4. nuestras abuelas	propiedades	

21·3
1. Mi ropa está sucia.	6. Nuestro apartamento no es muy grande.
2. Tu idea es buena.	7. ¿Quieres mis notas?
3. ¿Son estos tus zapatos?	8. Sus platos están sobre la mesa.
4. Vuestra casa no está limpia.	9. Sus sillas están aquí.
5. Estos no son sus documentos.	10. ¿Dónde están mis lentes?

21·4
1. nuestro	5. suya	9. nuestra
2. suya	6. tuyas	10. tuya
3. suyo	7. suyas	11. suyos
4. mías	8. tuyos	12. mía

21·5
1. Un amigo mío es profesor universitario.
2. Quiero conocer a una prima suya.
3. Esta obsesión tuya con los pájaros es muy rara.
4. ¡Este equipo de béisbol nuestro es fabuloso!
5. En esta exposición de arte veo dos cuadros suyos.

21·6
1. Es el pijama de ella.
2. Son las zapatillas de ellos.
3. Éste es el peine de él.
4. Son las medicinas de ellos.

21·7
1. la suya
2. las tuyas
3. el suyo
4. la mía
5. las suyas
6. La mía
7. Las suyas
8. las tuyas
9. el suyo
10. las nuestras
11. las mías

21·8
1. de él
2. de ella
3. de ellos
4. de ellas
5. de Uds.
6. de Uds.
7. de Ud.
8. de Ud.

21·10 Algunas personas son raras. Olvidan su pluma en casa y quieren usar la tuya. ¡Entonces ponen tu pluma en su bolsillo! Probablemente piensan que lo mío es mío y lo tuyo es mío también. Eso me molesta. Mi buen amigo Paul es un ejemplo. Él lee mis libros siempre. Si yo no puedo encontrar un libro mío, yo sé que está en la casa de Paul o en su oficina. ¿Dónde está nuestro diccionario bilingüe? No está en mi escritorio. Está en el escritorio suyo, por supuesto. ¿Y dónde está la biografía del Presidente Kennedy? No, no está en nuestra biblioteca municipal. Está en ese escritorio suyo, en su sala de estar. Nuestro sobrino Allan siempre compra libros para mi cumpleaños. Si Paul está aquí, él lee mis libros primero. ¿Es despistado Paul? Probablemente. Pero estoy enojado(a). Quiero mis libros. ¡Son míos!

21·11
1. este
2. estos
3. este
4. este
5. estas
6. esta
7. estos
8. estos
9. esta
10. estas
11. este
12. esta

21·12
1. esos
2. aquella
3. ese
4. aquellas
5. ese
6. aquellos
7. esa
8. aquel
9. esos
10. aquel
11. ese
12. aquel

21·13
1. este
2. esas
3. aquel
4. Estas
5. ese
6. aquellas
7. esta
8. ese
9. Aquellos
10. esta

21·14
1. Muchos niños vienen a este parque con sus padres.
2. Algunas mujeres corren en aquella área temprano por la mañana.
3. Estos columpios son nuevos y bonitos.
4. Mi perro, Max, juega con aquellos niños.
5. Puedes reciclar botellas de plástico en esos cubos.
6. Me gustaría patinar contigo en esa pista.
7. Mira, aquel hombre está durmiendo debajo del árbol.
8. ¿Quieres participar en ese partido de béisbol?

21·15
1. ésa
2. ésas
3. ésa
4. ése
5. ésas
6. ésa
7. ésa
8. ése
9. ésos
10. ése
11. ése
12. ésas

21·16
1. Este auto es nuevo pero ése es usado.
2. Tu cámara está aquí y éstas son de Julia y de Mark.
3. ¿Es ésta tu mochila o aquélla?
4. Éste es mi bolso y ése es mío también.
5. Ése es mi edificio de apartamentos.
6. Aquéllos son los turistas de México.
7. Este banco y aquél abren a las nueve.
8. Ese monumento es más interesante que éste.
9. ¿Qué es aquello?

21·17 Mi cumpleaños es mañana. Eso es bueno. Pero tengo que limpiar la casa, cocinar la cena y limpiar la pecera. Y eso es malo. Los cumpleaños son días para celebrar. ¿Qué es eso? ¡Es un aviso con información acerca de un servicio especial de limpieza! ¡Eso es fantástico! ¿Y eso por qué? ¡Porque voy a marcar este número de teléfono ahora mismo! ¡Eso es! Voy a comprar mi propio regalo de cumpleaños. Y voy a pedir un descuento con este cupón. ¡Esto es fantástico!

22 Adverbs

22·1
1. lejos
2. nunca
3. bien
4. cerca
5. todavía
6. debajo
7. mal
8. poco

22·3
1. Siempre hay una razón para ser feliz.
2. Nunca tengo suficiente dinero.
3. Todavía tengo esperanzas de ganar la lotería.
4. Bueno, sueño mucho.
5. Espero demasiado de mis amigos.
6. También tengo dolores de cabeza frecuentemente.
7. Además, no me quejo a menudo.
8. Luego voy a tomar dos aspirinas.
9. Pero todavía no, quiero esperar.
10. Entonces continuaré hablando de mi personalidad.

22·4
1. ansiosamente
2. definitivamente
3. lentamente
4. tímidamente
5. ágilmente
6. fácilmente
7. dulcemente
8. desgraciadamente
9. profundamente
10. inmediatamente
11. totalmente
12. obviamente
13. claramente
14. hábilmente
15. alegremente
16. desafortunadamente
17. violentamente
18. completamente
19. fuertemente
20. rápidamente

22·6
1. Hacemos los ejercicios lentamente.
2. ¿Siguen Uds. las instrucciones cuidadosamente?
3. Usualmente no nos gusta trabajar los fines de semana.
4. Evidentemente este perro no protege su casa.
5. Por suerte / Afortunadamente, Uds. no tienen muchas joyas.
6. Uds. pueden proteger fácilmente su casa con una alarma.
7. Lisa habla despacio y claramente.
8. También habla brevemente.
9. Francamente, no me gusta esperar.
10. Por suerte / Afortunadamente, no tengo mucha tarea.

22·7
1. de noche
2. de día
3. al mismo tiempo
4. Por suerte
5. con frecuencia / a menudo
6. A veces
7. Sin duda
8. de nuevo

22·9
1. Por suerte
2. Por desgracia
3. con tristeza
4. con rapidez
5. de día

22·10
1. Por lo visto, queremos una vida mejor.
2. De vez en cuando tenemos que considerar que la vida es corta.
3. Hasta ahora, hemos trabajado mucho.
4. De ahora en adelante vamos a cambiar nuestro estilo de vida.
5. No nos vamos a levantar al salir el sol.
6. Al anochecer podemos relajarnos y olvidarnos de mañana.
7. Desde aquí, tenemos una vista del río.
8. Hasta aquí, este plan es muy aburrido.
9. ¿De veras tenemos que cambiar nuestro estilo de vida?
10. De ahora (hoy) en adelante no podemos quejarnos más.

22·11
1. bajo
2. más rápido / más rápidamente que
3. rápido
4. fuerte
5. alto
6. claro
7. más alto que

22·12 ¡Por fin! El mensaje está claro en el contestador automático. El editor de "Publicaciones Maravilla" aceptó mi novela. Estoy muy contento. Quiero llamar a Lila ahora mismo. Obviamente ella cree que no tengo bastante talento para escribir un libro. Naturalmente, está celosa de mi éxito. Lila siempre dice que ella puede hacer todo mejor que yo. Ella habla a menudo acerca de un libro misterioso que va a publicar pronto. Sin duda, Lila exagera con frecuencia. De vez en cuando también miente. ¿Puedes guardarme un secreto? Ella es definitivamente la inspiración de Chloe, la bruja mala que todos mis lectores van a odiar.

23 Prepositions

23·1
1. entre
2. con
3. ante
4. por
5. sobre
6. hacia
7. desde
8. sin
9. en
10. Según

23·2
1. F
2. F
3. V
4. V
5. V
6. F
7. F

23·3
1. Luisa no puede vivir sin Jacob.
2. Jacob le envió una tarjeta a Luisa desde Lima.
3. Jacob viajaba a/hacia/para Ecuador.
4. Desde el aeropuerto, llamó a Luisa.
5. Él no llegó a Quito hasta la medianoche.
6. Jacob encontró una moneda debajo de la almohada.
7. Según Luisa, él es supersticioso.
8. Con suerte, Jacob venderá muchos de sus productos en Quito.

23·4
1. en una semana
2. en vez de
3. a cargo de
4. En cambio
5. además de
6. de ahora en adelante
7. a pie
8. a tiempo

23·6
1. Las tiendas están lejos de nuestra casa.
2. Mi auto está fuera del garaje.
3. En vez de azúcar, la receta dice miel.
4. De vez en cuando corro diez millas.
5. Esta reunión termina dentro de una hora.
6. Hay alrededor de quince pájaros en ese árbol.

23·7
1. por
2. antes de
3. dentro del
4. a través de
5. al lado de
6. en vez de
7. alrededor de
8. hacia
9. hasta
10. sobre

23·9
1. T
2. M
3. L
4. T
5. O
6. L
7. O
8. O
9. M
10. L

23·10
1. Esta casa huele a pescado.
2. ¿Llamas a Rosa o a Manuel?
3. ¡Yo amo a mi canario!
4. Ellos no invitan a nadie a su aniversario.
5. Mi sopa sabe a perejil.
6. ¿Conocen Uds. a alguien en esta clase?
7. Las flores son a tres dólares la docena.
8. La estación de trenes está a diez millas de mi casa.
9. Luisa cuida a mi gato.

23·11
1. en lugar de / en vez de caminar
2. Después de entrar
3. Al terminar
4. sin hacer
5. con rapidez
6. en paz
7. al llegar
8. En lugar de / En vez de lavar

23·12
1. e   5. a
2. h   6. c
3. f   7. d
4. g   8. b

23·13
1. Para ser un liberal tiene ideas tradicionales.
2. ¿Te entrenas para los juegos olímpicos?
3. Necesito una lámpara para mi dormitorio.
4. Deben estar aquí para las cuatro.
5. Este café es para nosotros.
6. Lucille lee el periódico para encontrar un apartamento.
7. ¿Es para Susan esta carta?
8. Vamos para San Francisco.
9. ¿Para qué necesitas este dinero?
10. Necesito el dinero para una computadora nueva.

23·14
1. ¿Vas al trabajo por tren o por carro/auto?
2. ¿Estás por terminar tu trabajo ahora?
3. ¿Envías tus saludos por correo electrónico?
4. ¿Corres por el parque a menudo?
5. ¡Caramba! ¿Compraste esos zapatos por trescientos dólares?
6. ¿Conduces/Manejas en la autopista a sesenta y cinco millas por hora?
7. ¿Regresas a casa por la tarde o por la noche?
8. Y por último, ¿estás por los liberales o los conservadores?

23·15
1. por ahí   5. Por cierto   9. Por fin
2. Por favor   6. Por Dios   10. por eso
3. Por supuesto   7. Por lo menos
4. Por lo visto   8. Por favor

23·16
1. para   5. Por
2. por   6. Para
3. por   7. por
4. Para   8. por

23·17
1. Trabajamos por Lidia.
2. Ellos pasan por el túnel.
3. Él tiene por lo menos dos autos.
4. Por su enfermedad no está aquí.
5. Mi amigo pasa por mi oficina.
6. Viene por tren.
7. Él estará aquí para las cuatro (en punto).

23·19
1. destination
2. "by means of"
3. deadline, time in the future
4. exchange
5. comparison
6. purpose or goal
7. moving through
8. reason, "because of"
9. duration of time
10. idiomatic expression with **por**

23·20
1. huele a   4. se atreven a
2. suenan a   5. montar a
3. inspira a   6. se oponen a

23·21
1. de   5. de
2. con   6. de
3. con   7. en
4. en   8. de

23·22 Bajo las escaleras, entro a la sala, pongo la tele y escucho las noticias. Sueño con un día lleno de buenas noticias. Por ejemplo, los líderes extranjeros no amenazan con un nuevo conflicto internacional, los expertos financieros no reportan detalles horribles acerca de la economía y yo dejo de pensar en los problemas del mundo. No soy egoísta, por Dios. Yo solamente quiero un día de paz y pensamientos felices. ¿Qué noticias quiero escuchar? Por ejemplo, que todos estamos por la paz y en contra de la guerra, y que nos alegramos de las cosas simples de la vida. Hoy voy a apagar la televisión y voy a buscar mi pala para trabajar en el jardín.

24 Indefinite and negative words and expressions

24·2
1. Nadie trabaja en esta oficina.
2. Algunas personas son más agradables que otras.
3. Nunca hago preguntas.
4. No hablo mucho tampoco.
5. A veces necesito ayuda.
6. ¿Habla Ud. alemán también?
7. Ella come o papas/patatas o arroz solamente.
8. Ni tú ni yo.

24·3
1. algo
2. Nunca
3. nadie
4. O, o
5. Algunos
6. Alguien
7. Siempre
8. Ni, ni

24·4
1. No hay refrescos en la nevera.
2. No quiero ni dormir ni jugar al fútbol.
3. No van a ningún lugar interesante este fin de semana.
4. No tenemos ninguna esperanza de encontrar el anillo perdido.
5. No sé dónde están ni las preguntas ni las respuestas para la tarea.
6. No tenemos tiempo para ayudarte.
7. Nunca voy a visitar a mis suegros.
8. No voy a saludar a mis tíos tampoco.
9. No celebramos ningún día especial esta semana.
10. No conocen a nadie de nuestra familia.
11. No tengo nada que añadir.

24·6
1. Estoy algo preocupado(a).
2. ¿Hay alguien en esta habitación?
3. Nadie quiere hacer nada.
4. Manny ni sacó las fotos ni filmó la reunión.
5. ¿Tenemos que encontrar a Peter o a Sandra?
6. Algún día vamos a terminar este trabajo.
7. No les gusta nada este trabajo.
8. Nunca harán esto.

24·7
1. e
2. c
3. a
4. d
5. f
6. b

24·8
1. El sol no es un planeta sino una estrella.
2. Blanca Nieves no es un personaje real sino ficticio.
3. La astronomía no es un deporte sino una ciencia.
4. El inglés no es la lengua oficial de Portugal sino de Inglaterra.
5. La paella no es un plato típico mexicano sino español.
6. El ballet no es un juego sino un arte.
7. Un crucigrama no es un problema sino un pasatiempo.
8. Un perro no es una persona sino un animal.
9. La luna no es una estrella sino un satélite.

24·9
1. pero
2. sino
3. pero
4. pero / sino que
5. pero
6. pero
7. pero
8. sino que
9. pero
10. sino que

24·10 Te voy a decir algo pero no le reveles esto a nadie, ¡a nadie! ¡Carmen tiene novio! Ni tú ni tus amigos lo conocen. Ella dice que nadie la comprende. Carmen nunca cuenta sus secretos. Ah, pero yo sé algunos de sus secretos. Carmen dice que tiene veintinueve años. Pero ella tiene algunos años más. Jamás celebra su cumpleaños. O tiene miedo a la vejez o es muy tonta. No, no es tonta, es obsesiva. ¿Y sabes qué? Carmen fue a un cirujano plástico para eliminar algunas de sus arrugas.

25 Interrogative and exclamatory words

25·1
1. Dónde
2. Cuáles
3. Qué
4. Cuándo
5. Cuántas
6. Cuánto
7. Cuántos
8. Cuál
9. Cómo
10. Cuánta

25·2 *Possible answers*:
1. ¿Cuál es su nombre? / ¿Cómo se llama Ud.?
2. ¿De dónde es Ud.?
3. ¿Es Ud. dentista? / ¿Su profesión es la odontología?
4. ¿Cómo es Ud.? / ¿Cuáles son sus características?
5. ¿Es Ud. puntual?
6. ¿Qué hora es? / ¿Qué hora tiene?

25·3
1. En octubre.
2. De México.
3. Sancho Panza.
4. Montevideo.
5. Español y guaraní.
6. Santiago y San Juan.

25·4
1. ¿Quién es el próximo?
2. ¿Cómo se llama Ud., señor?
3. ¿En qué puedo ayudarlo?
4. ¿Cuál es su fecha de nacimiento?
5. ¿Dónde trabaja Ud.?
6. ¿Cuánto tiempo puede quedarse?

25·5
1. d
2. c
3. b
4. a
5. f
6. e

25·7
1. Pregúntale a tu amigo quién está sentado allá.
2. La policía pregunta dónde estuviste anoche.
3. El/La detective pregunta a qué hora llegaste a la discoteca.
4. Tu mamá pregunta adónde fuiste después de la medianoche.
5. Preguntan cuándo terminará este interrogatorio.

25·8
1. Qué
2. Cuánto
3. Cuántos
4. Quién
5. Cuántos
6. Qué
7. Cuánto
8. Qué

25·9
1. d
2. f
3. e
4. a
5. c
6. b
7. h
8. g

25·10 Mario no me puede llevar hoy a mi doctor/médico. ¿Por qué no me llamó anoche? ¡Qué mala suerte! Ahora tengo que tomar un taxi. ¿Por qué hay tantos autos/carros en la autopista? ¡Cuánto tráfico! La consulta del Dr. Domínguez está/queda lejos y la tarifa es más o menos veinticinco dólares. ¡Cuánto dinero por este servicio! ¡Ah! Y ahora llueve también. ¡Qué día tan horrible! Por fin, ahora estoy en la consulta de mi doctor/médico. Hay muchos pacientes en la sala de espera. Probablemente voy a pasar aquí dos o tres horas. ¡Qué rabia! / ¡Qué pesado! / ¡Qué desagradable! Ahora puedo acercarme a la ventanilla. ¿Qué? La recepcionista me dio / me ha dado malas noticias. ¿Mi cita es mañana? ¡Qué día!

26 Numbers

26·1
1. treinta y cinco
2. dos mil trescientos cuarenta y un
3. trescientos veintidós
4. dieciséis
5. sesenta y siete
6. setenta y un
7. cien
8. quinientas dos
9. veintiséis
10. cien mil
11. treinta y un
12. setecientas
13. un millón
14. cincuenta y una

26·2
1. el quince de marzo de mil ochocientos noventa y ocho
2. Son las tres y media de la tarde.
3. el catorce de julio de mil setecientos setenta
4. el primero de junio de dos mil dos
5. Son las diez y quince de la noche. / Son las diez y cuarto de la noche.
6. el treinta y uno de enero de mil novecientos noventa y nueve
7. A las nueve y media de la mañana.
8. el treinta de noviembre a las siete de la tarde

26·4
1. 55; Cien menos cuarenta y cinco son cincuenta y cinco.
2. 37; Veinticinco más doce son treinta y siete.
3. 90; Treinta por tres son noventa.
4. 43; Doce más dieciséis / diez y seis más quince son cuarenta y tres.
5. 50; Doscientos entre / dividido por cuatro son cincuenta.
6. 231; Setenta y siete por tres son doscientos treinta y uno.

26·5
1. V
2. F
3. F
4. V
5. F
6. V
7. F
8. V
9. F
10. V

26·6
1. Hay más de cien canales de televisión.
2. Muchas familias americanas tienen solamente un hijo.
3. Muchos hogares norteamericanos tienen tres televisores.
4. Uno no puede comprar mucho con veinte y cinco (veinticinco) dólares.
5. Hay treinta y dos piezas en un juego de ajedrez.
6. Trabajamos cincuenta semanas cada año / al año.
7. El cumpleaños de Lincoln es el 12 de febrero.

26·7
1. primera
2. quinto
3. décimo
4. octava
5. primer
6. tercera
7. séptima
8. veinte
9. cuarta
10. segunda

26·9
1. Esta es mi tercera visita al museo.
2. Pero es la primera vez que saco fotos.
3. El décimo capítulo es difícil.
4. Daisy siempre llega la segunda, después de Julia.
5. Ellos/Ellas apuestan en la quinta carrera.
6. Picasso vivió en el siglo veinte.
7. Hoy es el primer día del resto de mi vida.
8. Diciembre es el mes doce del año.
9. Afortunadamente, hoy es el séptimo día de la semana.
10. Vivimos en el cuarto piso.

26·10
1. un tercio de la población / la tercera parte de la población
2. una ración doble
3. media naranja
4. medio día
5. dos tercios de mi salario
6. la sexta columna
7. un octavo de yarda
8. ganancias cuádruples

26·11 Todos los días vemos números: sumamos, multiplicamos, restamos y dividimos. Vemos un letrero en la pista de peaje y leemos: "Sesenta y cinco millas por hora". Vamos a una tienda y queremos comprar toallas y otro letrero dice: "Segundo piso". Queremos multiplicar nuestra fortuna con un billete de lotería o con acciones en la bolsa de valores. Nos sentamos frente a la computadora y buscamos la base de datos. El precio del oro puede subir un veinte por ciento para el segundo mes del año que viene / del próximo año. Podemos doblar nuestro dinero. Pero, si ganamos el cinco por ciento, ¡tenemos suerte! Probablemente gastamos el veinticinco por ciento de nuestro tiempo comprando, buscando gangas y gastando dinero. Y tenemos que recordar las fechas de cumpleaños. El mío es el 11 de febrero. En este siglo veintiuno tenemos computadoras y teléfonos celulares con calculadoras. Podemos hacer las tareas aritméticas fácilmente. ¡Ten cuidado: gasta menos y ahorra más!